A New Social Contract for Peru

An Agenda for Improving Education, Health Care, and the Social Safety Net

Edited by Daniel Cotlear

THE WORLD BANK
Washington, D.C.

World Bank Country Studies are among the many reports originally prepared for internal use as part of the continuing analysis by the Bank of the economic and related conditions of its developing member countries and to facilitate its dialogs with the governments. Some of the reports are published in this series with the least possible delay for the use of governments, and the academic, business, financial, and development communities. The manuscript of this paper therefore has not been prepared in accordance with the procedures appropriate to formally-edited texts. Some sources cited in this paper may be informal documents that are not readily available.

ISBN-10: 0-8213-6567-3   ISBN-13: 978-0-8213-6567-0
eISBN: 0-8213-6568-1
ISSN: 0253-2123   DOI: 10.1596/978-0-8213-6567-0

Cover photos by RECURSO team, The World Bank.

Library of Congress Cataloging-in-Publication Data has been requested.

Contents

LIST OF TABLES

LIST OF FIGURES

LIST OF BOXES

Foreword

There is a growing consensus in Peru that the country needs to increase its efforts to achieve greater equity and that a strong social policy must be part of those efforts. The objective of this book is to make available an analysis of the issues that need to be tackled to improve the delivery of education, health care, and antipoverty programs, and to describe the main options available to deal with those issues. The book is being published in the months prior to the 2006 elections to make this information available to inform the debate about social policy and suggest options for the design of a more equitable social policy.

The book is the result of two years of the collaborative work of many people. It summarizes the main findings and conclusions of a project that examined issues of accountability in the delivery of public services. The project, known by its Spanish acronym, RECURSO (*REndición de CUentas para la Reforma SOcial*), was financed by the World Bank and the Department for International Development (DFID), and had four characteristics.

First, it brought together people with a detailed knowledge about the issues confronting the delivery of education, health care, and social protection services in Peru with people with knowledge about how similar issues are being managed in other countries. The identification of the issues and of the possible solutions to those issues in each sector was based on a technical analysis of the available data and on a detailed review of the literature produced by Peruvian analysts. The teams that produced the analysis summarized in each chapter involved Peruvian professionals and international experts.

Second, the project attempted to go beyond a purely technical and economic analysis of each sector. Each chapter of the book incorporates, in addition to a technical, economic, and statistical analysis, an analysis of the institutional context for service delivery. In some instances some elements of anthropological analysis were also incorporated. A common theme that cuts across sectors is the attempt to discuss issues of accountability in each sector using a common framework. This framework, described in Chapter 1, was originally developed by the World Bank in its *World Development Report: Making Services Work for Poor People* (2004) and first applied to Latin America in *Citizens, Politicians, and Providers* (Fiszbein 2005). This book is the first attempt to use this approach in a single country, and the Bank is now likely to replicate the approach in other countries.

Third, there was a significant effort to go beyond the typical analysis that results from a review of each individual sector on its own. Instead, a comparative approach was used, seeking lessons by looking for historical patterns that are similar in several sectors and for other similarities and contrasts among the sectors. Specifically, there was an effort to systematically review each sector: the trends and the distribution of public expenditure, the impact of social participation in the delivery of services, and the incentive framework for the management of human resources.

Finally, the project attempted to develop the analysis and recommendations in a participatory manner that incorporated the views of as many stakeholders as possible. Policymakers, academics, civil society leaders, and providers of services were consulted at the planning stage of the project and again when the initial results became available. The book does not seek to give the "definitive answer" to or the "international recipe" for the various problems it identifies; rather, it seeks to support the national debate from which a "Peruvian solution" owned by the country's stakeholders, could arise.

The project was implemented by a team divided into six groups, each of which specialized in a sector or theme: education, health care, social assistance, public expenditures in the social sectors, social participation in the delivery of social sectors, and the incentive framework for teachers and doctors. Each of these groups included a World Bank staff member (who was also in charge of writing the final report) and Peruvian consultants. Each team developed its plan of work in consultation with the authorities and technical staff of the relevant ministries and with civil society organizations of each of their sectors. The ministries involved included the Ministry of Finance, the Ministry of Education, the Ministry of Health, and the Ministry of Women and Social Development, and the Prime Minister's office.

The whole project team is described in the acknowledgments section. The core team which summarized the results, managed the process, and wrote the chapters of the book was led by Daniel Cotlear and included Betty Alvarado Pérez, Leah Belsky, Livia Benavides, Luis Crouch, Pablo Lavado P., Rony Lenz, José R. López-Cálix, William Reuben, Cornelia Mihaela Tesliuc, Sofia Valencia, and Richard Webb.

The first chapter of the book presents a general overview of the findings, the conceptual framework, and the main policy options identified by the project. The main conclusion of the book is that while Peru has made significant progress in both education and health care, there remain significant challenges to achieving greater equity and better quality of services, particularly for the poor. The book finds that Peru has achieved high levels of coverage in all levels of education and in some programs of basic health care and of social assistance. While coverage is high, the average quality of most of these programs is low, and the health and education outcomes are extremely inequitable. The crux of the problem is that Peru has fallen into a trap, or a "low-level equilibrium," in the provision of education and health care services. This is a trap, because the outcomes are poor, but none of the actors in the system has an incentive to change their behavior, so the outcomes do not improve.

In order to improve outcomes, three types of interventions are needed: (a) standards of quality and quantitative goals need to be established, and there needs to be a permanent effort of monitoring progress toward those goals; (b) accountability lines need to be established so that providers become responsible for reaching the goals established for them; and (c) investments are needed to create the capacity to reach those goals. In order to begin this process, it will first be necessary to break out of the trap, or low-level equilibrium, and this will require measures that lead the users to become aware of the poor quality of services and to become vigilant about their right to better services. These interventions are complex and ambitious and will not be easy to implement in Peru or, indeed, in any country. But the moment has come. And the World Bank, with its 40 years of accumulated experience supporting Peru's development, stands ready to continue contributing to that process.

Marcelo M. Giugale
Country Director
Bolivia, Ecuador, Peru, and Venezuela
Latin America and the Caribbean Region
The World Bank

Evangeline Javier
Director
Human Development Department
Latin America and the CaribbeanRegion
The World Bank

Acknowledgments

This book summarizes the main findings and conclusions of a project that examined issues of accountability in the delivery of public services in Peru. The project was known by its Spanish acronym, RECURSO (*REndición de CUentas para la Reforma SOcial*). The core RECURSO team was led by Daniel Cotlear, who was also editor of the book, and included the authors of the different chapters of the book and an implementation group. The authors were Betty Alvarado Pérez, Leah Belsky, Daniel Cotlear, Luis Crouch, Pablo Lavado P., Rony Lenz, José R. López-Cálix, William Reuben, Cornelia Mihaela Tesliuc, Sofia Valencia, and Richard Webb. The implementation group was led by Livia Benavides and included Patricia Bernedo, Pablo Lavado, and Luisa Yesquen. Diane Stamm was the English language editor of the book.

The project was co-financed by the World Bank and the Department for International Development (DFID) of the UK. In DFID, we would like to thank Marfil Francke, Mark Lewis, Marianela Montes de Oca, Jennie Richmond, and Víctor Zamora. In the World Bank the project benefited from the strategic guidance of Marcelo Giugale, Country Director for Bolivia, Ecuador, Peru, and Venezuela; and Evangeline Javier, Sector Director for Human Development in Latin America and the Caribbean; and from the technical guidance of Jorge Luis Archimbaud, Cristian Baeza, Ariel Fiszbein, Vicente Fretes-Cibils, John Newman, Rossana Polastri, Helena Ribe, Jaime Saavedra, and Eduardo Vélez.

The project had the support of many government authorities who provided access to information and promoted an open exchange of information with their technical teams. The Ministers that had a direct participation in the project were Pilar Mazzetti Soller, Minister of Health; Ana María Romero Lozada, Minister of Women and Social Development; Javier Sota Nadal, Minister of Education; and Fernando Zavala, Minister of Finance. Beatriz Merino, supported the design phase of the project during her tenure as Prime Minister, and later, when she became ombudswoman, she encouraged the team to present its results as a potential tool for promoting the rights of the poor to quality public services.

The authors are also grateful to the authorities and officials of the Regional Government of Lambayeque, the Metropolitan Municipality of Lima, and the Provincial Municipality of Callao, all of which shared their concerns about the social sectors, and to the officials and consultants of the donor community in Peru who support the findings and the policy proposals, especially the Inter-American Development Bank (IDB), the U.S. Agency for International Development (USAID), the United Nations Population Fund (UNPF), Kf W, the German Agency for Technical Cooperation (GTZ), and the United Nations Children's Fund (UNICEF).

Chapter 1 provides an overview of the book and summarizes the main conclusions of the project; as such it is a synthesis of the work of the whole RECURSO team. It was written by Daniel Cotlear with support from Pablo Lavado. Peer reviewers (these are formal commentators from within the World Bank who are assigned to review an analytical piece) were Barbara Bruns, Yasuhiko Matsuda, and Halsey Rogers. External comments were received from Lorena Alcazar, Pedro Francke, and Juan Fernando Vega.

Chapter 2, on public expenditure in the social sectors, was written by José R. López-Cálix with input from Lorena Alcázar (public employment and payroll issues), Miguel

Jaramillo (pensions), Juvenal Díaz and Pablo Lavado (incidence analysis), and Jorge Shepherd (fiscal trends and pensions). Pablo Lavado also provided accurate and timely research assistance. Peer reviewers were Kathy Lindert and Eduardo Vélez. Valuable comments were received within the Bank from all the members of the RECURSO team, and from Vicente Fretes-Cibils, Ariel Fiszbein, Marcelo Giugale, Evangeline Javier, Kathrin Plangemann, Helena Ribe, and Rafael Rofman. Excellent production support was received from Michael Geller. The chapter also benefited from the collaboration and comments of Peruvian officials, especially Fernando Zavala (current Minister of Economy), Bruno Barletti, Luis Carranza, Hillman Farfán, Linette Lecussan, Julio Mejía, Cristina Mendoza, Waldo Mendoza, Augusto Portocarrero, Carlos Ricse, María del Carmen Rivera, Juan Pablo Silva, Nelson Shack, Milton Von Hesse, and Edgard Zamalloa.

Chapter 3, on education, was written by Luis Crouch of RTI International, with input from Lorena Alcázar and Nestor Valdivia from the Group for the Analysis of Development (GRADE) (*Fe y Alegría* and effective schools, and dropout problems); Flavio Figallo (analysis of voice); and Marcela Echegaray, Ingrid Guzmán, Lilliam Hidalgo, Consuelo Pasco, and Jessyca Sampe of TAREA (reading standards and *Educación Intercultural Bilingüe*). Helen Abadzi of the World Bank provided useful input and some text on reading standards. At the World Bank, peer reviewers Barbara Bruns, Ernesto Cuadra, Robert Prouty, and Kin Bing Wu provided valuable insights and comments. Barbara Hunt, an external peer reviewer, did likewise. Gratitude goes out to Peruvian colleagues and counterparts who participated in various policy sessions. Minister of Education Javier Sota Nadal and his Vice Ministers Idel Vexler and Helen Chávez and the advisory team extended a warm welcome to and collaboration with the RECURSO process. Giuliana Espinosa, Luis Paz, Enrique Prochazka, and Patricia Valdivia provided feedback and facilitated access to data. Commentators and interlocutors from civil society included Sigfredo Chiroque, Santiago Cueto, Jesús Herrero, Manuel Iguiñiz, Nicolás Lynch, Ricardo Morales, Jorge Oroza, Grover Pango, Pepe Rivero, Pepe Rodriguez, and Juan Fernando Vega. USAID's AprenDES project leader Antonieta de Harwood facilitated a site visit to schools in San Martín. Baltazar Lantarón Nuñez, Regional Education Director in Abancay, facilitated the visits to and analysis of the schools in Apurímac. We are grateful to Patricia Salas and Martín Vegas for enabling the opportunity for an exchange with the *Consejo Nacional de Educación* and the *Proyecto Educativo Nacional*.

Chapter 4, which explored the diagnosis and policies on the health sector, was written by Rony Lenz and Betty Alvarado Pérez, with inputs from Oscar Arteaga, Pablo Lavado, and Francisco Volante. It includes input from a World Bank study carried out by April Harding and Betty Alvarado (*Comites Locales de Administración de Salud*, CLAS). Valuable comments were provided by the peer reviewers, and other colleagues in the World Bank including Cristian Baeza, Livia Benavides, Rafael Cortéz, José Pablo Gómez-Meza, Yasuhiko Matsuda, and John Newman. Pedro Francke, an external consultant, enriched the dialog. Special thanks to the authorities of the Ministry of Health (MINSA), especially Dr. Pilar Mazzetti Soller, her advisory team, and other professionals from MINSA, *Seguro Integral de Salud* (SIS), *Direcciones de Salud* (DISAs), and the CLAS facilities (Cuzco and Lima). Likewise to the *Consejo Nacional de Salud*. The Bank is grateful to outside organizations including the *Consorcio de Investigación Económica y Social* (CIES), Future Generations, *Foro Salud*, PHR Plus, and to the specialists who attended the workshops and enriched the discussions: Laura Altobelli, Carlos Bardalez, Midori de Habich, Danilo Fernández, Ana

Guezmez, Alfredo Guzmán, Augusto Meloni, Margarita Petrera, Augusto Portocarrero, Maria Inés Sanchez-Griñán, and Oscar Ugarte.

Chapter 5, on the social safety net, was written by Cornelia Mihaela Tesliuc with input from Lorena Alcázar and Rodrigo Lovatón (decentralization of basic social infrastructure and community kitchen programs), Pedro Francke (decentralization of social programs), Juvenal Díaz (benefit incidence), Anja Linder (review of social protection programs), and *Propuesta Ciudadana* (an NGO that implemented a qualitative survey on empowerment, participation, and service delivery in 18 municipalities in the departments of San Martín, Cusco, and Piura). Pablo Lavado provided invaluable assistance in conducting research and analysis. Peer reviewers were Margaret Grosh, Edmundo Murrugarra, and Laura Rawlings. Comments were received within the Bank from Kathy Lindert, John Newman, Carolina Sánchez Paramo, Helena Ribe, and David Warren. The chapter also benefited from the collaboration and comments of Peruvian officials Minister of Women and Social Protection Ana Maria Romero, Vice Minister Mario Rios and staff, and specialists. Valuable comments were also received from Roxana García Bedoya, Cecilia Blondet, Juan Chacaltana, Martín Tanaka, and Maríin Valdivia.

Chapter 6, on human resources, was written by Richard Webb and Sofía Valencia. Rafael Basurto, Elizabeth Linos, Verónica Minaya, and Rocio Trinidad carried out interviews and provided written reports. Too numerous to mention are the many teachers, health professionals, officials in the Education and Health Ministries, and other governmental authorities who shared information and ideas during long hours of interviews. April Harding of the World Bank and Luis Crouch were our guides to the literature and experience in other countries on health and education, respectively, and provided helpful insights on health systems. At the World Bank, peer reviewers Gilles Dussault, Christoph Kurowski, and Halsey Rogers offered valuable comments and references. Barbara Hunt, as an external peer reviewer, contributed with guidance and suggestions. Patricia Ames, Bruno Barletti, Manuel Bello, Sigfredo Chiroque, Dante Cordova, Santiago Cueto, Hugo Diaz, Giovanni Escalante, Jorge Ferradas, Midori de Habich, Father Jesús Herrero, Miguel Jaramillo, Carmen Montero, Ulises Nuñez, Luis Paz, Margarita Petrera, Pierina Pollarollo, Eliana de Sanchez Moreno, Pablo Sandoval, David Tejada, Cecilia Thorne, and Juan Fernando Vega shared with us their specialized knowledge and experience in these sectors. We deeply appreciate the opportunity for exchanges with the *Consejo Nacional de Educación*, the *Colegio Médico del Perú*, the *Colegio de Enfermeras*, and the *Sindicato de Enfermeras del Ministerio de Salud*.

Chapter 7, on voice in the accountability of the social sectors, was written by William Reuben and Leah Belsky, with input from Annika Silva-Leander (enabling environment for voice and support on the methodological framework), and from the following authors of background papers: Levy del Aguila (national voice), Javier Aspur (legal framework), Eduardo Ballón (historical overview and regional voice), and Carlos Monge (overall synthesis). Eliza Wiener prepared the report of *Grupo Propuesta Ciudadana's* fieldwork team led by Carlos Monge. José Pablo Gómez from the World Bank (LCSHH) delivered a short background report on voice mechanisms in the health sector, as did consultant Flavio Figallo in the education sector. Pablo Lavado of the World Bank provided valuable assistance with secondary data analysis, and Elizabeth Dasso suggested relevant literature and sources of information. Daniel Cotlear, Team Leader of the RECURSO project, provided critical advice and insights, as did the other members of the RECURSO team. Ariel Fiszbein chaired the review meetings and provided useful advice, as did Katherine Bain, Reiner Forster, Yasuhiko Matsuda, and Roby Senderowitsch as peer reviewers. John Newman, Peru Country Manager, and other members of the Peru Country Team, also provided useful advice and feedback. Federico Arnillas from the *Asociación Nacional de Centros*, Carmen Lora and Maruja Boggio from the *Mesa Nacional de Concertación para la Lucha Contra la Pobreza*, Elias Szczytnicki from the *Conferencia Mundial de Religiones por la Paz*, and Juan Carlos Cortés from *Ciudadanos al Día* provided valuable feedback at various stages of the study.

The collective efforts of this talented team have resulted in what we hope will be a valuable contribution to improving the delivery of public services to the poor in Peru.

Author Biographies

Betty Alvarado Pérez is an economist. She was a Fulbright Fellow and holds a Masters of Public Administration and a Masters of Philosophy (PhD [abd]) from New York University. She has been a consultant to Peruvian national agencies and international bodies including the World Bank, the United States Agency for International Development, the Pan-American Health Organization, and the Inter-American Development Bank. She is a part-time professor and researcher at the Universidad del Pacífico in Lima. Her areas of interest are social and urban development, municipal finance, and fiscal decentralization.

Leah Belsky is a Junior Professional Associate at the World Bank. Before joining the Bank she was a Fellow in the Department of Clinical Bioethics at the National Institutes of Health. She has degrees from Brown University in Political Science and Human Biology and has performed research in Africa, East Asia, and throughout Latin America on governance and bioethics.

Livia Benavides is a Senior Social Sectors Specialist at the World Bank. She holds a B.Sc. from Trinity College, an M.Sc. from MIT, and a Post-Graduate Diploma in Economics from the University of London. She works mainly in Peru where she participates in the preparation and supervision of Projects in the Health, Education, and Social Protection Sectors. Prior to working for the Bank, she worked for the Pan-American Health Organization— Pan-American Center for Sanitary and Environmental Engineering, as an Environmental Health Specialist and as an independent consultant for various international organizations. Her areas of interest include monitoring and evaluation of social sector policies and programs.

Daniel Cotlear is the team leader for the *Rendición de Cuentas para la Reforma Social de Perú* (RECURSO) Project leading to this book. He is an economist (PhD Oxford University 1986; M.Phil. Oxford and Cambridge Universities; Bachelors Catholic University of Peru). He is currently Sector Leader in the World Bank's Human Development Department covering the Andean Countries, and as such is in charge of coordinating all activities in education, health, and social protection in Bolivia, Ecuador, Peru, and Venezuela. Prior to that, within the World Bank he was senior health economist and Task Manager of health projects in most South American countries. He has also served as macroeconomist in the Central America Department and as an Agricultural Economist in the Southern and Eastern Africa Department. Before joining the Bank he was an advisor at the Ministry of Agriculture of Peru and author of a book on poverty reduction in the Peruvian Sierra.

Luis Crouch is senior economist (PhD Berkeley 1981) and currently Research Vice President at RTI International in North Carolina, USA. His areas of interest include education finance, indicators and statistics, and planning, particularly in decentralizing countries. He has worked in almost all areas of the world, specializing more recently on South Africa, Indonesia, and Peru.

Pablo Lavado P. is an economist (BA Universidad del Pacífico 2003) and currently a Junior Professional Associate at the World Bank. Before joining the Bank he was Research Assistant in the Area of Social Policy and Human Development at the Universidad del Pacífico Research Center. He is currently a Teaching Assistant at the Department of

Economics of the same university. His area of interest is statistical analysis in education, health, and poverty.

Rony Lenz is an economist (Catholic University of Chile 1984) and holds a Masters in Economics (Georgetown University 1992). Currently, he is lecturer in Health Financing at the Public Health School of the University of Chile, and is a private consultant in health financing. His areas of interest include health economics, health financing, and management of health institutions. He has been Chief of Budget and Planning in the Chilean Ministry of Health, Director of the *Fondo Nacional de Salud*, and has worked in most Latin American countries as consultant to the World Bank.

José R. López-Cálix is a lead economist at the World Bank (PhD The Catholic University of Louvain 1994) and is currently in charge of Morocco and Algeria in the Middle East and North Africa region. His areas of interest include public finance, public expenditure tracking surveys, growth, trade, labor, and exchange rate policies. He has worked in most Latin American Countries, but especially in Central America and the Andean Countries. Before joining the Bank he was Chief of Advisors at the El Salvador Ministry of Planning during the Cristiani Administration, which concluded the peace agreements.

William Reuben is a Costa Rican social scientist (M.A. and Drs. Institute of Social Studies, the Netherlands) and is currently Senior Social Development Specialist at the Latin America and the Caribbean Region of the World Bank. He is the founder of important civil society networks in Latin America, like the *Asociación Latinoamericana de Organizaciones de Promoción* and the *Fondo Latinomaricano de Desarrollo*, and taught Economic and Development Anthropology at the University of Costa Rica. Areas of expertise include rural development, civic engagement and governance, and social analysis.

Cornelia Mihaela Tesliuc is a social protection specialist working in the Latin America and the Caribbean Region of the World Bank. Before joining the Bank she worked as economic advisor of the Romanian Minister of Labor and Social Protection, contributing to the reform of the universal child allowances and the guaranteed minimum income program in Romania. Her areas of interest include public expenditure reviews, poverty assessments, at-risk youth, and the social safety net.

Sofía Valencia is an economist with bachelor's degree from the Catholic University of Peru and a Masters in Public Management and a Ph.D. [abd] in Public Policy from the University of Maryland. Currently, she is a private consultant and her areas of expertise include organizational development, human resources management, and public sector reform. She has worked in the Latin America Region, particularly in Chile, Ecuador, and Peru. She has held high-ranking positions in the Peruvian public sector and has worked as a consultant to the World Bank and the United States Agency for International Development.

Richard Webb is senior economist (PhD Harvard 1974) and currently Director of the Economic Research Center of the University of San Martín de Porres in Peru. His areas of interest include monetary economics, international finance, poverty, and employment in poor countries. He was Governor of the Central Bank of Peru and has been a visiting lecturer at Princeton University, an economist at the World Bank, and a Fellow at The Brookings Institution.

Acronyms and Abbreviations

AETA	Extraordinary Bonus for Health Care Provision—*Asignación Extraordinaria por Trabajo Asistencial*
AFPs	Pension Fund Administrator
AIDS	Acquired Immune Deficiency Syndrome
APAFA	Parents Association—*Asociación de Padres de Familia*
APRA	*Alianza Popular Revolucionaria Americana*
BCG	Anti-tuberculosis vaccination
BIS	Beneficiary identification system
CAFAE	*Comité de Administración del Fondo de Asistencia y Estímulo*
CBO	Community-based organizations
CCL	Local Coordination Council, also Municipal Coordination Council
CCLD	Local Coordination Council—*Consejo de Coordinacion Local Distrital*
CCR	Regional Coordination Council
CENAPAFA	Centralized National Association for Parents—*Central Nacional de Asociaciones de Padres de Familia*
CLAS	Local Committees for Health Administration—*Comités Locales de Administración de Salud*
CMP	Doctors College of Peru—*Colegio Médico del Perú*
CND	National Council on Decentralization
CNE	National Council of Education—*Consejo Nacional de Educación*
CNS	National Health Council—*Consejo Nacional de Salud*
CONEIs	School Governing Councils—*Consejos Educativos Institucionales*
CONSUCODE	Superior Council for State Hiring and Acquisitions—*Consejo Superior de Contrataciones y Adquisiciones del Estado*
CP	*Comedores Populares*
CV	*Cédula Viva*
DE	*Desayuno Escolar*
DESCO	Center for Development Research and Promotion—*Centro de Estudios de Promoción del Desarrollo*
DFID	Department for International Development
DHS	Demographic and Health Survey
DIRESAs	Regional Health Office—*Direcciones Regionales de Salud*
DISAs	Health Directorates, also Regional Health Office—*Direcciones de Salud*
DM	District Municipality
DNPP	*Dirección Nacional de Presupuesto Público*
DPT	Diphtheria, pertussis, tetanus
DRE	Region-level School Management and Supervisión Unit—*Dirección Regional de Educación*
ECA	Europe and Central Asia
EGS	Employment Guarantee Scheme

EIB	Intercultural and Bilingual Education—*Educación Intercultural Bilingüe*
ELITES	Itinerant Local Team for Extramural Healthcare
ENAHO	Household National Survey—*Encuesta Nacional de Hogares*
ENDES	National Demographic and Health Survey—*Encuesta Nacional de Demografía y Salud*
ENNIV	Living Standards Measurement Survey—*Encuesta Nacional de Niveles de Vida*
EPS	Private Healthcare Providers
ESSALUD	Social Security in Health of Peru
FFAA	Armed Forces—*Fuerzas Armadas*
FONCODES	National Compensation and Social Development Fund—*Fondo Nacional de Compensación y Desarrollo Social*
FORMABIAP	Bilingual Teacher Training for the Peruvian Amazon—*Formación de Maestros Bilingües de la Amazonia Peruana*
FS	National Health Forum
FyA	*Fe y Alegría*
GDP	Gross domestic product
GOP	Government of Peru
GRADE	Group for the Analysis of Development
GTZ	German Agency for Technical Cooperation
GUE	Large School—*Gran Unidad Escolar*
HIS	Health Information System
INABIF	*Instituto Nacional de Bienestar Familiar*
INEI	*Instituto Nacional de Estadística e Informática*
INS	National Institute of Health—*Instituto Nacional de Salud*
ISP	Teacher Training Institute—*Instituto Superior Pedagógico*
LAC	Latin America and the Caribbean
LCSES	Latin America and the Caribbean Social and Economic Sector
LCSHH	Latin America and the Caribbean–Human Development, Health
M&E	Monitoring and evaluation
MCLCP	*Mesas de Concertación para la Lucha Contra la Pobreza*
MDGs	Millennium Development Goals
MECEP	Program for the Improvement of Quality in Primary Schooling—*Programa de Mejoramiento de la Calidad de la Educación Primaria*
MED	Ministry of Education
MEF	Ministry of Economy and Finance—*Ministerio de Economía y Finanzas*
Mesa	Roundtable for the Fight Against Poverty—*Mesa de Concertación de Lucha Contra la Pobreza*
MIMDES	Ministry of Women and Social Development—*Ministerio de la Mujer y Desarrollo Social*
MINSA	Ministry of Health—*Ministerio de Salud*
MINTRA	Ministry of Work—*Ministerio de Trabajo y Asistencia Social*
MMR	Maternal mortality rate
MRTA	Tupac Amaru Revolutionary Movement

NE	*Nucleo Ejecutor*
NGO	Nongovernmental organization
NPSs	Non-Personnel Services
OAS	Organization of American States—*Organización de Estados Americanos*
OECD	Organisation for Economic Co-operation and Development
OPDs	Organismos Públicos Descentralizados
PAAG	Program to Administer Management Agreements—*Programa de Administración del Acuerdos de Gestión*
PAC	Shared Administration Program—*Programa de Administración Compartida*
PACFO	Supplementary Food Program for Groups at Risk of Malnutrition
PANFAR	Food and Nutrition Program for Families at Risk of Malnutrition
PARSALUD	Program for the Support of Health Reform—*Programa de Apoyo a la Reforma en Salud*
PB	Participatory Budget—*Presupuesto Participativo*
PD	Pedagogical Degree
PIA	*Presupuesto Inicial de Apertura*
PISA	Programme for International Student Assessment
PLANCAD	National Plan for Teacher Training—*Plan Nacional de Capacitación Docente*
PROMUDEH	*Ministerio de Promoción de la Mujer y del Desarrollo Humano*
PRONAA	National Food Assistance Program—*Programa Nacional de Alimentos*
PRONAMACHCS	*Programa Nacional de Manejo de Cuencas Hidrográficas y Conservación de Suelos*
PSBPT	Program for Basic Health for All—*Programa de Salud Básica Para Todos*
PSPs	Priority Social Programs
QPVSD	Qualitative Power, Voice, and Service Delivery Study
RECURSO	Accountability in Social Reform in Peru—*Rendición de Cuentas en la Reforma Social de Perú*
SDV	Social Development
SECIGRA	*Servicio Civil de Graduandos*
SEG	Schoolchildren Insurance Plan
SEPS	Superintendency for Private Healthcare Providers
SERUMs	Rural and Marginal Urban Services—*Servicio Rural y Urbano Marginal de Salud*
SIAF	Integrated System for Financial Administration—*Sistema Integrado de Administración Financiera*
SIME	A monitoring and evaluation system for social programs
SINAMOS	*Sistema Nacional de Movilización Social*
SIS	Health Insurance for the Poor, also Integral Health Insurance—*Seguro Integral de Salud*
SIS-MI	Mother-Child Insurance—*Seguro Materno Infantil*
SNCDS	*Sistema Nacional Coordinado y Descentralizado de Salud*

SNED	Chile's National Teacher Performance Evaluation System
SNIP	National System of Public Investment
SNP	National Pension System
SPP	Private pension system
SSER	Social Sector Expenditure Review
SSN	Peruvian social safety net
SUTEP	United Education Workers Labor Union—*Sindicato Único de Trabajadores en la Educación del Perú*
TAREA	*Asociación de Publicaciones Educativas*
TB	Tuberculosis
UBN	Unmet basic needs method
UGEL	Local Educational Management Unit, also Province-level School Management and Supervision Unit—*Unidad de Gestión Educativa Local*
UIS	UNESCO Institute for Statistics
UNESCO	United Nations Educational, Scientific and Cultural Organization
VdL	Glass of Milk—*Vaso de Leche*
WDR	*World Development Report*

CHAPTER 1

Improving Education, Health Care, and Social Assistance for the Poor

Daniel Cotlear

Executive Summary and Introduction

This book identifies the achievements and challenges of social policy in Peru. Its objective is to provide the new presidential administration of Peru with a diagnostic of the main problems that need to be overcome to improve education, health care, and anti-poverty programs, and with recommendations on how to overcome these problems. The diagnostic uses international comparisons that put in context the achievements in coverage, quality, and equity, and presents an analysis of the evolution and distribution of public expenditures and of the service delivery institutions. In recent decades, there have been several attempts to solve some of the problems identified in this study through the introduction of reforms; the analysis of the success and limitations of these reforms is used to obtain lessons and to make recommendations. The analysis of each sector uses a combination of quantitative data from surveys and administrative information systems and qualitative information from hundreds of interviews with parents, children, teachers, nurses, doctors, and municipal, regional, and ministerial authorities in different regions of the country. Before the publication of the book, the recommendations were discussed with government authorities, political groups, academics, and representatives of civil society. This first chapter summarizes the findings and recommendations of the book.

The main conclusion is that Peru needs a change of culture to shock the system out of the low-level equilibrium in which it finds itself. The change of culture would be reflected in a society where all the stakeholders of the social services would demand more from each other. To make that possible, it is necessary to lift the veil that prevents society from recognizing the poor quality of results that prevail in many parts of the system. Lifting the veil requires establishing transparent standards of service and systems to measure the quality of service. Every parent needs to know whether their children are reading well for their ages, and whether the nutrition program in which their children are enrolled is improving their children's chances of success in life. Mothers need to know whether they are entitled to health insurance that will cover the delivery of their baby in a hospital and whether their local hospital performs deliveries safely.

There are many important achievements in education, health care, and some social assistance programs. In all these sectors there have been significant achievements in coverage. Basic literacy has improved and, according to the latest available data, infant mortality rates are rapidly improving. The quality of the services, however, remains a major challenge. Unless the quality of education improves, Peru will not be able to compete in an increasingly global economy, and graduates arriving in the labor market will be met with frustration instead of success. Unless the quality of health care improves, it is unlikely that health outcomes will continue improving, especially because the next stage will require not only population-based interventions such as immunizations or malaria control, but also better clinical services. Finally, the existing evidence suggests that the antipoverty programs are not having an impact on reducing malnutrition, which is perhaps the most transparent measure of poverty in Peru. Low quality of service is especially common among the poor. Outcomes—of learning and infant mortality—are very unequal—more than in most other Latin American countries. So a special concern is about the services that are provided to the poor. It is important to recognize, however, that even among the services provided to the poor, there are bright spots—good schools in poor areas, good nutrition programs, and good health care interventions. These give grounds for optimism. This book describes some of these success stories.

While it is true that Peru spends little on the social sectors, this is not the main cause for the low quality of services, and adding money to the system without first improving the way it works is unlikely to bring better results. The crux of the problem lies in the relations that have been established within the "corporations of providers." Frontline providers (teachers, nurses, doctors), their local-level supervisors (whose job should be to support the frontline providers), the middle managers (the regional or municipal authorities), and the senior administrators of their ministry are all tied up in an "equilibrium" where none of the actors has incentives to change their behavior. This equilibrium is the result of a combination of complex rules based on legislation, norms, and agreements with unions; practices (that often violate the formal rules); and, crucially, in low expectations of each other's performance. Untying the knot within the corporations would require not only changing the special legislation governing teachers and doctors, and not only finding a new balance with the unions—those would be enormous challenges on their own. In addition, it would require redefining the role of the local, regional, and national administrators.

While the knot created by the rules, practices, and low expectations remains untouched, there have been successful partial reforms that have contributed to some of the achievements in social indicators noted above. To explain this, the book uses a conceptual framework that looks at the relationships of accountability that go beyond the corporation. The framework suggests the existence of a triangle with three sets of agents: the citizens, the State, and the corporations of providers. The partial reforms consist of interventions that circumvent the failures in the system of accountability instead of attempting to fix them. Many of the partial reforms described later achieve results, and an important recommendation emerging from this book is that those reforms should be supported and expanded and that the efforts of the corporations to reverse these reforms should be resisted. The evidence discussed in this book also suggests that many of these reforms are only temporary solutions because they are often reversed after relatively short periods of time. These valuable reforms would become stronger and would last longer if the gains in quality of service could be measured and publicized by the reformers.

Measuring quality of service requires standards. Standards are the "metrics of accountability." Without standards, users, administrators, and policymakers have no objective way to judge whether services are of acceptable quality or if quality is improving. Standards are resisted by the corporations, so at least initially they should be produced and measured from outside the corporation—possible options would include an independent public agency, a nongovernmental organization, or a private-public partnership. At the initial stage, the key is to avoid complexity because that makes it impossible to develop understandable and measurable targets. This book suggests focusing initially on a few simple standards. For education, there should be emphasis on measuring reading achievement in the early grades. All students in all schools should be evaluated every year, and parents, school administrators, regional authorities, and national policymakers should be provided with the data in easily understandable form. For health care, the book suggests clarifying the rights of users by stating clearly what services are included in the benefits package of Health Insurance for the Poor (*Seguro Integral de Salud*, SIS), who is entitled to those services, and what providers offer those services with acceptable results. The nutrition programs should include an integrated package of interventions, mothers should be able to monitor the progress of their children, and the criteria for eligibility should be transparent. Just as the sectors should operate with transparent standards, the financing of the sectors should also follow transparent rules. In a decentralized context this would clarify why some regions and municipalities get higher per capita transfers from the central government than others.

The book makes three recommendations that, to be successful, would need to be implemented sequentially. First, it is necessary to establish basic standards, targets for service quality, and systems of measurement of quality. Second, once quality is measurable, accountability systems should be established based on the use of the standards and the quality targets. Users would play a central role in these systems by demanding their right to quality services, but this will only be possible once there are standards and targets that would clarify the rights of the users. Third, once standards and accountability systems exist, there will be a need to invest in strengthening the institutional capacity of the providers. The investments would need to cover several areas, including: (a) information systems; (b) training of frontline providers, administrators, and user associations; and (c) incentives for providers who have proven capacity and are willing to work within a system based in standards and accountability.

The rest of this chapter is organized as follows. The next section describes the achievements of the sectors in terms of coverage, quality, and equity. The third section discusses public expenditures using international benchmarks for comparison, analyzing the institutional changes that accompanied the fluctuations of expenditures over the last two decades and examining whether the distribution of the benefits of the social programs is pro-poor. The fourth section explains the low-level equilibrium that exists within the health and education sectors. The fifth section presents the accountability framework, and the sixth section uses the framework to review the attempts to improve service delivery for the poor. The seventh section explains in more detail the need for standards. The final section presents the conclusions and discusses the main recommendations of the book.

Coverage, Outcomes, and Equity

Peru distinguishes itself within Latin America and the Caribbean (LAC) by having made impressive gains in all areas of coverage in formal education, in some areas of health care, and in the total number of people receiving some benefit from social assistance programs. There is a big gap between the achievements in coverage and the results in terms of quality, as many measures of quality of service show Peru below the same neighbors it surpasses in coverage. The distribution of the benefits of the three services is also more unequal than in many countries similar to Peru. This section describes these findings in more detail.

Education: Coverage, Learning, Inequality

In education, enrollment levels are higher than in many other Latin American countries— even higher than in other countries with higher income per capita. Gross enrollment ratios in pre-primary, secondary, and tertiary education are higher in Peru than the LAC average, and the ratio in primary is over 100 percent. Furthermore, despite having a per capita income lower than the LAC average, Peru has been ahead of the rest of Latin America, with regard to coverage, for decades (see Figure 1.1). Completion rates at the primary and secondary levels are also quite high.[1] In short, Peru has already achieved a mass education system of nearly developed-country standards, in terms of coverage.

The gap between enrollment and achievement levels is high. In most countries producing large numbers of high-school graduates, the skill levels of those graduates are also fairly high, so the labor market can absorb them. In Peru, there is a very large gap between the large numbers of graduates being produced and their skills. Quality of education, as proxied by learning levels measured by international assessments such as the Programme for International Student Assessment (PISA), is not impressive. In the combined reading scale in PISA, for example, Peru scored 327, while the rest of Latin American countries scored, on average, 411.

Is there a tradeoff between coverage and quality of learning, and has Peru chosen a path of high coverage with low quality? Chapter 6 suggests that there is some evidence supporting this hypothesis. Low quality is partly the result of a policy that consisted of allowing standards to slip in order to maintain a rapid expansion of school coverage. Examples include reducing the number of hours in a school day to allow two "shifts" in a school, reducing the entrance requirements for entrants to teacher-training schools, and reducing the years of formal training for teachers. Less visible but possibly more important is the loss of quality in classroom activities. However, Chapter 3 shows that Peru's record is not

---

1. Figure 1.1 shows that the gross enrollment in primary education, which reached around 125 percent in 2000, has fallen (but remains over 100 percent). This indicator compares the number of students in primary education with the number of children of primary-school age. Its decrease in recent years could reflect improvements in the primary completion rate and the very high rates of enrollment in secondary education that have been achieved.

Figure 1.1. Gross Enrollment Rates in Peru and Latin America, 1970–2004 (percent)

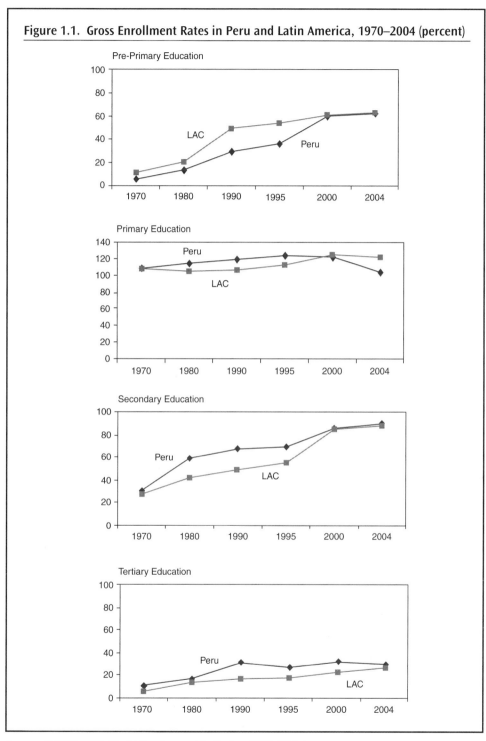

Source: ENAHO 2004; *World Development Indicators 2005*; Edstats.

as bad as is often thought if the broader context is considered: the other Latin American countries that participated in PISA have twice Peru's per capita income, some of them achieved mass literacy decades ahead of Peru, and Peru has a fifth more children per adult than the rest of the Latin American countries participating in PISA. Controlling for these factors, Peru's average level of quality may not be too far below its expected level.

Among PISA countries, Peru also had the most inequality, taking as an index of inequality the ratio of performance at the 95th percentile to performance at the 5th percentile. In Peru this ratio was 2.8. In Mexico and the Republic of Korea, this ratio was 2.0 and 1.6, respectively. Even in Brazil, a country with more income inequality than Peru, this ratio was 2.1. While inequality of learning is generally problematic, the Peruvian data on inequality point to a feature that may turn into an opportunity. Even though the poor as a group learn less than the rich, there are a significant number of poor children who obtain relatively high scores on learning tests. This suggests that there exist success stories in some schools attended by poor children. Chapter 3 investigates what makes these schools successful, in an attempt to obtain lessons that can be used in other schools. The main conclusion of that chapter is that in education there is a lack of standards, and a lack of accountability pressure and systems, built around learning, and as applicable in particular to the poor and multilingual.

Health Care: Coverage, Outcomes, Inequality

Internationally, the supply of health services tends to increase with the level of income of countries. Peru's per capita income is 70 percent of the Latin American average, and its supply of health services, measured by hospital beds per 1,000 population and by physicians per 1,000 population, are a third lower in Peru than the Latin American average (World Bank 2005a). Despite this lower supply, Peru has achieved relatively high levels of coverage for some public health interventions. Starting in the 1990s, coverage of key population-based collective health interventions, such as immunizations and treatment of acute respiratory infections among children, increased rapidly, surpassing the levels achieved by richer Latin American countries. At the same time, Peru continues to lag behind its neighbors in the coverage of basic clinical interventions, such as coverage of births by professionals, although the trend has improved significantly for some of these services (Figure 1.2).

Health outcomes are the result of many factors that affect quality of life, including education, access to water and sanitation, and health care. Some of the key health outcome indicators have improved in Peru, most notably indicators that respond to population-based health interventions such as the mortality of children under age 5. This indicator, which has been significantly worse in Peru than in neighboring countries for decades, has improved significantly and may already have reached the Latin American average (Figure 1.3).[2] Other indicators that depend more on hospital care, such as the maternal mortality rate (the MMR) or the perinatal mortality rate have improved in recent years, but remain significantly higher than the Latin American average (the MMR in Peru and in Latin America is estimated at 164 and 85 maternal deaths per 100,000 live births, respectively).

---

2. The most recent data are based on a small sample and are subject to a large statistical error.

Figure 1.2. Selected Health Intervention Trends in Peru and Latin America, 1990–2004

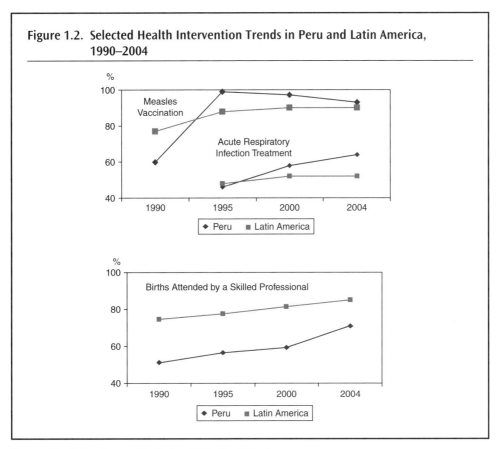

Source: *World Development Indicators 2005*, World Bank.

Figure 1.3. Under-5 Mortality in Peru and Latin America, 1970–2004 (Per 1,000 live births)

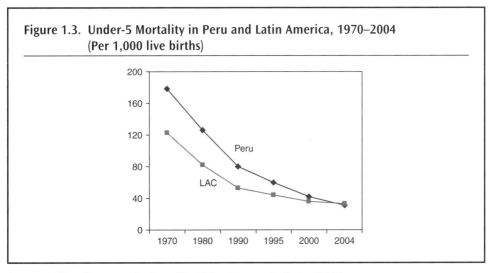

Source: DHS, various years for Peru (*World Development Indicators 2005*).

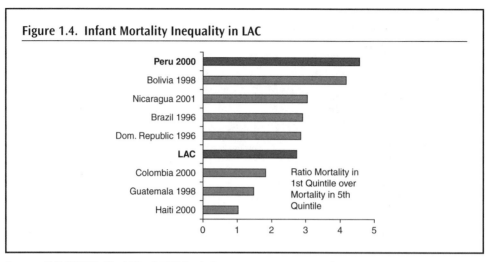

Figure 1.4. Infant Mortality Inequality in LAC

Source: ENDES 2000; World Bank DHS Statistics.

While there is much to celebrate in terms of improved average outcomes, inequality in health outcomes and in access to health care remains a top concern in Peru. Among the eight Latin American countries for which there is a demographic and health survey, Peru has the greatest inequality in infant mortality (Figure 1.4). A large fraction of the population has little access to health care. According to the Living Standards Measurement Survey (*Encuesta Nacional de Hogares*, ENAHO), in 2003, 13.4 million people (about half the population) had an episode of illness, of which only 62 percent received health care. Almost two-thirds of those who could not get care stated that the reason for not getting care was that they could not afford to pay for it. Lack of geographic access has become a less-important obstacle than in the past—it was stated as the main reason for not getting care by only 17 percent of respondents. Among the poorest 20 percent of the population, almost two-thirds did not receive care, compared with 13 percent among the richest 20 percent of the population.

Chapter 4 analyzes these trends and discusses a number of initiatives designed to improve coverage and quality of service. The chapter emphasizes the need for clearer standards and for greater transparency to strengthen accountability.

Social Assistance

As in health care, the coverage of social protection is high in some programs and low in others. The coverage of contributory social insurance schemes is very low—only 2.5 percent of the population in Peru receives pension benefits and only 5 percent of the population uses health services financed by social security.[3] This is less than half the average for Latin America

---

3. These estimates are based on ENAHO 2003/2004. Among the population over 65 years of age, only 22 percent are pensioners. ESSALUD claims that the number of users of its system is twice as high as the estimate based on household surveys.

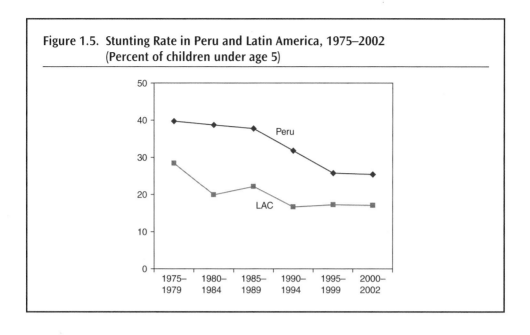

Figure 1.5. **Stunting Rate in Peru and Latin America, 1975–2002**
(Percent of children under age 5)

(Lindert, Skoufias, and Shapiro 2005). By contrast, the coverage of noncontributory social assistance programs is very high, reaching 44 percent of households. Benefits paid to the small fraction of the population with access to the social insurance programs are high and comparable to benefits paid by similar programs in other countries in LAC. Benefits of the social assistance programs (also known in Peru as antipoverty programs) by contrast are very low in value; the monthly value is estimated to be equivalent to 12 percent of the average value of similar programs in neighboring countries. The small benefit per program has led to a significant group of households that participate in multiple programs.

There is a strong debate about many aspects of the antipoverty programs. Many studies have focused on the quality of targeting, the fragmentation of the program, and their impact on nutrition. Chapter 5 reviews the evidence and concludes that the existing programs do reach the poor, but could have a greater impact on poverty reduction if they were designed to have an impact on improving the nutrition, education, and health care of young children. Malnutrition in particular continues to be an area were Peru lags significantly in relation to its neighbors (see Figure 1.5). To improve their impact, the programs should be more transparent in their objectives and targets, and should measure their progress in reaching those targets. That would allow greater accountability, and that would be translated into results.

Public Expenditures in Education, Health, and Social Assistance

Some of the main features of the social programs can be understood by an analysis of expenditures in the sector. This section analyzes the level of spending, comparing Peru with Latin America. Then, it describes the fluctuation in expenditures of recent decades, linking these fluctuations with institutional change. Finally, it looks at the distribution of expenditures across population and geographic groups.

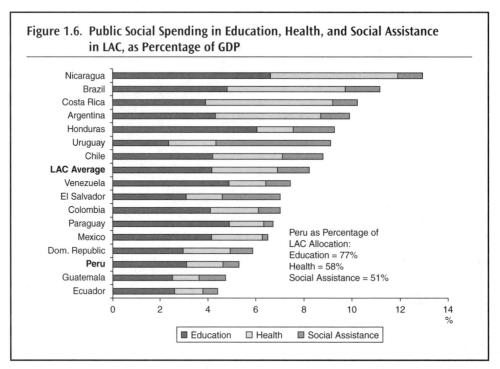

Figure 1.6. Public Social Spending in Education, Health, and Social Assistance in LAC, as Percentage of GDP

Source: DNPP-MEF; Lindert, Skoufias, and Shapiro (2005).

How Much Does Peru Spend on Social Programs Compared with Other Countries?

In 2004, public spending in Peru was 5.5 percent of gross domestic product (GDP) in the three sectors—significantly less than the unweighted average of 8.2 percent of GDP for Latin America that year. Spending was lower in Peru than the average for LAC in each of the three sectors: in education, health, and social assistance Peru spent, respectively, 3.2 percent, 1.6 percent, and 0.7 percent of GDP compared to the continental average of 4.2 percent, 2.7 percent, and 1.3 percent, respectively. Of 16 countries for which comparable data are available, only Ecuador and Guatemala spent less than Peru as a proportion of GDP. While Peru's GDP allocation to social sectors is smaller than the LAC average for each of the three sectors, the difference is less in education (where Peru's allocation was three-fourths of the LAC average) and largest in social assistance (where Peru's allocation was half of the LAC average; Figure 1.6).

Why does Peru spend less than its neighbors? Is the lower allocation due to a lower fiscal priority assigned to the social sectors, or is it the result of having a smaller tax effort? Table 1.1 shows the LAC countries divided into three similar-size groups in terms of fiscal priority (measured as a percent of the total public expenditure assigned to a sector) and in terms of tax burden. In terms of tax burden, Peru is in the lower group. In terms of fiscal priority, Peru is in the intermediate group in education and in health care, but it is in the lower third of countries in terms of fiscal effort for antipoverty programs. In other words, the main reason for the low social expenditures is that tax revenues as a percent of GDP are low in Peru compared with other Latin American countries. Fiscal priority is not the main culprit (except for social assistance).

Public Expenditure and Institutional Change—A Medium-term View

Public expenditures in the social sectors (education, health, and social assistance) have fluctuated significantly as a percent of GDP during the last 35 years. The fluctuations in expenditure were accompanied by institutional changes that have contributed to shaping the sectors into their present form.

Total social spending was around 4.5 percent of GDP in the early 1970s, after which there was a slow decline from the mid-1970s, until the mid-1980s, when social expenditures were around 4 percent of GDP. Inflation grew during the 1980s, reaching extreme levels by the middle of the decade. There were drastic cuts in social spending after 1986 in the attempt to stabilize the economy. During 1986–91, spending in education and in health care was cut in half as a proportion of GDP, while spending in social assistance programs increased slightly (Figure 1.7). This drastic cut in public spending pushed the education and health care systems into a serious crisis. Teachers and health workers saw their real salaries fall, while investment in and maintenance of schools, health posts, and hospitals stopped almost completely, and inputs for hospitals and schools virtually disappeared. In addition to the economic crisis, these were years of significant political violence, especially in rural areas. Some health posts and schools, especially in rural areas, closed their doors. Most hospitals and some schools, especially in urban areas, began to charge for their services, initially to replace medical inputs or teaching materials, and later to complement the drastically reduced salaries of their staff.

The imposition of fees, especially in health care, restricted access of the poor to most services. Paxson and Schady (2005) find an increase of about 2.5 percentage points in the infant mortality rate for children born during the crisis of the late 1980s, which implies that about 17,000 more children died than would have in the absence of the crises. The article shows that this was caused mainly by reduced public expenditures in health, and not by the contraction in household incomes.[4]

During the 1980s, a number of social assistance schemes were developed, particularly in urban areas, to provide food and other necessities to the unemployed and to refugees who migrated to the cities to escape rural violence. These schemes later expanded and became institutionalized as groups of women got organized around community kitchens, combining their work and a small monetary contribution with food aid provided initially by church groups, nongovernmental organizations (NGOs), and bilateral donors, and later by government agencies.

In the early 1990s, inflation was brought under control, public finances began to recuperate, and the government was able to reestablish social expenditure in an environment of great need to strengthen social cohesion weakened by the political violence. Social expenditures increased very rapidly after 1991. As a percent of GDP, expenditures on education doubled, peaking by 1995 at 3.3 percent of GDP and then remaining stable at around 3 percent

---

4. The authors also found that the temporary reduction in education expenditures did not impact educational results.

Table 1.1. Fiscal Priority of Spending on Education, Health, and Social Assistance in Latin America

(Figures in parentheses correspond to the percentage of GDP allocated to social expenditure on education.)

Fiscal Priority: Share of Total Public Spending Going to EDUCATION Sector

Spending as a Percentage of GDP (budgetary pressure)

		Less than 16%	Between 16% and 21%	More than 21%
More than 24%		Colombia (4.1) Brazil (4.8) Uruguay (3.2) Nicaragua (3.7)	Venezuela (4.9)	
Between 19% and 24%		Ecuador (2.6)	Chile (4.2) LAC (4.2)	Paraguay (4.9) Honduras (6.1) Costa Rica (4.7)
Under 19%			Peru (3.2) El Salvador (2.6) Dominican Republic (3.0) Guatemala (2.5)	Mexico (4.1) Argentina (4.3)

Fiscal Priority: Share of Total Public Spending Going to HEALTH Sector

Spending as a Percentage of GDP (budgetary pressure)

		Less than 7%	Between 7% and 13%	More than 13%
More than 24%		Colombia (2.0) Uruguay (3.7) Venezuela (1.5)		Nicaragua 3.7 Brazil (4.9)
Between 19% and 24%		Ecuador (1.2) Honduras (1.5)	Chile (2.9) LAC (2.7) Paraguay (1.4)	Costa Rica (5.7)
Under 19%			Dominican Republic (2.0) Peru (1.6) El Salvador (1.5) Guatemala (1.1)	Mexico (2.1) Argentina (4.4)

Fiscal Priority: Share of Total Public Spending Going to SOCIAL ASSISTANCE

Spending as a Percentage of GDP (budgetary pressure)

		Less than 4.5%	Between 4.5% and 7%	More than 7%
More than 24%		Colombia (0.9) Venezuela (1.0) Venezuela (1.5)	Nicaragua (1.1) Brazil (1.4)	Uruguay (4.7)
Between 19% and 24%		Paraguay (0.4) Ecuador (0.6)	Costa Rica (1.1) LAC (1.3)	Chile (1.7) Honduras (1.7)
Under 19%		Peru (0.7)	Argentina (1.2) Mexico (1.1) Dominican Republic (1.0)	Guatemala (1.1) El Salvador (2.4)

(continued)

Table 1.1. **Fiscal Priority of Spending on Education, Health, and Social Assistance in Latin America (*Continued*)**

Fiscal Priority: Share of Total Public Spending Going to Education, Health and Social Assistance			
	Less than 34%	**Between 34% and 40%**	**More than 40%**
More than 24%	Venezuela (7.4) Uruguay (11.6) Colombia (7.0)	Nicaragua 8.5 Brazil (11.2)	
Between 19% and 24%	Ecuador (4.4)	LAC (8.2) Honduras (9.3) Paraguay (6.7)	Chile (8.8) Costa Rica (11.5)
Under 19%	Peru (5.5)	Dominican Republic (5.9) Guatemala (4.7)	El Salvador (6.5) Argentina (9.9) Mexico (6.5)

(Row label along left side: Spending as a Percentage of GDP (budgetary pressure))

Source: Lindert, Skoufias, and Shapiro (2005).

of GDP for the rest of the decade. Expenditures in health tripled by 1998 reaching 1.5 percent of GDP and remained stable. Expenditures grew by a factor of 5 in social assistance (although from a very low base), peaking in 1999 at 1 percent of GDP.

The recuperation of social spending in the 1990s was accompanied by a significant change in the composition of spending within each sector. Only a small part of the increase was used to raise salaries. Legislation was passed, freezing the hiring of teachers and health

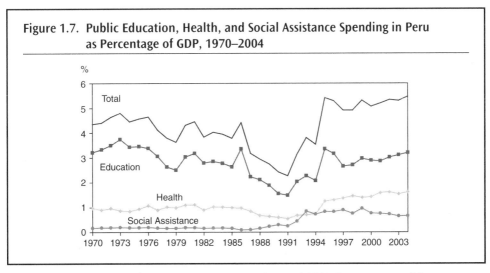

Figure 1.7. **Public Education, Health, and Social Assistance Spending in Peru as Percentage of GDP, 1970–2004**

Source: Francke (1998, 2003); *Peru en Numeros 1991, 1997,* and *2004*; Portocarrero and Romero (1994); OGP–MINSA webpage; DNPP–MEF database; PRONAA database; PRONAMACHCS webpage at: www.pronamachcs.gob.pe; INS webpage at: http://www.sisvan.gob.pe/web/progproy.htm.

workers as tenured civil servants (*nombrados*). Teachers and health workers were, however, hired, and in significant numbers, through nontenured contracts. Also, while some of the increase in spending went to strengthen the budget of traditional hospitals and schools, most went to finance new infrastructure in education and new programs in health and social assistance. Much of the new expenditure was directed to rural and peri-urban areas and to programs that were implemented by community groups, instead of by government agencies. In other words, most of the new funds were used to finance programs that circumvented the traditional corporation, particularly in health, education, and social assistance.

In health, there was little investment in urban hospitals, but massive investment in setting up and paying for the operating costs of rural and peri-urban primary care facilities. Between 1992 and 1996 the number of clinics in operation doubled. These new clinics were supported by a program that reached US$100 million per year to pay for vaccines and other medical inputs required to strengthen population-based collective health interventions and for health workers (who were hired as contract workers to circumvent the hiring freeze). A new program of government-financed, community-run health clinics was also established (Local Committees for Health Administration, *Comités Locales de Administración de Salud*, CLAS).

During the late 1990s, in education, much of the new expenditures went to the construction and rehabilitation of existing schools. New antipoverty programs were created targeting the rural population, including the National Compensation and Social Development Fund (*Fondo Nacional de Compensación y Desarrollo Social*, FONCODES) and the *Programa Nacional de Manejo de Cuencas Hidrográficas y Conservación de Suelos* (PRONAMACHCS), two social funds that provide financing to community groups to build small-scale infrastructure. The food programs were also expanded during these years. New programs were developed targeting the rural areas of the sierra that suffered most from terrorist violence (the Supplementary Food Program for Groups at Risk of Malnutrition [PACFO] and the Food and Nutrition Program for Families at Risk of Malnutrition [PANFAR]). In urban areas, the programs created during the 1980 were maintained (*Comedores Populares*) or expanded (*Vaso de Leche*).

After a small reduction in social spending in 2000, social expenditures grew moderately from 5.1 to 5.5 percent of GDP in 2004. This increase involved assigning a greater fiscal priority within the overall budget to the social sectors because it took place during a period of fiscal contraction (see Chapter 2). There was a small reallocation among sectors, as spending in social assistance fell by 30 percent and spending in education and health care slightly increased. The largest cut in social assistance took place in the social funds and in the food programs for the poor operating in the rural sierra. The cut in financing for the social funds was expected to be compensated by higher investment by municipalities and regions in the context of decentralization. Unfortunately, the municipal investment did not materialize.

The most significant change in spending after 2001 took place within the sectors. The programs created during the 1990s have been reduced to make space for significant increases in the payroll. In education, from 1999 to 2005 (estimates based on actual expenditures incurred until August), the payroll increased from 71 percent to 80 percent of total education expenditures. During this period, investments were reduced by 60 percent and the purchase of goods fell by 28 percent. A similar pattern took place in health, where from 1999 to 2005 the payroll increased from 36 percent to 54 percent of total spending, while investments were cut by half and goods were cut by a third. In both health and education, part of the increase in payrolls is due to the hiring as civil servants (*nombrados*) of thousands of teachers and health workers who previously had been working under various types of contracts, and partly due to increases in wages and benefits. The change in status from contract worker to *nombrado* implies a reduction in the hours of work, and in the health sector in some cases this has required the hiring of additional staff to avoid large reductions in the hours of operation of key services. In health, there also seems to have been a change of emphasis away from population-based programs of collective health to strengthening hospital-based treatment. This translated into a temporary loss of coverage of several collective health programs (including immunizations and family planning). The reduction in the availability of medical inputs has also led to an increase in tariffs charged to users of medical services.

Benefit Incidence Analysis

A benefit incidence analysis was performed to understand who benefits from the expenditures in education, health care, and social assistance, and how government spending affects the welfare of the different income groups. The analysis includes 20 programs: 6 programs in education, 4 programs in health, and 10 programs in social protection. The analysis was performed for each program in two ways: first, using administrative expenditure data to analyze to what degree the geographical distribution of expenditures across jurisdictions (regions or municipalities) is pro-poor according to a measure of poverty of the jurisdictions; and second, using household survey data combined with expenditure data to measure to what degree the distribution of public expenditures was pro-poor across households. Figure 1.8 shows the concentration coefficient of each program across households (the

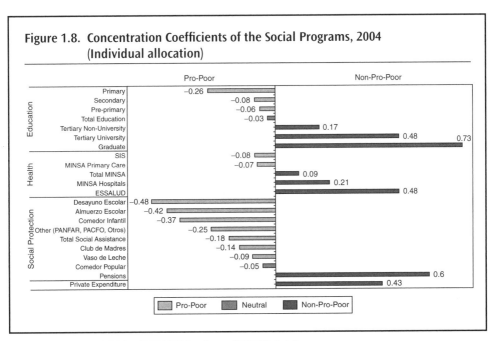

Figure 1.8. **Concentration Coefficients of the Social Programs, 2004 (Individual allocation)**

Source: ENAHO 2003/2004; SIAF-MEF database; PRONAA database.

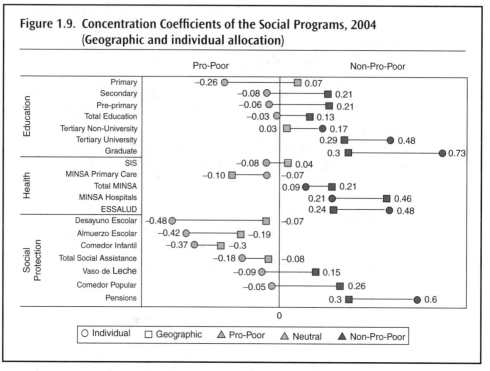

Figure 1.9. **Concentration Coefficients of the Social Programs, 2004 (Geographic and individual allocation)**

Source: ENAHO 2003/2004; SIAF-MEF database. DNPP database for *Vaso de Leche*. PRONAA database for food programs. ESSALUD (2005).

smaller the coefficient, the more pro-poor the program), and shows the coefficient of private expenditures as a comparator.

Of the 20 programs, 13 are pro-poor (with concentration coefficients in the negative range). The most pro-poor programs are the food programs that operate in rural schools (*Desayuno Escolar, Almuerzo Escolar, Comedor Infantil*), followed by primary education.[5] The least pro-poor programs (with large positive concentration coefficients) are: tertiary education (non-university, undergraduate university, and graduate university); Ministry of Health (MINSA) hospitals; the contributory Social Security in Health of Peru (ESSALUD) program; and pensions (which receive a large subsidy from the State).

Among the pro-poor programs, the distribution is even more pro-poor when it is measured at the household level instead of at the jurisdiction level (Figure 1.9). The reason for this is that these programs are not only pro-poor in their geographic distribution, but that they mostly benefit the poorer households within the jurisdiction in which they operate. This pattern exists for school education (pre-primary, primary, and secondary), all MINSA programs (SIS, primary care), and for all the social assistance programs for which data are available. In education and in health care, the pro-poor distribution of the programs is the results of household behavior: the poorer households have more children than the richer

---

5. The household surveys do not include independent information about PACFO, which is thought to be among the most pro-poor programs.

households, so they benefit more from public schools and clinics. The pro-poor distribution that occurs within jurisdictions is also the result of the low quality of the services: the richer households prefer to pay for private services and the poor cannot afford to do that. Two of the larger food programs (*Vaso de Leche* and *Comedores Populares*) are often thought to be non-pro-poor in their distribution. These programs have a geographic distribution that is not pro-poor; however, within their jurisdictions, they seem to be well targeted to the poor, so that the end result is a pro-poor distribution for *Vaso de Leche* and a neutral distribution for *Comedores Populares*.[6]

By contrast, for the programs that are not pro-poor, the end result is even more regressive at the household level than in the geographic distribution. This is true for post-secondary education, ESSALUD, and pensions. These programs are concentrated in the richer regions of the country, and within each region the higher-income households benefit more than the lower-income households.

The previous paragraphs discuss the question of how much of the public expenditures go to the poor (the question of "targeting" or "absolute incidence"). There is also a question about the importance of a given program for a group ("relative incidence"). This is measured by the average benefit received by a group or a household as a percentage of the total consumption of the group or household. Education and health constitute giant subsidies for the poor. For the extreme poor, the education and health subsidies are equivalent, respectively, to 24 percent and 7 percent of their household income. Those estimates are an average of all households in extreme poverty, including beneficiaries and nonbeneficiaries. If only beneficiaries are included, the education subsidy is 27 percent and the health subsidy is 20 percent. By contrast, the social assistance subsidy is equivalent to only 5 percent of the income of the beneficiary households.

Looking at the individual subprograms, the largest benefits (as a percentage of the household incomes of the beneficiaries) accrue to users of tertiary education and MINSA hospitals. While only 17 percent of university students come from poor families, for them the university subsidy is equivalent to 30 percent of household income. For the non-poor, the subsidy is also very large—16 percent of their average household income.

In MINSA hospitals, about half of the users are from poor households and half are from non-poor households. For all households, having access to the MINSA hospitals constitutes a form of catastrophic insurance. In any given year, the average benefit from these services is small, reflecting an average estimated for the whole group that includes a small number of users and a large number of non-users. However, when there is a need to use the hospitals, they provide a huge subsidy, equivalent to over 20 percent of the income of both poor and non-poor households.[7]

The analysis in this section is about average incidence, so we need to be careful in drawing conclusions about which programs would benefit the poor the most on the margin. For example, secondary education is mildly pro-poor now, but if most non-poor youth are already attending secondary school, any marginal investments in secondary schools could have strongly pro-poor effects. Also, the analysis focuses on the degree of targeting rather

---

6. The quality of the targeting of these programs is analyzed in detail in Chapter 5.

7. A similar proportion implies a higher dollar value for the richer households. This probably implies that they use the MINSA hospitals for higher-cost interventions.

than on its costs, and it is possible that the costs of improving the targeting of a program are greater than the additional resources that are transferred to the poor. Despite these limitations, three tentative conclusions can be drawn from the analysis in this section.

First, contrary to the prevailing view among critics of the social assistance programs, most of the social assistance programs are mildly to strongly pro-poor. Chapter 5 suggests that the problem with these programs is not so much the quality of their targeting as their lack of impact on long-term poverty determinants such as the nutrition and basic health of young children. Second, the main gains in terms of improved targeting are likely to come from efforts allocated to the non-pro-poor programs, specifically to public subsidies assigned to pensions and to higher education. These subsidies combined have a total value of around US$2 billion, or almost 20 times the total cost of the often-criticized *Vaso de Leche* program. Third, while there are many problems surrounding the way the antipoverty programs are distributed to households in the jurisdictions where they operate (see Chapter 5), they mainly benefit the poor households within their jurisdictions. This suggests that a decision to introduce new costly ways of targeting through administrative means should be carefully considered against their likely benefits.

Teachers and Health Workers: A Low-level Equilibrium

Why is there a low quality in the provision of social services? Given the importance of human resources in the provision of education and health services, it is useful to analyze the performance of human resources as a starting point to understand the quality of services. Chapter 6 suggests the hypothesis that there is a low-level equilibrium—a situation where standards of quality have fallen to a low level and the actors of the health and the education corporations have no motivation to change the existing state of affairs. Low quality is the result of a complex process triggered by the rapid expansion of coverage during several decades that featured a contraction in public expenditures per capita. This process transformed the "rules of the game" for the interactions of the actors in the education and health systems. With a base year of 1959 = 100 for all indexes, by 2002 population grew to 277, school enrollment to 575, and government teachers to 628. In other words, coverage grew very fast, as services expanded much faster than population. The employment of teachers grew even faster than coverage, so that their average workload was reduced (either class sizes fell, or hours and days of work were reduced, or both). There are also indications that teachers' salaries fell significantly during much of this period—between 1982 and 2002 public spending in recurrent costs grew by 5 percent while the number of teachers grew by 85 percent.

The "rules of the game" are crucial in the social sectors, which involve very large numbers of frontline professionals and managers, as well as unions and government authorities. The Ministry of Education estimates that in 2004 it employed 297,000 teachers and administrators, a third of whom worked in rural areas and 83 percent of whom had a pedagogical degree. The Ministry of Health estimates that it employs 65,000 health professionals, 44 percent of whom are in Lima. Among doctors, 58 percent are in Lima. An unknown number of teachers and health workers hired by municipalities and communities, and volunteers (in the tens of thousands) also work in primary schools and in primary care clinics.

Chapter 6 concludes that the rules of the game have deteriorated, leading to behaviors that produce low quality of performance by the frontline providers. The government succeeded in expanding coverage without increasing taxation and public expenditures. The unions, unable to prevent wages from falling, focused successfully on an agenda that has allowed professionals to compensate their low wages through engaging in other economic activities. Teachers and doctors seek alternative sources of income. About two-thirds of teachers have a second job. As a source of income, on average the teaching job provides only 41 percent of the household's income and 53 percent of the income of health professionals. The implication is that work and career decisions of education and health professionals, such as location, schedules, investment in training, or acceptance of administrative duties, will be determined by the overall economic strategy of the household, and the public sector career is only one of several considerations.

To be able to spend time and effort on their outside job, dedication to the public sector job had to fall. Successive governments have accommodated this need by granting rigid job tenure security, by reducing the hours of work, and by reducing work discipline. This was partly achieved by changes in the legislation that diluted the rules of selection of new entrants, delinked performance from remuneration, and granted rigid tenure rights. Vega (2005) provides a careful description of the dilution of standards in legislation related to the education sector during the last 50 years. As early as 1959 the government reduced the required number of years of training for a teaching degree; in the early 1970s the school week was reduced to five days and the school day to five hours, and teachers were allowed to work two shifts per day. In the early 1980s, a law elevated the value of non-university degrees to the same level as university degrees. In the late 1980s teachers were given stability "in their job, level, function and place of work."

Chapter 6 shows how most of the time, the changes were not the result of changes in legislation, but of lack of enforcement of norms designed to ensure career development and quality in work performance. This in turn led to a loss of self-respect that created a spiral of degradation and demoralization of these professions—workers feel entitled to lax discipline, which they deem necessary for them to have parallel careers; unions have established a cadre of officials that prevent administrators from attempting to establish discipline. Administrators feel that they cannot ask for more effort, given how little professionals are paid. Disorder is aggravated by a judicial system that undercuts the efforts of directors to impose discipline. Administrative actions are paralyzed and often reversed when employees resort to the courts, accusing directors of "abuse of authority." Chapter 6 quotes evidence showing that the success rate of directors attempting to discipline teachers is less than 10 percent (compared with a third in private schools). Worse, most directors who attempted to discipline teachers are now facing legal suits.

In the long run, the most important effect is not the adjustment of individuals, but the change in the quality of entrants into the profession. Chapter 6 presents indications that suggest that top professionals have dropped out of public service.

Users have contributed to this process by adding pressure for the expansion of coverage. Because quality is hard to measure, parents identified success with the promotion of their children to ever higher grades, and in health care, communities request access to facilities of higher complexity of care. For the poor in rural and peri-urban areas, demand focused on visible inputs, notably the construction and staffing of schools and clinics. Once a primary school became available offering the first three years of education, the next objective was to expand it to five grades. Because the rate of primary completion was high, the next aspiration was access to a secondary school. As early as the 1970s, the next level of aspiration in education was post-secondary schooling. For most parents, the only measure of quality is the promotion of their child to the next level of education. As long as expansion continued, their perception of quality was satisfied.

A third response by providers has been a turn to self-financing. To an increasing extent, users are paying for services provided by the public education and health systems. The methods range from the legal to the illegal, with a great deal that is dubious. In one way or another, service professionals are generating more and more self-financing as a way to supplement government salaries. There is little systematic information on self-financing, even funds generated by legitimate and published fees, but there are clear indications that is has grown—in health, where there are data about this, they are thought to have doubled after 1980 as a proportion of revenues, reaching 13 percent of total revenues in 2003.

Users, unions, and administrators all gained by the expansion of coverage, and none had a strong incentive to resist the decline in quality that took place to accommodate the expansion. Webb and Valencia in Chapter 6 describe the resulting outcome as a "low-level equilibrium." Box 1.1, reproduced from Vega (2005), describes the political equilibrium by analyzing in more detail the incentives faced by the various actors in the educational system.

As mentioned, the hypothesis of the low level of equilibrium suggests that the actors within the health and the education corporation have no incentive to change their behavior. In education the teachers, principals, regional authorities, unions, and the ministerial administration are all part of the low-level outcome. Inside the corporation, the equilibrium requires lax accountability among members of the corporation—doctors cannot expect much from nurses, hospital directors from doctors or from regional managers, or national managers from regional managers. The implication is that any changes can only come from outside the corporation as external shocks. There is evidence from other countries that, at least at the level of individual schools, institutions that have made substantial improvements in performance over the years have one thing in common: an external shock. In the next section a conceptual framework is described broadening the relations of accountability beyond the limits of the corporation. This framework is then used to interpret the mechanics of several reforms under way in the social sectors. Although social assistance is different from education and health in that it involves a much smaller bureaucracy, this sector has piloted some of the reforms that have then been applied to health and (in a more limited way) to education, and its institutional arrangement can also be described with the use of the framework.

The Accountability Framework

This section describes the conceptual framework of accountability in service delivery developed by Devarajan and Reinikka in the *World Development Report 2004: Making Services Work for Poor People*. The framework explains why the service delivery chain for social services often fails for poor people, and identifies possible forces of change. There are three sets of actors: (a) the citizens or clients of the system; (b) the corporation of service providers, including the frontline providers, the administrators, the local and regional authorities, and the top echelons of the administration at the ministerial level; and (c) the

Box 1.1: The Low-level Equilibrium in Education

Actor	Interest Expressed	Other Interest	Current Balance
Parents	To ensure that their children develop the skills required to better perform in a modern society, and as such improve the children's opportunities for social progress.	Many parents built their children's schools with their own hands. These individuals seek to ensure that their children are kept busy and safe, and that they receive complementary health and nutrition services.	The parents are content with the fact that they have a nursery that can take care of their children for several hours a day while they pursue other activities. They do not perceive that their children do not learn.
Teachers	To work professionally according to high moral standards while ensuring that the children of the community receive an education that enables them to improve their personal opportunities and collective development of the country.	To ensure the best possible working conditions and the highest feasible income to secure the well-being of their families. For almost all of them, being a teacher has enabled them to improve their social status and income possibilities compared to their father's earning capacity.	Teachers are content because they have stable, part-time employment with a negotiating capacity that allows them to increase their earnings or better their working conditions without being evaluated regarding their offered services or professional capacities.
Directors and academic authorities at schools	To encourage the members of the educational community—parents, teachers, and students—to obtain the highest possible formative achievements.	To ensure the best possible working conditions and income to secure the well-being of their own families. To obtain recognition for service rendered. To circumvent controls imposed by the administrative structure.	The directors are content as long as they encounter no problems with the Parent Association (APAFA), the teachers, or administration. They get a *nombramiento* post in the civil service that allows them to retire with a higher income (however modest) and with few demands.
Trainers, teachers, and graduate students of education	To improve the quality of service by promoting best practices so that the system continually improves performance despite a changing and increasingly demanding environment.	Increase the supply of teachers in such a way that allows them to teach and others to study. Trainers: To ensure better working conditions and income to secure the family's well-being. Graduate Students of Education: To obtain a degree that allows them to find stable public employment.	Trainers and graduate students are content because many institutions have openings for them. They do not perceive that the system and current consensus will impede the overhaul of public education and that the majority of the education students (even if they are better than current teachers) will not find employment.
The union	Like all professional unions, this group defends the professional prestige of its associates and seeks to obtain economic recognition and improved working conditions for its members.	The union is an instrument for the economic (*Derrama Magisterial*, Teachers Social Security and Credit Union Fund) and political benefits of a political party.	The union heads are content because they enjoy both leadership and legitimacy, and can hold office without general elections, in exchange for reaping economic benefits for their members without expecting any compensation from the teachers.
Public education administration	To provide support to schools in the implementation of education policies aimed at achieving learning objectives, building citizenship, and development of equal opportunities.	Obtain recognition for public service they render. To ensure better working conditions and income to secure the well-being of their families. To exploit for personal benefit the relationship with the administrative authority.	The administrators are content because they have achieved a small space that permits them to enjoy monetary benefits, prestige, and client access.

(continued)

Box 1.1: The Low-level Equilibrium in Education (*Continued*)

Actor	Interest Expressed	Other Interest	Current Balance
Experts and formers of public opinion including think tanks	The informed intelligentsia creates and maintains the public opinion consensus on the priority of education in the construction of a society that promotes responsibility and individual and collective development.	To obtain recognition for the public service rendered. To collaborate with governance. To ensure better working conditions and income to secure the well-being of their families.	The intellectuals or think tanks and political forces are content to produce documents on education, such as the National Agreement or the New Social Pact of Reciprocal Commitments, because they have built a consensus and secured a voter base. They are incapable of judging whether the consensus is useful in solving the problems at hand. Almost all of these individuals educate their children in private schools.
Local authorities	To facilitate support to the community to administer educational centers with the needs of the inhabitants in mind; they coordinate and direct the services they provide in their ambit and represent community interests before regional and national authorities.	To obtain recognition for the public service provided. To collaborate in governance. To ensure better working conditions and income for the well-being of their families.	The local authorities have no clear responsibilities and do not know what to do besides making some type of investment. They do not wish, given that many are teachers, to be responsible for the performance control of teachers and schools.
Government political authorities	The government fulfills the three tasks assigned to the State by the Constitution in the area of education: to define objectives, ensure that no one is left out of the loop, and guarantee quality by making any necessary decisions.	To ensure social peace and governability. To manage the nation's budget with austerity.	The government, and particularly those individuals responsible for the public budget, obtains "governability" by making a meagre per capita investment. This means that neither the teachers nor parents nor citizens are able to adversely affect the authorities' fragile legitimacy and leadership with strikes,* denunciations, or other methods.
Students	Younger primary-school children frequently express that they are uncertain why they have to go to school at all. Older children and university students declare that they are interested in acquiring skills that will allow them to fulfill their dreams of personal, family, and even national achievement.	To learn the rules of social coexistence and develop a circle of friends. To obtain recognition from their peers. To obtain accreditation backed by a certificate or degree. To fulfill the expectations of their teachers and parents.	Many students are satisfied because they have managed to learn the social rules of survival (although this appears to contradict the values expressed) and are able to obtain certificates and degrees with a minimum of effort in a scenario in which neither their teachers nor parents make significant demands or have high expectations of or for them

* The political authorities responsible for these areas are satisfied because the consensus allows them—in negotiations with the union—to grant benefits without demanding an increase in educational quality as guaranteed by the Constitution.
Source: Vega (2005).

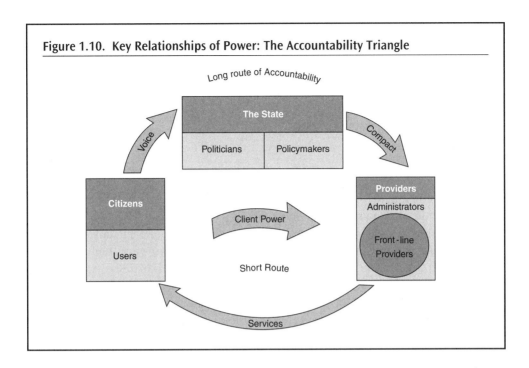

Figure 1.10. Key Relationships of Power: The Accountability Triangle

state (including regional or subnational levels), which includes politicians and policymakers in both the legislative and executive branches. The relation among these three actors is sometimes referred to as the "accountability triangle" (see Figure 1.10).

People—as patients in clinics or students in schools—are the clients of services (the bottom of the triangle). They have a relationship with the frontline providers, schoolteachers, and doctors. For the services considered here—health, education, and social assistance—society has decided that the service will be financed not through a market transaction but through the government taking responsibility. Hence, there is no direct accountability of the provider to the consumer through the market.[8] However, as the following sections will describe, a number of experiences are under way to empower users in relation to the frontline providers to create a "short route of accountability" to improve services. An example of this in the health sector consists of community leaders who have established nonprofit boards that direct the management of over 2,000 primary care clinics.

The role of the government in the provision of services requires the establishment of a "long route" of accountability—by clients as citizens influencing policymakers ("voice" at the left side of the triangle), and policymakers influencing providers ("compact" at the right side of the triangle). Consider "voice"—the link between citizens and policymakers or politicians. People contribute to defining society's collective objectives, and they try to

---

8. Users can also opt out of the public sector by choosing to pay for private schools and clinics. When they do so, however, they do not take with them any public funds, so their market choice has no impact on the public providers they abandon.

control public action to achieve those objectives through votes, through influence in Parliament, through demonstrations, and through the use of the media. In practice, this does not always work. In Peru, there exist today a number of institutional innovations that have developed with the objective of strengthening the voice of the citizens in the design and regulation of social services. Some of these innovations consist of improvements of the electoral system or the development of new forms of electoral representation created in the context of the process of decentralization. Other innovations attempt to influence the policymakers directly through forms of direct participation. These instances of "voice" are discussed below.

Even if people can reach the policymaker, services will not improve unless the policymaker can ensure that the service provider will deliver services to them. This relationship between the policymaker and the provider embodies the creation of laws and regulations and the provision of resources. While in theory these should be powerful tools that should give policymakers significant power over the providers, in practice very often policymakers have little influence over the providers. The low-level equilibrium described in the previous section is partly the result of this lack of influence. Legislation, regulation, and the power of the purse are often not enough to change the behavior of providers. The administrators of the health and education systems respond to health workers and to teachers much more than they respond to users. Officials at the Ministry of Education are more concerned with the problems of teachers than with the problems of learning by students. Officials at the Ministry of Health respond first to the demands of health professionals and later to the needs of users. Often administrators and frontline providers behave as closed "corporations." Health and education workers have a strong weight as voters and are very well organized.

Users, by contrast, are not well organized, are not sufficiently aware of the problems of quality in the system, and have no benchmark of what a good system should deliver. Solving the problem of users requires mentally, and sometimes physically, separating the administrator from the provider—and thinking of the relationship between the two as a contract or "compact." If the separation is achieved, the provider agrees to deliver a service, in return for being rewarded or penalized depending on performance. The compact may be an explicit contract between tiers of government, or it could be implicit, as in the employment agreements of civil servants. Separating the policymaker from the provider is not easy, because those who benefit from the lack of separation resist it. The separation of administrators and providers would require a profound reform of the State. There have been some mild attempts to do this in recent years, but without much success. Faced with the inability to do this, there have been several attempts by policymakers to shock the system by creating a parallel cadre of frontline providers or by dealing with the existing frontline providers in ways that circumvent the corporate administrators. Those attempts are described in the next section.

Attempts to Break the Low-level Equilibrium

In recent years, there have been several attempts to shock or reform the system. Using the accountability triangle, we can classify the reforms of recent years into three groups: (a) reforms that seek to strengthen the short route of accountability by placing users as

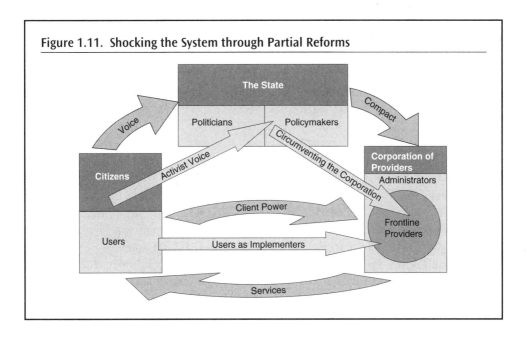

Figure 1.11. Shocking the System through Partial Reforms

implementers of services (empowerment of users); (b) reforms that establish a parallel system of frontline providers or that establish procedures to circumvent the rigidities of the existing corporations by reaching directly to the frontline providers; and (c) reforms that attempt to give citizens a stronger influence in the design and implementation of social programs ("Voice"). These attempts to shock the system are illustrated in Figure 1.11 and are described below. The section then discusses the potential shock value of the ongoing process of decentralization.

Users as Implementers

In recent decades, users have established a direct influence on service provision in many ways. Chapters 3, 4, and 5 suggest that the direct participation by users in the implementation of social programs led to significant shocks in three ways: (a) forcing a physical expansion of the health and education systems to poor areas; (b) implementing social assistance programs without the intermediation of a state corporation; and (c) managing a large number of primary care clinics outside the procedures of the health corporation. These reforms are described below.

Users and Infrastructure. Much of the expansion of education and health care coverage that has occurred in the last 50 years in rural and peri-urban locations has been the result of pressure by communities to obtain such services. Most communities in remote areas have a history that began with an effort to get organized to request from the relevant authorities a first-level establishment—a single–teacher, multigrade school or a basic health post staffed by an auxiliary nurse. To emphasize their interest in the service and put pressure on the line ministry for the allocation of staff, for many decades communities would build the infrastructure, usually with support from an outside agency. In the 1960s, *Cooperación Popular* helped communities build their schools and health posts. In the early 1970s, the *Sistema Nacional de Movilización Social* (SINAMOS) helped obtain building material for organized communities, and these activities were later pursued by NGOs that channeled external funds helping communities build their facilities. Many of these schools and health posts suffered greatly during the 1980s as a result of violence and fiscal crisis.

In the 1990s, there was a frenzy of construction of simple infrastructure financed by FONCODES, a social fund. The government passed special legislation that allowed FON-CODES to circumvent the rigidities of planning and executing public investment through line ministries. This legislation allowed the transfer of funds to *Núcleos Ejecutores*, community groups that could choose from a simple menu of investments and would be in charge of the procurement of works using simplified rules. The agility of the new legislation allowed community groups to implement about 40,000 small-scale projects with a value of more than US$2 billion in a decade—mostly rehabilitation and construction of schools, health posts, water and sanitation systems, rural roads, secondary electrification schemes, and small irrigation systems. Once the infrastructure is built, communities put pressure on the relevant authorities to assign staff. Often in the initial years the local community or municipality finances the hiring of the first teacher or auxiliary nurse. It is common for young professionals to volunteer their services for some time to establish a right to be hired for the position once it is opened.

While these programs produced important benefits, they also created problems. They compete with the line agencies (the Ministries of Education, Health, and Water and Sanitation) that criticize them, stating that there is lack of coordination that sometimes creates an excessive number of schools or health posts in a certain area. In health, they often lead to the construction of small rural hospitals that cannot be staffed and end up being underused. They also compete with local governments that criticize them, stating that in a decentralized context the local governments should be in charge of organizing these activities. In recent years, the government has been cutting the funding of these programs with the expectation that municipalities would increase their investment activity and would cover the areas formerly covered by the social funds. This has not happened because the rural municipalities that benefited from the social funds did not increase their investment levels due to lack of access to the special legislation that had been developed for the social funds and due to lack of capacity to develop and implement projects.

Users and Social Assistance Programs. Food assistance programs in Peru today reach 9.5 million beneficiaries, spending around 0.4 percent of GDP. The largest of these programs are implemented by community groups that receive food and require the community to organize to cook and distribute the food. These programs originated in the early 1980s. They were energized by the reestablishment of democracy after a long period of military government, and were prompted by the economic crisis of 1983, which led GDP to fall by 9 percent and inflation to reach 125 percent per year. They were independently championed by the First Lady, who promoted *Cocinas Populares*, and by the left-wing mayor of Lima, who promised a million glasses of milk and created the *Vaso de Leche* program. During the 1980s, these programs received food donations from bilateral aid agencies, international NGOs linked to the church, and the World Food Program.

Vaso de Leche is the largest of these programs, with over 5 million beneficiaries. The beneficiaries organize in groups that receive the food from the municipality and then cook it (or in some cases distribute it uncooked). The cooking is done in the house of one of the beneficiaries in the early morning by two or three women who rotate the task. The mothers who are not in charge of cooking collect the food every morning. The benefits are relatively small (US$2 per month per beneficiary) and the effort of participating in the group is relatively large, leading to self-selection. The central government funds the program and covers only the food. Other costs must be paid for by the municipality or by the beneficiaries.

The use of beneficiary groups for these programs has important advantages for the beneficiaries, including the creation of social capital and an effective protection of the budget—by law the funds of these programs cannot be used to pay for salaries, so there is no bureaucracy that could grow at the expense of the benefits. The programs, however, also have significant drawbacks. One is the difficulty in managing a graduation of beneficiaries. Because the beneficiaries govern themselves and government support is limited to providing them with food, the beneficiaries become a closed group with an interest in extending the benefits for themselves and not for the rest of the community. Chapter 5 shows how the mothers of *Vaso de Leche* have continuously extended the age limit of beneficiaries to keep their children in the program. This is done at the expense of other younger children whose nutritional status could be improved. In recent years some of the beneficiaries have been receiving the food uncooked. This has worsened since 2001 and is a serious concern, because it eliminates the main instrument of self-targeting in the program. Finally, because these programs are implemented with little contact with government services, they lack the coordination with complementary services such as education, health care, and nutritional guidance, necessary for the programs to have an impact on the nutritional status of the beneficiaries.

Users and the Provision of Primary Health Care: The CLAS. Following on the success of community groups in making investments financed by the social funds, and in implementing the social assistance programs, in the mid-1990s there were various attempts to involve communities in the management of schools and health facilities. In education, the government passed a decree in 1991 to implement a system that would give parents a strong role in the management of schools. The decree was met with a teacher strike that lasted five months, until the effort was abandoned.

In health, a lower-profile attempt was more successful. In 1994 a new program was developed to transfer the management of health posts to community groups. Hundreds of new health posts were rehabilitated, and many of them were not staffed. The *Comités Locales de Administración de Salud* (CLAS) were established as nonprofit institutions created by community members to manage a primary-care clinic. They receive public funds to produce services specified by a three-year contract, and agree with the health authorities on targets and activities. At present, about a third of public clinics are managed under this system.

Given their nongovernmental nature, the CLAS achieved substantial flexibility in the management of funds and in the management of health workers. During the initial years of operation, the CLAS were not subject to the slow procedures of public sector budget management. Also, they had direct management of their funds, unlike conventional health clinics the funds of which are managed by subregional administrators located outside the clinic. The CLAS could also hire staff under private sector legislation. The use of short-term contracts and bonuses provided staff with a strong incentive framework.

A number of studies have attempted to evaluate the performance of the CLAS, described in Chapter 4. Comparisons between CLAS and conventional clinics in similar geographic and social settings suggest that the CLAS: (a) have a 30 percent higher productivity per health worker (Harding and Alvarado 2005), (b) provide 61 percent more access to low-income users financed by Health Insurance for the Poor (*Seguro Integral de Salud*, SIS) in urban areas and 20 percent more access in rural areas (Altobelli, Sovero, and Diaz 2004), and (c) achieve 9 percentage points higher user satisfaction rates (Cortez 1998). There are also indications that waiting times are lower in CLAS than in conventional clinics.

Despite these positive results, the CLAS system encountered significant resistance from the public sector and from the health worker unions. During the last several years, MINSA administrators resisted an expansion of the system, irrespective of numerous requests from local groups. More crucially, the flexibility of the CLAS in the management of funds and of human resources has been curtailed. The Ministry of Finance pressed to establish public accounting and procurement rules for the CLAS, reducing their flexibility and agility to process purchases. In December 2004, legislation was passed granting all physicians working for the CLAS the right to become *nombrados*, subject to the legislation of the civil service for health workers. Over 3,000 physicians have changed status under this legislation, reducing their hours of work per day and their days of work per month, and increasing the cost of payrolls. The future of the CLAS system looks uncertain because the union representing the rest of the health professionals is demanding similar treatment as that given to the physicians.

Circumventing the Corporations

This section describes three attempts to solve the problem of the low-level equilibrium by circumventing the corporations: an example of outsourcing the management of schools, an experience with hiring contract workers outside the rules of the corporation, and a new way of financing health care.

Outsourcing Service Provision. Fe y Alegría (FyA) is a Catholic organization that manages schools financed by the public sector. It began work in 1955 in Venezuela and is now established in several Latin American countries. In Peru, FyA has 71,000 students, 3,200 teachers, 62 large schools, 97 rural schools managed under 4 networks, and a number of technical and vocational venues. The FyA schools aim to reach children, who are typically from the bottom two quintiles of income distribution. Performance evaluations regularly show results better than those in public schools, even though costs are about the same, because the system uses teachers paid on the same salary scale as public school teachers and at about the same pupil/teacher ratio.

Chapter 3 analyzes the possibility of expanding the experience by enlarging the number of schools outsourced or by taking the factors that explain the success of FyA and applying them to public schools. It concludes that a number of the factors that make FyA successful are replicable, but that others are not. Replicable factors include: Clearer curricular and achievement standards, more monitoring and evaluation, more continuity in leadership, more use of universalized measurements as feedback to individual schools, and the realization that Head Offices (such as the Province-level School Management and Supervision Unit, *Unidad de Gestión Educativa Local* [UGELs] in the public sector) are meant to provide services to the schools.

Other factors are not replicable: many FyA principals, for example, are unique individuals not in very elastic supply to the public sector. Some are foreign, are extremely well educated, are religious, and have experience managing modern, large schools in developed countries. There is some selection of parents. Schools are placed largely where communities demand them. All of these factors suggest that one should be cautious about how much the whole system could improve via outsourcing or contract models such as FyA. This is not to say that outsourcing of this sort is unpromising; on the contrary, experimentation should continue, but it should be cautious and well documented, and should pay particular attention to researching the nonreplicability issues.

Hiring Temporary Workers. In health care, there is a huge concentration of human resources and equipment in Lima. This has improved in recent years—the availability of physicians was five times higher in Lima than in the rest of the country in the mid-1960s. Since then, the supply has grown almost four times faster outside Lima. Much of this improvement was brought about by urban growth outside Lima, which provided a natural pull for physicians. Part of it, however, particularly in rural areas, was achieved through government interventions.

One such intervention was *Servicio Rural y Urbano Marginal de Salud* (SERUMS), a voluntary internship program created in the 1980s to replace an earlier program that required all medical students to work without pay for a year in rural establishments as a condition for graduation. SERUMS is not a requisite for graduation, but it provided young medical graduates with extra points to apply for employment in the public health sector and to apply for admission to government internship programs for further specialization. In recent years, SERUMS has provided over 1,000 health professionals to health clinics in poor locations.

Another such intervention was the *Programa de Administración de Acuerdos de Gestión* (PAAG). This program was started in 1994 to hire health workers for newly rehabilitated primary care clinics.[9] The program was managed centrally, health workers were hired under temporary contracts that were not subject to the civil service legislation, and the staff was assigned to specific clinics in poor locations. Contracts were renewed based on performance criteria. Initially, the program also paid bonuses to regular MINSA staff to extend their hours of operation beyond their regular hours of work. In 2000, the program employed over 10,000 health workers; about half were doctors and nurses and the rest were auxiliary nurses and other health technicians.

Both PAAG and SERUM have been subject to much opposition. In 2004, after a long strike, the government agreed to designate the doctors working under the PAAG program

---

9. The original name of the program was *Salud Básica para Todos* (Basic Health for All), and it financed staff, inputs for core public health programs, and some construction.

as *nombrados*, without undergoing the requisite of an open competition. In 2005, the nurses requested similar treatment. Once these professionals become *nombrados*, they soon move from their rural locations to urban hospitals. Another result of the conflict of 2004 was to eliminate the advantage that SERUM used to confer on young professionals interested in applying to specialization programs. Given these changes, the government that will take office in 2006 will face a significant challenge in maintaining the staffing that has been achieved in rural areas. There is a big risk that the gains in outcomes of recent years could suffer as a result.

Health Insurance for the Poor. In 2001, the government created Health Insurance for the Poor (*Seguro Integral de Salud*, SIS), in an effort to help overcome the economic barrier that prevents the poor from accessing health care. SIS was created based on smaller-scale experiences that had proven successful in previous years. It works on the premise that there is an underuse of capacity in public hospitals and clinics and that with the correct incentives the existing providers could increase their productivity and provide service to a larger number of people. The infrastructure, equipment, and staff are already paid for through the budget of the Ministry of Health, and SIS pays a fee for each service provided to predefined beneficiaries based on tariffs that are estimated to cover medical inputs, medicine, and a markup. It circumvents the "corporation" by paying directly to frontline providers and by doing it as payment for services effectively provided (and involving a system of audits), instead of following the traditional route that would add resources to a budget line provided to the ministry. SIS has five benefit Plans: A for Children up to four years old; B for children ages 5 to 17; C for maternal services; D for emergencies; and E for selected beneficiary groups, which include the leaders of several antipoverty programs and other politically influential groups that have been added to the lists of beneficiaries without adding funds to the budget of SIS to pay for these services.

While SIS has a budget equivalent to only 7 percent of the budget of MINSA (including the cost of the regional offices), its influence consists of opening the doors of MINSA to people who might not be able to afford a user fee. It is thought to have contributed to a significant improvement in the coverage of services to the poor. While there is no rigorous impact evaluation of the program, several analysts associate the implementation of SIS with the rapid expansion of institutional births from 58 percent in 2000 to 70 percent in 2004 as measured by household surveys (INEI 2004). While SIS is not as well targeted to the poor as similar schemes in other countries, it is significantly more progressive than all other health programs in Peru. Of each SIS dollar, 67 cents go to the poor; of each MINSA primary care dollar, 58 cents go to the poor; of each MINSA hospital dollar, 33 cents go to the poor; and of each ESSALUD dollar, 17 cents go to the poor. These results are the consequence of the emphasis placed by SIS on providing coverage outside Lima, in rural areas, and in limiting the financing it provides to high-complexity hospitals.

Like all the other attempts to reform the system described in this book, SIS has encountered resistance from many fronts. MINSA would like to manage SIS funds through its traditional budget, and SIS and MINSA have been at loggerheads over many issues, including the regulation of services, the setting of tariffs, and the choice of benefits included in the benefit plans. The frontline providers are under pressure to increase their productivity and resist having a larger number of patients per day (even if productivity per professional per day is thought to remain at levels equivalent to less than 20 percent of what they are in the private sector). Frontline providers also resist SIS because it imposes tariffs that are often smaller than what the providers would charge to the public (the services covered by SIS are provided free of charge to the user). The Treasury also resists SIS because it exposes the government to a loss of discretion in the execution of the budget: once a service that is covered by a plan is provided to somebody entitled to coverage, SIS incurs a debt to the provider of the service. While in theory this is manageable—all insurance schemes work this way—it requires a huge change of culture in the Treasury. In 2004 there was a large increase in the MINSA payrolls and a large cut in the SIS budget. The cut in SIS implied that many providers did not receive payment for services already provided. In addition to the financial costs to the providers, this might have created a longer-term problem of trust in the new system.[10]

Strengthening Citizen Voice

The 1990s were the heyday of the reforms that encouraged users to engage directly in the provision of services. At the same time, that decade saw few developments in the area of "citizen voice." Communities were encouraged to take action in their local sphere and to direct their energy to the implementation of specific projects, but were discouraged from active participation in broader areas of decisionmaking. By contrast, in the 2000s the government has encouraged participation in "voice activities" aimed at discussing plans and activities that are ambitious in their scope and time frame, while it has reduced the scope for direct participation on service delivery, leaving that activity to the formal providers and to the new regional and municipal bureaucracies.

In the last five years the environment for citizens to influence policymakers has been strengthened in two significant ways described in detail in Chapter 7. First, while the 1990s were characterized by secrecy, since 2000 the right of citizens to access public information has been greatly expanded through legislation, and through a rapid expansion in the use of information technologies. Second, various institutions have materialized to influence social policy and social budgets at the national, regional, and municipal levels. This initially occurred as a spontaneous response to the vacuum created by the dismantling of the political system that existed until 2000, and later as part of the new institutionality mandated by the decentralization legislation.

Access to Public Information. The Law of Transparency and Public Information of 2002 and subsequent legislation related to transparency, to sectoral organization, and to decentralization require central, regional, and municipal governments to regularly publish information on numerous areas. The Ombudsman Office (*Defensoría del Pueblo*) has been actively monitoring this policy. Helped by an explosive growth in the use of the Internet by government agencies and by the public at large, information is today widely available on many areas. By the end of 2004, 23 ministries, all regional governments, and many municipalities had implemented Transparency Portals. The Ministry of Finance's financial

---

10. Chapter 4 includes a number of recommendations to strengthen the capacity of SIS to behave as an insurer and to limit the uncertainty in the total cost of SIS to the Treasury.

information system (Integrated System for Financial Administration, *Sistema Integrado de Administración Financiera*, SIAF) has established a fairly user-friendly portal with useful information for anyone interested in monitoring the central government's budget. Many regional and municipal governments are complying with the legal requirement to make public information available on open hearings on a regular basis. A number of civil society organizations have developed programs dedicated to monitoring the use of some of this wealth of information.

The availability of this information has significant potential value, but in its current form much of the information cannot be used as an instrument of accountability. With few exceptions (such as the SIAF) much of the information is not systematic, and in very few cases it is directed at monitoring progress in the implementation of programs. The quality and usefulness of the information is likely to improve as it is used by people and institutions interested in monitoring.

Institutions that Influence Social Policy.   A large number of organizations and institutionalized participatory processes have developed at the regional and local levels during the transition government and in the context of the implementation of the various laws issued after 2001 to promote decentralization. The main organizations and processes today are the *Mesa de Concertación para el Alivio de la Pobreza* (Roundtable for the Fight against Poverty), the Regional and Local Coordination Councils, and the *Presupuesto Participativo* (Participatory Budget). The first organizations that spread widely were the *Mesas*, which were constituted by government officials, representatives of religious groups, NGOs, and other civil society groups to fill the coordination vacuum that followed the dismantling of some of the centralized decisionmaking controls of the late 1990s. Local-level *Mesas* were established during the transition period to coordinate and monitor the social programs of the Government.[11] By December 2003, 1,283 *Mesas* were operating in the country. The rapid organization of the *Mesas* is a reflection of the appetite to participate in decisionmaking for social policy that characterized the political transition. This appetite led to the passing of legislation in 2002 that attempted to formalize participation in many areas of public life. The legislation that created the Regions required the new Regional Government to have a Regional Coordination Council (CCR), and the new Municipality Law requires municipalities to have a Municipal Coordination Council (CCL). These Councils are composed of various combinations of elected officials and of representatives of various civil society organizations.

The ultimate attempt to formalize participation was the passing of legislation in 2004 (and complementary norms in 2005) requiring all Regions and all Municipalities to produce Participatory Budgets. The Participatory Budget is based on the now-legendary participatory experience of the municipality of Porto Alegre in Brazil that allows the population to provide input on key development decisions that become implemented

---

11. The *Mesa* mechanism was inspired by the success of the National *Mesa de Diálogo Democrático* that was established by the Organization of American States, political parties, and civil society to manage the process that led to the resignation of the Fujimori Government in September 2000 and to the orderly organization of elections in April 2001. The *Mesa* has national, regional, and municipal structures that promote the coordination of social policy and participate in various social policy processes, some of them informal and others linked to specific government processes.

through the budget. The process was piloted by officials in the Ministry of Finance in nine Peruvian regions in 2002 and was immediately expanded to the whole country and made mandatory in 2004. Chapter 7 analyzes the Participatory Budget, finding that it focuses on the design of the budget and of the development plan, giving no attention to monitoring the implementation of the budget or of the results of the development plan. While it might be too early to assess its costs and benefits, there is an incipient impression that it can lead to frustration because it demands a lot of social energy and, until now, it has shown relatively little impact in return. The small impact is partly the result of having a process that affects only a small part of the budget: estimates range from 1 percent to 6 percent of the municipal budgets (these are the new investments; the recurrent budget and all the ongoing investments are not included). Frustration can result from the lack of a visible impact and from the large gap that develops between the expectations that get reflected in the budget proposal and the results that are obtained as the budget is implemented. Typically, the Participatory Budget process ends up in a big budget proposal that reflects the wishes of the participants. This proposal is later trimmed down by the local government and many of the specific proposals are turned down by the National System of Public Investment. As a result, the final budget that gets approved bears little resemblance to the proposal made by the Participatory Budget. Further, many of the initiatives that are approved are not implemented, either by design or by lack of capacity of the local governments.

In summary, the appetite to participate that developed after 2000 led to the creation of numerous instances of "Voice." These instances today do not have clearly defined roles and there is substantial overlap among the roles of the *Mesas*, the Regional and Local Councils, and the bodies involved in the Participatory Budgeting. These overlaps, the lack of clarity of function, and the large amount of social energy that is being invested in these activities may be leading to "participation fatigue." Worse, all the energy goes into designing the budget or an ambitious development plan, and none to monitoring its implementation. Some analysts associate an increase in "conflictive participation" with fatigue with "institutionalized forms of participation" (Remy 2005).[12] Chapter 7 concludes that one of the weaknesses of the participatory setup of the voice mechanisms in Peru is its exclusive orientation toward influencing policy design. It recommends that social participation in voice institutions should turn its attention to monitoring public expenditures, service performance, and quality standards. With this orientation, voice could play an important role in the effort to break the low-level equilibrium in service delivery diagnosed by this study.

Decentralization as an External Shock for Service Delivery

Is decentralization the external shock needed to break away from the low-level equilibrium? International experience suggests that there may be four channels through which

---

12. Remy presents a careful account of both types of participation. She suggests that there are high transaction costs in most forms of participation, that high expectations were created during 2000–03, and that there is now a growing sense of frustration with some of the instances of institutional participation. Since 2004, there have been 90 cases of local populations violently attempting to remove their local authorities (this is in addition to the 189 municipalities that held special recall elections to oust their elected official in 2004).

decentralization can serve as a shock to improve accountability in the provision of social services. First, decentralization can favor the development of competitive benchmarking. In Brazil, for example, the open comparison of states' performance has created a "competitive" source of pressure for performance improvement, because state governments are pressed by their populations to do better than comparable states in their results, and also because the federal government has to make explicit the formulas used to assign funds to the different states. Second, decentralization can open the door to experimentation and to innovations that better respond to local needs. The more reform-minded states tend to innovate, and the lessons learned from that experience can then help the other states reshape their own systems. Some innovations in Medicaid in the United States and in health care in Brazil have started that way. Third, decentralization can lead to a "separation of functions" if the federal–provincial relationship is reconfigured so that the federal government plays a stronger (or exclusive) role focused on norm-setting, funding equalization (cross-regional equity), and performance monitoring. Some analysts suggest that this has been the most positive change in the education sector in Brazil over the past decade. In Brazil, the federal government has moved away from the provision of services and closer to regulation and financing of services provided by states and municipalities. Fourth, citizen voice can have a greater impact on local authorities than on national authorities. The evidence for this last channel, however, suggests that it depends on how clearly the local authorities assume responsibility for the service; when that responsibility is ambiguously distributed between the local and national governments, as in Ecuador or Venezuela, decentralization can make matters worse, not better.

According to the Framework Law for Decentralization, there should be four stages in the process of decentralization in Peru. Social assistance would be decentralized in the initial stages and would become mainly the responsibility of municipalities. The decentralization of these programs was started in 2003 and should be greatly advanced in 2006. According to the Framework Law, health care and education would be decentralized in the final stage of the process and would become mainly the responsibility of regional governments.

Various chapters in this book are very optimistic about the potential impact of the first two channels: greater decentralization may improve service delivery by creating an environment where benchmarking can lead regions to "compete" to improve their relative performance. Also, some regions are already showing an innovative spirit—such as Lambayeque, which carried out a referendum to establish its health priorities, and San Martin, which is experimenting with a new system of primary teaching in multigrade schools.

By contrast, the third and fourth elements will be harder to obtain in Peru because of the way decentralization has occurred in reality. The main function of the Ministries of Health and Education today is the provision of services in Metropolitan Lima—since they have a small role in policymaking nationally and no role in the provision of services outside Lima. It will be politically difficult to change that configuration because the ministry officials, the municipal authorities, the unions, and many other organizations in the service corporations are opposed to the change. Without releasing the function of provision in Lima, it will be difficult for them to develop a national role focused on norm-setting, funding equalization (cross-regional equity), and performance monitoring. The debate about decentralization that has taken place since the Framework Law was passed has neglected this aspect.

Also, it will be difficult to encourage the regions and municipalities to assume greater accountability for education and health. Typically, decentralization entails the transfer of some rights that the regions want to obtain (such as being in charge of hiring future teachers) together with responsibilities that the regions would prefer not to have (such as being responsible for a politically painful rationalization process needed to improve the system). The money should only be transferred to the regions once the regions agree to also be assigned responsibilities (rights should only be transferred together with responsibilities). In Peru, most of the rights that are attractive to the regional authorities have already been transferred—especially the right to decide who is hired when the payroll is expanded. For almost two decades, the payrolls and many of the goods and services used to provide health and education services outside the Lima Region have been managed by the regional offices of the Ministries, while the headquarters of the Ministry of Health and the Ministry of Education manage the payroll and the services in the Lima Region (which includes Metropolitan Lima and Callao). In the 1990s, the regional administrators were officials appointed by the central government, so the deconcentration of power kept the decisions within the central government. After the elections of the regional presidents in 2003, the regional health and education authorities were appointed jointly by the regional president and the sector ministry, but they increasingly respond to the elected regional authority.

While most of the budget transferred to the regional governments must be used to pay the payrolls of existing health and education workers (which are mostly *nombrados*), the regional authorities have the primary role in the decisions concerning new hires. Beyond the choice of individuals, the regional authorities are also now defining key policies—for example, in 2004 two regions (Iquitos and Puno) decreed that only teachers who were originally from the region could be hired. While pay policies are managed by the central government, the field research conducted for Chapter 6 found that some regions apply the national pay policy with great flexibility—specifically bonuses (which can add up to more than half the take-home pay) are assigned in different ways by different regions.

Also, a large fraction of the future tax revenues of the government from exports of natural resources have already been assigned to the regions and municipalities without requiring them to assume any new responsibilities in service provision. Finally, large wage increases have been given to the teachers and health workers without making that part of a package of increased performance or without making it part of an agreement to transfer authority to the regions. Under these circumstances it will be difficult for the next government to convince the regions to take on more responsibilities for health and education or to convince the unions to accept any changes in their status. Under those circumstances, one should not expect greater accountability from the system because the regional governments will continue to blame the central government for any problems that may occur in the sectors.

The Need for Standards of Service

When the challenge of service delivery was to increase coverage, as it was in previous decades, progress or lack of progress was obvious to all—the number of children in school, the percentage of children who are immunized or get treatment for pneumonia, the number of children benefiting from food programs—can all be easily measured. Policymakers can track progress in coverage through statistics that are relatively easy to produce and to interpret. Parents know if their children are getting the service or not, and if they are not getting the service, it is relatively obvious what is needed to increase coverage—build a school or a health post, put pressure on for a teacher or a nurse to be hired, lobby the responsible government agency to be included in a food-aid program.

The difficulty of measuring the performance of a social program increases drastically when the challenge becomes improved quality. How can policymakers, administrators, or parents know if children are getting a good education, if medical care is of acceptable standards, or if a food-aid program is improving the nutritional status of a child? How do you measure quality?

Measuring quality of service requires standards. Standards are the "weights and measures" needed to measure service delivery. Without standards, users, administrators, and policymakers have no objective way to judge whether services are of acceptable quality or if quality is improving. Users often base their expectations for the quality of service on comparisons. Schools, hospitals, and social programs are impossible to compare unless the quality of their services can be measured. Similarly, the quality of the educational or health system in one region cannot be compared with that of another region without standards of quality. A National Evaluation of parental satisfaction with the schools of their children showed that over 80 percent of parents are satisfied with the service their children are receiving; satisfaction surveys on health care often find equally high levels of satisfaction. Chapter 3 analyzed the relation between parental satisfaction and objective quality measures, and found no correlation.

Why have clear standards not been developed? Part of the answer it that it is technically difficult to define standards of quality, but another part of the answer is that standards are resisted by the corporations. Standards make accountability possible. Users and policymakers can bring the corporations of providers to account with the use of standards. Hence, the corporations reject standards and measurements of quality to avoid being accountable. Users need to know the quality of the services they are getting to be able to demand their rights to education or health care. Thus, standards are key to a rights-oriented approach to improving services. Similarly, policymakers need standards to establish if a municipality is executing the nutrition programs in an effective way. No contract can be established unless the units of measurement and the targets are clarified.

In education, the implementation of measurable standards has been resisted in many ways. First, while tests to measure quality have been developed, they continue to be applied on an irregular basis, to only a subset of schools, and the use of the results continues to be restricted (so, for example, a parent does not have access to the data from their children's school to compare it with the school in the next district; or the results from each region are not published in a way that would allow voters from region A to compare their schools with those of region B). Second, the official curricular guidelines are designed to be so complex that they cannot be understood or measured. Chapter 3 compares the official guidelines with those of *Fe y Alegría* (a nongovernmental network of schools). A second-grade student in a *Fe y Alegría* school should be able to: "read audibly, respecting exclamation and question marks and without sounding out syllables." Compare that clear and measurable objective with the official guidelines, which are complex to the point of being impossible to understand or measure: second-grade students should "construct the comprehension of the text being read by … anticipating the type of text and the purpose of the writing, according to context … formulates hypotheses about the meaning of text and tests his or her hypotheses against those of classmates and draws conclusions."

Clear standards are also nonexistent in health. As described in Chapter 4, information systems are very weak in most areas that are needed to measure health outcomes—for example, the system of vital statistics is totally unreliable and maternal mortality and infant mortality are monitored very poorly. The measurement of health care outputs is also very weak; for example, there is almost no information centrally available about the production of services by the public hospitals. Without this information, there is no way to measure the efficiency in the use of public funds or to compare the quality of results among regions. There are also no standards concerning the rights of users: it is not sufficiently clear what services are financed by SIS or who is entitled to such coverage; there is also no definition about what services can be charged to users or what tariffs can be charged for specific services by the public hospitals. Without this information, users in reality have no rights.

A similar problem exists in social assistance. The social assistance programs discussed in Chapter 5 have unclear objectives—most of them are based on the distribution of food and claim to have among their objectives the improvement of nutrition, but there is no effort to monitor the nutritional status of the beneficiaries. Eligibility for the programs is also blurred; the beneficiaries of the *Vaso de Leche* program were originally defined as children up to age 6, but they increasingly include older children. Given this ambiguity about the objectives of the program or the intended beneficiaries, it is not possible to monitor the benefits of the program. It is also not possible for those poor families who are currently not beneficiaries to demand their right to be included.

Conclusions and Recommendations

This book analyzes many reforms that have been tried to improve services in Peru in recent decades. Many of these reforms have been successful at increasing coverage, and sometimes also at increasing the quality of services and the outcomes in the population. However, most of the successful reforms were successful on a small scale or for only brief periods of time. A few remain successful and have a potential for scaling up, but many are not replicable or are being dismantled. How can more permanent solutions be found? Which reforms can be scaled up and what is needed to do that?

The different chapters of this book make specific recommendations on how to achieve that goal. These recommendations can be stated as follows: (a) develop standards and set goals, (b) strengthen accountability relationships, and (c) build capacity for service delivery. These recommendations are summarized below. Before discussing the longer-term recommendations, however, it is useful to emphasize again the need for a shock to break the low-level equilibrium that prevails in the system. Without that shock, the long-term recommendations are unlikely to have a significant effect.

Develop Standards and Set Goals

The development of standards of service is a complex task. Standards and targets are needed in three areas: outcomes/outputs, process, and resource allocation. In education, learning standards should be developed for every course and every grade of instruction, taking into account the cultural and regional diversity of the country. Process standards are also needed. Province-level School Management and Supervision Units (UGELs) should set standards of service to schools and schools to communities. Standards for teacher selection, embodied in exams that would have to be passed before individuals can become teachers, should also be created and enforced and coordinated with standards for pre-service teacher training. In health care, there is a very sophisticated industry world-wide that produces standards of quality, and another complex industry that provides accreditation to facilities based on those standards. In social assistance, programs may have several objectives and several target groups and each may require a complex set of standards. Funding standards are also needed, particularly as the country decentralizes. This should take the form of a formula-based transfer of funds from the national level to regions and municipalities and from the regions to the providers. Producing these standards will be necessary to improve the quality of services, but it will be a long and complex process.

Peru cannot wait for that long process to take place. There must be a short-term strategy linked to a longer-term strategy. Given that the system is in a low-level equilibrium, a prerequisite for any reform is the creation of a shock to break the inertia. The shock would consist of new behaviors triggered by a widespread recognition of the poor quality of results in the system and the realization that improvements can be achieved if providers are made accountable. The short-term strategy must focus on generating the elements needed to produce the shock, specifically it should produce simple, easy-to-understand standards and goals that can capture the imagination of the population and of the politicians and motivate them act to extract accountability from providers.

The initial set of standards and targets should be designed to ignite the shock. It would not substitute for the development of a wider and more thorough set of standards that would have to be developed over the long run to sustain the momentum of change after the process of change has started. This initial set of standards and goals would constitute proxies (or "banners") for a fuller set of standards that would take longer to create.

The initial set should include simple and understandable standards that users can apply to their everyday life. For example, Chapter 3 suggests that 8-year-old students in the second grade should be able to read 60 words per minute with a good level of comprehension. All parents of second graders should know whether their children meet this standard. They should also know how well their school compares with other schools in their region, and how well their region compares with other regions. The data should be presented in a way that allows comparison without losing sight of cultural and ethnic diversity, but cultural diversity should not be an excuse for mediocrity. A national secondary-school exit exam could also provide a simple measure for quality at the secondary level.

Chapter 4 suggests focusing on clarifying the rights of users of health care services by making a clear statement of what services are included in the benefits package of SIS and who is entitled to those services. This information, which today seems to be a well-kept secret, should be widely available, including in posters that could be placed next to the cashier window of all hospitals and clinics. The criteria for eligibility for the SIS should also be available to all. Regional targets should be published for each region and progress toward these targets should be reported quarterly.[13] Similar to the recommendations in

---

13. The challenge involved in making the rights of users more transparent in health care is that the government would have to make promises that are no bigger than the budget it can provide for SIS. Once the promises are made it would no longer be able to cut the budget provided to SIS.

education, the report suggests that information systems be developed that allow comparisons among hospitals and clinics within a certain region, and across regions. Indicators should include the safety record of providers (for example, rate of perinatal mortality) and measurable indicators of client satisfaction, such as waiting times (or even simpler proxies such as number of consultations by professional, by day).

Chapter 5 shows that food programs in Peru, even when they are well targeted, have no measurable impact on nutrition, partly because they lack the link with education and health care interventions. It suggests that all nutrition programs should have an integrated package of interventions. To make the systems work, all mothers (including those that are currently not beneficiaries of any program) should be able to know if their child is chronically malnourished and how to monitor the progress of the child.

The initial set of standards should also include funding standards with two objectives: first, to bring transparency to the distribution of funds to the regions and to municipalities in the context of decentralization; and second, to protect funds required to ensure a supply of key inputs (such as vaccines or Internet connections) because, since the total budget is fixed, every time the payroll increases, money is cut for vaccines.

The announcement of an initial set of standards would strengthen other processes that are already under way. Reforms that attempt to give users a more direct role in the governance of providers would be strengthened if users could measure the quality of their school or clinic using common indicators and working toward known benchmarks. Parents armed with the knowledge of how their child is doing could support their children more effectively and could be more effective members of school councils. The development of voice and compact mechanisms discussed above would also benefit from clearer objectives— imagine how different the debate in education would be if the focus changed from just measuring the share of GDP assigned to the education sector or from the percent increase in the salary of teachers, to why second graders in a certain region are reaching the target in reading fluency, while others are not. The dialog with the unions could also be more effective if improvements in remunerations could be linked to improvements in the reading capacity of children or in the access of pregnant mothers to health care services subject to waiting-time limits.

Other forms of reform that have failed in the past could become more feasible to implement. For example, there have been attempts to start the process of change by developing standards for the selection of teachers and health professionals and requiring that these standards be passed before individuals are granted permanent positions in the public sector. Recent history includes many attempts to impose these standards, and each attempt has been met with failure. For decades, the legislation in both health and education has required that the process of hiring include careful selection according to exams and academic credentials. In practice, these requirements are almost always waived. In 2002, the Ministry of Education opened a large number of new positions meant to improve the quality of teaching. A careful exam was designed and very few applicants passed. This led to conflict, change of ministers, and the hiring of most of the applicants— at the end of the process 90 percent of the teachers hired had failed the exam. In 2004, after a long strike by doctors, the government agreed to the *nombramiento* of several thousand doctors. The legislation that requires *nombrados* to pass specific standards was waived and the main criterion used was time worked as contract workers. Perhaps the main lesson from this is that unless there is support for a revolt by the users, policymakers will not be able to make changes, despite the good intentions of a minister.

Compare the failures in reform described above to the success achieved in closing the legal loophole that forced the government to subsidize a highly regressive pension system. Closing the loophole required that many Congressmen that were beneficiaries of the scheme would vote to change the Constitution to close the loophole. A national information campaign created enormous public pressure and the reform was passed.

Strengthen Accountability

Previous sections have described a number of initiatives already under way to strengthen accountability in the three sides of the accountability triangle. Many of those initiatives should be strengthened and others that have not yet been developed should be introduced. Experimentation with different forms of accountability should be encouraged.

Accountability to Users by Individual Providers. Chapter 3 suggests that parent groups at the school level have the power to hold schools accountable by, for example, ensuring parents statutory majority on School Governing Councils (*Consejo Educativo Institucionales*, CONEI), and by requiring schools to report to parents on standards of achievement and resources received and used, according to simple preset formats. Parents should participate in the promotion and selection of principals and teachers. Chapter 4 suggests that the CLAS organization should be preserved and if possible enlarged to cover an ever greater fraction of primary care clinics. Community leaders should retain a majority vote in the CLAS, and the CLAS should continue to make decisions about the promotion and selection of all staff. Users should also acquire a role to oversee the quality of care in hospitals, particularly in relation to maternal or perinatal deaths.

Accountability to Citizens by Local and Regional Governments. Chapter 7 suggests that social participation should complement and not substitute for the role of the elected representatives. Specifically, civil society organizations should strengthen their role in monitoring the implementation of services. To make that possible, the existing obligation of regional and municipal governments to periodically report on their activities should be made more precise. Governments should report to citizens on standards of achievement and resources received and used, according to simple, preset formats. The indicators should be chosen carefully, they should be few, and the same indicators should be used by all governments to ensure comparability.

Accountability to Policymakers by Providers. Policymakers should experiment more widely with nongovernmental administration of service providers with public funding, similar to the scheme followed by *Fe y Alegría* schools or by the CLAS clinics. To do that, they should reduce the current ad hoc nature of such experiences by creating more standardized formats and contracts for such management, and improve the comparative evaluation of the experiences according to results and cost measurement. They should also disseminate the results so they can also become relevant for public providers.

The administrative units that operate immediately above the providers are supposed to have a support role to the providers. The evidence suggests that the UGELs in education, the REDES (networks) in health, and the municipalities in the municipal-run social assistance programs do not play a significant role of supportive supervision, classroom and clinic observation, and one-to-one advice. Instead their current emphasis is on mechanical control functions based on checklists of formal requirements and on group training courses and seminars. The supporting units should set standards of service and schools, clinics, and social assistance providers should rate the supporting units. Comparative data should be publicized. Policymakers should also consider the possibility of contracting out on an experimental basis some of the services provided by these units.

Accountability to Subnational Governments by MEF. More transparent financing standards are also needed; these need to be developed for the regional and municipal levels to allow for comparisons as the country decentralizes. Also, if efficiency of individual providers is to increase, there needs to be an effort to clarify costs and productivity for each school and hospital. This will require major changes in the way the public budget is structured, because the existing budget system makes it almost impossible to identify the inputs and costs at the level of the provider. The use of transparent formulas to distribute the budget will lower transaction costs and increase trust. The lack of census data for over a decade made it difficult to implement these types of formulas before, but once data from the 2005 census become available, the use of formulas will be feasible. The use of formulas will also put pressure on the data systems, creating a virtuous cycle.

Capacity Building

There is evidence of some slack in the production of services in Peru. In that sense, in the short run a shock of accountability would be enough to produce some gains in quality. Over the long run, however, accountability pressure built around standards will lead to improved results only if providers develop the capacity to respond to the higher demands. Hence, capacity building is the third component required to improve the quality of services. Each sector has different requirements for capacity building, but most needs can be classified into four categories.

Improved information systems are needed in many areas in all sectors. Monitoring the evolution of the quality of services will demand the development of a variety of new information systems. Some of the systems already exist and need to be upgraded; others will need to be developed from scratch. On an optimistic note, it should be noted that many people, especially many young people, are ready for this upgrade as witnessed by the hundreds of Internet cafés that can be found wherever communications reach, even in the remotest villages of Peru today.

Training will be needed in most sectors and may be required for many players in the system. Certainly the frontline providers will need training to be able to provide services according to standards. School principals and hospital managers will also need training to learn how to discharge their new accountability to parents and how to perform to outcome and process standards. Officials from UGELS, REDES, and municipalities will also need training to change their role from one of bureaucratic control to one of technical support. Users—parent bodies, community groups—will also need training in how to hold providers accountable for performance to standards and for budgetary and financial issues.

Achieving greater capacity may also require further outsourcing of services. In some cases it can be experimental with the objective of learning. In these cases a major component of the required investment should be in rigorous evaluations of the experiment. In other cases, it may be to provide specialized services that cannot be developed locally at competitive rates, such as specialized services for small municipalities that do not have the scale to produce the services efficiently.

Finally, significant financial incentives may be needed to improve the behavior of the existing pool of frontline providers in the short run, and, perhaps more important, the composition of the pool over the longer run. These incentives, however, should be conditioned on the existence of rigorous quality control at entry, because there is ample evidence that without establishing a link between pay and quality, higher pay does not improve quality. Chapter 6 shows that salaries for teachers and doctors have increased in recent years. Yet, Peru already has an oversupply of teachers and doctors. Increases in pay, if not tied to improved selection, incentives, and skills development, will not result in better teachers or more committed doctors. It will result in further oversupply. On the other hand, once the incentives are right and a group of highly motivated and highly qualified individuals choose to dedicate their efforts to improving the health and education of Peru's children, greater resources should be assigned to sustain their efforts.

CHAPTER 2

Public Expenditure in the Social Sectors

José R. López-Cálix

> When public services fail poor people, a good place to start looking for the underlying problem is almost always how the government spends money. If politicians and policymakers spend more than they can sustain, services deteriorate. If budgets are misallocated, basic services remain underfunded and frontline providers are handicapped. And if funds are misappropriated, service quality, quantity and access suffer. The budget is the critical link on the long route of accountability connecting citizens to providers through politicians and policymakers.
>
> —*World Development Report 2004*

During the Toledo administration, Peru's poverty reduction strategy has essentially relied on the trickle–down effects from economic growth. Successful efforts to restore fiscal discipline have been critical to promoting economic recovery. Fiscal discipline—reflected by lower fiscal deficits—has been obtained through a combination of dramatically reduced capital spending, modest increases in taxation, and some debt service savings from an active public debt management. Growth has averaged around 4.5 percent per year, but its impact on poverty reduction has been mitigated, at best. The question is, Why?

First, social spending remains low, at around 5.6 percent of gross domestic product (GDP), only modestly increasing by end-period. Economic growth by itself is a major determinant of poverty outcomes, but, according to international experience, it is public spending that makes most dramatic improvements possible. Thus, fiscal discipline has not translated into additional social outlays, and budget rigidities need to be explored.

Second, the particular mix of measures implemented for restoring fiscal discipline has resulted in a double-edged outcome for poverty. On one hand, lower deficits have led to low inflation, higher growth, and a strong external position, all of which have contributed to improving living standards—measured by income per capita levels—and by some social indicators nationwide. On the other hand, lower deficits have been obtained by a significant reduction to floor levels in the already small fiscal space[14]: non-wage spending devoted to pro-poor programs. Certainly, capital cuts have taken place and additional savings have occurred from tax revenue gains and lower interest payments on debt, but these savings have mostly financed significant payroll increases, especially among teachers and health workers.

The decentralization process has also reinforced these trends. Fiscal neutrality has been preserved throughout the creation of regional governments by following the same spending patterns. The creation of additional bureaucracies in regional governments has been mostly financed by scarce resources formerly allocated to regional capital investment.

Consequently, at 1 percent of GDP, Peru's most pro-poor public expenditures—resources allocated to Priority Social Programs (PSPs)—are at floor levels, and overall social expenditure remains low by international and regional standards. Capital spending on education and health has shrunk to virtually nil. Payroll levels of public school teachers, health workers, and subnational civil servants have reached unsustainable levels.

Third, the continuous change in the definition of social policies and poor implementation of social programs by weak institutions has taken its toll on the delivery of social services and on poverty outcomes. Despite perceived efforts by current government officials, significant inefficiencies, poor targeting, and leakages remain in the execution of social programs, which has made social policies ineffective. In addition, subnational governments still have little or no accountability for the resources they spend, and most of their investments have little to do with pro-poor programs. Short of adequate training, subnational governments have reproduced or aggravated institutional shortcomings, a feature of the Central Government. Thus, nationwide, the allocation of the remaining small fiscal space to poverty reduction programs is neither optimal nor accountable.

Fourth, the current mix of adjustment measures is obsolete. During the next administration, the likelihood that tax revenue gains will dissipate, strong pressure for payroll growth will continue from education and health workers, requests for additional investment transfers from subnational governments will materialize, and only small gains will be obtained even from a sound public debt management, makes continuity of the present policies not an option. Simple math tells us that the original adjustment strategy implemented to recover and maintain fiscal discipline is no longer an option.

Fifth, in this context, it is clear that simply increasing inputs (social spending) without reforming institutions that produce inefficiencies will not lead to sustainable improvements. If the incoming officials opt to place at the top of their agenda preserving fiscal discipline to achieve poverty reduction, and this agenda centrally relies on completing a sound decentralization of education, health, and social protection sectors, then a different mix of policy components that generate a sustainable fiscal space, coupled with perceived improvements to the institutional framework, is needed. That is what this report is about.

---

14. Fiscal space is defined as the share of flexible non-wage, non-financial, and non-pension spending in the budget.

Main Policy Recommendations

This chapter is framed in a new accountability framework that combines a set of mutual accountabilities among three main actors: citizens, policymakers, and service providers, but focuses on a particular link, known as the "Compact," the one between policymakers and providers. Under this relationship, the provider agrees to deliver a service in return for being rewarded or penalized. It can be a very explicit relationship, such as a contract with the government, or not be too explicit, like the hiring of teaching services the performance of which is very difficult to measure. Critical elements of the Compact are norms, standards, target outcomes, and the information required to enforce and monitor them, which will allow officials to measure progress in their policies and citizens to learn about the actual use of resources involved.

In the context of severely constrained fiscal resources for social spending, the next government is in a position to strengthen the Compact in a fiscally responsible way, by following these five recommendations:

1. Devoting additional resources to social needs only to the extent that new fiscal space is created. Since Peru can hardly find additional savings in further cutting public outlays, it has no choice but to increase its social spending pari passu with additional tax revenue gains and budget reallocations. Finding additional revenue is urgent, given the incoming phaseout of several temporary taxes. Expenditure reallocations should follow a thorough review of budget priorities toward progressive and pro-poor social programs. Reorienting the budget toward pro-poor expenditure requires the next three actions.

2. Developing a medium-term strategy and a monitoring system for the social programs, defining targets for specific outcomes in education, health, and nutrition. The strategy should identify key priority programs required to meet those outcomes, and a social sector multiyear expenditure framework with explicit minimum allocations assigned to the priority programs. It should also define a small number of annual and quarterly indicators to monitor progress in the priority programs. These indicators should be available to the general public through a user-friendly Internet interface that would allow beneficiaries, municipalities, and regions to measure the progress in budget execution and in the achievement of the intermediate indicators. Impact evaluations of all key programs should be produced by third-party analysts using internationally recognized methodologies, and should be made public before each annual budget is sent to Congress.

3. Curbing the crowding out of non-wage expenditure by a heavy, unsustainable, and growing public payroll, particularly among public-school teachers and health workers, and a fiscally neutral and accountable decentralization of the social sectors. In the short term, this implies a temporary freeze in both the hiring of and the level of public salaries, and, in the medium term, a comprehensive civil service reform. At the subnational level, additional hiring of staff should go pari passu with additional revenue-raising capacity at the subnational level and concomitant minimum reporting requirements on executed expenditure by regional and municipal governments.

4. Introducing performance budgeting at the subnational level, with a special focus on implications for the upgrading of the present budgetary protection policy. To do this first requires the definition of policy outcomes to be regularly tracked with the support of the Integrated Financial Management System (SIAF). This is particularly relevant for spending on the PSPs, which are being decentralized. Then, following the example of food aid and the Integral Health Insurance (SIS) programs, it requires the gradual introduction of conditioned transfers through annual "performance contracts" with subnational authorities. Performance budgeting should be the rule rather than the exception in the future management of decentralized social spending. Such a technical tool would help optimize returns on every dollar spent and enhance accountability and efficiency in service delivery in health, education, and social protection programs, especially at the subnational level. It would also involve an annual independent review of budget outcomes that should be regularly monitored and published. Such review should be the basis for defining annual budget reallocations, eliminating staff redundancies, and completing staff decentralization to subnational offices. If needed, the implementation of performance budgeting could be outsourced.
5. Continuing to improve the effectiveness of social expenditure with the elimination of programs that are poorly targeted, with low coverage or high leakages, and higher allocations to programs that are progressive and pro-poor. This involves filling the gaps in coverage of the beneficiary population, especially in pre-primary education; enhancing targeting that is especially poor in most health programs; and reducing leakages that are particularly acute in the food programs. Peru has excellent geographic targeting tools, such as a poverty map that reaches the municipal level, but their use is not generalized. Because extreme poverty is concentrated in rural areas, its reduction requires an improved targeting of social programs on the extreme poor, who mostly live in those areas, rather than on the non-poor, who mostly live in urban areas and do not need them. Correcting leakages in the management of social programs requires remedying their defective technical design and/or problems in their management.

The complementarities behind these five components are straightforward. First, maintaining low fiscal deficits is the foundation for sustainable fiscal and social policies. They are also needed to preserve price stability, higher growth, and viable countercyclical fiscal and social policies.

Second, keeping social expenditure as the top budget priority and continuing to shift it to pro-poor programs is essential for achieving desired social outcomes in the medium term. Budget reorientation, however, requires tackling long-standing problems of low tax revenue and budget rigidities.

Hence, and third, the government has no choice but to reopen fiscal space both by increasing revenue and curbing inertial current expenditure, especially the wage payroll. Because the civil service regime is in total disarray, a short-term solution is insufficient. The myriad of salary supplements and benefits (cash and in-kind) now prevailing must be consolidated and replaced by rational and transparent personnel management and pension systems.

Fourth, the lack of a medium-term expenditure framework that would set clear inter- and intrasectoral spending benchmarks has made budgetary protection policy helpful as a second-best policy, but it deals only with a very small share of the total budget, and its implementation has been mixed: tagging key social programs has not prevented deviations to non-priority spending (that is, to teachers' salaries), and its weak monitoring has not guaranteed adequate targeting. Besides, this policy requires adjustments in a context of decentralized, autonomous, and participatory spending decisions.

Fifth, making most efficient and effective use of scarce resources is essential for a country in the midst of fiscal retrenchment. This implies reducing anti-poor disparities in sectoral budget allocations; eliminating duplications in social projects; minimizing leaks of public funds, particularly in food supplementary programs and at the bottom level of service delivery and, if feasible, considering their gradual downsizing or replacement by other tools (that is, cash-transfer programs); and improving self-promoted or geographically based targeting of resources, especially in the rural areas addressing the most vulnerable.

Sixth, education, health, and social assistance expenditure needs must be resolved addressing complex decentralization questions, particularly those related to accountability. For instance, what functions and responsibilities must be gradually decentralized? With what timing and outcomes in mind? An ill-designed decentralization process, especially if developed through novice regional and weak municipal governments, has considerable potential for provoking not only fiscal imbalances but also severe disarray in service delivery. Thus there is a need to proceed cautiously.

Main Diagnostics

Social Sectors Expenditure Trends

Peru experienced a virtuous circle in the 1990s: increased social spending accompanied by improved social outcomes. During that decade, total private and public social spending rose by 50 percent in the three years after 1992, from 6 to 9 percent of GDP, and remained at that level until the end of the decade. In parallel, social outcomes markedly improved. On the *health* front, the supply of health services increased sharply, especially in primary care; and the employment of health professionals rose, mostly for primary care positions. The demand for services also increased, especially in rural areas. Infant mortality and child malnutrition fell by almost 25 percent during the first half of the decade and have continued to improve. On the *education* front, a similar pattern occurred. On the input side, unlike many countries where most of the budget increase was absorbed by personnel costs, Peru shifted additional resources to educational infrastructure, quality-enhancing materials (such as textbooks), teacher training, and capacity building. As a result, the percentage share of personnel costs (payroll and pensions) of total education spending was significantly reduced to 60 percent, one of the lowest ratios among low-to middle-income countries. On the outcome side, universal enrollment was reached, even though wide variations prevailed among urban/rural, gender, and socioeconomic status. On the *social assistance* front, temporary safety net programs were created or were strengthened outside the ministries. Programs like the National Compensation and Social Development Fund (FONCODES), the National Food Assistance Program (PRONAA), *Vaso de Leche*, and *Comedores Populares* were strengthened as direct transfer programs for food supplementary aid, and temporary employment creation programs were created as contingent aid relief. Gains in coverage and outcomes were also significant. Unfortunately, the fiscal situation markedly deteriorated by the end of the 1990s, when large fiscal deficits appeared as a result of a significant fall in tax revenue and lax expenditure.

Facing a fragile fiscal stance, the Toledo administration opted for the paramount objective of recovering growth and restoring fiscal discipline. To correct this, since 2003, primary surpluses (and declining deficits) have resulted mainly from the combination of three measures: (a) dramatic public investment cutbacks, (b) small tax revenue gains from tax policy and administration reform, and (c) mild interest savings from debt restructuring. Highly relevant for the social needs, the investment ratio, as a percentage of GDP, dramatically halved between 1999 and 2004, and a negative correlation developed between the fiscal deficit and public investment, a correlation that did not exist in the 1990s. Given the commitment and actual compliance to meet annual fiscal benchmarks, investment cutbacks (and their associated fiscal space) were essential to offset expenditures originating from budget rigidities in current spending, especially in rising wages, and more recently nascent decentralization, which together absorbed about 60 percent of the total savings generated from the fiscal adjustment process.

The gradual recovery of fiscal discipline has had important implications for social expenditure trends. This includes: (a) a modest increase in the level of social spending from 5.2 percent of GDP in 2000 to 5.6 in 2004; (b) a modest reorientation of the budget by reducing military spending and increasing social spending to close to one-third of the budget; (c) a renewed search for efficiency and effectiveness, with the merging of a myriad of social programs, followed by their gradual decentralization, and the application of pro-poor targeting tools; and (d) the implementation of an active budgetary protection policy to non-wage allocations in selected programs, aimed initially at offsetting the social cost of adjustment programs, but later to targeting minimum inputs needed to achieve poverty reduction goals. We examine these implications in detail.

However, the budget composition, especially among core social—education, health, and social protection—sectors, has changed significantly. Driven by successive payroll increases in the social sectors, two main outcomes have followed. On one hand, current spending has escalated to above 90 percent of the budget in 2004, offset by a significant decline in capital expenditure. On the other hand, those social sectors with a higher share of their budget allocated to wages have gained weight. Between 2001 and 2004, led by teacher salary increases, wages in the social sectors have increased from 56 to 65 percent of the total budget payroll. A direct consequence of the fall in capital outlays is that Peru has certainly increased its gap in infrastructure. While there are no reliable data on its size, according to Ministry of Education officials, school maintenance by the Central Government has all but disappeared, and rehabilitation and equipment of school and health facilities is reduced to co-financing of external assistance projects. Similar trends are observed in spending patterns by regional governments.

During the same period, Peru has made remarkable improvements in budget management. Budget performance, measured by the total executed/budgeted spending ratios, has improved, although performance is less stellar when comparing budget performance in investment ratios, especially in the health sector. There are several reasons for this improved performance, including the update of the SIAF, its expansion to subnational governments, and the creation of a performing National System of Public Investment (SNIP). By issuing a "seal of approval" the SNIP has been critical for providing "quality at entry," while managing a rationed pipeline of public investment projects in the social sectors.

Fiscal decentralization has not derailed fiscal neutrality, the latter being defined as the absence of deviations of the actual fiscal deficit from its annual declining benchmark.

However, fiscal neutrality has been achieved by reducing capital investment, because financing of new regional bureaucracies required it. A weak and incomplete regulatory and accountability framework for the decentralization of health and education sectors persists. Currently, overlapping areas among levels of government are leading to an increased fragmentation of spending authority, waste of resources, lower capital investment, and increased non-pro-poor spending.

Employment, Pay, and Pensions Management

Civil service reform continues to be the missing link of a results- and poverty-reducing-oriented modernization of the State in Peru. There are clear reasons behind the aggravating trends in current expenditure, particularly in payroll and pensions in the education and health sectors. The past 15 years witnessed a severe deterioration of Peru's civil service, with strong implications for the fiscal accounts and the costs of the pension regime. There is an entrenched disregard for the provisions of the existing civil service law and its associated regulations. Civil servants are employed under a variety of legal regimes with a wide disparity in salaries for similar tasks. The existing formal structure of salary and pensions has not been revised in over a decade, so base salaries are increased through a variety of supplements and benefits in cash and in–kind. With the proclamation of a ban on hiring for permanent positions more than a decade ago, institutions have resorted to hiring on a contractual basis, a process that is not subject to any required procedures for recruitment and selection and that has severe fiscal implications. All these factors have contributed to the existing legacy of a workforce that is poorly prepared, poorly trained, poorly supervised, and, consequently, of very low productivity.

The fiscal burden of the public labor force is now very high and unsustainable. Wage expenditures in the education and health sector had been growing in recent years. The international recommended share of current spending devoted to teachers' wages is 66 percent for primary education (World Bank 2004). Peru reached 88 percent in 2004, placing it at the top of a list headed by African countries like Nigeria (96 percent), Congo (90 percent), and Tanzania (89 percent). Although no one denies teachers are a key part of the schooling system and that paying them adequately is important, there is simply too little money left for other important inputs, such as textbooks, school materials, and training, which obviously should have an impact on education quality (Figure 2.1).

The wage bill is also a major contributor to making Peru's budget among the most inflexible in the region—less than 5 percent of the total budget in net terms—ranking alongside Brazil, India, and other highly indebted poor countries (Figure 2.2). The shrinking of the fiscal space is largely explained by: (a) an increased share devoted to wages and social obligations; (b) to a lesser extent, increased pre-committed outlays in goods and services and capital expenditure, often as counterpart funding for external credits; and (c) the removal of the contingency reserve. Government officials and legislators currently have almost no discretion to reallocate expenditures.

Perhaps the most notable distortion aggravated during the Toledo administration is the approval of teacher salary increments through special bonuses. The teachers' salary structure is severely distorted—almost 90 percent of total teachers' salaries come from bonuses, including those for preparing classes. In nominal terms, the total salary increase during 1999–2004 was about 44 percent, or an annual average of about 7.6 percent (Crouch 2005). There is an urgent need for a thorough reform to reestablish some semblance of control over

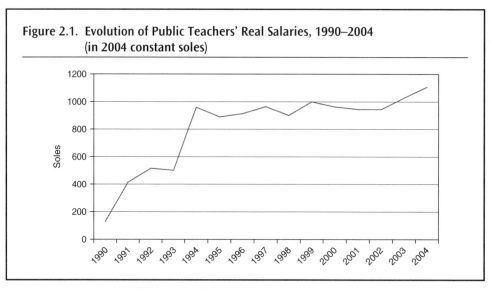

Figure 2.1.   Evolution of Public Teachers' Real Salaries, 1990–2004
              (in 2004 constant soles)

Source: Saavedra (2004), until 1999, and Ministry of Education for 2000–04.

the wage bill and to promote the creation of a more efficient government. For its part, the health sector is widely characterized by informality payments and lack of transparency, and up to 90 percent of total salaries is composed of bonuses not subject to social benefits, non-pensionable, and not included in the payroll system. In addition, MINSA is the ministry that

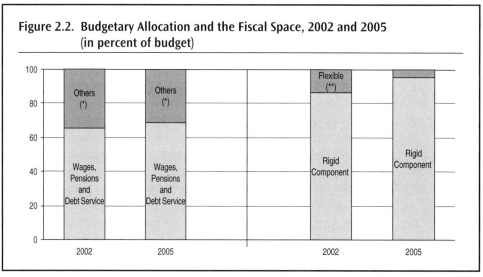

Figure 2.2.   Budgetary Allocation and the Fiscal Space, 2002 and 2005
              (in percent of budget)

*Refers to the "gross" fiscal space available: non-wage, non-financial, and non-pension spending in the budget.
**Refers to a "net" fiscal space, taken as the flexible share from the "others" portion in left columns of Figure 2.2.
Source: Budget Directorate of the Ministry of Finance (2005).

registers the largest number of workers under the non-personnel services hiring modality. In sum, it is hard to provide exact quantitative estimates of what has happened to total salaries in both sectors, but any initiative designed to improve the performance of government must include a major overhaul of the institutional framework that governs public sector employment and of the management of its human resources.

Employment expansion in the social sectors, especially teachers, has also occurred in the last 14 years, but it has escalated since 2000. As a result, the number of teachers has grown more than the number of students in the public education system (the ratio of students in primary education per teacher decreased from 25 in 2000 to 23 in 2004). In addition, the number of non-regular teachers decreased, as regularization processes took place, resulting in a reduction of the percentage of teacher *contratados* (temporary contractors) in the system. In the public health sector, the number of doctors and health workers has also grown. In addition, it is well known that most health employees have been hired under non-regular labor modalities (mostly Non-Personnel Services, NPSs), and this situation was also aggravated during the 2000s. In parallel, a promising regularization process was initiated at the Ministry of Education in 2004. On the other hand, wage remunerations in the health and education sectors have been larger than in the rest of the public sector due not only to additional regularized workers, but to special bonuses obtained through strikes.

Institutional shortcomings compound salary distortions. Because of the weaknesses of the legal framework, disorganization, lack of control, and non-organized information, payroll leakages, ghost teachers, and absenteeism prevail. Currently, the Ministry of Education is implementing new and unified payroll and information systems that will result in important savings for the sector. Human resources management in both sectors has not yet experienced major legal changes as a consequence of the ongoing decentralization process. However, there has been some de facto decentralization since regional governments now have more power over the Regional Sector Directorates and over their budget management. Because the Ministries of Education and Health do not have much control over the intermediate regional units, and there is no adequate centralized register of the existing vacant posts, each intermediate unit is following its own hiring procedures, which has brought the de facto decentralization of personnel management to regional government.

In a similar vein, a large challenge lies ahead for the Peruvian State to reduce the fiscal burden of pensions while improving social services and expanding coverage of protection to the elderly poor. Like in many other countries, public employee pensions are a significant fiscal problem in Peru. There is a disparity between collections and current liabilities, widening the gap to be covered with transfers from Treasury (Figure 2.3). Measures of the long-term fiscal burden (the net present value of future pension payments minus contributions) indicate that the size of the problem is larger than that of the stock of external debt. Most of these costs (about 60 percent before the recent reform) are associated with the *Cédula Viva* (CV), although beneficiaries of this regime (both present and future) are only one of every four in the National Pension System (SNP) regime. The recent reform of the CV is an important step toward moderating fiscal costs, but even after this reform, costs are still large.

Within this context, the analysis of the fiscal effect of public employees' pensions in Peru's Education and Health sectors provides mixed results. One aspect to consider is that it is difficult to assess basic indicators such as ratios of active to passive participants because the system is in transition. First, the presence of the private sector is relatively recent—a

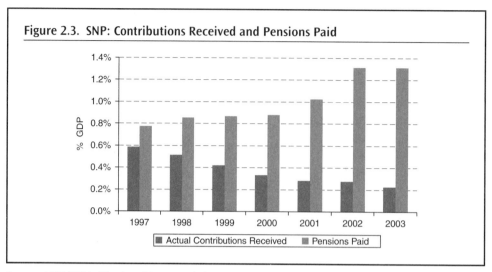

Figure 2.3. SNP: Contributions Received and Pensions Paid

Source: MEF (2004a,b). Dirección General de Asuntos Económicos y Sociales.

little more than a decade—though affiliations grew quickly, particularly among those higher on the income scale. Second, new affiliations to the CV regime have been restricted during the last decade, and a very recent reform has closed the possibility of new affiliations to the system. It should be noted, however, that this is not the first time this regime has been closed, although this time it would take a constitutional reform to reopen it. In addition, the reform provides ample room for changes in the characteristics and management of the regime. Thus, imbalances in the current pension system are to a significant degree the result of these policy-induced institutional changes. Overall, however, the central result is that in the short and medium term the system still produces a significant fiscal burden, even after the reform of the CV regime.

Most active workers in the health and education sectors (close to two-thirds) are already in the private pension system (SPP); in the health sector the proportion is 82 percent. Affiliates to the CV regime are a small proportion (5 percent), though they make up most of the remaining active workers in this regime. Even before considering that according to the new legislation some of these will have to migrate to either SPP or the SNP, were all these workers to retire tomorrow, they would add only 6 percent to the number of pensioners in this regime. This allows for cautious optimism regarding the long-term prospects. The situation is better in the health sector not only because it is smaller, but also because a larger portion of members are in the SPP, and only a small portion (4 percent) is in the CV. This allows for a cautiously optimistic medium-term outlook.

In relation to pensioners, a large part of the burden the CV currently represents—48 percent in number of affiliations—is likely less in financial terms due to low benefits paid. Almost all the new workers that will be added are from the education sector. Finally, the active workers affiliated with the SNP represent a relatively small portion (14 percent) of the total, and pensioners even less. Moreover, here the ratio of active workers to pensioners is almost 50 to 1. The central challenges for these sectors are to reduce the CV burden in the short and medium term and to improve SNP management, where the retiree population will grow quickly for at least the next decade.

The recent CV reform passed by Congress is promising and has opened the way to a more sustainable, fiscally less onerous, and more equitable public pension system. However, our central findings suggest cautious optimism about short-term prospects for big fiscal saving of CV reform, because the private pension system has already absorbed a large part (close to two-thirds) of the active workers in the health and education sectors, and savings to be obtained from the reforms will be used to improve the lowest pensions. In any case, reforms should focus on the remunerations systems and employment practices of these sectors as part of more comprehensive human resources management upgrading, and on financial management of the public pension funds.

Fiscal Space, Budgetary Protection, and Public Investment under Decentralization

Fiscal adjustment in a context of high budgetary rigidity has minimized the fiscal space for financing poverty reduction programs in Peru. The fiscal space has reached floor levels: three years after decentralization, poverty reduction programs barely represent 4.5 percent of total budgetary resources, and less than 1 percent of GDP. The fiscal space for investment in education expenditure is close to nil. This prompts the urgent need for preserving budgetary protection in the social sectors. Preserving critical outlays in a context of nascent decentralization mitigates the adverse effects of payroll expansion on a highly squeezed social expenditure, but urges improved targeting and monitoring of protected inputs and social outcomes embedded in the social policies.

In the last four years Peru quietly developed an innovative budgetary protection policy. In a context of increasingly rationed resources for other than payroll increases, and sizable cuts to public investment, the budgetary protection policy has been very helpful in raising (from 1999 to 2002) and then preserving (from 2003 to 2005) priority social spending on non-wage and capital spending assigned to six PSPs: pre-primary, primary, and secondary education, individual and collective health, and social assistance (Figure 2.4). Overall, spending on the PSPs has doubled from 0.5 percent of GDP to a projected 1.1 percent of GDP in 2005.

There is a strong rationale for making a case for budgetary protection policy in Peru. The three main reasons are: (a) creating contingencies for preserving income of the poor during a heavy recession; (b) maintaining human capital during a fiscal adjustment; and (c) supporting expenditure shifting toward key poverty reduction programs, while developing results-oriented budget mechanisms. These reasons are not mutually exclusive, as the Peruvian case illustrates, because there can be overlaps among them.

What spending should be protected remains the key question. Once the country decides it needs budgetary protection at multiple levels, the next question Peru faced was how to select the programs to be part of a budgetary protection policy. This requires: (a) identifying pro-poor expenditure in the overall budget, (b) defining whether it will apply to one or multiple budgetary levels, and (c) choosing among those programs (and project/activities) according to certain criteria.

Several rules of thumb to follow are: (a) During a recession or natural disaster, the *top priority* should be those programs that benefit the poorest and that should not to be cut back, even if public spending is reduced—namely, basic health and education; (b) poorly targeted or universal welfare programs are often regressive and fiscally impossible to sustain,

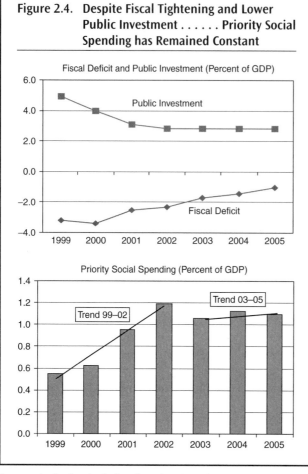

Figure 2.4. Despite Fiscal Tightening and Lower Public Investment . . . . . . Priority Social Spending has Remained Constant

Fiscal Deficit and Public Investment (Percent of GDP)

Priority Social Spending (Percent of GDP)

Source: Author's calculations based on SIAF data.

particularly during a crisis, so an alternative procedure is to opt for a *negative list* on poorly targeted or lower-priority universal programs, such as infrastructure subsidies; (c) an important caveat is that *most existing health and education programs*, some of them not necessarily targeted to the poor, should be preserved and not be part of the negative list because they have positive externalities on human capital development, as in the case of hospitals. As the crisis deepens, the unemployed shift from private to public hospitals. Finally, (d) there are decisions to be taken on a *case-by-case* basis. For instance, comparing what to choose among cash transfers, direct food delivery, or tax subsidies to agricultural products requires a thorough local assessment.

Budgetary protection policy in Peru has made use of very refined policy tools. These include: (a) overall floor amounts at the aggregate function and program level, published in the social chapter of the Annual Macroeconomic Framework; (b) introduction of legislation to ban deviations from protected resources; (c) contingency clauses ("ceilings") allowing budgetary transfers intra-PSPs from underperforming to overperforming programs; (d) user-friendly and transparent monitoring of executed resources through SIAF; (e) pilot introduction of performance contracts in selected activities grouped under a program, like Mother and Child Health Insurance (SIS-MI); and (f) pilot introduction of conditioned transfers (programmatic transfers) to food-aid programs.

The performance of the budgetary protection policy has been positive. Despite strong political pressures, resources have been preserved and allocated accordingly (Table 2.1). However, multiple problems have occurred, including continuous deviation of protected resources to teachers' salary increases; underexecution of some individual programs, short of projected external financing; transfers above the ceilings agreed; delays in the design of a user-friendly *Ventana Amigable* for monitoring PSPs performance, and in the approval of regulations for conditioned transfers; and poor targeting in a few programs.

Table 2.1. Budget for Protected Social Programs Non-salary Current and Capital Budget (Million soles)

Sector	Target 2001	Executed 2001	Percent Executed	Target 2003	Executed 2003	Percent Executed	Target 2005
Pre-primary education	132	66	50%	107	128	120%	63
Primary education	467	151	32%	182	154	85%	197
Secondary education	467	107	23%	230	146	63%	291
Collective health	180	152	84%	173	105	61%	116
Individual health	471	660	140%	754	743	99%	908
Social and community assistance	331	682	206%	773	898	116%	1245
Total	2,048	1,818	89%	2,219	2,174	98%	2,820
% of GDP	1.1	1.0		1.0	1.0		1.1

Source: World Bank staff estimates supported by MEF.

None of these shortcomings has prevented budgetary protection policy from playing its central role, but rather illustrates the need for enhancing their monitoring, targeting, and management tools.

Budgetary protection policy has to be tailored to the reality of decentralization. The next government faces a dilemma: either to continue increasing fiscal revenue or curbing currently expansionary spending, especially in teachers' and health workers' payrolls, in order to increase its fiscal space and keep key spending protected. The rationale for budgetary protection of priority social spending still prevails, but under decentralization there is an additional reason: it is perhaps the only policy tool available to preserve national spending priorities among autonomous decisions by regional or municipal governments, which might have different views on their budget priorities.

Efficiency and Effectiveness of Social Expenditure

Perhaps the major task in poverty reduction for the coming years for Peru, given the reduced fiscal space and the need for tight control of fiscal expenditure, is to keep improving the efficiency and effectiveness of social expenditure under decentralization. Peru devotes low amounts to social expenditure and, given fiscal constraints, there is no reason to believe the fiscal space will increase significantly in the rest of the decade. Hence, policies to improve efficiency should reward the best-performing programs, and policies to improve effectiveness should aim to eliminate programs that are poorly targeted, with low coverage or high leakages, while increasing allocations to and expanding coverage of programs that do have not only a clear progressive bias, but are pro-poor.

Efficiency is measured by calculating the distance between observed input-output bundles and an efficient frontier constructed using an innovative technique widely used in efficiency and productivity analysis: Data Development Analysis. This technique identifies efficient input-output combinations from a convex production frontier, and ranks countries

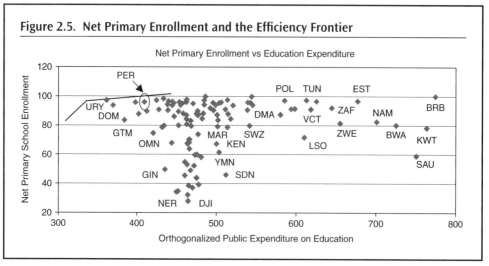

Figure 2.5. Net Primary Enrollment and the Efficiency Frontier

Source: Herrera and Pang (2004).

according to their distance to the efficiency frontier. We applied this technique for different social outcomes in Peru, while using a single input: public spending. Our main findings follow.

- In *education*, Peru ranks better than the average for Latin American countries; that is, it is more output efficient in gross and net primary enrollment, in average years of school, and in youth literacy. The country scores at the top of Latin America and the Caribbean (LAC) regional averages in net primary enrollment (Figure 2.5), and also ranks high in the first- and second-level completion ratios (Crouch 2005). This suggests the presence of students remaining after the early stages of education, despite perceived quality problems in primary education.
- In *health*, Peru's scores are also mixed. They are above the LAC average in DPT (diphtheria, pertussis, tetanus) (Figure 2.6) and measles immunization, but below regional averages in life expectancy at birth and in disability-adjusted life expectancy.

Although the results should be interpreted with caution, the need for less focus on access and rather for an overarching focus on improving quality in the education sector is relevant. In health, however, there is a less clear-cut message. Indeed, education and health outcomes can be explained by multiple supply and demand factors not examined here, so this approach contains an explicit omission bias due to the lack of relevant information. Hence, the main contribution of both approaches is to identify areas of significant achievements or, alternatively, underachievements, and to look for possible explanations of departures from benchmark countries that are located over the efficiency frontier. In this respect, Herrera and Pang (2005) search for statistical associations between efficiency scores and policy environment variables. By estimating correlation coefficients, three general findings are that: (a) countries with higher expenditure levels have lower efficiency scores, so that the focus on quality is at least as important as the focus on the level of spending; (b) countries with a wage bill that is a large share of the total budget tend to have lower efficiency

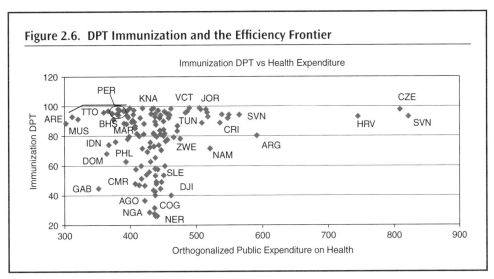

Figure 2.6. DPT Immunization and the Efficiency Frontier

Source: Herrera and Pang (2004).

scores, so that a high payroll must be curbed; and (c) countries with higher inequality (income distribution) are associated with lower educational efficiency scores, but not necessarily to those of health, so that proper targeting to the poorest is required to improve the pro-poor content of social expenditure, which is relevant for the discussion on the effectiveness of social spending that follows.

Effectiveness is measured by benefit incidence analysis. It shows who benefits from public services and describes how government spending affects the welfare of different groups of people or individual households. It does this by combining information about the unit costs of providing those services (obtained from government or service-provider data) with information on the use of these services (obtained from households through a sample survey). Results for all three sectors—education, health, and social assistance programs—address the following three concepts: absolute incidence, relative incidence, and leakages.

- *Absolute (target) incidence* of a program is defined as the average benefits (herein called transfers) received by any particular group as a percentage of total public transfers to such program; that is, the targeting outcome of the program.
- *Relative incidence* is defined as the average benefit received by each beneficiary group as a percentage of the average total consumption of each group; that is, the relative "importance" of such program.
- *Leakages* are understood either as (a) the percentage of non-targeted beneficiary population in a program, or as (b) the share of the non-poor beneficiaries receiving the benefits of a program.

Comparison of spending concentration curves with the Lorenz curve shows how progressive/ regressive transfers are and their pro-poor bias or anti-poor bias. Concentration curves lying above the Lorenz curve, which is defined in per capita expenditure, are progressive. This indicates that spending is more equally distributed than expenditure per capita. Furthermore, by

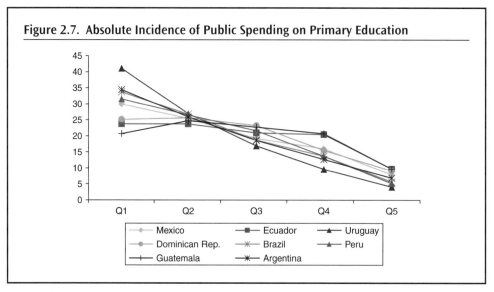

Source: Lindert, Skoufias, and Shapiro (2005).

comparing the concentration curves with the 45 degrees diagonal, targeting on the poorer groups can be judged. If the curve lies above the diagonal, it means that the poorest quintile gains more than 20 percent of the total spending allocated to such program. In contrast, curves below the diagonal indicate non-pro-poor targeting.

In Peru, public expenditure in the three social sectors is, in *absolute incidence* terms, more progressive in the case of the food programs, followed by education (Figures 2.7 and 2.8) (with the exception of the tertiary programs). Although the expenditure on tertiary education

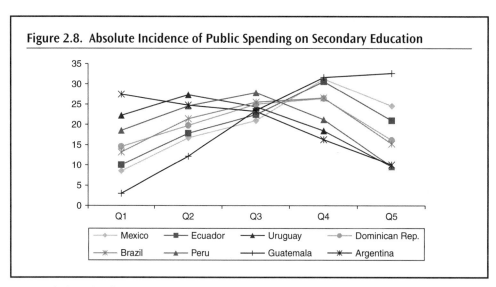

Source: Lindert, Skoufias, and Shapiro (2005).

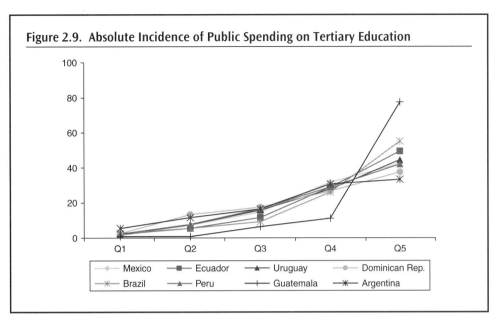

Figure 2.9. Absolute Incidence of Public Spending on Tertiary Education

Source: Lindert, Skoufias, and Shapiro (2005).

is highly regressive, the ratio in Peru (27.56) is about the average for selected countries (Figure 2.9). Public health spending is, in contrast, highly regressive, since the top quintile receives almost 40 percent of all outlays. Regressivity is even more acute in the case of ESSALUD programs. Only Integral Health Insurance (SIS) spending in health shows some progressivity (and pro-poor targeting in the second and third quintiles), but still does not reach the extreme poor population.

In terms of pro-poor targeting, there are significant differences between rural and urban programs. Spending is pro-poor only in the case of rural spending. All urban education programs are non-pro-poor, whereas all rural programs, except those for university and non-university education, have a pro-poor focus. In the same vein, all rural health programs, except the one for hospitals (including MINSA) have a pro-poor focus, whereas all urban health outlays are not well targeted to the poor. In the case of the food programs, *Desayunos Escolares* is clearly the program that has achieved a better pro-poor targeting; 52 percent of its spending reaches the poorest quintile and more than 75 percent reaches the rural population, followed by the *Almuerzo Escolar* program (39 percent reaches the poorest quintile). By contrast, about one-third of the resources of *Comedores Populares* and *Vaso de Leche* benefit the non-poor. In fact, the *Comedores Populares* program is relevant for only the middle-to-low-income urban population located in the fourth, third, and second quintiles (Table 2.2).

Public expenditure in the three social sectors is, in *relative incidence* terms, progressive for education and regressive for health. However, the relative incidence of MINSA spending is progressive, and this is also the case of the SIS program, while it is regressive in the cases of ESSALUD and the health services of the armed forces (FFAA) (Table 2.3). This certainly has to do with the relatively high cost of health services in average household consumption. Indeed, the share of consumption allocated to the top quintile by ESSALUD is

Table 2.2. Absolute Incidence of Food Program Expenditure, 2003 (Average transfer as percentage of total spending received by each group)

Food Programs	Quintiles					Poverty Level			Area	
	I	II	III	IV	V	PX	PNX	NP	Urban	Rural
Vaso de Leche	17.6	23.4	28.7	23.5	6.9	22.1	44.3	33.6	74.7	25.3
Comedores Populares	16.0	19.0	33.2	26.3	5.5	14.0	53.6	32.4	70.1	29.9
Desayunos Escolares	52.6	24.4	15.9	5.0	2.1	53.2	30.2	16.6	23.2	76.8
Club de Madres	8.1	29.7	54.1	5.4	1.4	6.8	56.8	35.1	47.3	52.7
Almuerzo Escolar	38.9	37.6	15.0	7.1	1.3	41.6	42.0	16.4	26.1	73.9
Comedor Infantil	27.9	42.5	23.7	5.9	0.0	31.1	53.9	15.1	42.9	56.6
Other (Panfar, Pacfo, others)	22.8	41.3	13.7	19.7	2.6	24.1	49.8	26.1	35.1	64.9
Total Food Programs	**23.7**	**26.4**	**25.3**	**19.5**	**5.0**	**26.3**	**44.7**	**29.0**	**59.2**	**40.7**
Memo for comparison										
Share of total population	20	20	20	20	20	22	33	45	65	35
Share of poor population	37	36	23	4	0	40	60	0	51	49
Share of total consumption	5	10	14	21	50	6	20	74	83	17

PX = Extreme Poverty; PNX = Non-extreme Poverty; NP = Non-poor.
Note: Only households that benefit from at least one food program are considered.
Source: ENAHO 2003 IV Term–INEI.

roughly equivalent to the share assigned by private spending to health; that is, both service providers have equivalent relative incidence and similar weight in terms of their share in household consumption of the less poor.

Table 2.3. Relative Incidence of Health Spending by Quintile, 2003 (Average transfer as percentage of total spending received by each group)

	Quintiles				
	I	II	III	IV	V
MINSA	6.7	6.3	6	3.8	1.3
ESSALUD	0.4	1.3	2.7	3.6	2.5
FFAA	0	0	0.2	0.2	0.4
PRIVADO	2.2	2.4	2.8	3.5	2.8
SIS	0.7	0.7	0.4	0.3	0.2
Total	**9.4**	**10.1**	**11.6**	**11.1**	**7.0**

Note: SIS is part of MINSA.
Source: Author's calculations based on ENAHO 2003 IV Term, MEF-SIAF and ESSALUD.

Coverage of education programs is very extensive, but also very unevenly distributed. Basically 100 percent of the extreme poor population receives primary education, but such percentage halves when it comes to secondary education, a result consistent with our efficiency analysis. Tertiary education reaches only about 3 percent of the extreme poor. Primary education has the highest coverage of the rural population. Of food programs, *Vaso de Leche* and *Desayunos Escolares* have the best coverage (Table 2.4).

Leakages in most health and food programs increased between 2001 and 2003. Health programs have the highest leakages of all social

Table 2.4. Social Program Leakages, 2001 and 2003 (Percent of non-poor beneficiaries in the program)

Social Program	National Level		Urban Areas		Rural Areas	
	2001	2003	2001	2003	2001	2003
Food Programs						
Vaso de Leche	29	30	39	38	16	23
Comedores Populares	30	32	36	34	18	26
Desayunos Escolares	14	18	27	32	10	13
Almuerzo Escolar	17	18	30	25	13	15
Comedor Infantil	17	16	32	13	7	18
Health						
Control de Crecimiento del Niño	39	32	52	46	19	20
Seguro Integral de Salud	31	32	40	39	20	26
Planificación Familiar	43	48	51	53	30	41
Education						
Textos y Utiles Escolares	25	24	36	33	14	16

Note: Percent of non-poor beneficiaries.
Source: Author's calculation based on ENAHO 2001–2003.

programs, and these increased between 2001 and 2003, particularly in the rural areas. The degree of leakages is non-negligible: no less than one-third of beneficiaries of health programs are non-poor. Food programs have the second-highest leakages of all programs, and this is particularly relevant for *Vaso de Leche* (30 percent) and *Comedores Populares* (32 percent). Leakages are higher in urban than in rural areas, where they also increased between 2001 and 2003. Just for *Vaso de Leche*, subsidies lost in leaks to the non-poor population represent about NS/100 million per year. Furthermore, leakages in education programs (textbooks and materials) are also, surprisingly, non-negligible—close to one-quarter nationwide—and show marginal improvement between 2001 and 2003.

Review of Research-based Peruvian Literature

Many of the previous findings are not news to Peru. Indeed, there is a vast literature on partial diagnostics of problems dealing with the different angles of the Compact. The challenge, then, is putting all the richness of the diagnostics together and finding a comprehensive set of messages that define a new social policy for the incoming officials.

To do this, Table 2.5 summarizes the existing set of policy recommendations of distinguished Peruvian scholars that have ventured into the fields dealt with in this chapter. Then, in Table 2.6, we present a summary of the main diagnostics on Compact issues found that converge with the issues raised here and that broadly guide the recommendations.

Table 2.5. Summary of Key Policy Recommendations on Compact-related Matters in the Peruvian Literature

Issue	Alcázar (2004)	Hunt (2001)	PREAL (2003)	RESAL (1999)	Francke (2004)	Mendoza (2003)	Vasquez (2004)	Vega (2004)	Rivero (2004)	Du Bois (2004)
Increase social spending.	✓	✓	✓	✓					✓	
Target spending toward the poor, create more targeted programs, not just targeted spending.	✓	✓	✓	✓		✓			✓	
Create a "lower bound" level of priority "basic" social expenditure that mainly addresses rural-poor living standards.				✓		✓	✓			
Reduce the role of the State in the provision of social services and increase the participation of those that receive such services at the local level, mainly in education.										✓
Reduce fragmentation of social programs.										✓
Improve the quality of education.										✓
Clarify and finalize powers and functions under decentralization, including school autonomy, with fully specified and non-overlapping responsibilities.	✓	✓	✓		✓					
Increase coverage of pre-primary schooling and food programs.		✓				✓	✓		✓	
Clarify, in particular, formulas for resource allocation to subnational entities.					✓	✓	✓			
Adopt an effective monitoring system at the decentralized levels, supported by an improved SIAF and the SNIP.	✓									
Reduce leakages and other forms of non-provision of services such as teacher absenteeism.	✓						✓			

Source: World Bank staff.

Table 2.6. Main National Findings on Previous Research Related to the Compact in Peru

Factor	Discussion	Sources of Evidence and Range of Application of the Research	Possible Policy Implications
Social expenditure trends and budget management	Between 1990 and 1997 there was an increase in social spending. Low spending in social sectors. Increasing current expenditures. Decreasing capital expenditures and large infrastructure gaps. Inertial structure in the composition of expenditure. High household contributions and an extended private education.	Saavedra and Suarez (2002) Francke and Paulini (2003) Francke and Mendoza (2001) Francke, Castro, and Ugaz (2002) Vasquez (2004) Shack (2000) Francke (2001, 2002) Mendoza (presentation 2003) Ortiz de Cevallos and others (1999) IPE (2003)	Reduce military expenditure and increase social expenditure.
Procyclical fiscal policy	During the last three decades, fiscal policy has been procyclical and volatile. Shortcomings in Fiscal Transparency and Prudence Law in order to diminish the effects of recessions.	Vidaurre (2000) Ormeño (2002) Jimenez (2002, 2003) Pereyra (2003) Francke (2002)	Fiscal countercyclical rule in a context of a permanent primary surplus.
Fiscal space for social spending and budgetary protection of social spending	Tributary system not very progressive. 41.5% of total expenditure is spent on pensions and debt services. Few studies on earnings generation, collection capacity, and borderline regions. Transferences create a perverse result in local management: they reduce tax collection efforts.	Iguiñiz and Barrantes (2004) Iguiñiz (2000) Cortez (2002) Francke and Mendoza (2001) Vasquez (2005) Francke, Castro, and Ugaz (2002) Alvarado (2003) Larios, Alvarado, and Conterno (2004)	Reduce tax burden on labor income and poor population consumption. Eliminate tax exonerations and special schemes. Create a health fund to which non-poor should contribute (a percentage of their incomes), and the government should contribute for the poor. Choice of provider.

(continued)

Table 2.6. Main National Findings on Previous Research Related to the Compact in Peru (*Continued*)

Factor	Discussion	Sources of Evidence and Range of Application of the Research	Possible Policy Implications
			Revise the tax scheme. Co-participation of subnational governments in social sectors spending and transfers, mostly in the higher tax collection regions.
Use of public resources	Public resources have not been used adequately, they have not reached those they wanted, and they have not generated the expected results. Moreover, there is an increase in administrative costs. Incentives on spending are political rather than priorities.	Du Bois (2004) Jaramillo and Parodi (2003)	Reduce government participation in provision and management of services. The government must focus on financing, regulation, and participation of beneficiaries. Use of conditional cash transfers and constitution of one public social fund.
Information and Monitoring Systems	Lack of a consensual definition of social spending. Good advance in information systems and management monitoring. Poor performance in monitoring results and targeting. Government has to be aware of transferences to subnational jurisdictions.	Francke (2003) Vasquez (2004) Alcazar (2004)	Define goals and monitor and evaluate efficiency and performance. Expand budget information systems to subnational governments. Train subnational authorities in budget management. Use of an individual targeting mechanism.
Efficiency and effectiveness of social spending	Lack of objective mechanisms of elaboration, formulation, and execution of social policies. Social policies are not adequately transparent and technical driven. Low impact of nutritional programs.	Vasquez, Cortez, and Riesco (2000) Ravina and Paulini (2002) Gajate and Inurritegui (2001)	Promote pro-poor growth. Give incentives to social sectors professionals. Monitor and evaluate performance.

Equity of social spending	High level of leakages. Spending concentrated in Lima–Callao. Overlapping efforts and perverse cross-subsidies. Spending in education and health is not progressive. Lack of suitable legislation.	Alcazar, Lopez, and Wachtenheim (2003) Vasquez (2002, 2004) Chacaltana (2001) Tanaka and Trivelli (2002) Francke (1998, 2002, 1999) Portocarrero (2000) Petrera (2002) Cortez (2002) Jaramillo and Parodi (2003) Francke and Mendoza (2001) Gonzales de Olarte (2000) Saavedra, Melzi, and Miranda (1997)	Focus expenditure to the poorest departments and zones. Active participation of civil society, which assures service delivery to the poor. Efficient targeting mechanisms: geographic or individual. Develop public infrastructure outside Lima–Callao.
Decentralization and transferences of social spending: (Changes in budget composition)	Decentralization of budget without limits would cause fiscal imbalances in subnational governments. Combination of old management deficiencies with those that come with the decentralization process. Low degree of decentralization of resources and responsibilities: additional resources are concentrated at central level. Amounts of money transferred have been small.	Carranza and Tuesta (2003) Francke, Castro, and Ugaz (2002) Francke (2001, 2002, 2004) Perla (2002) Iguiñiz and Barrantes (2004) Caballero (2004) Larios, Alvarado, and Conterno (2004)	Create "hard" budget constraints and subnational indebtedness limits. Discourage growth of current expenditure and encourage capital expenditure. New management mechanisms and conflict resolution in the local government. Interaction with civil society.

Source: World Bank staff elaboration.

Table 2.7. Peru: Tasks Required to Strengthen the Compact

Key Issues	Policy Recommendations
In the context of limited fiscal space, how should the next government proceed with social expenditures?	Preserving fiscal discipline by not committing additional social expenditure unless there are new revenues or budget reallocations. In addition:

■ Develop a medium-term strategy and a monitoring system for the social programs, defining targets for specific outcomes in education, health, and nutrition. The strategy should identify key priority programs required to meet those outcomes, and a social sector multiyear expenditure framework with explicit minimum allocations assigned to the priority programs.

■ The strategy should also define a small number of annual and quarterly indicators to monitor progress in the priority programs. These indicators should be available to the general public through a user-friendly Internet interface that would allow beneficiaries, municipalities, and regions to measure the progress in budget execution and in the achievement of the intermediate indicators.

■ Impact evaluations of all key programs should be produced by third-party analysts using internationally recognized methodologies and should be made public before each annual budget is sent to Congress.

■ Expand progress achieved on budget management in the areas of (a) integration of the budget formulation module into SIAF; and (b) development and implementation of a monitoring and evaluation system for social programs by SIAF, with the creation of a user-friendly website tracking core priority social expenditures.

■ Introduce performance-based contracts between the *Ministerio de Economía y Finanzas* and the main executors of social programs, based on the pilot *Convenios de Administración de Resultados*.

| Should the government continue protecting the Priority Social Programs through decentralization? | Yes, but tailored to the new institutional setup. Indeed, there is a need to provide further institutionalization to budget protection, which implies a transparent, consensus-building, and participatory political negotiation, rather than just technical or institutional decisions: |

■ The central recommendation is to keep protecting at least key programs and/or "projects" and "activities" the resources of which (a) belong to well agreed national priorities; (b) if decentralized, are administered through management contracts; (c) if centrally managed, are implemented by a reduced number of Executing Units; (d) include effective targeting mechanisms (pro-poor) and monitoring tools by SIAF; and (e) are supported by complementary training, evaluation, and participatory tools.

■ Shift the expenditure allocations in favor of the most efficient, better-targeted, and accountable activities/projects belonging to the PSPs, such as SIS or revamped food-aid programs.

(continued)

Table 2.7. Peru: Tasks Required to Strengthen the Compact (*Continued*)

Key Issues	Policy Recommendations
How urgent is negotiating and reforming the public payroll system?	Short of fiscal space, there is hardly a sustainable social agenda if there is no civil service reform. This implies short- and medium-term measures, including:
	■ Curbing the growth in the wage payroll while freezing hiring and resisting salary increases and further pressures from regional and municipal governments to increase investment.
	■ Making sure that social expenditure increases only pari passu with the materialization of additional fiscal space (savings) generated from payroll downsizing or other sources of public savings, such as tax revenue increases.
	■ Watching for significant contingent liabilities in the fiscal system with the pending regularization of teachers and health workers by regional governments, and with excessive subnational debt, part of it nonregistered, in some municipal governments.
	■ Simplifying and unifying the remuneration structure. Consolidate sources of payment to reduce transaction costs; consolidate bonus payments, aiming to have as much or 100 percent of the paycheck disbursed as regular, pensionable salary; and institutionalize the "informal" *Comité de Administración del Fondo de Asistencia y* Estímulo (CAFAE) payment mechanism, making it subject to pension contributions.
	■ Commissioning detailed staff surveys and studies of the remuneration structure for both the health and education sectors to guide the construction of a new wage structure.
Would completing reform of the pension fund system help?	Definitely, especially if it contributes to reducing future contingent liabilities for the State. This would involve:
	■ Deepening private sector involvement, both domestic and foreign, in fund management.
	■ Modernizing information technology pension systems.
	■ Reducing the significant levels of arrears in contributions to SPP, particularly in the public sector.
	■ Defining a new tax scheme for pension contributions. Currently, savings (contributions) are taxed and consumption (pensions) exempted. If long-term savings are to be incentivized, the inverse would be a much better scheme.
	■ Allowing Pension Fund Administrators (AFPs) to manage different funds with different mixes of risk and profitability to better accommodate individual preferences.
	■ Integrating and centralizing the registration and financial planning functions, while formally linking them through an information system with the General Accounting Office.
What specific actions are needed to improve the effectiveness and efficiency of program deliverables?	Policies should aim for continuous monitoring and evaluation of surviving programs to correct those that are poorly targeted or that have high leakages or low coverage of the poor. This implies:

(continued)

Table 2.7. Peru: Tasks Required to Strengthen the Compact (*Continued*)

Key Issues	Policy Recommendations
	Education. Fill the gaps in coverage, especially at the pre-primary and secondary stages, and reduce expenditure on most tertiary education programs in real terms, while shifting expenditure toward inputs, rural schools, and quality-enhancement programs.
	Health. Promote the expansion of a renewed SIS, and self-targeted services to the poor, through more health posts rather than on additional hospitals.
	Food Programs. Fine–tune their implementation through new accountability mechanisms at the municipal level leading to (a) building a database of beneficiaries, (b) developing regular social auditing procedures, (c) reducing high prices of food supplies, (d) installing adequate monitoring and control systems, and (e) eventually considering their total or partial conversion to a cash-transfer mechanism. By monitoring progress toward target outcomes on an annual basis with the support of SIAF, the *Instituto Nacional de Estadística e Informática* (INEI), and the Ministry of Women, their annual evaluations would indicate whether those programs meet their objectives.
Should decentralization continue with a closer eye on effectiveness, efficiency, and fiscal neutrality?	Yes, a sound decentralization process has no choice but to complete the accountability and regulatory framework to preserve quality of social services under decentralization. This involves a series of possible actions to:

- Use simple formulas for transferring resources, introducing a rule-based transfer system for regional government as a revenue-sharing arrangement in amounts proportionate to actual amounts of budget transfers.
- Avoid high transactions costs in management.
- Improve local revenue collection.
- Limit subnational debt to sustainable levels.
- Introduce ceilings on personnel expenditure (in percent of regional government or municipal budgets), and improve human resources management practices.
- In the medium term, regional governments should introduce their own taxes, perhaps piggybacking on a national tax such as on gasoline or on the income tax (but at flat rates).
- Develop a social sector multiannual budgeting framework that integrates inter- and intrasectoral spending priorities shared between the Central and subnational governments.
- Unify debt concepts throughout the public sector, improve monitoring and information flow by developing an SIAF-Local Government debt module, and apply sanctions for overindebted municipalities.
- Introduce debt rescheduling programs for the 30 most overindebted municipalities, which entails, among other things, a program of own revenue collection improvement (commitments for improving property tax collection, among others), rescheduling of investments, privatization of municipal assets, a hiring freeze, and limiting severance payments.

Policy Recommendations

Based on the findings of this report and the Peruvian literature explored above, it is possible to formulate a coherent set of policy recommendations to serve as a basis for a Compact framework of social policy by the next government. These recommendations assume that preserving fiscal discipline continues to be the paramount objective of fiscal policy and that the medium-term target fiscal deficit of 1 percent of GDP is reached in 2005 and maintained during the rest of the decade (except during years when major negative shocks occur).

Preserving social expenditure as the top priority of the budget is welcome, but the present current/capital expenditure composition needs to be changed. Curbing payroll growth is among the top priorities of the social agenda in the short term, followed by a comprehensive civil service reform in the medium term. Moreover, priority focus should be on improving the quality rather than the quantity of social spending, which implies preserving core priority spending and shifting the expenditure mix in favor of the most efficient, better-targeted, and accountable social programs, such as SIS or revamped food-aid programs. This implies tailoring the current budgetary protection policy to a results-oriented, accountable, pro-poor, transparent, and participatory decentralization process. All this is easier said than done, and must be understood as actions belonging only to the Compact—actions that cannot be isolated from the other sides of the Accountability Triangle. More specifically, it implies strengthening of the Compact, outlined in Table 2.7.

CHAPTER 3

Education Sector: Standards, Accountability, and Support*

Luis Crouch

Main Policy Recommendations

Peru has made great strides in education coverage. Quality, as measured by actual cognitive achievement of children, and particularly the distribution of quality among social groups, remains the problem to which a solution has been elusive. In order to move forward on quality and its distribution, the following steps are needed.

First, Peru needs to establish much clearer, more specific learning standards.[15] Specificity needs to refer to both grade level and clarity of goals. For example, goals should exist at a

---

*This chapter is a summary of a longer background technical report entitled, *Recurso Perú. Education Sector: Standards, Accountability, and Support*. The report can be obtained at http://www.worldbank.org/ or by writing to Daniel Cotlear, at dcotlear@worldbank.org.

15. Since the word "standards" is used throughout this document, it is important to offer some definitions. First, in the context of learning, by "standards" we mean both a system of measurement or "metrics," such as a way of measuring a student's performance (for example, words read correctly per minute), and specific numerical goals to be achieved (for example, being able to read 70 words per minute by the end of grade 2) or non-numerical skills to be learned (for example, learning letter-sound recognition). Other such metrics and goals exist, of course. Second, in the context of management and funding processes, we refer to standardized ways of proceeding, such as funding via formulas, and specific goals such as saying that each school should receive so many soles per child for purchasing learning materials. Having standardized ways for schools to report on budget use to parents is another example of a process standard. Third, in the context of bilingual education, we refer to standardization of languages of instruction in order to discuss the limits to such standardization. It would be possible to state, each time the word or concept is used, the exact meaning used. However, given the pervasiveness of the use of the concept, it would also be tedious. The expectation is that the context will make it clear enough. In any case, what the appropriate notion of standard might be is, in any case, open to discussion and interpretation. For example, while we believe we should recommend that children be able to correctly read 70 words per minute by the end of grade 2 (a standard as an actual goal), the policy dialog process in Peru might determine that for now it is wisest simply to get teachers to track students on this measurement and try to improve it (a standard as a metric).

minimum by grade, and ideally by semester. Goals should be stated in specific terms, such as levels of comprehension, fluency, and speed of reading, words read correctly per minute, and specific numerical skills. Reading materials of standardized grade or age appropriateness need to be created and distributed. Quality goals for secondary education should be embodied in a national secondary-school-leaving exam or certification. Peru also needs to establish service and process standards; that is, standards of behavior (such as hours of effective and active learning per year) and reporting to the client, in a process of downward accountability of schools to communities and of the Province-level School Management and Supervision Unit (*Unidad de Gestión Educativa Local*, UGELs) to schools. Provision standards need to be developed whereby, for example, funding formulas are developed for the national level to fund regions and for regions to fund schools. Funding according to formulas is more transparent, more equitable, and more efficient. Finally, clear and rigorous standards for teachers are needed as part of a strategy for upgrading teacher quality significantly over time. Standards for both recruitment and professional behavior are needed, and can include the accreditation of teacher training approaches at colleges and universities. These standards should include subject-matter knowledge. They can be incorporated in the *Carrera Pública Magisterial* or its regulation.

The need to create standards is related to the need for developing a culture of evaluation in Peru. There is currently a pervasive fear in Peru's education sector of anyone being evaluated. This creates a vicious cycle. The fear of failure creates a fear of evaluation, but the lack of evaluation condemns almost all efforts to failure, because there is no serious way to detect when anything is going wrong. Failure and lack of evaluation against any kind of standard become self-fulfilling prophecies of each other, and create an environment of intense pessimism, fatalism, and lack of accountability. The fear of evaluation and standards has been turned into a virtue, and it has become popular to question evaluation and measurement as intellectually suspect, non-modern, regressive, or inequality-inducing. However, this pessimism is largely unjustified. It is shown in this study that there are many schools that perform well, and that high expectations are often met by high performance. Having clear and reasonably high expectations is an important way of breaking the vicious cycle of pessimism and the blame-the-child or blame-the-society game that seems to be pervasive in Peru.

Second, Peru needs to develop much clearer lines of accountability pressure and consumer or parental power. Without accountability pressure and rewards (incentives), agents will not come to standard. (And, without standards, accountability pressure would not know what direction to seek.) Given the situation of low accountability that has developed in Peru in recent decades, most teachers will not, for example, expend the hours of effort required unless they are supervised and motivated by both communities and bureaucracy, and unless expectations are made clear. Some will make the effort needed, and already do so, motivated by intrinsic professionalism and pride (as documented in the background technical report), but most do not. Parents should have more say in what happens in schools, such as the use of school budgets and the selection and careers of teachers. Options such as giving parents a statutory majority in the School Governing Council (*Consejos Educativos Institucionales*, CONEIs) and giving the CONEIs more power in determining teacher selection and teacher evaluation should be considered. An important tool of accountability will be to strongly encourage (or even find ways to dismiss) the less-motivated and less-capable teachers to leave the profession. This increases the turnover rate and allows new teachers into the system, and if the latter have met knowledge standards, the quality of the profession will improve faster. Finally, more systemic and evaluated experimentation in outsourcing of education for the poor, such as the *Fe y Alegría* model, should be carried out.

Third, support needs to be improved so that actors can come to standard. Accountability pressure is not enough if agents lack appropriate information on how to come to standard, and will only frustrate agents. Teacher training, both in-service and pre-service, has tended to be too generic and (in the case of in-service training) episodic, precisely because there are no sufficiently clear learning standards. Instead, much more specific in-service training is needed—training that accompanies the teacher throughout the year and that is oriented at helping the teacher go through a year's work in trying to achieve the end-of-year learning goals. Similarly, much more and better learning materials, in particular reading materials, libraries, stationery, and supplies are required. This will be expensive. Thus, general financial support is also needed; education expenditure as a share of gross domestic product (GDP) will likely have to increase.

The Accountability Triangle Approach in Education

This chapter takes as its point of departure an accountability framework that says that for any social system to work well there must be a well-defined and well-exercised framework of mutual accountabilities among three sets of actors. These actors are: (a) the State (including regional or subnational levels), which includes politicians and policymakers in both the legislative and executive branches; (b) the service providers (including organizations such as the ministerial bureaucracy, regional bureaucracies such as Region-level School Management and Supervision Units (*Dirección Regional de Educación*, DREs) and UGELs, and the actual service providers, such as schools; and (c) the citizens or clients of the system. This is sometimes referred to as the "accountability triangle" (see Figure 3.1).

The relationship between political actors and service providers (the right leg of the triangle) is often referred-to as the "compact" or "contract." This relationship embodies the creation of laws, norms, standards, and regulations. It also embodies the provision of resources and support. In return for funding, the providers give back information to the policymakers on the results of provision—for example, whether such provision is in fact taking place to norms and standards. The relationships at the base of the pyramid are relationships of "local participation," "local voice," or "consumer choice." These relationships are particularly necessary in situations, common in most developing countries, where the capacity of the policymakers to extract, from service providers, behavior according to standard is weak. Yet, it should be noted that without standards it is difficult for "local participation" to work very well, particularly when the problem is quality. When the problem is educational access, parents and local citizens are easily able to see whether schools exist, and their children enroll. When the problem is quality and cognitive development, then unless standards of learning are specified and popularized, it is difficult for parents and citizens to know whether they are being provided with the standard of service they are entitled to.

These relationships at the base of the triangle work either through direct parental or citizen input into school affairs (such as the setting of overall direction, approval of budgets, input into teacher selection, and teachers' annual performance reviews), or through

Figure 3.1. The Accountability Triangle

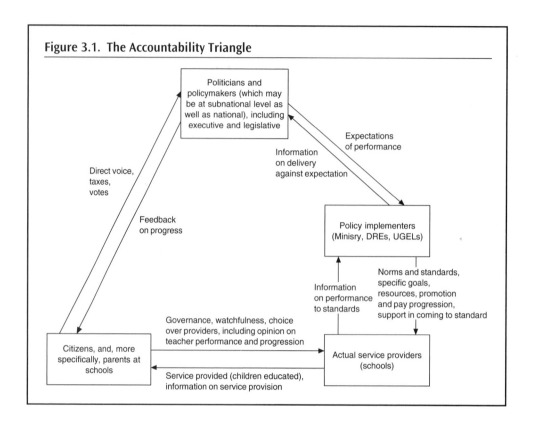

consumer choice. In either case if there is no "market information" as to which providers are providing to standard, it is difficult for this relationship to work. Thus, there is dependence between the base of the triangle and the right leg: if the right leg cannot generate standards, the base will tend to not work very well.

Finally, the relationships in the left leg of the triangle are called "voice" relationships. (Sometimes it is called "national" or "aggregated" voice to distinguish it from the participatory voice relationship at the base of the triangle.) In this relationship voters provide votes and taxes, and direct citizen input through advocacy nongovernmental organizations (NGOs), protests, civil unrest, testimony to the legislature, and other actions, to the policymakers. In return, the policymakers periodically inform (or should inform) voters as to actions taken and results achieved.

For service provision to work well, all relationships must function. More important, the flow of relationships should be circular. Every actor should be part of two circular flows. A clockwise (outer) flow typically sends resources, support, and information on what is wanted (such as norms and standards) from one actor to another; a counterclockwise flow sends information about performance that has been achieved, and on actual outputs, from one actor to another. The flow between citizens and politicians, and between politicians and service providers, is called the "long route" of accountability. This route has developed over decades, even hundreds of years, in developed countries, and can often work very well even without the relationship at the base. The direct flow between citizens and service providers is called the "short route" of accountability. When the "long route" fails, for reasons too complex to describe here, societies can opt to strengthen the "short route." In fact, historically, accountability at the base of the triangle is where most societies start. However, this is typically seen as an interim or incomplete solution, because some central "referee" is needed to create the standards or metrics whereby citizens transact with service providers, and because such a referee is also needed to take care of equity problems and problems that arise when the transactions of some citizens with service providers damage (or help) other citizens and service providers, and the latter cannot find ways to either discourage those damages or stimulate those benefits.

In Peru, many of these relationships work, at best, imperfectly, and in some cases they barely work at all, as this chapter documents. Two relationships are emphasized in this chapter: (a) the relationship between the citizens—that is, the parents who have children attending schools—and the providers—that is, the schools; and (b) the relationship between the politicians and policymakers of all levels with the policy implementers—that is, the ministries, DREs, and UGELs.

Issues and Analysis

Current Status of the Sector

Gains in Coverage: Peru has made impressive gains in education coverage. Enrollment levels are higher in many other Latin American countries—even higher than in countries with higher income per capita. Gross enrollment ratios in pre-primary, primary, secondary, and tertiary education are 60 percent, 116 percent, 82 percent, and 33 percent, respectively, in Peru, and 63 percent, 110 percent, 72 percent, 18 percent, respectively, in Latin America as a whole. Furthermore, Peru has been ahead of the rest of Latin America, with regard to coverage, for decades. Given that the gross enrollment ratios at the post-primary levels are higher in Peru than for the rest of Latin America, completion at the primary and secondary levels has to be quite high. This is indeed the case. In short, Peru has already achieved a mass education system of nearly a developed-country standard, in terms of coverage.

Problems with Quality. Quality, measured by international assessments such as the Programme for International Student Assessment (PISA), is not as impressive. On the combined reading scale in the PISA, for example, Peru scored 327, where the rest of Latin American countries scored, on average, 411. Furthermore, Peru's own internal learning assessments produce results that analysts consider quite unsatisfactory. However, average learning levels in international assessments are not much lower than one would expect given Peru's per capita income, demographic burden, and how recent a phenomenon widespread literacy is. The other Latin American countries that participated in PISA have twice Peru's per capita income, and some of them achieved mass literacy decades ahead of Peru (so that more of the parental and grand-parental generations are literate). Peru has 20 percent more children per adult than the rest of the Latin American countries participating in PISA, and, as is logical, it is harder to provide education when there are more children per adult. Thus, Peru's average position on international assessments such as PISA is really not surprising. Figure 3.2 shows this.

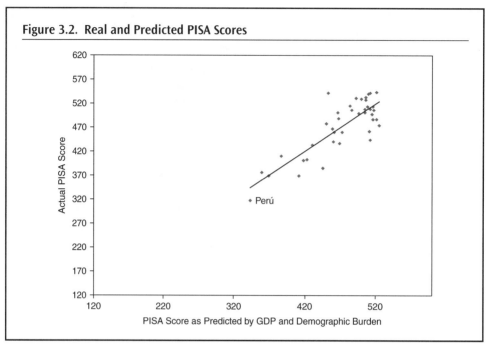

Figure 3.2. Real and Predicted PISA Scores

Source: For scores, OECD/UIS 2003, Table 2.3a, Annex B; for predicted scores, author's analysis.

However, there are at least four specific problems related to quality. First, the gap between enrollment and achievement levels is high. In most countries producing large numbers of high-school graduates, the skill levels of those graduates are also fairly high, so the labor market can absorb them. In Peru, there is a very large gap between the large numbers of graduates being produced and their skills, and this could be problematic. Second, among PISA countries, Peru also had the most inequality, taking as an index of inequality the ratio of performance at the 95th percentile to performance at the 5th percentile. In Peru this ratio was 2.8. In Mexico and Korea this ratio was 2.0 and 1.6, respectively. Even in Brazil, a country with much more income inequality than Peru, this ratio was 2.1. Third, in Peru, educational inequality seems to be unrelated to income inequality, but is more determined by sociological and pedagogical issues, as in South Africa. Fourth, in a related manner, even though the poor learn less than the rich, the inequality of learning among the poor is higher than the inequality of learning among the rich, and this is not accounted for by greater inequality in input distribution *among* the poor. This is shown in Figure 3.3. Variability of results, as shown by the distance between the two lines, is twice as high among the poor as among the better-off. Relative variability among the poor is even higher, given that their average results are worse.

Learning inequality is to a significant degree associated with sociological, managerial, and pedagogical factors such as the lack of an effective pedagogical model and standards for reaching students whose first language is not Spanish, and lower accountability to poor citizens. The result is that poor children receive education of a more variable quality, and not just lower quality, and this depends on the random personal devotion or skill of teachers or principals, or on the fact that there is greater variability in language spoken at home among the poor than among the rich (many of the poor are from Spanish-speaking homes,

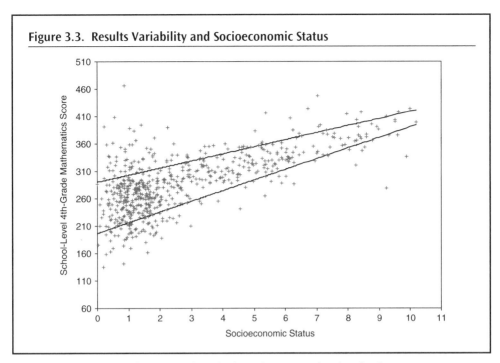

Figure 3.3. Results Variability and Socioeconomic Status

Source: Authors' analysis of school-level results from the 2001 National Evaluation.

but relatively few of the middle class and above are from non-Spanish-speaking homes). How to solve the problem of quality, and particularly quality among the poor and bilingual, is, then, the main task. A main hypothesis is that there is a lack of standards, and a lack of accountability pressure and systems built around learning, and as applicable in particular to the poor and multilingual. For example, there is a lack of a scientifically proven and consensually accepted approach to bilingual education, even after more than 10 donor projects (related to a lack of a culture of evaluation and accountability). This lack of standards thus hurts the poor most of all. These issues are discussed below.

While quality is the main problem, there are many dropouts from high school. Only a minority of rural children finish high school. This appears to be largely an economic or demand-side problem, not a problem related to unavailability of high schools (though if demand increased unavailability could become a problem). Only a small percentage of dropouts give "lack of school nearby" as a reason for dropping out. In this sense, experimentation with conditional cash transfers, though possibly conditional on achievement rather than on mere attendance (given the quality problem in Peru), is suggested. Care would have to be taken in the design of such an approach, in order to prevent various possible perverse incentives and possible unfairness. It should be possible to create, for example, a substantial prize given to last-year students in secondary schools in poor areas, who sit for a voluntary exam, and who, for instance, get the highest 3 or 5 or 10 marks in their school. This removes bias against the poor. Such a system could also be useful in beginning to create social acceptability for the notion of a secondary-school-leaving exam. Thus, voluntary at first, the system could be made mandatory if it meets acceptance. It would also be a good way to get the private sector involved in education: it could underwrite part of the (necessarily large) prize fund. While there would be some unfairness in this system because not everyone has equal quality of teachers, this unfairness could be greatly reduced or entirely eliminated by giving prizes only to those in poor areas, and to the top grade earners in *any* given school or *any* given community (thus correcting for location bias). It is also likely that the system should act as an incentive for students and parents to demand more accountability from their teachers, thus reducing teacher shirking. Furthermore, dropping out in Peru does not have simple economic determinants, but has complex sociological determinants at this point, similar to those of advanced countries (anomie, alienation, unstable homes, youth gangsterism, and so forth). These require special treatment.

Financing of Basic Education and its Relationship to Results

Peru's spending patterns are ineffective. Too much is spent on labor inputs in the education sector, and not enough on non-labor inputs. In the last few years, expenditure on personnel as a proportion of total education expenditure has reached levels higher than 80 percent. This should be unacceptable, a reasonable norm being somewhere in the range of 65 percent. The recent trend toward increased total expenditure on labor is clearly driven by three factors: 70 percent of the pressure is from salary increases, 20 percent is from decreasing pupil-teacher ratios, and 10 percent is from increases in student numbers. Further increases in salaries, if any, should be strictly keyed to agreements on some form of teacher accountability and improved teacher management. Further decreases in the pupil-teacher ratio should be controlled; there is little justification for further decreases in the near term.

Subsectoral distribution in Peru (the division between primary, secondary, and tertiary levels) is broadly reasonable and in line with international benchmarks.

Part of the pressure of personnel expenditure on total expenditure is created by the fact that there is a tight ceiling on total expenditure. Peru spends relatively little on education, as a share of GDP—only some 3 percent in recent years (that is, public expenditure as a proportion of GDP). Furthermore, as a "producer" of raw access to education, Peru has been a reasonably efficient spender. Access to education has been expanded at low cost. In spite of this, this report does not recommend an unqualified expansion of education expenditure, because Peru's task is no longer to increase access as much as it is to improve quality, and this is harder to drive through mere spending. Increases in expenditure, without first improving standards and accountability, would most likely be taken up simply by salary increases or infrastructural improvements that are unrelated to productivity of quality and learning. Until the systems of accountability that are needed to drive performance up to quality standards are in place, it would not be wise to increase expenditure by much. This is not to say that increases in expenditure should take place only when quality is already improving. But such increases in spending do need to await the development and beginning usage of systems of standards-based accountability. Until then, increases in funding should be spent almost solely on development of such systems, and this is not very costly in relation to total spending, though it will require technical imagination and consensus-building skill. To summarize: at around 3 percent of GDP over the recent past, Peru spends too little on education. But increasing spending will not, by itself and as a first step, improve matters. If funding is simply increased, it will tend to seek its "natural" channels—salaries and infrastructure—and these bear little relation to learning outcomes, as is shown both by Peruvian research and by international evidence. Thus, first, or at least in lockstep, improved systems of quality accountability and fiscal control over the distribution of spending are needed, as are agile and results-oriented teachers and an in-service support systems. Only then should spending be increased substantially but gradually. Immediate, but very modest, increases in spending might be useful, if they were oriented at improving the systems needed to support *further* spending, or at facilitating the social and political bargaining needed to get serious accountability systems in place. (However, it could be argued that with the large increases in salaries over the past few years, the increases needed to create a favorable bargaining position have already taken place, but have not been used, in fact, to bargain.) After a few years, spending should reach the Latin American average of approximately 4.5 percent of GDP.

In both the public and private education sectors, input distribution and spending are largely pro-poor, particularly in pre-primary and primary education. Overall, some 25 percent of education expenditure reaches the poorest 20 percent of households, and only 9 percent reaches the richest 20 percent. At the primary level, the poorest 20 percent receive six times the proportion of public spending that the richest 20 percent of households receive (32 percent compared to about 6 percent). But this is to a significant degree not a matter of policy at all. There has been no conscious effort to distribute educational resources in a pro-poor fashion. The current pro-poor distribution is simply an unintended consequence of various other policies and of private choices.

First, the poor have more children (two to three times more) than the rich. Second, the poor are "trapped" in public schools, whereas the more affluent frequently send their children to private schools, which they perceive to be better. Half the children of the richest 20 percent of families are in private schools, compared to essentially zero percent of the children of the poorest 20 percent of families. Third, within the public sector, and if one looks at the school rather than region or district level, spending is slightly pro-poor because all teachers get paid essentially the same, and the pupil-teacher ratio in poor areas tends to be a little lower, because population density is lower in poor areas. Thus, there is some pro-poor spending on personnel *within*, say, the public education sector, at the primary school level, that is the result of (a) a relatively perverse salary scale such that well-qualified teachers do not earn much more than poorly qualified ones; and (b) geography, rather than the result of a conscious policy of improving the quality of education provided to the poor.

Thus, the relative pro-poor nature of public spending on education is not really a policy accomplishment, but is the result of other policies and private choices. Spending and resource allocation need to be thoroughly analyzed and reformulated along the lines of explicit policy choices aimed at improving quality among the poor. This should be done via simple and transparent per capita funding and physical resourcing formulas that explicitly provide extra support to the poor. In addition, public reporting on resource transfers and use should be linked, via reporting and public policy discussions, to the results of spending. This should be done via simple formats in ways that encourage accountability at school, regional, and national levels. Parents, the public, civil society, and the State should all be made aware, via appropriate reporting linking spending and results, of what resources are being used, and how this leads, or fails to lead, to results.

While the most expensive input (teacher labor), and hence (most likely) total cost, is not distributed in an anti-poor fashion, the distribution of measured learning results favors the rich. Not only do the poor have worse results, but the *distribution* of results *within* the poorer groups is wider than the distribution of results within the richer groups. Thus, results for the poorest children are worse than for the richest children, but this is not surprising. More interesting is the fact that results among the poor are twice as variable as results among the rich.

This implies that, with currently inefficient spending (that is, without accountability for learning standards), further input equalization or even pro-poor spending is unlikely, by itself, to improve learning results among the poor. Making spending more explicitly pro-poor, using explicit funding formulas, however, is still worthwhile, for the sake of transparency; for the sake of equity (even if certain inputs are not directly or obviously associated with learning, but make lives better for children, it seems unjust for some children to have those inputs and others not to); and to remove spending as a justification for poor results. But while this is being done, accountability to standard, particularly among suppliers of education to the poor, needs to be increased many-fold.

Finally, it is to be noted that while learning results are anti-poor, they are distributed more progressively than either income or private spending on education. Learning results have a concentration index of some 0.10 to 0.15 at the primary level (at the secondary level the concentration of results is hard to measure, because by then quite a few students have dropped out, but it is likely that the concentration of results is greater at the secondary level), whereas the income of parents is three to five times more concentrated than this. This suggests that, against much opinion in Peru, education, even with the current inequalities and inefficiencies, is probably contributing to social equalization in a fairly strong manner. But it could be contributing much more if there were improved standards and accountability.

Learning and Standards: An Illustration in Early-grade Reading

The fact that learning results are distributed unequally, and especially that results are more unequally distributed among the poor than among the less poor, was hypothesized to result from a lack of specific standards around learning goals, and a lack of use of any outcome standards for accountability and support, with the result that teacher support is nonspecific. Standards of bureaucratic control and certain management processes do exist, and tend to get used discretionarily and in a harassment mode rather than in a true accountability and support mode. In order to assess these hypotheses, a simple survey of schools was carried out. While too small to offer definitive conclusions, the conclusions derived from the survey should be sufficiently alarming to motivate concern and further study.

The focus of the study was on early reading development, because inequality and poor performance on early reading is likely to be an underlying factor in determining both low and unequal performance later on (in the fourth grade as in the national evaluations, or at age 15 as in the PISA assessments). It was found that, indeed, there are many schools where few if any children are able to read *at all* by the end of first grade or even second grade. We applied a reading passage from the official first-grade communications textbook (adapted to three languages) to first- and second-grade children (some 250 children in total), at the end of the school year. The reading passage was found approximately two-thirds of the way through the textbook. Overall, and noting that our sample is not meant to be entirely scientific, and is concentrated on the poorest 40 percent or so of the population, we found that as few as 25 or 30 percent of the children in first grade, and only about 50 percent of the children in second grade, could read at all.

Reading speed and comprehension were tested as a way to get a quick idea of early literacy acquisition, as a proxy for quality of instruction. Methods of introductory reading instruction have been the subject of heated debate, but in recent years many thoughtful reading specialists have converged on what is often called a "balanced" approach to the teaching of early literacy. For example, the National Reading Council in the United States recommends that early literacy instruction include the following components in addition to writing: language and vocabulary development, phonemic awareness, phonics, fluency, and comprehension. In this study a measure of oral reading fluency was used as a proxy for a more in-depth reading assessment. (For an explanation of this approach, see the background technical report.) Taking reading speed of those who could not read to be zero, average reading speed was only 9 words per minute for first grade and 29 for second grade. Minimalist expectations would be that all children should be able to read at the end of first grade, and the reading speeds at the end of the first two grades should be about 30 and 60 words per minute, respectively, even for relatively poor children. (These *goals* would be *half* of the achieved levels in developed countries, which is why they are minimalist.) Though these would be considered speeds typical of at-risk children in developed countries, they might be a reasonable interim (average, national) goal in a country such as Peru, and are consistent with informal standards established by Chilean organizations that cater to the poor.

The evaluated children in Peru thus seem to perform at one-third to one-half of a reasonable goal. Problems with reading were clearly found to have a linguistic and cultural aspect, but we also found large variability in achievement even for schools of approximately the same sociological type. There seems to be a great deal of essentially random variation among schools, due to idiosyncratic factors having to do with, for example, personal motivation on the part of individual teachers—a sign of poor *institutional* effectiveness, that is, a lack of effective and effectively enforced standards.

Teachers themselves are clearly aware of the need for standards, in that they report having them, and actually seem to have them. Ninety-four percent of the teachers report that they have goals or standards, and are typically able to explain how they set them (72 percent of them could state some specific approach whereby they set goals), which suggests they truly are aware of the need. However, their standards are low, as is their ability to measure achievement. Thus, their concept of goal achievement is not very correlated with achievement as measured in the survey—teachers seem to not be good at setting standards, and do not teach to standards. Worse, not being able themselves to establish useful standards (or measure and teach to standard) they find little support in official standards, as the official curriculum is reported by teachers to be too difficult to use, too expert-based, and inapplicable to their situation. Only some 41 percent of teachers use official curricular guides as a way to set goals, and in any case some 80 percent of teachers, and even more principals, think the curricular structure is too hard to apply. Teachers reportedly rely mostly on each other as a way to set goals and find support. Most teachers (78 percent) also report that there are no useful ways to seek support around specific teaching problems from UGELs, and very few (only 13 percent) of them report ever having received specific support from the system, in direct response to reported pedagogical problems.

Finally, it is noted that accountability is a problem, and that this lack of standards makes it difficult for parents or the State to hold schools accountable. Indeed, most parents are happy with their schools (80 to 90 percent, both in our survey and in the 2001 National Assessment). This happiness, partly due to the lack of publicized standards and publicized data on achievement against standard, will make it very difficult to rely on parental participation to improve learning results.

The recommendation is that much simpler and practicable learning goals be established, particularly in the early grades, and that these be universally measured (although the actual measurement can be school based as long as it is based on standard measurement tools and there is some auditing of how that is done). The results of such measurement should be used to develop specific support rather than generic training. This will require that intermediate units (for example, UGELs) have the capacity to respond, including stable personnel with technical abilities and knowledge of teaching and learning. It will also require that much more funding be devoted to support systems. Finally, the results should be distributed to parents, and should be used as a means of putting pressure on schools to perform. Both (specific rather than generic) support *and* pressure have to be applied.

Confirmation of the difficulty and vagueness of curricular guidance in Peru can be sought by comparing the official curricular guidance to that of other countries, or, perhaps more appropriately, to that of institutions, other than the State, within Peru. Table 3.1 shows the official curricular guidance found in official curricular statements, compared to a document of similar level or stature, but within the private educational organization *Fe y Alegría*. The latter appears considerably more user-friendly. Other countries have recently found that their curricular statements are too vague, on one hand, and overambitious, on the other hand, and have sought to make much more practical guidance available to teachers, by providing further specificity and goal orientation. The implicit recommendation here is not that Peru should deprive itself of lofty goals and high-level thinking on the cognitive skills children should have. The recommendation is that Peru urgently needs to go beyond this, and needs to specify goals or standards that teachers and teacher trainers find useful as concrete goals and guidance. Thus, the high-level, abstract statement can coexist with high-quality documents where specific standards, that tie back to the broader curriculum, are presented to the community. Other countries manage to do this, though it takes considerable leadership and consensus-building effort, because it is the attempt to get specific that brings out differences in point of view. All this is, of course, no guarantee of quality, since having clear standards is only part of a three-legged strategy (the other two legs being accountability to standard, and specific goal-oriented support so that teachers and institutions can discharge their accountability).

It is difficult to guess what a poorly trained teacher is to make of phraseology such as "constructs the comprehension of the text." Moreover, the official curricular statement is even more ambitious, and at the same time vague, than Table 3.1 shows. For example, one of the skills children in the first cycle (through second grade) are expected to achieve, in a country where many children in this cycle are *not reading at all*, is: "the ability to reflect on the linguistic functioning of the text . . . ," and this is to be tracked by things such as whether the child "is acquiring consciousness that the meaning of the text is constructed as the text is read and is reconstructed, each time it is read anew, because it allows for new information to be added to the sense given it initially." This mixture of high ambition combined with

---

Table 3.1. Official and Fe y Alegría Curricular Guidelines

Official Curricular Statement: Abilities and Attitudes at the End of the 1st Cycle (1st and 2nd Grades), Given Jointly for the Whole Cycle[a]	FyA Curricular Statement, by Grade
■ Constructs the comprehension of the text being read by: ● Anticipating the type of text and the purpose of the writing, according to context (situation, motives, and the means whereby the text arrives at his hands). ● Reads individually and silently; identifies signals and cues such as: title, subtitles, shapes, known words. ● Formulates hypotheses (suppositions) about the meaning of the text. ● Tests his or her hypotheses against those of classmates and draws conclusions. ● Creates a synthesis on the meaning of the text. ● Confronts the constructed meaning with the reading of the text, as carried out by the teacher. ■ Reads with pleasure self-selected texts: poems, stories, jokes, comic strips, etc. ■ Reads diverse texts: stories, legends, poems, recipes, letters, cards, posters, news in line with his or her purposes and the needs of the moment. ■ Recognizes and can classify, according to function and profile, different types of text such as posters, recipes, cards, advertisements, etc. ■ Can read and use double-entry tables of use in daily life (attendance charts, responsibility charts, achievement charts).	**First Grade** ■ Reads audibly. ■ Pronunciation is adequate. ■ Reads individually and in groups. ■ Reads in groups following models for tone and rhythm. ■ Respects exclamation and question marks. ■ Does not sound out syllables. ■ Reads short (3 paragraphs) texts fluidly. **Second Grade** ■ Adapts tone of voice according to audience and type of text. ■ Respects commas and periods. ■ Does not sound out syllables. ■ Does not change letters or words. ■ Does not add or remove words. ■ Does not skip paragraphs. ■ Reads without difficulty words up to four syllables. ■ Reads short (3 to 5 paragraphs) texts fluidly.

a. The official curricular statement notes that, "It is expected that by the end of 1st grade, children will be able to read and produce texts, and that in 2nd grade they will consolidate these skills." This statement is, however, still relatively vague about how to gauge these skills, and is found in a section on teaching methodology, not in the main section on expectations.

Sources: Ministerio de Educación (2000); Equipo Pedagógico Nacional de Fe y Alegría (2003). Author's translation.

nonspecificity is generally absent from curricular materials in, for example, *Fe y Alegría*. Similarly, other countries are reformulating curricular statements to make them more practical. While the nonspecific but high ambition in such statements is surely well intentioned, it is unlikely that it serves the poor very well, because it is high ambition only in vague and theoretical terms.

There are also very low standards in other respects, although success has been achieved in some areas. One area of key success, for example, is the coverage of textbooks. In our survey, which confirms official data, essentially 100 percent of schools have books, and the vast majority of schools have books for all their children. However, the books are arriving, on average, a quarter of the way through the school year. This is a significant wastage. Furthermore, anecdotal evidence suggests the books are not widely used, perhaps because they are too ambitious and/or impractical. The reading passage we used to assess children's reading skills was from the official first grade communications textbook, and was found approximately three-fourths of the way through the book (and the testing was at the very end of the school year). While it is true that the passage was somewhat altered to make it more applicable to poor children (the official book uses the word "vacation," for example, which seems culturally inappropriate to poor rural children), only 5 percent of children recognized it. This is consistent with other studies that report extremely low curricular coverage. Both the lateness of arrival and the low curricular coverage suggest poor application of standards and poor time management, such as low time-on-task.

Similarly, classroom practice seems to follow very poor standards. Only some 12 percent of class time was used in what one could recognize as highly-productive activities. (See the technical background report for a classification of activities and further data on this matter.)

In summary, there is a problem with goals or standards, and performance to goals.

Accountability and Clear Goals are Possible in Peru

Effective models of schooling already exist in Peru, and individual schools are frequently willing to compete and accept accountability. Whether schools are using effective behaviors is easy to detect, and hence accountability for behavior (or "process"), and not just for results, should be quite possible if the technical ability to establish (and the will and mechanisms to demand) such accountability existed. Effective behaviors do not seem to be complex, but do require much hard work and perseverance, as opposed to a "feel-good" (nonevaluated) approach to teaching that seems too common in Peru.

Because there is considerable variation in school performance in Peru, especially in schools that serve the poor, there may be useful lessons in that variation. Furthermore, because there is little effective zoning of children into specific public schools in Peru, children are in practice free to attend any public school, and in urban areas this choice can be effectively used. To the degree that parents tend to prefer certain public schools, and to the degree that this preference has behavioral effects on "schools-of-choice" (or the other way around: certain schools have certain behaviors that attract parents), there may be something that the rest of the public sector can learn from these schools. Finally, because there is some outsourcing or subsidization of schooling for the poor to various religious bodies, such as *Fe y Alegría*, and this schooling seems to produce good results, there may be managerial lessons in this as well.

Small studies were carried out in public schools that seemed to have a good reputation or to produce good results, and in *Fe y Alegría* schools, to ascertain whether there were certain behaviors that characterized these schools, that might be replicable to other schools, and that, if replicated, could lead to improved results. In the case of public schools the research was specifically done within urban schools only, not because these are in any way more important, but because the idea was to ascertain the relationship between choice and school behavior, and choice is easier in urban areas. The emphasis was on ascertaining the nature of the behavior, rather than understanding or recommending choice per se. Thus, the findings could be replicable to other settings where choice is not possible, as long as there is some accountability mechanism, other than parental choice, to enforce the behaviors. The findings suggest there are some behaviors that could be replicable to other public sector schools, with some reforms. Other behaviors most likely would take such profound public sector reforms that the easiest thing might be to continue experimenting with a contracting system and growing it if it is successful. Other behaviors are replicable, but if replicated would not improve learning in the whole system, because they are largely selection behaviors, or rely on fixed inputs. Finally, since "choice" already largely exists, the most important thing is not so much to experiment with choice, as to ensure that choice has consequences and is well informed.

Characteristics of Good Public Schools. The following conclusions were derived from the assessment of public schools.

Reputation matters, is known, and choice is exercised. Some schools have a clear reputation for being better than others, they are oversubscribed, and parents do take some pains to send their children to the better schools. Reputation, however, has an imperfect correlation with measured good performance.

Behavior affects reputation, but enhanced reputation is not always the main motivation for effective behavior. We found that, often, good education behavior on the part of teachers and schools is caused by largely intrinsic motivation, not by a desire to enhance reputation. Having a good reputation and being chosen by parents is, in those cases, a consequence of teacher and school behavior, not a cause. However, whichever way the causality runs, there is little doubt that there is a causal link between reputation and behavior, and that both parents and teachers see and understand the causal link. The link, while clear in the schools where it exists, is not always operational, because accountability pressure is not sufficient. Thus, because this link (a) is so *analytically* clear and important, (b) is so managerially detectable when it is operational, but (c) is not always operating, then: in schools where the intrinsic motivation does not exist, some form of extrinsic accountability pressure has to be applied, and could be applied, in principle, precisely because the needed behaviors are fairly clear.

Behaviors that seem to be associated with effectiveness and good reputation were fairly easy to identify, they cluster, and many are in principle replicable. Thus, they should be amenable to systemic policy and management action. The clearest such factors, and those that seem to distinguish certain schools the most, were:

- Clear and widely shared vision and goals (classifiable as "standards")
- Central focus on teaching and learning
- Much monitoring and evaluation around goals
- Teachers engaged in goal-oriented teamwork and showing little factionalism
- Motivation and sense of mission
- Clear norms and organization
- Orderly and disciplined school environment
- Support to students falling behind
- Existence of extracurricular activities.

Schools, but in particular those trying to improve, seem to actually relish competition and objective comparisons. They seem to seek standards, and seem to create them if they do not exist. Athletic competition, competition in parades, academic olympiads, winning Ministry competitions for special projects, and rates of entry into university, were all used by schools to compare themselves to each other, and to signal to parents. (Some of these signaling mechanisms are also intrinsically quality-enhancing tools, not just signaling mechanisms.) Many types of information get used to fill the informational vacuum created by lack of objective standards and measurement from the Ministry. (This may be one reason why the existence of extracurricular activities looms so important in effective schools in the Peruvian context: in a vacuum of information about other factors, winning at, or even just competing in, extracurricular activities is one way for schools to signal their quality to parents. Of course, extracurricular activities are worthwhile for their own sake.) In this sense, fear of publicly available information on individual school performance seems possibly misguided. However, a sudden and unplanned introduction of universal and public information could induce despondency among the least able to perform, especially if the information is not presented in a value-added or improvement-over-time form, that is, if information is not somehow normed for poverty and other social issues.

Schools with better reputations do engage in some pupil selection behaviors, and there is also pupil self-selection. Thus, caution is needed about how much the whole system could improve if poorer public schools were simply to "do what the good public schools do."

Lessons from Fe y Alegría. The analysis of *Fe y Alegría* schools led to the following conclusions.

There are more selection and fixed-factor issues in *Fe y Alegría* schools than in public schools of choice. Many *Fe y Alegría* principals, for example, are unique individuals not in very elastic supply to the public sector. Some are foreign, are extremely well educated, are religious, and have experience managing modern, large schools in developed countries. There is some selection of parents. Schools are placed largely where communities demand them. Teacher selection was hard to ascertain—there seems to be more post-entry teacher molding than there is selection-into-entry, according to the teachers themselves. All of these suggest that, as in the case of public schools, one should be somewhat cautious about how much the whole system could improve via outsourcing or contract models such as *Fe y Alegría*. This is not to say that outsourcing of this sort is unpromising; on the contrary, experimentation should continue, but it should be cautious and well documented, and should pay particular attention to researching the nonreplicability issues. However, just as in the public schools, there are some behaviors that are clearly replicable with or without outsourcing of this sort, and that, if replicated, could improve the whole education system, because the behaviors are not related to selection. The following are the key behaviors.

There is an emphasis on monitoring, feedback, and learning from experience, both in day-to-day instructional management and in medium-term improvement in teaching approaches. This is used in a gradual improvement, rather than a discontinuous-reform, approach to change. There is little sense of "fashion" in *Fe y Alegría* schools, whereas fashions seem to come and go very quickly in the public sector. This stability provides teachers and systems with time to learn and practice. Furthermore, the fact that improvements are based on feedback from teachers, and on observation of the better teachers as they teach in actual situations, means that implementability tends to be built into the improvements.

Financial and staffing autonomy allow managers more freedom to deploy resources and shape resources to maximize quality. It also allows managers to gather extra resources which, while not large in absolute terms, make a difference at the margin because they are discretionary. However, because such freedom exists in a context of tight accountability and intrinsic trust, there is little fear of favoritism, nepotism, or corruption due to such flexibility.

The commitment to involve the community and to respond to communities is genuine and pervades all managerial action. The school, not the head office, is seen as the front line, the face of the system to the country. There is no "generic" face of the system to the country, as in the Ministry of Education; instead the face of the system is each single school and its interaction with parents and community.

The Head Office (the equivalent of an UGEL, DRE, and Ministry all in one) sees each school as providing the guarantee of quality and commitment to the community, and sees itself largely as supporting that commitment. This, it is realized, requires some control, and there is little hesitancy to use that control. But there is a clear sense of "downward commitment" of school to community and of Head Office support to schools in meeting that downward accountability. In the public sector, on the other hand, the sense is not that UGELs exist to support schools in their mission to serve parents, but that they exist largely to control or, since standards are complex and hard to apply (and hence get applied selectively), to harass.

Instructional goals, or at least indicators, are more specific than the Ministry's, and the evaluation methods are more correlated with the instructional goals. Standards are clearer. While specific *Fe y Alegría* schools can adapt standards to meet the needs of their specific communities (as in the public sector), there are clear standards frameworks and the learning goals are linked to assessment goals (unlike in the public sector).

Summary of Recommendations from Good Public Schools and Fe y Alegría.   Several policy implications or recommendations stand out from our analysis.

1. Clearer goals and standards should be created for the public sector as a whole. Adaptations by individual schools should be allowable, but all schools should be required to have specific measurable and measured learning goals, particularly (for now) in early-grade literacy. They should be helped to establish specific, measurable baselines using as much standardization as reasonable, but much more than is currently the case. The need for cultural specificity can be respected without allowing it to become an excuse for mediocrity, though this will require some skill in standard setting and monitoring.
2. Individual school (and teacher) performance should be universally measured in terms of children's learning results, and information (at least about schools) should be disseminated. Schools should know where they perform relative to statistically determined peer groups, and parents should know this. It may take many years for this information to start affecting behavior, but it is important to start.
3. Mechanisms that induce a more responsive relationship to communities and parents, and where individual schools, rather than "the system," feel pressure to maintain a good relationship of accountability to communities, need to be developed in all schools.

4. This information should be used to design and drive specific support to teachers, and the support and professional development functions should be routinized, as opposed to being based on a "training" model.

5. UGELs and DREs should be partially transformed into support organizations (or into organizations that can contract out to NGOs or universities, and bring support to schools), not simply control organizations. Experiments where schools rate UGELs and DREs, based on agreed standards of service from UGELs to schools, should be instituted. These standards of service from UGELs to schools could be based on schools' own standards of service to parents and children.

6. Autonomy around some spending and staffing issues, and more direct and standardized accountability to parents, should be extended to all public schools. In *Fe y Alegría* this autonomy tends to work smoothly, and there is considerable trust among funders (including parents) and school authorities, but this is partly due to intrinsic reasons, such as the religious background of many principals. Because this cannot be replicated in the public sector, more systemic and extrinsic accountability mechanisms (for example, more public transparency in budgeting and more auditing) would be needed to go along with the autonomy and flexibility.

7. There is a need for more ongoing experimentation with models whereby the public sector can contract with NGOs, foundations, or other private and religious groups (and, possibly, nontraditional public sector groups) to provide education, but with more evaluation and more analysis of replicability issues. An important step would be the creation of standardized contracting approaches, as opposed to having to have a specific *convenio* with each different provider. The latter makes evaluation and transparency either impossible or very expensive.

Intercultural Bilingual Education: Special Standards and Accountability Problems

The importance of bilingual education in Peru is indicated by two factors. First, for some 26 percent of children, a language other than Spanish is their first language (as determined by the answers of fourth-grade students in the 2001 National Evaluation, probably the most reliable source on this subject). At the school level, in the average school, for 31 percent of children, a language other than Spanish is their first language (the difference between the child-level value and the school-level value is due to the fact that schools frequented by children from non-Spanish-speaking households are smaller). Second, there is a significant correlation between Spanish being a first language and school achievement. The bivariate correlation between being Spanish-speaking and mathematics achievement in fourth grade is 0.35, and with Spanish achievement the correlation is 0.42, at the level of the individual child. The school-level correlation between percentage of children of non-Spanish origin in the school and the school's average achievement in Spanish is 0.57 (and our own research showed that such children are extremely slow at acquiring reading skills even in their own languages). In a multivariate context, being of a non-Spanish speaking origin is also a source of reduced school achievement, independently of poverty and other socioeconomic characteristics (even though poverty is usually a more important determinant). School achievement is not only lower among the poor, but is also less predictable.

Language issues, and the problem of delivering a predictable "package" of learning in languages other than Spanish, are part of the reason for this greater variance of achievement among the poor. While Peru took leadership among many other Latin American countries in getting started in Intercultural and Bilingual Education (*Educación Intercultural Bilingüe*, EIB), its current efforts fall short of what is needed, in many respects. Table 3.2 shows how far short Peru falls on a set of areas needed if improvement is to be generated.

From an accountability point of view the thorniest problem is the development of what might be called "decentralized standards" or "standards with diversity." The languages other than Spanish are not naturally standard; there are varieties of Quechua, for example, that are quite distinct from each other. In the case of other languages they are only recently written languages, and agreement on how they should be written is not universal. These issues present at least two problems. First, without some standards it is difficult to achieve economies of scale. Second, and more important, without standards there is little scope for accountability (or it becomes too expensive), yet accountability for results (and for processes) is clearly a desirable thing in the use of public funding.

This problem shows up in, for example, the design of standardized assessments. However, the solution is unlikely to lie in complete standardization of, for example, the language of instruction to be used in textbooks, since if the written version does not match the locally spoken one, then the advantages of EIB are likely to be lost, and one may as well teach directly in Spanish, since Spanish is likely to be almost as foreign as a version of (for example) Quechua that has been so artificially standardized that the children cannot recognize it in any case. With an excessively (or artificially) standardized language, the theoretical advantages of EIB are essentially lost.

Peru has not yet done sufficiently creative, public, and high-level thinking around how to resolve these problems, nor devoted the resources needed to do this thinking and then proceed to implementation. Decentralization represents an opportunity. Options such as matched earmarked funding of language development efforts, taking advantage of decentralization, could be considered. The source of matching funds need not be own-source revenue—it could be block grants, both because own-source revenue formats take a long time to develop, and because they may be inequitable. Thus, being willing to use a part of one's block grant to match an earmarked funding of language development would signal to the national government that the community in question is serious about standardizing its approach to language and assessment. Communities (for example, provinces or districts) could then use their funds to appoint their own linguists and commissions to create localized standards. If the language is spoken in more than one province, bottom-up agglutination of efforts could also be encouraged if the funding mechanisms are sufficiently clever. This would allow a localization of standards that would, as implied, respect both the need for some standardization and the need to respect variation. These sorts of options need to be more deeply analyzed, and above all discussed, and then funded, in Peru.

Voice and Participation

Parents in Peru appear basically happy with the quality of their children's education. In our analysis, and in other surveys, about 80 percent of parents feel their children's education is of good quality. If parents are basically happy, it seems unlikely that, in the absence of certain improvements in parental overview of schools, parental pressure and

Table 3.2. Tasks Required to Implement Proper EIB in Peru

Task or Requirement Needed to Successfully Implement EIB	Degree of Presence in Peru
Development of mother tongue as a base for second language and other cognitive skills.	Recognized officially. However, compared to Bolivia, for example, the policy is weak, in that it does not sufficiently promote indigenous languages as important national languages by, for example, calling for Spanish speakers to learn indigenous languages (see Hornberger 2000; Ministerio de Educación 1989). Other multicultural societies, such as South Africa, call for all youth to learn at least one other national language.[a]
Parental and community support.	Not sufficient, as programs currently implemented, though there is support from indigenous leadership. Degree of parental support would most likely increase if EIB was properly implemented and paid off as the research suggests it would, and if it was localized. The poor quality alienates the parents. (For example, children would learn Spanish better in a proper EIB program, and parents most likely would then be satisfied.) (See Orr Easthouse 2004; Lopez 2002; Uccelli 1999; Oliart 2002; Zúñiga, Sánchez, and Zacharías 2000.) Furthermore, it is important to realize what "community support" might mean in a country like Peru. This chapter shows that parents are often happy with the level of quality of education their children receive, even if it objectively seems poor. Nonetheless, parents do seem to have concern over their children's acquisition of Spanish.
Teachers able to understand and use both languages, and prepared in bilingual instruction and intercultural competence.	Minimal, but public discourse on EIB is very aware of the need. Progress is being made, as teacher training institutions take on the need. However, until now only nine teacher-training colleges (out of several hundred) officially offer this specialty, and the first cohorts of graduates are only now exiting. Furthermore, four of these are in the Amazon region, which appears to be an imbalance (see Oliart 2002; Trapnell and others 2004.) Teachers themselves often do not actually know how to use the language they are supposed to teach for writing. Worse, many of the trainers in EIB do not speak or use the languages (Lopez 2002). Some apparently actually undermine EIB with parents (Lopez 2002). One hopeful sign is the increased self-organization and interest of teachers as in, for example, national meetings on EIB which are not state based (Lopez 2002).
"Localized standardization" of approaches within the indigenous languages, to include standardization of the language used for instruction, and discovery and diffusion of standard, effective pedagogical models.	Minimal and public discourse does not seem cognizant of the need. Standardization is achieved in a bureaucratic manner and seems unrealistic because of lack of attention to local variants. Furthermore, standardization appears not to have been created yet with a proper degree of understanding of the complexities involved. In the opinion of some researchers, it appears as if the standardization proposed is similar to what would result in Europe if one were to standardize, say, Spanish and Italian around Latin, to economize on the production of books and materials in Spain and Italy. (See Orr Easthouse 2004; Hornberger 2002; Zúñiga, Sánchez, and Zacharías 2002; Vigil 2004; Kuper 1988; Red EBI Perú 1999; and Lopez 2002, who comment on lack of systems, standards, and indicators, and a big gap between theory and practice.) The studies, taken together (with varying opinions among the authors) could be synthesized as recognizing the need for some standardization but within localized variants,

(continued)

Table 3.2. Tasks Required to Implement Proper EIB in Peru (*Continued*)

Task or Requirement Needed to Successfully Implement EIB	Degree of Presence in Peru
	in the case of language itself, and for standardization of pedagogical approaches based on solid research and local participation.
Thorough national research and evaluation processes that allow "cycles of discovery" rather than importation of models or dependence on a "once-and-for all" approach.	Weak, not just in EIB, but in education in general. Though there is a very good education research industry in Peru in general, there is weak linkage between research and policymaking and policy enforcement, and, specifically, EIB-oriented research is incipient. There are some examples of an incipient cycle of discovery (research and feedback) such as in PEEB-Puno and FORMABIAP. But in general the opinion of key informants and the literature is that there is very little evaluation-based learning going on (see Zúñiga, Sánchez, and Zacharías 2000; Jung and Lopez 1989; and Trapnell and Neira 2004). There is little evaluation of results against any reading and literacy targets (Trapnell and others 2004). Considering the large number of EIB projects that have been funded, this is a considerable waste. Had there been a serious interest in a cycle of evaluation and learning, there would now be powerful lessons, instead of widely dispersed opinions, and there could be strong national programs.
Proper planning and resourcing commensurate with the task; availability of materials teachers would actually want to use.	Weak. Education spending in Peru is low, in general, and human resourcing is weak (great instability in positions). EIB is also poorly resourced, and seems to be resourced too much at the insistence of donors, and with donor funding. A common complaint among key informants and in much of the literature is that most of the support seems to come from international organizations (see Lopez 2002; Trapnell and Neira 2004).
A decentralized system characterized by "decentralization with standards" that can provide the space for diversity while respecting the need for accountability.	Incipient, though actors are keenly aware of the opportunity decentralization represents and are beginning to take advantage of it. However, there seems to be very little clarity about how to achieve "decentralization with standards," how to have standards with diversity, etc., though there is some increasing awareness of this (see Trapnell and Neira [2004] on the notion of procedural rights to produce localized norms). EIB itself is still a centralized program. Key informants were of the opinion that indigenous groups are consulted and do give opinions (which is progress) but are not involved in crafting solutions in a decentralized manner.

a. See: http://www.polity.org.za/html/govdocs/policy/edulangpolicy.html?rebookmark = 1, sourced on March 20, 2005. Interestingly this aspect of the policy actually predates democratization. During apartheid, among whites, those of the Afrikaner (Dutch-origin) group were required to learn English, and those of the English group were required to learn Afrikaans, even though the media of instruction were separate and citizens had the choice of schools specializing in either medium of instruction. Typically, the better-off Afrikaners, traditionally the exploited group, learned English better than the well-off English learned Afrikaans. This relative "within-White" openness to multilingualism during the pre-democratic past may help in opening up the society to "White/non-White" multilingualism, though of course the cultural gap that must be bridged now is much greater.

Sources: Compiled by the authors from the reports cited and key informants as noted.

"local participation" could be relied on to improve quality. At the national level, there is a real florescence of spaces for participation and voice, yet quality remains low.

The main explanation for these paradoxes is that that while in Peru there is a great deal of *potential* participation and voice, because there are, formally, many "spaces" and opportunities for the expression of voice, in reality there is little *effective* voice in the education sector for parents and ordinary citizens (including the private sector and the poor). The main reasons for this appear to be:

- Unsolved collective action problems. Parents' associations at the national level seem to get little support from local parents' associations since it may not be rational for parents to personally take an interest in the education of "all" children.
- Lack of standards and a perception of rights specifically around quality issues, which makes it difficult for citizens to know when their rights or entitlements are being violated and hence prevents organization and the expression of grievance; in short, lack of effective demand for quality. This is reflected in the fact that parents are mostly happy with the current status.
- There is almost complete capture of "participation" organizations by providers. The national parent-teacher association is closely allied with the teachers, and takes positions that do not differ from those of the main union; in fact the leader of the parents' association is a teacher and unionist. The plurality of members of the national legislature's education commission is teachers, and members of the *Foro Educativo* are mostly educators.
- Weak legislation (contradictory, overlapping, complex, and unclear duties and powers) regulating the bodies implementing voice. While there are some promising initiatives in regional and local organizations, the norming is confusing and contradictory, and these organizations tend to be subservient to the Executive Branch of government, by design. Representation is corporatist rather than democratic, again suggesting that these organizations will tend to get captured by providers.
- Lack of effective power to go along with voice and participation. There is little effective citizen power over, say, school budgets or personnel selection and promotion, or regional and local budgets.
- The private sector in Peru is relatively absent from public policy debates on education (though this may be improving slightly), compared to countries such as Colombia or El Salvador, and seems a weak source of accountability pressure on the Government.

In short, there is a dearth of opportunities for political and economic pressure for change from "voice" mechanisms. The only real opportunity for action is likely to come from an implicit coalition of a few progressive politicians and officials, and NGOs, that can push through an agenda that involves the creation of standards, the effective funding of a standards-measurement agency, the creation of awareness among parents about the low quality of education their children receive, and their capacity to pressure schools for change. Other possible actors might include the private sector organizations, but they remain thus far relatively unmobilized. Current legislation actually creates the basis for almost all of the needed changes. Creating effective implementation regulation, funding the necessary capacity-building and systems development, and staffing the institutions that can lead the changes are the challenges that remain. Donors could be of assistance by continuing to provide technical and financial assistance and organizational focus to institutions willing to work for such changes, at both the policy and implementation levels.

Opportunities and Dangers Created by Decentralization

Educational decentralization in Peru has started; a basic legislative and normative framework is either in place or is taking shape. As of the writing of this book, however, the state of decentralization in practice (and even in regulation) is sufficiently fluid and confused that it is impossible to forecast whether decentralization is likely to make all of the problems listed here better or worse. There are various options for using decentralization to improve quality, but also some dangers. Neither the dangers nor the opportunities are real yet. Maximizing the potential is likely to require significant work in crafting a regime of accountability at the regional level. The work required is discussed below.

On the positive side, decentralization could have a beneficial impact if both the regional leadership (the regional president, the *gerente social*, and the head of the Region-level School Management and Supervision Unit [*Dirección Regional de Educación*, DRE]) are forced to take responsibility for the quality of education in their jurisdictions, are forced to compete with each other (or at least compare themselves to each other), and are given the authority to address the problems. This would require that, for example, comparative information on school performance be available on a region-by-region basis (since presumably most of the authority will be at that level and at the school level), be disseminated to citizens and regional representative bodies (both general, namely the *Consejo Regional* and the *Consejo de Coordinación Regional*, for example, and the *Consejo Participativo Regional de Educación*) for them to hold the local executives (such as the DRE) accountable for school performance, and if they are also used by the national government (or civil society) to enhance the accountability of regional authorities to their local citizenry by publishing comparative data. However, the regional authorities would have to have full ability to respond to problems that show up in comparative performance data. For example, they would have to be able to move personnel around, allocate resources to particular problems, and be able to innovate. In this sense, decentralization could take advantage of the fact that some regional leaders are likely to be more innovative than others, and are likely to be more interested in education than others. With decentralization, the country will have a larger variety of approaches to tackling problems; regions can experiment with a variety of practices, and the likelihood that best practices will emerge is enhanced. Yet, for the country as a whole to benefit from this variety of practices, a centralized process for studying good practice, and spreading it, is needed. Few (if any) countries in Latin America have been able to craft such systems in order to benefit from decentralization. It is far from clear that, as it is shaping up, decentralization in Peru is going in the direction needed for quality improvement.

There are also various dangers. A clear one is confusion. Current legislation in Peru is creating such a variety of participatory and parliament-like bodies, and with such vague language, that confusion over roles and conflict over jurisdictions is all but inevitable. In many cases, in practice, one jurisdiction is given control over a neighboring jurisdiction, if one of them is considered weak, instead of control reverting to the higher-level government.

Thus, some "stronger" UGELs have executive authority over other, "weaker" UGELs, instead of control of the weaker UGELs reverting to the DRE. This is a recipe for chaos and conflict, and indeed this is what one finds, repeatedly, throughout Peru. At the same time, Executive Branch bodies (such as the DRE and the UGEL) have both horizontal (to their own regional government) and vertical (to national ministries, in particular education and finance) accountability lines that overlap and are not at all clear. This can, and does, lead to confusion and evasion of responsibilities. Finally, though (most of) education, as a sectoral competence, is allocated to regions, the reality is that a region is so large that, in terms of the accountability triangle discussed above, the citizens are not sufficiently closer to the top of the pyramid to make the voice mechanism much more powerful than if the top of the pyramid is simply the national government. Nor are the policymakers and the regional level sufficiently closer to the delivery points (schools) to make the norms stronger or truly more sensitive to local conditions, or to make problem detection at the school level any easier. Whether a school is one of 1,500 or one of 40,000 will probably not make much practical difference to accountability, even if it does make some difference to local adaptation and client preference.

In these regards, it is some form of school autonomy (contemplated in the current education law, but largely unimplemented) oriented at autonomy of management prerogatives such as control over teachers, but with centralized standards and testing, that might ultimately render the service sufficiently close to the citizens to make a significant difference to learning achievement. Most of the recommendations in the rest of this chapter are oriented at enhancing this sort of localized accountability.

Good Sets of Recommendations and Research-based Diagnostics Already Exist

Good diagnostics on the problems discussed in this chapter already exist, and because they do, more research on what the problems are and what to do about them could help. The main remaining problems appear largely related to politics, policymaking, and knowledge of how to *implement* a modern education system.

In the last 10 years Peru has developed an impressive set of analytical and research results that spell out the nature of the problems that remain in the education sector. This chapter takes advantage of the previous work by Peruvian researchers and summarizes the main conclusions. In addition, some original work is carried out that synthesizes much of what is known. Given the quality of what has been done already, however, it is difficult to add much. This chapter owes a great deal to what Peruvian researchers have already accomplished.

Existing Recommendations. Table 3.3 shows the key set of policy recommendations. This table represents perhaps only one-third of the literature of equal quality, and is meant only to give a flavor of the completeness of the policy reviews that exist. There are many current lists of policy suggestions, including many that have not yet been taken up. They vary from those produced by Peruvian and individual foreign expert analysis and opinion, to those based on analyses of international organizations, to those derived from consensus-building and large-scale consultation exercises within Peru. Most of these converge on a fairly consistent set of recommendations. Just within the 1990s and 2000s, Alcázar (2004),

Table 3.3. Summary of Policy Recommendations in Peruvian Literature

Issue	Alcázar (2004)	Hunt (2001)	PREAL (2003)	Foro Acuerdo Nacional (2004)	Francke (2004)	World Bank (2001)	Vega (2004)	Rivero (2004)
Establish more detailed and clearer performance expectations.	✓	✓	✓			✓	✓	
Increase capacity to demand and use standardized achievement testing, perhaps universalize testing in some grades; some recommend dissemination of schoolwide information.	✓	✓	✓	✓ (?)		✓	✓	
Make parents and/or principals more responsible for schools, including teacher evaluation.	✓	✓	✓		✓		✓	
Increase spending on education.	✓	✓	✓					✓
Target spending toward the poor, create more targeted programs, not just targeted spending.	✓	✓	✓			✓		✓
Clarify and finalize powers and functions under decentralization, including school autonomy, with fully specified responsibilities.	✓	✓	✓		✓			
Improve teacher pay (in some cases stated thus, in other cases stated only in relation to performance).	✓ (?)	✓	✓	✓		✓		
Simplify teacher reward system, based on some measure of performance, including school-level evaluations.	✓	✓	✓	✓		✓		
Rationalize and accredit pre-service teacher training, and make it more selective.	✓	✓	✓	✓				

(continued)

Table 3.3. Summary of Policy Recommendations in Peruvian Literature (*Continued*)

Issue	Alcázar (2004)	Hunt (2001)	PREAL (2003)	Foro Acuerdo Nacional (2004)	Francke (2004)	World Bank (2001)	Vega (2004)	Rivero (2004)
Increase coverage of pre-primary schooling.								✓
Evaluate existing and past pilot projects and initiatives, and force accountability to absorb lessons that work and reject those that do not.		✓	✓		✓	✓		
Simplify and clarify organization of the sector. Reorient it so it serves the pedagogical functions.	✓	✓						
Ensure communitarian or administrative systems to guarantee attendance of teachers and students.		✓		✓				
Take steps to ensure continuity of policies and perhaps of Ministers.			✓					
Social mobilization around learning, specifically reading.				✓				
Focus in particular on early-grade literacy through expectations and programs.		✓						
Establish better methods and tools, including more reliable and standardized approaches, for education in non-Spanish-speaking areas.						✓	✓	
Clarify in particular formulas for resource allocation to subnational entities.					✓			
Ensure competitive selection and evaluation of sector managers.					✓			
Develop more specific, problem-oriented teacher support, instead of generic in-service training.		✓						

Source: Compiled by the authors.

Foro del Acuerdo Nacional (2004), Francke (2004), Hunt (2001), PREAL (2003), Rivero (2004), Rodriguez (2004), Vega (2004), and World Bank (2001) can be cited as examples of sets of policy suggestions. Table 3.3 emphasizes the range of agreement of all the various diagnostics and sets of recommendations. In the table, the fact that a symbol does not appear under an author's name does not imply that the author does not support the idea; it implies simply that he or she does not discuss it—some of the papers do not present comprehensive lists of what the author thinks ought to be done to improve the system. In some cases (for example, Cruz and others 2002) the authors do not lay out recommendations as such on the theme in question, but their description of a problem is so pointed and specific that it can be taken as an implicit recommendation. Finally, in a few cases the interpretation of the authors' recommendations is not clear. This is indicated with a question mark.

Existing Research Base. This literature on policy recommendations is not based on opinion. Very good studies of the factors associated with learning production in Peru already exist, and most of the recommendations listed above are based on this research literature. (Some of the recommendations listed above are based on professional experience and direct observation.) Table 3.4 shows the main results of these studies.

To summarize the literature, this study re-estimated a "typical" statistical model, similar to many of those mentioned in Table 3.4. These statistical models identify the key factors that are associated with learning results. (Full details can be found in Volume 2 of this report.) A model was estimated for four cases: communications and mathematics in fourth grade primary and fourth grade secondary, using the 2001 National Assessment results. Factors that are statistically significant and at least minimally significant (using a very low threshold) from a substantive point of view were counted. Factors were also reclassified into broad groups, and the numbers of cases in which each broad set of factors appears in the models are listed:

1. Poverty and socioeconomic issues (13 cases)
2. School and classroom management, pedagogy, having norms and standards (10 cases)
3. Ethnic and gender disadvantage (above and beyond poverty, 5 cases)
4. Resources and resource use (3 cases).

The most important factors, listed in order of decreasing importance, are: (a) poverty and general socioeconomic factors; (b) variable and generally poor management quality that is particularly unreliable in poor areas, and is associated with an inability to develop and enforce standards; (c) ethnic and gender disadvantage and the nonexistence of appropriate pedagogical models to overcome this disadvantage; and (d) lack of resources. The order of importance of these factors is reasonably rigorous. However, these studies, including our own re-estimation of a standard statistical model, leave nearly 40 percent of variation in learning unexplained, even when many managerial factors, not normally accounted for in these sorts of studies (and in this sense the Peruvian literature is superior to that of most other developing countries) are accounted for. Most of the unexplained variation is likely due to management and pedagogical factors (and possibly some poverty or cultural issues) too subtle to measure quantitatively. Thus, taking account of the unexplained variation, most likely the "real" priority order in causal factors is: (a) management (including, most importantly, pedagogical management in the classroom and the existence of pedagogical management tools for bilingual education); (b) poverty; (c) ethnic and gender issues; and (d) resources.

Table 3.4. Factors Associated with Improved Learning Results in Peru

Factor	Discussion	Sources of Evidence and Range of Application of the Research	Possible Policy Implications
Coverage of the curriculum.	Coverage is very low but low coverage does not appear to be very related to poor achievement in a few studies, perhaps because higher coverage with poor quality does not add to achievement.	Cueto and others (2003); 6th grade mathematics, Lima. Multivariate analysis. Equipo de Análisis de la Unidad de Medición de la Calidad Educativa (2004). Multivariate analysis. Galindo (2002). Multivariate analysis.	Poor teacher preparation for certain areas, and poor accountability and supervision.
Use of materials provided by Ministry, lack of materials other than textbooks.	Materials are distributed but underused. Coverage (percent of materials used) is associated with achievement. In addition materials arrive late. Learning materials are reported to be not very usable or used. Other supplies and stationery are not supplied.	Cueto and others (2003); 6th grade mathematics, Lima. Multivariate analysis. Data from the present report suggest that students do not recognize text from the reading materials and the materials are late. Based on nonrandom but "representative" quantitative sample and field visits. Hunt (2001). Expert opinion based on nonrandom sample, nonquantitative samples.	Review and assess use and appropriateness of materials, reform and redesign materials.
Gender.	Being male is associated with higher achievement, all other things being controlled for, particularly in mathematics.	Cueto, Ramírez, and León (2003). Language and mathematics, Lima and Ayacucho, 3rd and 4th grades. Multivariate analysis. Cueto and others (2003); 6th grade mathematics, Lima. Multivariate analysis. Benavides (2002). Multivariate, large sample.	Pedagogical practices might discriminate against girls. Cultural expectations may also play a role.
Date school opens.	Positively associated with achievement. Most likely a proxy for overall good management and time on task.	Equipo de Análisis de la Unidad de Medición de la Calidad Educativa (2004). Multivariate analysis. Cueto and Secada (2001). Multivariate analysis.	Policies on time-on-task (campaign for 1,000 hours of effective instruction) exist but are weakly enforced.

Time-on-task, and time-on-task devoted to high-value activities.	Time-on-task generally very low, unenforced, and unsupervised. It impacts learning.	Cueto and Secada (2001). Multivariate analysis. Hunt (2001). Expert opinion based on nonrandom sample, nonquantitative samples. Data from this report suggest that teachers use time very unproductively. Quantitative, "representative" but nonrandom sample.	Policies on time-on-task (campaign for 1,000 hours of effective instruction) exist but are weakly enforced.
Amount of homework.	Amount of homework positively associated with results.	Montero, Ames, Cabrera, Chirinos, Fernández Dávila, León. 2002. Small sample quantitative. Benavides (2002). Multivariate, large sample.	
Level of teaching and problem setting in mathematics, poor or no feedback on problem sets.	Teachers correct problems lightly, often give incorrect feedback to students. Quality of feedback and problems are associated with more achievement.	Cueto, Ramírez, León, and Pain (2003); 6th grade mathematics, Lima. Multivariate analysis.	Teacher's own education is poor, due partly to selection of personnel into the profession. Support to teachers is insufficiently specific.
Teacher lack of confidence and incapacity in specific skills in reading and evaluation.	Teachers do use standards, but they are informal and lower than they should be. On the other hand, instructional strategies and texts may be more complicated than necessary.	Hunt (2001). Expert opinion based on nonrandom sample, nonquantitative samples. Data from the present report suggest that teachers do use standards, but even if they were meeting goals fully, reading would still be below where it should be.	
Teachers are badly prepared in general.		Arregui, Díaz, and Hunt (1996).	
Spanish ability (and Spanish mother tongue)—affecting mathematics achievement as well.	Generally highly correlated with achievement. In some models this is the only really significant factor. Tends to appear significant even when general socioeconomic status and other educational factors are controlled for.	Cueto (2003). Rural. Transition 4th to 6th grade. Controls for initial achievement. Multivariate analysis.	Lack of strong enough programs and methods for non-Spanish-speaking children. Need for value-added analysis and reasonable expectations.
	EIB programs are generally poor, and education in areas where Spanish is not an ancestral language is generally poor.	Equipo de Análisis de la Unidad de Medición de la Calidad Educativa (2004). Multivariate analysis. Cueto and Secada (2001). Multivariate, rural.	
	The indigenous/nonindigenous gap is worse in Peru than in Bolivia or Mexico.	Sakellariou (2004), multivariate analysis based on LLLECE results.	

(continued)

Table 3.4. Factors Associated with Improved Learning Results in Peru (Continued)

Factor	Discussion	Sources of Evidence and Range of Application of the Research	Possible Policy Implications
Socioeconomic status of family.	Often quite correlated with achievement. Probably co-linear with Spanish ability or language spoken at home, but often has significance independent of the latter. In some studies this is the most important measurable factor in driving student learning.	Cueto, Ramírez, and León (2003). Language and mathematics, Lima and Ayacucho, 3rd and 4th grades. Multivariate analysis. Benavides (2002). Multivariate, large sample. Similar original results are also reported in Chapter 2 of the background technical report to this chapter.	Lack of compensatory mechanisms and resource targeting. Need for value-added analysis and reasonable expectations.
Cultural capital in the home (e.g., number of books).	Associated with increased achievement.	Benavides (2002). Multivariate, large sample.	Lack of compensatory programs and resource targeting. Need for value-added analysis and reasonable expectations.
Child labor.	Negatively associated with achievement even when socioeconomic status is controlled for.	Equipo de Análisis de la Unidad de Medición de la Calidad Educativa (2004). Multivariate analysis.	Lack of compensatory mechanisms and resource targeting. Need for value-added analysis and reasonable expectations.
Level/quality of teacher training.	Somewhat associated with achievement. Could be a proxy for overall general knowledge and status of teachers.	Cueto (2003). Rural. Transition 4th to 6th grade. Controls for initial achievement. Multivariate analysis.	Teacher recruitment and retention.
Resources such as school libraries, reading materials at home, etc.	Some impact from these factors is found, as would be expected. Many of these factors probably have an effect, but the statistical significance is masked by the presence of other factors that are correlated, such as socioeconomic status of the family.	Benavides (2002). Multivariate, large sample. Similar original results are also reported in Chapter 2 of the background technical report to this chapter.	Unclear. Conclusion should not be that material inputs do not matter.
Parental involvement in homework.	Could be a proxy for parental involvement in general.	Equipo de Análisis de la Unidad de Medición de la Calidad Educativa (2004). Multivariate analysis.	Parental involvement in the past has generally been postulated as involving only assistance with infrastructure. Need for value-added analysis and reasonable expectations.

Source: Compiled by the authors.

Thus, while most of what is needed, in terms of research results, is already known, particularly with respect to "factors" or the "what" of educational interventions needed, a few lacunae exist in the knowledge base on the "how" issues: (a) more cost-effectiveness analysis is needed, as are (b) more analysis of the management and implementation problems likely to be confronted in trying to improve quality, especially in a decentralized setting; and (c) more evaluated, large-scale experimentation with programs that actually boost student learning among the poor. On the latter, good ideas exist for how to do this, and there are quite a few exemplary schools, but there is also much romanticism and idealism, and, as yet, there is little "proof-of-concept" regarding how a very business-like, outcome-oriented approach can yield results in a large subsystem of the education sector, thus leading to replicable ideas and pressure to replicate. It would be wise to create such large-scale, evaluated experiments, with the emphasis on large scale and evaluation. The evaluation ought to concentrate not just on whether the pilots produce results, but on how. Finally, there is a need for more work on the political economy of change, to overcome policy barriers to implementing quality improvements.

Recommendations in Greater Detail

Standards

Standards are needed in three key areas: learning (outcome standards), service to communities and to schools ("process" standards), and resource allocation. Without standards, accountability is either impossible or consumes too much social energy in transactions cost; standards are the currency, or the "weights and measures," of accountability; they economize on the informational content of transaction costs. Similarly, it is only the application of standards that gives meaning to the notion of a right to education once mass-scale enrollment exists. Thus, standards are the key not only to efficiency, but also to a rights-oriented approach to quality and equity of quality. "Standards" refers generically to three sets of things: (a) standardized, simplified, and transparent ways of doing things, in a manner that reduces discretion and transaction costs, such as allocating resources via formulas based on enrollment (or attendance) and poverty; (b) setting metrics of performance, such as performance on reading as measured by a test, or service standards for UGELs to provide services to schools, but without setting actual goals for a level on that test; and finally (c) actually setting goals, such as reaching a certain level on a reading test.

Peru needs much clearer learning standards, especially in the early grades, and especially focusing on reading achievement. These need to be developed and disseminated. The current approach is too vague. The need for local and regional adaptation is, currently, being used as an excuse for mediocrity. It is possible to develop standards that are locally adapted yet that provide both ambition and a metric for accountability. The ambition to develop standards for the whole system, all at once, should be resisted. Peru needs to start with *reading* (and perhaps writing) standards, and with the *early grades*. Standards should be simple, should emphasize skill, and should be meaningful particularly to teachers and parents. With regard to reading, Peru should at first develop a simple and universal metric applied to every child in every school (and publicize school-level achievement against this metric), without setting actual, specific goals. Within five years, the country should move to goals for each school. Standards could focus on comprehension as a goal, and on speed (or fluency) of reading as an instrument. Standards should be grade specific, or perhaps even specific to semesters within the school year. As the simpler ones, in the earlier grades, are developed, the system can catch up to the later grades. The idea is not to fixate the system on literacy in the early grades, but to *start* there, both chronologically and in terms of priority, because this is the basis of all other later skills, and if these standards cannot be set and met, the prognosis for the more advanced ones will not be good.

Standards need to allow for cultural and regional diversity, while still being standards. This can be done in a variety of ways to which Peru has not yet devoted sufficient attention. Matching-grant systems that require local effort, for example, could be developed as a way to stimulate standards that are applicable to particular regions, or adaptation of standards to intercultural and bilingual education (EIB).

One possible focus on learning standards that Peru could consider is a secondary-school exit exam. It would be possible to generate this process voluntarily, by, for example, creating nationwide prizes for those that pass an exam that at first would be voluntary. Should this process find social acceptability, and as it leads to a refinement of the exit exam, the exit exam could be made mandatory. Such exit exams tend to drive parental and student pressure for school accountability, and this accountability pressure tends to trickle down to primary schools (as feeder schools), though this takes a long time. It would be possible to create prize systems that are sensitive to differential starting conditions, for example, by giving prizes at the school level (for instance, if a whole school volunteers for the system), and by giving prizes to the top grade earners at any given school, and for progress rather than actual achievement, or by using statistical controls that create peer groups (as in Chile's National Teacher Performance Evaluation System—SNED).

Service or process standards should be developed over time via observation of successful practice under difficult or average conditions. Schools that outperform others under similar conditions could be studied, and the good practices they engage in should eventually find their way into the procedural norms and standards. Current practice in Peru is for these procedural norms to be based on vague theories and bureaucratic needs, rather than school-level practice and need. The next wave of Peruvian education research should focus on this issue.

Standards for teacher selection, embodied in exams that would have to be passed before individuals can become teachers, should also be created. These should be coordinated with standards for pre-service teacher training. Peru is currently considering these issues in the drafting of the new law on *Carrera Pública Magisterial* and in debates on accreditation of teacher-training institutions. A new career ladder that promises better pay for better teachers will also help attract and retain better teachers.

Better funding standards are also needed, particularly as the country decentralizes and increases school-level autonomy under new legislation. This should take the form of a formula-based transfer of funds and physical resources from the national level to regions and from regions to schools. Formulas will lower transactions costs and will increase transparency and trust. They will also make it possible to target spending where it is needed most, in terms of both equity and results orientation. Finally, they enable a sense of "rights," in that schools and parents can have a clearer sense of the minimum funding to which they are entitled. The minimum per-student funding could be created such as to fund a basic minimum package of items such as stationery, classroom supplies, cleaning materials, and so forth. The package could be more generous in poorer regions.

Finally, UGELs, or the administrative unit above the school, should set standards of service to schools, and schools should set standards of service to parents and communities. Parents and communities should rate schools, and schools should rate UGELs. Comparative data should be publicized. After a few years, goals on these standards should be defined.

Accountability

While standards are needed for accountability, because otherwise there is no metric to which to hold anyone accountable, it is also true that without accountability pressure standards do not do much good. Coming up to standard requires effort; effort should be rewarded and lack of effort should be punished. Thus, incentives are needed to drive accountability. To increase accountability pressure, the following steps are needed.

- Measure results at all schools in key areas of knowledge, not just in a sample of schools, concentrating first on reading in the early grades. Start publishing data on learning results and on fiscal transfers on a regular basis, ideally down to the school level. Publish average results and expenditure data at the regional level. Ensure that data are presented relative to standards, but also relative to capacity and disadvantage using some simple "value-added" concepts, and put more emphasis on trends than on levels at any particular time. The system should avoid reporting on a "passed" basis, or using standards for grade retention of students.

- Ensure that parent groups at the school level have the power to hold schools accountable by, for example, ensuring parents a statutory majority on School Governing Councils (*Consejos Educativos Institucionales*, CONEIs), and by requiring schools to report to parents on standards of achievement and resources received and used, according to simple, preset formats. Parents' Associations (*Asociación de Padres de Familia*, APAFAs) should be equally accountable to the principals and the State. Parents should have a vote and voice in the promotion and selection of principals and teachers. This will act as an incentive for teachers to work toward satisfying the ultimate clients. However, as noted, it is important that the clients be realistically informed about learning standards.

- Encourage greater school-level autonomy for principals and parents, such as in procurement of materials and in allocation of inputs, as long as there is both budgetary and results accountability. This can be encouraged by formula-based fiscal transfers to schools, as opposed to direct input provisioning of physical inputs.

- Experiment more extensively with nongovernment administration of schools, with public funding, similar to the *Fe y Alegría* experience. Reduce the current ad hoc nature of such experiences by creating more standardized formats and contracts for such management, and improve comparative evaluation of the experiences according to results and cost measurement. Disseminate the results.

- UGELs should experiment with contracting out to service providers (see below). Schools should be explicitly asked to rate the services provided by UGELs or service providers, and this information should be used to modify provider behavior and to drive provider selection. The continuation and promotion of UGEL staff should be keyed to school ratings. Similarly the promotion and continuation of school personnel (principal and teachers) should be informed by parental rating of schools.

Support

Accountability pressure built around standards will lead to improved results only if one is willing to assume that all actors have all the information and skills needed to come up to standard. This appears not to be the case in Peru. Thus, support is the third important leg on which qualitative improvement is needed.

■ Support is the area that will require the implementation work, and hence the most funding. Setting standards and accountability systems will require technical skill and creativity, as well as consensus building and dialog ("political will"). But developing and using the support systems will, in addition, actually use up large amounts of scarce resources (particularly human resources), and is something that needs to be improved on over time.

■ Teachers need much more intensive support and "accompaniment" in how to teach to the learning standards. Generic and low-intensity "cascade" support is unlikely to work. Instead, week-by-week, or at least month-by-month "accompaniment," based on measured results, is needed, at least for a few years. Experiments with massive and intensive training that instrumentally take teachers through a whole year's curriculum, and with specific, measurable goals (the standards), are needed. This should start with reading and with the first few grades, and can then be expanded to other skills and later grades.

■ Parent bodies need training in how to hold schools accountable for performance to standard and for budgetary and financial issues. This should include the development of reporting formats, and the training of parent bodies in how to use the formats to put pressure on schools. On the other hand, a clear distinction between a governance or accountability role, which is positive, and a daily management role for parents, which is likely to be negative, needs to be drawn, and both parents and principals need to be educated about this.

■ School principals will need training in how to discharge their new accountability to parents and in how to perform to both outcome and process standards.

■ Support will also be needed in helping both schools and UGELs make cogent use of performance information in driving decisions on personnel progression and pay. This will not be an easy task.

■ UGELs and other such intermediary institutions (such as DREs) are grossly under-equipped to provide support on either pedagogical or administrative matters to schools. At this point they fulfill more of a control and harassment function, in the worst of cases, or a vertical reporting or upward accountability function, in the best of cases. Instead, UGEL personnel should be required, and trained, to support the accountability of schools to parents and community, realizing that schools are the frontline of service provision, and are the quality "face" of the system. The regional and national governments, in turn, should be accountable to UGELs and schools; there should be some clear "downward" accountability. Importantly, the capacity of UGELs to support schools pedagogically needs to be strengthened. In most cases this will take too long. In the meantime, experiments in outsourcing school support functions to NGOs or universities, in whole districts or even regions, can be developed. However, such support should be explicitly oriented at helping schools discharge accountability to standard; it should not be merely generic training on pedagogical theory and principles (as is all too common at present). Finally, this support should be rated, for accountability purposes (see above).

- Overall budgetary support, in the form of increased expenditure (to pay for the resources needed to provide all of the above-mentioned support, but to pay for other improvements not discussed here, as well), should be developed, pari passu, once the various systems discussed here start to be developed and applied. It is unlikely that all these forms of accountability will produce results if the current levels of total budgetary support to education are maintained. For example, the levels of support and training needed to improve performance of teachers is likely to be massive. But expenditure support, if provided before proper forms of accountability are developed, will tend to flow along the current channels (expansion of numbers of teachers and schools). It would not tend to flow toward standards-based accountability support. While these channels were appropriate when the goal was to increase coverage, they are quite inappropriate when the goal is to improve quality, but that is what the systems are "trained" to do, and that is where the interest groups are.

- Fiscal support should be standardized (or formula driven), as noted above. A simple way to do this is to make funding enrollment (or assistance) driven. Total funding (including personnel) from the national level to the regional level could be enrollment driven, with, perhaps, some differentiation for population density or poverty. For funding from the regional to school level, the formula could at first cover only nonpersonnel spending, and should provide more support to the poor, using simple targeting criteria such as geographical location of the school.

- Finally, and related to budgetary support, there is the issue of teacher costs. Since teacher costs consume the large majority of budgetary resources, the financing of teacher costs is the most important part of "support" to the education sector. Teacher costs have increased significantly in recent years. Yet Peru already had an oversupply of teachers. These teachers may not be of the quality and level of skills society needs. Increases in pay, if not tied to improved selection, incentives, and skills development, will not result in better teachers. It will result in further oversupply. At this point, instead of increases in pay, the focus should be on much more rigorous quality control at entry (selection through competition based on skills and knowledge, that is, standards-based selection and training) and improved selection over the career, including measures to encourage poor teachers to leave the profession.

CHAPTER 4

Pro-poor Policies in the Peruvian Public Health Sector

Betty Alvarado Pérez and Rony Lenz

This chapter analyzes the state of the health sector in Peru. It is an abbreviated version of a health study conducted by the World Bank for the Accountability in Social Reform in Peru (*Rendición de Cuentas para la Reforma Social de Perú*, RECURSO) Project, which includes a review of issues related to health, education, and social programs. Its objective is to contribute to the dialog and to include some pro-poor policies in the debate agenda with an eye to improving the performance indicators of the health sector and, more specifically, the health of the poor. The analytical framework that guides this investigation can be found in the World Bank's 2004 *World Development Report* (WDR). Within this framework, both institutional factors and accountability among actors in a country—policymakers, providers, and users—are crucial to improving health care services for the poor.

The evidence of inequality of access to health care is abundant. Access to health care is proportional to income level: the poor are 4.8 times more likely *not* to receive attention than the rich. Moreover, the percentage of the population lacking health insurance is 48.4 percent, and citizens are required to finance 39 percent of the system's costs, the majority of which goes to covering the purchase of medications.

Although the indicators of the state of the health system point to a significant reduction in the national infant mortality rate (approximately 23 for every 1,000 live births in 2003), indications still exist of inequities related to geography and income level. Perinatal and maternal mortality rates remain high due to the aforementioned inequities. While the Latin American average is 85.1 for every 100,000 live births, Peru's average in 2002 was 163.9. Peru's goal is to meet the Millennium Development Goal of 66.2 by 2015.

The Peruvian Health System is complex and includes both public and private providers. This study focuses on the public sector, and a specific analysis of the Ministry of Health

(MINSA) has been conducted, given its importance in providing health care for the poor—it provides 70 percent of the health care administered to the nation's poorest 40 percent.

The rest of this chapter is organized as follows. The next section presents a summary of recommendations. The section after that explains the conceptual framework for participation and accountability applied in the health sector in Peru. The third section includes a diagnostic of the heath sector in the country. The fourth section discusses the principal innovations in the sector. The fifth section presents a précis of studies on the health care sector conducted by Peruvians. The final section presents policy recommendations.

Summary of Recommendations

The evaluation of health care provision for the poor in Peru indicates that the channels and processes for accountability are weak and in some cases nonexistent. This is due to both the lack of clarity and responsibilities among actors and the absence of standards and goals related to determining what accountability to the population should consist of. What follows is a set of recommendations grouped into three general strategies associated with health care functions.

Regulatory and Decentralization Strategy

In principle, regulation of the health system is the responsibility of MINSA; in practice, however, the Ministry intervenes infrequently in the Social Security System (ESSALUD) and in the private sector. In addition, MINSA is currently encumbered with financial and operational functions that distract it from its regulatory role. The process of clarifying responsibilities at the governmental level, which is fundamental to achieving improved accountability, is progressing. As part of the decentralization process, the three basic functions of the health system—regulatory, financing, and provision—are slowly being separated. The regulatory function falls to MINSA and the financial function to Integral Health Insurance (SIS); provision is in the hands of the subnational governments. The challenge for the next five years is to provide MINSA with the information it needs to exercise its regulatory role. This information consists of:

- *Vital statistics of the population and the identification of the characteristics of demand.* MINSA makes estimates of the beneficiary population without precise information about the users of different services it manages (preventive and curative). A method based on access and impact analysis is needed to identify the population and facilitate adequate follow-up on its health status and the care administered.
- *Production of services in public facilities.* The statistics on outpatient care are poor, and those on hospital stays are good only in certain hospitals. This information, however, is not consolidated by MINSA. In addition, efforts must be made to coordinate the information bases generated by SIS with those managed by MINSA.
- *Supply of services.* Since the infrastructure census of 1996, only partial efforts have been made to identify the physical characteristics of the health care supply in MINSA facilities, and no attempts have been made with regard to other providers

in the sector. Due to the separation of functions, the task of maintaining up-to-date information on the supply will fall to the regions.

■ *Financing and budgeting.* The budget structure of MINSA is designed in such a way that the information it produces fails to provide a means to analyze the efficiency and quality of spending. For example, no differentiation is made between primary, secondary, and tertiary care, or according to an equitable distribution of funds among jurisdictions. MINSA's information is also not useful for establishing the cost-effectiveness of the service units (cost and production of specific hospitals, geographic networks, or individual services).

■ *Follow-up on the productivity of human resources.* The lack of information on productivity impedes efforts to build a culture of accountability from human resources to manager, facilities to networks, and network to the Regional Health Offices (DISA).[16] Currently, MINSA and DISA conduct no follow-ups on the productivity of human resources, and are unable to do so due to an inadequate health information system and problems with the Master List of Personnel (the database managed by the statistical department).

■ *Cost-tracking systems.* No information system exists that gathers data on expenses, salaries, and the location of health personnel. As such, it is difficult to determine the relationship between the availability of human resources and production, and to conduct an analysis of costs to subsequently determine fees. Without information on costs and fees, SIS is unable to determine reimbursement amounts based on real costs; nor is it feasible to set the standards under which providers must operate.

Financial Strategy

This strategy complements the regulatory and decentralization strategy in the sense that it helps clarify the responsibilities of different agents. This strategy consists of:

1. *Maintaining a protected and independent budget for prioritized attention.* It is necessary to ensure protected and independent financing for public health programs with population goals. This will lessen the risk that funds for purchasing vaccines and other key materials will be diverted to cover other expenses.

2. *Strengthening SIS institutionally as an insurance provider.* SIS should be in charge of health service purchases nationally so that MINSA can concentrate on its regulatory function. An attempt has been made to separate SIS's financing function; as such, SIS is still incapable of acting as an insurer. Rather, it only reimburses insurance claims. In light of this, SIS's institutional capacities need to be strengthened.

3. *Financing a Guaranteed Priority Plan within SIS.* To accomplish this, it is essential: (a) to pass legislation to ensure the existence of a plan with identified costs that establishes national and regional goals for the number of beneficiaries and health care services it will cover, (b) to develop a budget capable of financing the Plan for the number of beneficiaries and the amount of coverage mandated, and (c) that SIS

---

16. DISAs, the Regional Health Office, is changing its acronyms to DIRESAs as result of the ongoing decentralization process, except in the case of Lima. We use DISAs or DIRESAs interchangeably in this book.

set aside an additional amount to finance the Fund for Catastrophic Illnesses, which is directed toward providing access to specialized institutes in Lima for the poorest families from the provinces.

4. *Developing a national fee policy.* This policy should regulate fee collection from users in hospitals, health centers, and posts, and generate equity and efficiency of access to services and ensure transparency in the use of funds.

Provision Strategy

Human Resources. Following civil service appointments (that is, *nombramientos*)[17] of *contratados* doctors (doctors under contract) in rural areas and the elimination of access to specialized residencies provided by Rural and Marginal Urban Services (SERUMs), the corresponding loss of health care personnel in these areas was foreseeable. This situation has created the necessity of developing new mechanisms and formulas to attract health care personnel to poor and isolated areas.

Infrastructure. What is needed is: (a) to strengthen the supply of primary health care in areas where it is currently scarce, primarily in the rural and poorer areas; and (b) to strengthen the supply of emergency obstetric care and emergency care in hospitals located in the poorest regions.

Empowerment of the Users. The management model developed by the Local Committees for Health Administration (CLAS) places administrative and supervisory capacities in the hands of the community. These functions are exercised through the community's Association and Administrative Council and revolve around a local health plan that incorporates job flexibility and autonomy in the management of resources. This model establishes effective channels for accountability that translate into increased user satisfaction, greater access for the population assigned to the facility, an increased number of intraorganizational and outreach activities, and so forth. It would be a good idea to assimilate the lessons that this model provides and promote its development.

Focus of the Accountability Triangle

The *World Development Report 2004* presented a conceptual framework for the analysis of the provision of social services. One of its purposes is to create a better understanding of the causes of persistently low performance in this area in developing countries. Traditionally, analysis was centered on the follow-up and analysis of the structure and level of public spending. Now, priority is placed on determining the institutional factors that affect the performance of services in order to highlight the relations among three principal agents: public policymakers, providers, and citizen-users.

In the case of the public health sector, the group of public policymakers is made up of MINSA, the Ministry of Work (MINTRA), and ESSALUD at the central government level, and the regional governments and municipalities at the subnational level.[18] The providers

---

17. With *nombramientos*, doctors receive tenure and social benefits.
18. As a result of decentralization.

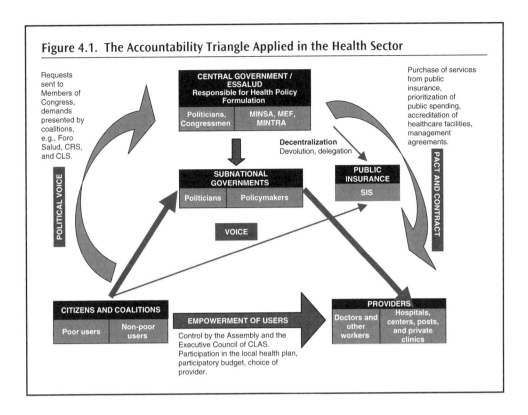

Figure 4.1. The Accountability Triangle Applied in the Health Sector

are public health facilities. This group includes frontline providers—managers and health personnel (doctors and nurses). The third fundamental actor is the population, in particular the poor beneficiaries of MINSA. The relations among actors are visualized within the so-called accountability triangle, or responsibilities (see Figure 4.1).

The political voice represents relations between citizens and public policymakers. It is in this very framework that attempts to influence the generation and adaptation of health policies must be made. The compact, or contract, frames the relations between policymakers and providers, and encompasses relations between MINSA or the subnational governments with the health facilities (centers and posts, and hospitals at different levels) and the frontline health care providers (managers, professional and technical health personnel). The empowerment of users is present in the relations between citizens—as users—and providers, whether through participation in production,[19] supervision, or the choice of a preferred provider.[20] As such, there are two routes that frame relations of responsibility and accountability: a short route (empowering users) and a long route (political voice and compact).

On the long route, the central, regional, and local governments are the intermediaries. They are also responsible to beneficiaries with regard to services that are offered and policies that are put into practice in favor of the poor (political voice). As such, these actors must generate policies and use the adequate instruments to regulate and supervise the providers' performance. Another chapter in this book presents a specialized study,

---

19. For example, through its active participation in prevention and promotion activities.
20. Low user empowerment can produce a situation where the user fails to seek out a health facility even though he or she needs one.

requested by the World Bank, on political voice. It analyzes the roles of the National Health Council, the Regional and Local Coordination Councils, the citizen forums, and the Round Tables in the Fight Against Poverty, among other bodies.

The long route also includes primary health care policies (compact or contract). The government, personified in the policymakers and executors, must be equipped with the necessary tools to request accountability and fulfill the sector's objectives. It must watch over the budget within an inclusive and equitable framework that is adequately focused on the poor, possess protective instruments against health risks, and eventually purchase services for the poor through insurance offerings. In addition, it must have access to instruments that generate incentives for adequate performance, such as management agreements, agile and transparent systems for information control, and *ad hoc* regulatory frameworks.

In the short route, the users or beneficiaries can influence the performance of providers so that the services are offered in a timely manner and in the quantity and quality required (empowerment). A clear example of this can be found in the CLAS in Peru.

This chapter focuses on the long route, involving the compact, or contract, and the short route, which involves the empowerment of users. The sector's policies, and in particular those of MINSA (and now the regions), must be sensitive to the necessities of the poor population and to the fact that the providers are accountable for their spending and operations (for example, coverage, equity, productivity, quality), and provide information on their actions with vulnerable groups, minimizing all types of barriers.

Principal Findings

Overall Vision of the Organization and the Fiscal Dimension of the Health Sector

The Peruvian health system is segmented; it is comprised of two subsectors (public and private) and various subsystems that work independently and lack coordination (Londoño and Frenk 1997). In addition, the current system fails to offer health insurance protection to all of the population, although some progress has been made in this area. MINSA, ESSALUD, and the health care units of the Armed Forces and the National Police make up the public sector, and each acts independently, covers different populations, and develops few relations with other actors. The private sector consists of private insurance companies and service providers, and nonprofit institutions, medical and health professionals, and providers of traditional medicine. All of these entities act according to market logic and are totally fragmented.

MINSA provides the majority of the country's primary health care services. More than 80 percent of the centers and health posts are part of MINSA, and they can even be found in areas not covered by ESSALUD or the private sector. Although MINSA is not the major hospital provider, it still accounts for a considerable percentage of beds—more than two-thirds of the total number available.[21] In 2004, MINSA registered 57 million visits, which represents 80 percent of the health care services provided to the public sector.

The poor population, particularly those living in rural areas, depend on MINSA for access to health care. In the two poorest income quintiles, 70 percent of the population that

---

21. MINSA has 9 hospitals with 250 beds, 28 hospitals with 100 to 250 beds, and 8 small facilities with less than 100 beds.

seeks health care does so through MINSA. This pattern is repeated in the three geographic regions. In addition, in 2003, 80 percent of quintiles 1 and 2 (the poorest) were hospitalized in MINSA facilities.

There are differences between the per capita spending of MINSA and ESSALUD. In 2003, MINSA spent approximately $139 per capita; ESSALUD spent 3.5 times that amount. This reflects the differences evident in health care access between distinct sectors of the population—the same differences that impede efforts to integrate the subsystems. A top-to-bottom leveling off in spending at ESSALUD is necessary to generate greater equity between the systems. Another alternative is to dramatically increase public spending on the poorest members of the population in order to lessen the enormous gaps that exist. Both of these alternatives will take a long time to implement.

Peru spends little on health compared with the Latin American average. Current spending is 3.5 percent of GDP, compared to 7 percent spent in Latin America in 2000. Peru spends $100 per capita on health and Latin America spends an average of $262 per capita (see Table 4.1).

According to the national accounts methodology, which distinguishes between sources, intermediation funds, and suppliers, it is evident that the final destination of the contributions from different financing sources is evenly distributed among the three large subsectors: private, public, and social security. The private subsector (private doctors' offices and pharmacies) receives 36.7 percent of the contributions from the different financing sources; households finance up to 78 percent of that amount. During 2003, the principal household expense on health was for medication, which constituted 46.5 percent of the household's total health expenses.

Access to and Use of Health Services and the Unequal Situation of the Poor. Despite the progress made in public health in Peru, gaps still exist in health care coverage, and the poor are the most affected. For example, in 2003, approximately 13 million people fell ill; of this number, 5.6 million did not want to be seen at a facility, and the other 7.9 million sought out or had the intention of seeking attention at a facility. Of this last group, 37.7 percent

Table 4.1. International Comparisons of Health Expenditure, 2000

Indicator	Peru 2000	Latin America	Bolivia	Ecuador	Mexico	Brazil	Chile
Public expenditure on health (percentage of GDP)	1.6% (2004)	3.3%	4.9%	1.2% (2004)	2.1% (2002)	4.9% (2004)	3.1%
Private expenditure on health (percentage of GDP)	2.0%	3.7%	1.8%	1.2%	2.9%	4.9%	4.1%
Total per capita expenditure (US$) 1997–2000	$100	$262	$67	$26	$311	$267	$336
GDP per capita	$2,050	$3,280	$900	$1,450	$5,910	$2,850	$4,260

Source: World Development Report 2004.

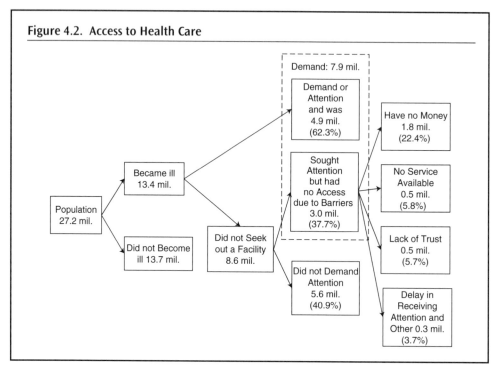

Figure 4.2. Access to Health Care

Source: Based on INEI (2003).

could not receive attention due to different obstacles, particularly the lack of money. The first group, which chose not to seek health care in a facility, may have chosen to self-medicate through pharmacy purchases, home remedies, or by visiting a local traditional health practitioner (see Figure 4.2).

A poor person is 4.8 times less likely to be attended to in a health facility than a wealthier individual. While in the poorest quintile 36 percent of individuals had no access to health care due to a lack of money, in the richest quintile, this percentage was only 6 percent. It is estimated that almost two-thirds of the population (63 percent) of those that requested attention in health care facilities did not access services. At the other end of the spectrum, almost 87 percent of those in the richest quintiles were able to access health care when they required it.

Equally, the difference in hospitalizations between the richest quintile (22.1) and the poorest (10.0) is 2.2 times greater (see Table 4.2). In addition, on average, the inhabitants of Metropolitan Lima were hospitalized twice as much as the inhabitants of the jungle; nevertheless, a more detailed comparison of hospitalizations between the poorest quintile and the richest in each geographic zone indicates that the most dramatic situation of intraregional inequity corresponds to Metropolitan Lima. This is due to the fact that the richest quintile has a prevalence of hospitalization that is 13.73 times higher than the poorest quintile, while in the jungle, the sierra, and the coast, these differences fluctuate between 5.6 and 8.2 times higher. Table 4.2 illustrates two important points: the primary provider to the poor for hospitalization is MINSA, and ESSALUD serves the less-impoverished quintiles (INEI 2003).

Table 4.2. Prevalence of Hospitalization According to Quintile in Peru, 2003 (percentages)

Quintile	MINSA	ESSALUD	Armed Forces, Private, and Others	Total
Q1 (poorest)	8.6	1.4	0.1	10.0
Q2	15.0	2.6	3.7	19.3
Q3	16.9	2.0	1.3	21.2
Q4	16.1	8.6	2.7	27.4
Q5 (richest)	5.9	10.1	6.2	22.1
Total	62.5	25.6	11.9	100

Source: INEI (2003).

Forty percent of the poorest population accounted for only 25 percent of the number of days of hospitalization, while the richest 40 percent, quintiles 4 and 5, comprised 47 percent of days of hospitalization. Metropolitan Lima accounted for 40 percent of the number of hospitalization days. This concentration can be explained by the fact that national hospitals and institutes are located in this area (see Figure 4.3).

One of the causes of inequality is the barrier imposed on the poor by the hospital fee structure, particularly with regard to hospital bed costs per day. The budgets of the hospitals in Lima depend in great part on the resources collected from fees, which on average represent 25 percent of their total income (SIAF 2004). In extreme cases, the percentage of income collected from patients in specialized institutes and large hospitals, which rely on direct collection of resources, is approximately 61 percent and 32.6 percent, respectively.

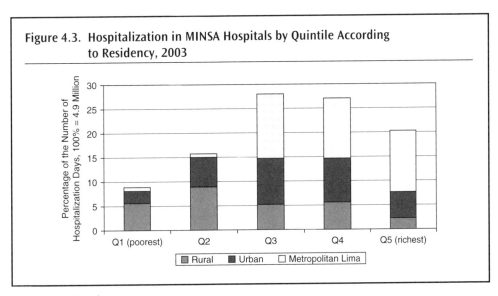

Figure 4.3. Hospitalization in MINSA Hospitals by Quintile According to Residency, 2003

Source: INEI (2003).

Figure 4.3 shows that both income level and geographic factors cause the inequities in hospitalization, with income being the primary factor.

Inequity also exists in the access of patients from the regions to care at specialized and high-complexity hospitals and institutes located in Lima. In the case of hospitals, there were 180,751 discharges in 2003, of which 96.9 percent corresponded to residents of Lima, and only 3.1 percent to residents of other departments. In the case of institutes, of 63,276 discharges in 2003, 87.1 percent were inhabitants of the department of Lima, and only 12.9 percent were residents of other departments. This situation is even more serious if we consider that the majority of those who were able to achieve hospitalization in Lima in these facilities belong to the richest quintiles (Q3, Q4, Q5).

Some Indicators of the Health Status of the Poor

The principal manifestations of health status in Peru are reflected in a new demographic context. During the last three decades, Peru—like other countries in Latin America—has experienced a decrease in population growth and an important tendency toward urbanization. Peru has gone from a population growth rate of 2.8 percent during 1961–72 to a 1.7 percent reduction during 1993–2002. The proportion of the urban/rural population, which in 1940 was 35.4 percent/64.6 percent, was inverted in 2002 to create a situation where for each inhabitant living in a rural zone, there were three living in an urban area. The population dynamic and the aforementioned reduction in growth can be explained by the decrease in the number of children per female over time.

In addition, while extreme poverty has diminished in rural zones, poverty has increased in Metropolitan Lima. This situation presents a significant challenge for the health system in a new and more complex scenario with new epidemiological manifestations typical of urban areas.

Communicable and Infectious Diseases. It is estimated that 85,000 deaths occur in Peru each year. The principal causes of death are circulatory diseases, malignant tumors, and communicable diseases, with similar relative frequencies that as a whole explain around half of all registered deaths (see Box 4.1 and Table 4.3). Nevertheless, differences exist if we consider income quintiles and areas of residence. While on the coast communicable diseases are the cause of 21 percent of deaths, in the sierra and the jungle they represent 44.9 percent and 40.5 percent of deaths, respectively. Among communicable diseases, respiratory and intestinal infections and septicemia stand out (MINSA 2004).

Although there has been a decline in communicable diseases, the relative frequency of tumors has increased, which is a tendency that is more than likely related to the aging of the Peruvian population and, as such, represents a difficult situation to successfully tackle.

The last analysis of the health situation in Peru—*Análisis de la situación de la salud del Perú 2003* (MINSA 2004)—concluded that the illnesses with the highest rate of reoccurrence during 2000 in the first income quintile were respiratory infections and other related conditions (24.4 percent), intestinal and parasitic infections (23.5 percent), and problems of the mouth cavity (10.9 percent). Although respiratory infections also affected the richest quintile, intestinal and parasitic infections are particularly prevalent in the lowest quintile due to a lack of sanitary services.

Not all of the cases of illness reported receive treatment: once again, gaps arise between population segments. In 2004, 68 percent of those affected by severe respiratory infections

---

Box 4.1: Summary of the Status and Tendencies of Communicable Diseases in Peru

- The incidence of malaria rose in 1998 and was brought under control in 2002.

- Dengue fever is considered reemergent and has affected 13 regions. In 2001, an increased number of classic dengue fever cases was registered, concentrated on the northern coast. In 2003, the number of cases was significantly reduced.

- Cases of bartonellosis (which comprises infections caused by newly emerging pathogens) have doubled over the last three years. In 2001, the number of cases reached 1,593 and increased to 3,390 in 2002 and 6,481 in 2003. Ancash, Cajamarca, and Cuzco are the departments registering the highest number of cases.

- Tuberculosis declined until 2002, when case numbers reached 155.5 per 100,000 inhabitants. In 2001, the number climbed to 189.7 per 100,000 inhabitants. Over the following two years, the number of cases again declined, to 139.1 cases per 100,000 inhabitants in 2002 and 119.1 in 2003.

- The number of AIDS cases reported from 1983 to 2003 was 14,640; of these, 756 were reported in 2001, 736 in 2002, and 918 in 2003. Analysis of the evolution of AIDS cases according to gender indicates that the male/female ratio declined from 11.3 to 2.6 in 2003. This means that the proportion of affected women is on the rise: currently, the figure is one woman to every three men.

Source: MINSA (2002, 2003a, 2003b, 2004).

---

sought treatment in Metropolitan Lima, and the remaining 64.6 percent and 64.2 percent sought care in the rest of urban areas and in rural zones, respectively. The gaps widen in the case of severe diarrheic illnesses, given that in Metropolitan Lima, 68 percent of the individuals affected seek treatment, and in the remaining urban areas and rural zones only 30 percent and 26 percent, respectively, seek treatment (INEI 2005).

Maternal and Infant Mortality. Although over the last decade infant mortality has declined in Peru, maternal mortality continues to be a serious problem. In fact, the mortality rates in Peru are almost double that of all of Latin America combined (see Table 4.4).

The reduction in infant mortality in the last decade in Peru has been proportionally higher than that experienced in Latin America (see Figure 4.4). Comparing the five-year

---

Table 4.3. Causes of Death in Peru, 1996–2000

Year	Total Deaths	Deaths Due to Communicable Diseases (%)	Deaths Due to Malignant Tumors %	Deaths Due to Circulatory Diseases %	Deaths Due to External Causes %
1996	92,674	19.8	13.8	16.2	8.8
1997	89,790	19.6	14.4	16.1	7.8
1998	91,471	21.0	14.4	16.9	7.7
1999	86,539	17.2	15.7	15.6	10.8
2000	84,393	17.1	17.2	18.2	10.6

Source: MINSA, Oficina de Estadística e Informática, various years. At: www.minsa.gob.pe.

Table 4.4. Selected Basic Indicators of Health for Peru and Latin America

| Indicators | Peru | | | | Latin America |
	1991	1996	2000	2004	(Last year available)
Life expectancy at birth (in years)	66.7	68.3	69.8 (1)	71[1]	72.1
Maternal mortality rate	308[2]	265	185	175[2,3] 163.9	85.1
Infant mortality (per 1,000 live births)	64	50	33.6	23	22.7
Perinatal mortality (per 1,000 live births)	29	24	23	16	34.4

1. INEI projections.
2. Calculated on the basis of variations reported by MINSA. At: http://www.minsa.gob.pe/estadisticas/estadisticas/indicadoresNac/download/estadodesalud323.htm.
3. Figure corresponding to 2002.
Source: MINSA (2004).

period of 1995–2000 with 2000–05, the reduction for Latin America is 20.6 percent, while for Peru it is 32.6 percent. Peru has achieved a rate of 23 deaths per 1,000 live births, thus reaching the Latin American average.[22]

The situation is similar for the mortality rate for children under age 5. In 1980, Peru's rate was similar to that of Latin America in 1970 (around 124 per 1,000); today its rate (50.8 per 1,000) is comparable to that for the region in 1995.

Although infant mortality has declined in Peru, some gaps and the concentration of deaths in the perinatal group must still be addressed.[23] Improvements have not been homogeneous and have not occurred at the same rate in all the country's departments (see Figure 4.5). Thus, the infant mortality rate in Puno, the department with the highest infant mortality rate (53.1 per 1,000), is 3.6 times higher than the infant mortality rate in Callao, the department with the lowest infant mortality rate (14.9 per 1,000). The intensity of the decline in infant mortality over time also reveals differences. For example, at the beginning of the 1970s, the infant mortality rate in Huancavelica was 50 percent higher than the national average, but in 2000 the rate jumped to 56 percent (33.8 per 1,000). In 1972, the infant mortality rate in Callao was 31.4 percent lower than the national average, and in 2000 it increased that difference to 55.7 percent. The control of infant mortality is also related to environmental causes and to an improvement in the population's standard of living (access to drinking water and education for mothers). Other factors include health interventions, including immunization programs, sanitary education, and adequate management of diarrhea.

---

22. In the National Demographic and Health Survey (ENDES Continua [2004]), the confidence intervals for a rate of 23 (per 1,000 births) are between 15 and 32 due to the sample size.

23. The perinatal mortality rate consists of deaths occurring in the period that begins at 22 complete weeks of pregnancy (death of a fetus of 500 grams or more), and for newborns that die before seven days after birth.

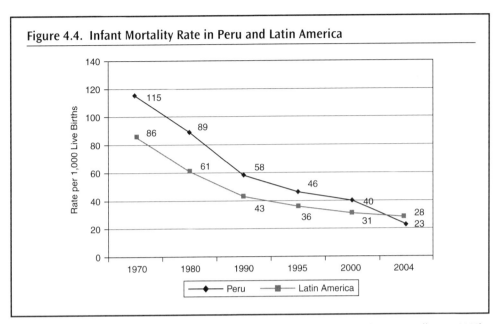

Figure 4.4. Infant Mortality Rate in Peru and Latin America

Source: Peru DHS Fact Sheet, based on the ENDES Continua (2004) (World Development Indicators 2005).

A more detailed analysis also reveals that the relative weight of the perinatal mortality rate increased as a cause of infant deaths. This component of mortality is difficult to reduce because it requires concentrated efforts to improve access to and the quality of health care (coverage for prenatal care, deliveries in health care facilities, premature births, neonatal care for premature infants, and so forth), which involves higher cost interventions.

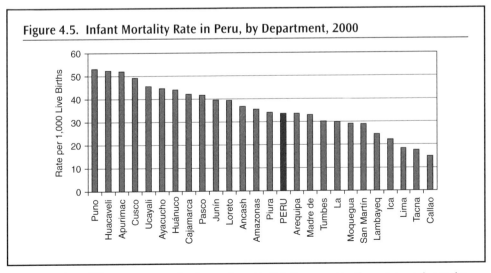

Figure 4.5. Infant Mortality Rate in Peru, by Department, 2000

Note: The slight differences among the data assigned in this figure and in Figure 4.4 are due to the fact that the sources for each were different.
Source: MINSA.

Table 4.5. Child Mortality in Peru According to Quintile, 1996 and 2000

Indicator	Q1 (poorest)	Q2	Q3I	Q4	Q5 (richest)	Average	Poorest/ Richest
Infant mortality (per 1,000 live births)							
Year 1996	78.3	53.6	34.4	36.0	19.5	49.9	4.0
Year 2000	63.5	53.9	32.6	26.5	13.9	43.2	4.6
Absolute rate variation 1996–2000	14.8	−0.3	1.8	9.5	5.6	14.8	
Percentage variation 1996–2000	18.9	−0.6	5.2	26.4	28.7	13.4	
Mortality in children under 5 (per 1,000 live births)							
Year 1996	110.0	76.2	48.0	44.1	22.1	68.4	5.0
Year 2000	92.6	75.5	43.9	34.5	17.6	60.4	5.3
Absolute rate variation 1996–2000	17.4	0.7	4.1	9.6	4.5	8.0	
Percent variation 1996–2000	15.8	0.9	8.5	21.8	20.4	11.7	

Note: The sample size of the *ENDES Continua* (2004) does not permit analysis of infant mortality based on spending quintiles, so only 1996 and 2000 are presented.
Source: Peru DHS Fact Sheet, based on ENDES (1996, 2000); World Bank (2002).

Analysis of child mortality rates by income quintile (see Table 4.5) confirms that the rates of infant mortality and the rate pertaining to children under 5 declined in all income quintiles during 1996–2000 (with the exception of the second quintile with regard to infant mortality, which in effect remained the same). Specifically, during 1996–2000, infant mortality declined 18.9 percent in the lowest income quintile and 28.7 percent in the highest quintile, and mortality for children under 5 declined by 15.8 percent and 20.4 percent in the respective quintiles.

However, maternal mortality continues to be a health problem in Peru. It has the highest rates in Latin America and no substantial modifications have been observed over the last few years. Estimates are that 1,074 women died in the country in 2002 due to pregnancy complications or related conditions.

The risk of dying due to complications in pregnancy, delivery, or puerperium[24] also depends on the poverty status of the population. In fact, death due to these factors is 11 times higher in poor departments such as Ayacucho and Puno (35.8 deaths and 35.7 deaths per 1,000 women in reproductive years, respectively) compared with Lima and Ica (3.2 deaths and 3.3 deaths per 1,000 women in reproductive years, respectively). An associated factor is the differentiated access to health care throughout the country. For example, in the departments Huancavelica and Puno, attention by qualified personnel for women in puerperium

---

24. The period between childbirth and the return of the uterus to its normal size.

reaches only 21 percent and 27.8 percent, respectively, while in Lima, health care for deliveries and prenatal control exceeds 90 percent.

The Millennium Developments Goals (MDGs) set for Peru for 2015 are: for children under 5 and those less than 1 year old, a mortality rate of 27 and 19 per 1,000, respectively; and for maternal mortality, a rate of 66.25 per 100,000 live births. The country is very close to meeting the goal set for infant mortality (national), but not for maternal mortality.

Estimates indicate that the MDGs set by Peru for maternal and infant health will not be met only through economic growth (it is not sufficient that the economy grow at rates as high as 7 percent per year). Instead, it must be reached by developing the necessary redistributive and specific social policies, such as programs to alleviate poverty or those related to education and basic water/sanitation services and prenatal health care provided by professionals (see Beltrán and others 2004).

Achievements in the Provision of Health Care Services

The health care policies implemented in Peru during the last decade have concentrated on maternal and infant health and have resulted in significant achievements in program coverage, including the immunization program. An increase in the coverage of deliveries of babies by professionals at health care facilities has also been achieved.

Immunizations. The effort to expand immunization coverage is valuable on two fronts: as a sanitary achievement linked to reducing the possibility of epidemics, and, since it is a public good delivered universally and free of charge, as a powerful instrument in the battle to reduce inequities among different segments of the population. Indeed, the success of the effort to improve population access to preventive care through measures such as immunization programs has resulted in an increase in the number of individuals protected. The advances in this area are noteworthy given that, at the beginning of the 1990s, coverage was only 70 percent.

Between 1998 and 2002, the coverage reached for the anti-polio, diphtheria, pertussis, tetanus (DPT), and the anti-tuberculosis BCG vaccines fell on average approximately 7 percentage points. This decline coincided with the introduction of changes in the Ministry of Health that were directed at replacing an organization based on vertical programs with an organization of integral program organization[25] (see Figure 4.6). During the same period, spending on other vaccines also declined. In 2000, spending on vaccines fell to $4.5 million but rose again in 2001 to $11.2 million. During 1998–2002, efforts were set in motion to improve the quality of some information registry systems, which explains part of the decline due to improved statistical registration. The sensitivity and importance of immunization programs demands the implementation of financing protection to prevent funds originally set aside for these programs from being used for different purposes.

Coverage of Childbirth Attendance. Current data show a significant improvement in the coverage of maternal health care in the country (see Table 4.6). *ENDES Continua*

---

25. The MINSA was successful in reducing communicable diseases through specialized programs that were identified as "verticals," because these programs each had their own administration, parallel to the ministry structure, which sometimes caused administrative inefficiencies and limited the decisionmaking process at the facility level.

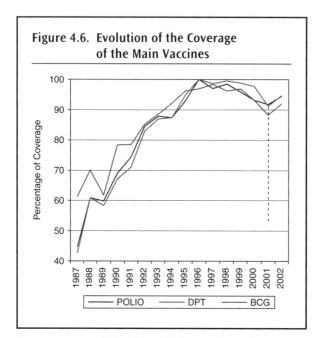

Figure 4.6. Evolution of the Coverage of the Main Vaccines

POLIO ——— DPT ——— BCG

Source: MINSA—Oficina de Estadísticas e Informática.
At: www.minsa.gob.pe.

data indicate that 91.2 percent of women received prenatal care during their last pregnancy, an increase of 8.7 percentage points over the 82.5 percent in 2000. Importantly, deliveries of babies in health care facilities increased considerably in Peru—from 57.9 percent in 2000 to 70.4 percent in 2004. The most significant indicator, however, is the increase in professional attention for deliveries, which rose from 57.5 percent of births in 2000 to 71.1 percent in 2004.

The national average hides the gaps between the poor and non-poor and between rural and urban areas, but the disaggregated data show an immense difference between these two groups. While 91.5 percent of those living in the urban zone receive professional attention, only 43.6 percent of rural women received such attention. The improved information system on maternal mortality has revealed that the majority of deaths are due to hemorrhaging resulting from

Table 4.6. Indicators of Maternal Coverage 2004

Concept	Professional Prenatal Attention (% of women)	Delivery at a Health Care Facility (% of women)	Delivery Attended by a Health Care Professional (% births)
Area of Residence			
Urban	97.2	87.8	91.5
Rural	82.0	43.9	43.6
Region			
Metropolitan Lima	99.0	91.5	97.1
The rest of the Coast	97.7	87.3	89.0
Sierra	86.8	50.0	51.4
Jungle	78.6	56.7	51.4
Total 2004	**91.2**	**70.4**	**71.1**
Total 2001	**82.5**	**57.9**	**57.5**

Note: Professional attention is care provided by doctors, skilled childbirth attendants, and nurses.
Source: INEI (2005). Preliminary report by ENDES Continua.

pregnancy or delivery (58 percent). Analysis of the specific causes of hemorrhaging reveals that 53 percent are related to retention of the placenta, 21 percent to uterine atony,[26] 7 percent to premature placenta separation, and 6 percent to placenta previa[27] (MINSA 2003a). The majority of these causes can be prevented and attended to only if the delivery takes place in a health care facility with adequate personnel and equipment.

Innovations and Challenges in the Management and Financing of Health Care

Since the beginning of the 1990s, the Peruvian health care system has been experiencing a slow but continuous process of change marked by progress and reversals. Some of these changes have positively impacted equity and the results of health outcomes, and at the same time have contributed to an improvement in the accountability process between policymakers/executors of policy and suppliers, and in the empowerment of the population.

A Summary of the Reforms

During the second half of the 1980s, a deconcentration effort was set in motion in the health area that served as the basis for the current decentralized DISA. In the 1990s, the DISAs of Lima and Callao were recentralized in MINSA, but the ministerial structure was not modified. Instead, vertical programs were developed parallel to the traditional structure. Once the economy stabilized in 1993, a series of changes took place:

- Strengthening of primary health care through the development of a basic package of services delivered by the Program for Basic Healthcare for All (PSBT; 1994).
- Promotion of the formation of community co-administration entities of primary health care facilities (Local Committees for Health Administration, CLAS; 1994).
- Structuring of a system for rural *rondas* (outreach visits by itinerant local teams for Extramural Healthcare, ELITES; 1998).
- Reorganization of social security,[28] currently ESSALUD, primarily through the incorporation of Private Healthcare Providers (EPS) to manage part of the plan (the basic plan for health care) of ESSALUD (1997). In addition, the Superintendence for EPS (SEPS) was created to fiscalize the private companies under the EPS regimen.
- Creation of insurance for school children (1997) and Mother-Child Insurance (1998).

---

26. Uterine atony is the failure of the uterus to contract with normal strength, duration, and intervals during childbirth.
27. Placenta previa is a condition wherein the placenta implants over the cervical os.
28. Law 26760, "Modernización de la Seguridad Social en Salud," published on May 17, 1997.

Unfortunately, no significant changes were made in the management of hospitals. Because of the nation's fiscal restrictions, the only area that was formalized was fee collections. This was meant to give hospitals a way out to their insolvency problems, but the poor were adversely affected. In practice, this has meant that hospitals are focused on fulfilling basic plan functions that should be dealt with by primary health care facilities, and, consequently, services have become more expensive. The hospitals enjoy unregulated autonomy; some provide services through private clinics that use the hospitals' infrastructure, and it is unclear whether the repayments to the hospitals by the clinic cover all the additional benefits obtained by the personnel that work in these clinics. In light of the extensive inequities within the hospital, measured by the composition of the hospitalized patients, of which the poor represent only 10 percent, it is necessary to regulate fees and ensure the transparent use of resources.

From 2002 on, the decentralization process received a new push, but MINSA has yet to benefit from internal reorganization. One of the most important measures has been the attempt to unify the vertical programs. The current administration has wisely concentrated its efforts on improving the maternal-perinatal coverage, diminishing the economic barriers to access through:

- The creation of an Integral Health Insurance (SIS) plan, a result of the merger of the Insurance for School Children Plan and the Mother-Child Insurance plan, and provides an additional incentive to extend coverage for deliveries in health care facilities.
- The incorporation of management agreements as monitoring tools for the management of regional health care entities within the MINSA structure.

No specific policies to improve ESSALUD management have been formulated. Instead, it has reinforced its position of autonomy vis-à-vis the central government. In addition, priority has been diverted from primary health care. This is due more to the narrow margin of financial sector growth and the subsequent allocation of funds to SIS than to a debate process by MINSA authorities on the model known as CLAS. Another factor is the increased union pressure that limits flexibility in the management of the sector's human resources.

None of these changes has generated significant reordering in the Peruvian Health Sector, but it is important to remember that some of these initiatives have been more pro-poor than others and have fostered very interesting accountability processes that are worthy of further consideration.

Next, we will focus on the experiences at PBST, the CLAS, and SIS, and will explore the challenges for the future, specifically the strengthening of the regulatory role of MINSA.

Program to Administer Management Agreements (PAAG)

The PAAG administers those funds destined for hiring personnel for primary health care centers and posts (51.4 percent). It constitutes one of the main articulating forces in MINSA and oversees efforts to develop primary care and the CLAS model. The PAAG administers three programs that support primary care, and all corresponding management costs:

- *Program for Basic Healthcare for All, ELITES, and outbreaks* (25.1 percent). It finances the human resources purchased in health centers and posts located mainly in depressed areas. This financing is for the development of primary health care activities and efforts related to local itinerant health equipment and brigades to fight epidemic outbreaks in populations located in isolated and extremely impoverished areas.
- *Program for Shared Administration* (25.2 percent). This program finances human resources corresponding to the CLAS.
- *Sanitary priorities.* These provide financing for collective health activities and for the acquisition of inputs and medication (vaccination campaigns, vector control, zoonoses,[29] sexually transmitted diseases, and so forth). The PAAG, according to the officials in charge of the programs, finance the vaccination campaigns and have maintained coverage efforts for vaccination. In 2003, around $8.1 million went to the acquisition of vaccines and needles. This amount was increased to almost $11 million in 2004. A new increase is expected, mainly due to prices for the incorporation of the PENTA vaccine[30] in 2005.[31]
- *Management support* (24.1 percent). This includes funds for the supervision of DISA program activities and the allocations for sectoral salary increases. These efforts distort PAAG's spending; in 2003, an extraordinary allocation was made for assistance work, and for management levels F4 and F5 (incentives for directors) (see Table 4.7).

Until 2004, PAAG administered almost 17.3 percent of MINSA's resources. These funds constituted around half of the financing that MINSA administers at a central level, not counting the DISAs in Lima and Callao.

Next, we will discuss the characteristics and contributions of PSBT and the CLAS model administered by PAAG.

Program for Basic Healthcare for All

In 1994, the Program for Basic Healthcare for All (PSBT) was created. It receives resources from the Ministry of Economy and Finance (MEF) to expand the availability of primary health care providers (doctors, nurses, obstetric nurses, and health workers) under a temporary contract scheme that permits a higher pay scale than the one for public employees. This created incentives to hire personnel in rural and poor areas. In addition, a transfer system was set up to directly pay personnel at health centers and posts as opposed to following standard fund transfer procedures channeled through MEF, the regional governments, and DISAs to personnel.

---

29. Zoonoses are diseases that are communicable from animals to humans.
30. A vaccine to fight diphtheria, tetanus, pertussis, polio, and influenza B.
31. Nevertheless, when this chapter was written, said increase had yet to be backed by the necessary budget. This may eventually compromise the continuity of other programs.

Table 4.7. Budget Execution of MINSA and PAAG (Millions of constant soles, base 2000)

	Millions of Soles		Percentage	
	2002	2003	2002	2003
MINSA structure				
MINSA	1.855.3	1.956.0	100.0	100.0
PAAG	298.3	339.0	16.1	17.3
SIS		219.0	0.0	11.2
INS	251.0	65.0	13.5	3.3
Administrative and Budgeting Units, Lima, and Callao	1.145.0	1.280.0	61.7	65.4
PARSALUD	151.0	39.0	8.1	2.0
Central administration, Institute de Recursos Humanos, SEPS, others	10.0	14.0	0.5	0.7
Structure of the PAAG				
PAAG	298.3	339.0	100.0	100.0
Sanitary priorities	93.0	83.0	31.2	24.5
CLAS	66.8	85.4	22.4	25.2
Basic health, ELITES, and outbreaks	93.1	85.0	31.2	25.1
Management support	39.2	81.8	13.1	24.1
Others and special requests	6.2	3.8	2.1	1.1

Note: The line of Support to Management involves the payment of an extraordinary stipend for Assistance Work, which was incorporated in 2002, and the F4 and F5 payments (incentives for management posts at F4 and F5 levels), supervisory activities in the DIRESA, and the operating costs of the central level of PAAG.

Sources: Sistema de Información del PAAG.
http://www.paag.minsa.gob.pe/sispaagnet/sispaag.aspx, información del SIAF.
http://ofi.mef.gob.pe/transparencia/default.aspx, DNPP.
http://www.mef.gob.pe/propuesta/DNPP/aplicativos/gob_nacional.php), SIGA.
http://www.minsa.gob.pe/siga/presentaciones.htm.

We have found that the personnel *contratado* (under contract) by the PSBT in non-CLAS facilities attended nine patients a day on average in 2004, while the rest of the personnel attended only five patients a day.[32]

Program for Shared Administration and the CLAS

Primary health care is important because it is the first point of contact between the population and the health system. As was evident in the review of the outcomes of health status, severe

---

32. Median of daily production per worker in each group. The median of daily production per worker was obtained by dividing the annual production of the worker by 220 days, according to the methodology of Waters (1998). Only personnel (doctors, nurses, and skilled birth attendants [*obstetriz*]) that worked more than eight months during 2004 were considered. The HIS, the Master List of Personnel, and the database of PAAG facilities were used as sources.

diarrheic illnesses and severe respiratory infections are the most prevalent diseases among poor children, and both must be prevented and treated at the primary-health-care level. Other key objectives, such as reducing maternal mortality, are also influenced by the performance of health centers and posts. As such, these facilities are key in the reform process. In this context, MINSA was on target in its move to create the Shared Administration Program (PAC) in the same year that PSBT was set up. The PAC sought to change the way the government relates to the community through the management of primary health care facilities through the CLAS. This model develops the possibility of financing primary health care centers that are organized under a quasi-private management scheme in which the community participates.

Table 4.8. Location of Primary Health Care Facilities According to District and Urban Poverty Levels, 2004 (percentages)

	No CLAS	CLAS	Total
Poverty			
Third of the poorest districts	37	38	37
Third of intermediate districts	33	34	34
Third of the richest districts	29	27	28
Total	100	100	100
Urban Population			
Districts the population of which is less than 33 percent urban	46	43	45
Districts the population of which is 34 to 66 percent urban	24	27	25
Districts the population of which is more than 66 percent urban	30	31	30
Total	100	100	100

Note: Structure based on the CLAS that existed in 2001.
Sources: For poverty, map of poverty with an index of MEF's resource distribution; for CLAS facilities, PAAG database; for the population, INEI projections, 2004.

There was a sustained increase from 1994 to 2003 in the number of health centers and posts operating with the CLAS system. In 1994, 432 facilities were working under this scheme, which represented only 8.3 percent of the total of MINSA health centers and posts; in 2002, the number increased to 1,927 facilities, representing 22.6 percent of the total of 8,521 centers and posts registered that year. According to recent information provided by the PAAG, there are currently 2,155 CLAS facilities, representing 25 percent of the primary health care facilities.[33]

A myth exists that the CLAS have been concentrated in urban or wealthy areas. In fact, these facilities have a distribution similar to that of traditional facilities and cover both poor and less-impoverished districts and urban and rural areas (see Table 4.8).

Attributes and Superiority

The model has three characteristics that differentiate it from a traditional establishment: community participation, human resources management flexibility, and autonomy in resource management.

---

33. From 2003 on, the growth rate declined; in 1998 and 2000, the growth rate exceeded 45 percent; in 2004, the growth rate was only 3.1 percent.

Community Participation. Each CLAS facility has an Association and a Managing Council. The Association is made up of six members of the community that are representatives of base organizations that are elected for a period of three years to oversee and participate in the facility's administration. Three of these individuals are approved by the Regional Health Office. The members of the Council (President, Speaker/Secretary, and Treasurer) are elected within the Association and are in charge of overseeing the facility's daily performance. The Association hires the head doctor or manager of the facility. This individual works closely with the Council.

The Association approves the annual Local Health Plan in conjunction with the community. The Association and the members of the Council in charge of supervision are generally better informed about what is happening in the facility than the supervisors of the networks or DISAs, and tend to be more motivated to supervise the facility. The CLAS signed two agreements or contracts—one for three years to manage the inputs including human resources and infrastructure, and one for one year to manage the services offered by the Local Health Care Agreement.

We believe that in the accountability triangle proposed by the *World Development Report* in 2004 (presented at the beginning of this chapter), the model used for the CLAS facilitates accountability along the short route—empowerment of the population—and the long route each time it is accountable to the sector through the DISAs.

The CLAS model stands out because it contemplates the empowerment of users in the planning and overseeing of the facility by increasing what is known as client power. It also has two attributes that make it superior to the conventional model: its flexibility in the management of human resources, and autonomy in the management of its resources with respect to both the fees charged to the public and the funds that come from SIS.

Human Resources. One of the most important instruments for influencing the operation of primary health care facilities is the financing and administration of human resources that work in these facilities (this can represent up to 80 percent of the facility's costs). In all non-CLAS facilities, a large number of health professionals, including the manager, have been employees under the civil service regimen (*nombrados*) and are under central administration schemes. The manager has very few tools to manage his or her personnel. The hiring, relocation, salary determination, promotion, office hours, medical specialties, medication to be used, services to be offered, and availability of equipment are determined by the network, the DISA, or the Ministry. The manager of the facility decides virtually nothing. Many interviews have confirmed that these managers have either none or few instruments to impact the conduct of appointed civil servants acting as personnel.[34]

In the face of this rigidity, a possibility of hiring personnel through the CLAS arises that contemplates either extending private contracts with social benefits (regimen 728) or temporary contracts (nonpersonnel services).[35] The first contract option is financed by the PAC and the second by PSBT or the CLAS through their own resources. The difference

---

34. Interviews conducted in Lima and Cuzco during February and March 2005. For more information, see Chapter 6, "Human Resources in Public Health and Education in Peru."

35. Few facilities have only *nombrado* personnel or personnel contracted by the PSBT. In traditional, non-CLAS facilities, one of the two groups may be more numerous than the other. It is important to distinguish between nonpersonnel service contracts with PSBT, which are signed between the worker and MINSA, and the contracts made in CLAS for both nonpersonnel and private services, which are signed with the Association.

between this hierarchy and authority and those described in the previous paragraph is that the performance of personnel, and in particular those hired under private contracts, is monitored and evaluated. The manager of the CLAS must be accountable to the Council and the Association concerning performance as measured by production, working hours, satisfaction, and fulfillment of the Local Health Plan.[36] This practice, if it ever really existed, has been lost in traditional facilities (MINSA 2004).

Table 4.9. Comparative Indicators of Productivity: Average Number of Visits per Day by Physicians, Nurses, and Skilled Birth Attendants, 2004

Performance Indicators	CLAS	Non-CLAS
Contrado Personnel	9.81	9.16
Nombrado Personnel	6.47	4.89
Total	8.65	6.65

Sources: MINSA, HIS (2004), and the database of the Master List of Personnel (2004).

Their status as a nonprofit organization gives the CLAS much more autonomy than facilities that have been organized under traditional schemes. The CLAS can manage or administer the majority of issues related to human resources (for example, hiring, salary and activity determination, working hours, and service to the public). In visits and interviews, the CLAS mentioned that a doctor was available 24 hours a day and that, unlike in traditional facilities, deliveries could be performed around the clock seven days a week (Harding and Alvarado 2005).

The restrictions that apply to all civil service employees also apply to managers (working hours, shifts, bases for promotion, salary determination, and so forth). At times, the facility may be left unsupervised when the manager has a free day following his or her shift. The CLAS are not subject to these limitations because the manager is in the position to adequately program shifts and is always present during coordination sessions with the CLAS Council.

A quick analysis of the productivity of human resources in the CLAS compared with those working in non-CLAS facilities reveals that the workers in the former are more productive (Table 4.9). We have two comments regarding this: the individuals who have been *contratados* always show greater productivity than those who have been *nombrados* to posts, but the latter always demonstrate greater productivity within a CLAS environment. This indicates that the job flexibility and the organizational environment at CLAS favor improved performance.

Management of Funds and Own Resources. All MINSA facilities collect funds through fees, and like any other Ministry unit, they have no budget independence. These funds are reported and returned to the DISA and administered by the DISA. The DISA decides the use of the funds and returns them in-kind whether through medication, materials, and inputs, or through petty cash. The same applies to funds from SIS: SIS reimbursements remain in the DISA and are returned to the facilities in-kind as determined primarily by the DISA.[37]

---

36. Nevertheless, according to the new norms, the Association must seek the "technical opinion" of DISA. These rules were established in 2003, which is why their application and effects on decisions relative to personnel are still uncertain.

37. In one interview in Cuzco, the personnel at a facility complained that the DISA had sent a water heater that they had not requested. This would have gone unnoted if the center had possessed a place to put the heater and the resources to connect it.

Table 4.10. Comparative Indicators of Performance Using the SIS According to the Plan and Health Care Attention for Children Under 5

Performance Indicator	Urban		Rural	
	CLAS	No CLAS	CLAS	No CLAS
Service per inhabitant. Plan SIS age 0–4[1]	3.58	1.99	1.74	1.05
Services per inhabitant. Plan SIS pregnant women and women in puerperium attention[1]	0.84	0.40	0.63	0.32
Services per inhabitant. Plan SIS age 5–17	2.94	1.73	2.32	1.32
Attention for all children underage 5[2]	7.0	4.35	5.84	4.88

Sources: Altobelli (2004) for footnote 1 and Health Information System results for footnote 2.
Note: Attention per child among all children under age 5 from the population assigned to the facility.

It appears that the CLAS's performance is better, given the fact that they have the power to administer their own resources by giving the manager the freedom to determine the best combination of inputs, including the possibility of covering personnel and extending the facility's working hours while fulfilling the stipulations of the Local Health Plan. Importantly, the Council supervises the use of resources, and the CLAS, as quasi-private entities, generate and audit their financial statements. Interviews have shown that the CLAS can finance transport costs for extramural activities, something largely unheard of at traditional facilities.[38] The CLAS also receive reimbursements from SIS in cash; the DISA retains only a percentage for administrative costs.[39]

An incentive exists for the CLAS to affiliate more beneficiaries to SIS (see Table 4.10). CLAS also have greater coverage in rural areas compared with urban non-CLAS. The additional financing that the CLAS generate appears not to adversely affect poor patients (the poor use the CLAS at a higher rate than traditional facilities). It is also clear that the CLAS use a portion of their income to subsidize those services that cannot cover their costs, such as attention provided to patients, with partial exemption of fees or costs, and preventive-outreach activities (Altobelli 2004).

Other Evidence of the Improved Performance of CLAS

A series of studies, including this book, indicate that CLAS users enjoy improved coverage, efficiency, and service compared with traditional primary attention facilities. Among the most significant results are: greater population coverage in CLAS facilities; greater access to health care for the population under the CLAS scheme than under traditional attention

---

38. The workers interviewed at the health centers and posts indicated that they had no petty cash to take patients in critical condition to hospitals, and often had to pay for taxis out of their own pockets.

39. Different studies have analyzed the autonomy of the management of resources in other countries and have found a positive relationship between performance and autonomy in primary care facilities (Audibert and Mathonnat 2000; Chawla and Ellis 2000).

systems (74.7 percent and 59.7 percent, respectively[40]); and a higher ratio of intramural services in the CLAS (1.7) compared with other facilities (1.5) (Altobelli 1998).

In addition, with regard to the quality of services offered, 85.9 percent of CLAS users indicate that the health care received was satisfactory, compared to 76.9 percent in the MINSA centers and posts (Cortez 1998). There are also signs that the waiting times are shorter in the CLAS than in other facilities, and that the CLAS facilities demonstrate a more rational cost-recovery policy compared with the collection policies used by traditional centers and posts, by exempting the majority of patients from the poorest income quintiles.

In addition to the average performance of the CLAS (measured by the quality perceived and the higher quality of the attention given), variations exist among the CLAS themselves. The CLAS perform better due to, among other factors, the support and supervision provided by the DISA, and whether they have more active Associations (Cortez 1998).

In summary, the CLAS's management and accountability mechanisms are unique with regard to their organization and ties to the population:

- The CLAS combine the supervision provided by the Association, made up of six representatives of the community and the manager of the facility, with DISA's supervision.
- Their status as nonprofit organizations run by the communities allows them to freely manage and maintain their funds in the facility, which attracts patients. This last factor allows us to conclude that the consumer's choice acts as another accountability mechanism to stimulate the CLAS's behavior.
- Another aspect of the autonomy of the CLAS is that the manager is directly supervised by the Managing Council and the Association, to which he or she is accountable for his or her performance. The Council meets frequently (weekly on average) and its members spend part of their time on a daily basis in the facilities. As such, the Council engages in direct supervision to ensure that performance reflects the communities' needs, which were set forth, for the most part, in the Local Health Plan.
- The Association indirectly "observes the facility," along with the community members who are users, and comments on the quality of services in community organizations such as the *Vaso de Leche* (Glass of Milk) program, *Comedores Populares* (Soup Kitchens), and *Asociaciones Vecinales* (Neighborhood Associations). The members of the Association must represent one of these entities.
- Their income (and the resources available to operate) is directly influenced by patient volume (and is related to SIS fees and reimbursements). CLAS facilities, in this sense, are more influenced by patient choice of facilities than traditional facilities; consequently, quality levels are higher.
- The manager, along with the Association and Council, can adequately handle personnel discipline or performance problems (such as hiring, salary and activity determination, schedules, and working hours).
- The process for accountability to the population is strengthened by other governmental mechanisms, the most important of which is the management contract between the CLAS Association and DISA. The agreement stipulates the Association's

---

40. Percentage of the population that received any service.

responsibilities with regard to the facilities' operation, and is part of the Local Health Plan. The CLAS also receive funds from the PAAG to cover personnel costs through the Program for Management Agreements, and must provide information on the use of funds according to the norms established for this purpose. The accounting and acquisition processes at CLAS are considered governmental activities and must be monitored by the General Controller of the Republic (*Controlaría General de la República*) and the Superior Council for State Hiring and Acquisitions (*Consejo Superior de Contrataciones y Adquisiciones del Estado*, CONSUCOD). This agency regulates government purchases.

Future Challenges

Unfortunately, the expansion of the CLAS model in MINSA has lost momentum despite extensive intellectual and academic support for its strengthening. The factors influencing this change of policy include the ministerial authorities' fear of losing control over primary health care, financial restrictions, increased union and health professional association pressures, and questions that the decentralization process poses for the future of the CLAS.

One of the major limitations is the change in the job status of the *contratado* to *nombrado* physicians, effective December 2004. The recent *nombramiento*[41] of 3,067 physicians affects the system in three ways:

- Reduction in production
- Reduction in the number of working hours without salary adjustments
- Reduction in management effectiveness.

The CLAS have the largest number of *contratado* personnel and thus will be the most affected by this measure. The CLAS and non-CLAS health facilities are taking measures to adapt themselves to the process of *nombramiento* of physicians. In the case of the CLAS, if the manager has been *nombrado*, he or she will work fewer hours as a physician and will not be present at the facility on a daily basis, leaving the facility without supervision. The *nombrado* manager will not be accountable to the Council, and instead will report to the DISA. This endangers the system of authority and accountability within the CLAS system. The total impact on the budget goes beyond the initial calculation for payroll purposes; resources will be needed to cover the additional personnel hours not covered by the newly *nombrado* personnel in order to fulfill the Local Healthcare Plan. It is more than likely that the urban CLAS will find it easier to adapt than the rural CLAS given that the latter find it more difficult to find funding. Some of the CLAS have mentioned that extramural activities will be the first to be cut to free up resources. Box 4.2 provides two examples of the CLAS's adaptations to change.

Integral Health Insurance and the Poor

At the end of the 1990s, the Peruvian government launched a program known as Mother-Child Insurance (SMI) to extend coverage to mothers and poor children. In 2001, this program was merged with the Schoolchildren Insurance (SEG) to create a new program called Integral Health Insurance (SIS). This insurance reimburses public providers

---

41. Law 28220 on the *nobramiento* of surgeon *contratados* across the country by the Ministry of Health.

Box 4.2: Adjustments after Personnel *Nombramientos* in the CLAS

In the Laura Caller Healthcare Center in Northern Lima, the *nombramiento* of a manager has produced changes in working hours and the time that the manager normally meets with the Council. The physician/manager's hours have been reduced to 30 per week. In addition, as a consequence of the *nombramiento*, the manager is unable to meet with the Council after 5:00 p.m. He is not obligated to work after his shift, and on the days he is absent, the center has neither a manager nor a physician. The Council has no influence over the manager's behavior or performance. This influence is critical to managing the facility well. The Council has decided to hire (with a contract) a new physician with whom it can coordinate.

In the Healthcare Center of Urubamba, following the *nombramiento* of two physicians, the total number of hours worked by doctors declined from 950 to 650 per month. To fulfill the objectives and activities of the Local Healthcare Plan, the Council has decided to redistribute its resources in order to hire more doctors to cover the lost hours. The appointment (with a contract) of a new doctor may cost an additional 16,800 soles in bonuses, which will delay equipment purchases for mother-child care, one of the highest priorities in the region. A skilled birth attendant working at the Center has also been changed from *contratado* to *nombrado* status and has been sent temporarily to another DISA facility. The Center has not received any compensation for this employee's lost hours.

Source: Interviews and visits to Lima and Cuzco by the RECURSO team, February–March 2005.

---

of MINSA for the variable costs of plans. SIS was created by Law 27657 and is considered a Decentralized Public Body that is attached to MINSA. Its objective is to protect the health of Peruvians without health insurance, giving priority to vulnerable population groups that live in extreme poverty or poverty to improve their access to health care services.

According to SIS estimates, the target population could reach 13 million Peruvians. Currently, SIS covers 33.4 percent of the population (approximately 9 million people in 2004), ESSALUD covers 16.5 percent, and private entities cover 1.7 percent. This means 48.4 percent of Peruvians are still without health insurance.

Reimbursement Plans and Tariffs. SIS offers five plans plus one in the implementation stage:

- Plan A for children age 0 to 4
- Plan B for children and adolescents age 5 to 17
- Plan C for pregnant women and women in puerperium
- Plan D for adults in emergency situations
- Plan E targeted to adult groups defined by law
- Contribution Plan (in the implementation stage).

The coverage of services and exams is extensive (see Annex). The benefits of plans A, B, and C have changed relatively little, but new plans and beneficiary groups have appeared. Plans A, B, and C came into existence after the unification of SMI and SEG; Plan D was added to these to cover adults in emergency situations. Plan E for adult groups defined by law was created later; it has an open-door policy that targets organized base groups (for example, members of the *Vaso de Leche* organizations, *Comedores Populares, Clubes of Madres, Wawa Wasis, Federación de Clubes de Calzados,* and individuals who have received a pardon). The Peruvian Congress is also interested in including poor adults over age 17 in an insurance plan.

The beneficiaries must register for affiliation at the primary care facility of their preference and pay 1 sol. The extremely impoverished are exempt from this fee, but the majority pay it.[42]

The DISA and the health care facilities offer insurance plans and coverage for users that request it; the SIS pays ex post as a typical "pay-for-service" mechanism. The problem lies in the fact that no precautions are taken not to exceed the financial ceilings available to SIS.

The reimbursement tariffs used by SIS in its dealings with the health care facilities have been set by using as benchmarks referential costs determined by various studies. These tariffs are not based on payment mechanisms that consider the risk of getting sick, the epidemiological profile of the regions, or actuarial calculation. In principle, the fees are the same for all primary-care facilities. This apparently favors urban over rural areas despite the fact that the former evidently have lower costs than the latter. Beyond variable costs, the facilities must absorb fixed costs for additional suitable personnel to attend to the demand generated by SIS. The information compiled in the interviews indicates that the reimbursement fees may leave a surplus in the basic plan, but the surplus might disappear when higher-complexity procedures are provided in regional hospitals. Moreover, while the primary care facilities receive reimbursements based on the fees set by the SIS and paid through the DISA either directly or indirectly, the hospitals in Lima and Callao are reimbursed for the complete expense as a variable cost without fee ceilings, which has generated greater financial pressure on SIS.

Budget

SIS is a Decentralized Public Body of MINSA that derives its budget from the mother organization, which has budget ceilings just like any other government entity. In contrast with its ambitious population goal, SIS's budget represents only 11 percent of MINSA's budget (or 7 percent when the regional budget is included). In 2003, the SIS budget was 219 million soles, and the MINSA budget was 1,956 million soles (without counting the regions).

Progress in Coverage and Targeting. SIS targets mother-child care. In 2004, almost 70 percent of its resources were directed to Plan A (age 0 to 4) and Plan C (pregnant women and women in puerperium), while 22.8 percent was concentrated in Plan B (age 5 to 17), and only 2.6 percent went to the rest of the plans. In 2004 (compared with 2003), SIS made an effort to more decidedly direct its resources to mother-child components, raising participation in Plans A and C to 69.3 percent.

Available information indicates that SIS has achieved wide coverage for maternal care. Attention for deliveries in health care facilities increased from 57.9 percent in 2000 to 70.4 percent in 2004. In addition, the professional attention for deliveries increased from 57.5 percent of the births in 2000 to 71.1 percent in 2004 (INEI 2005). Some MINSA indicators are consistent with these statistics and indicate that deliveries in health care facilities increased from 43.1 percent in 2000 to 59.8 percent in 2003.[43]

---

42. A survey conducted in Lima found that 70 percent of the beneficiary population of SIS was willing to pay 3 to 5 soles; in addition, it was determined that 61 percent of the beneficiaries had been attended to at the same facility on prior occasions and had paid for the service received (Universidad del Pacífico 2003).

43. http://www.minsa.gob.pe/estadisticas/estadisticas/indicadoresNac/download/recursos410.htm.

Table 4.11. Affiliated SIS Users per Department, 2003

Area	Population	Percentage	Affiliations	Percentage	Affiliations/ Population %
Prioritized DISA	4,684,390	17.3	1,737,815	23.0	0.371
Lima and Callao	8,679,569	32.0	1,422,701	18.8	0.164
Remaining DISA	13,784,142	50.8	4,410,786	58.3	0.320
Country total	**27,148,101**	**100.0**	**7,571,302**	**100.0**	**0.279**

Source: INEI estimates of their web page; SIS statistics to December 2003.

SIS coverage is heterogeneous across departments. In general, SIS has lower coverage in Lima and Callao (16.4 percent), primarily due to the presence of higher-income populations and the fact that ESSALUD's affiliation headquarters is located in the capital city. In those departments that have a prioritized DISA, the coverage is higher (37.1 percent; see Table 4.11).

The DISA's more extensive coverage also has a positive correlation on the spending side, given that it shows progressive growth. The per capita spending distribution per department is greater as the departmental poverty incidence rises (Figure 4.7).

In addition, SIS devotes 88 percent—a majority of its resources—to the attention provided to affiliated SIS members at Levels I and II, meaning in centers, posts, and regional and local hospitals. Some 21.1 percent of the activity is channeled to the eight prioritized DISA (Apurimac I, Andahuaylas, Ayacucho, Bagua, Cuzco, Huancavelica, Huanuco, and Puno), and 29.1 percent is directed to the population of Lima and Callao.

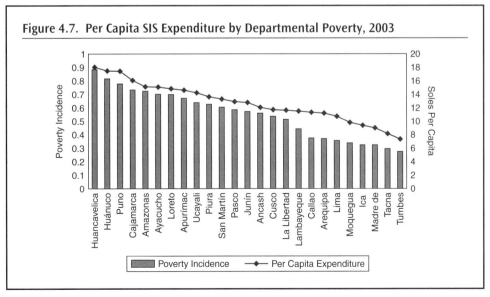

Figure 4.7. Per Capita SIS Expenditure by Departmental Poverty, 2003

Sources: MEF, poverty map with an index of public resource distribution; SIS, statistics for 2003. *Boletín Semana a Semana.*

Table 4.12. SIS Coverage by Plans According to Spending Quintiles, 2003

Groups Attended	%	Quintiles of per Capita Spending				
		1 (poorest)	2	3	4	5 (richest)
Children age 0–4	27.5	26.4	30.4	23.4	14.5	5.3
Children age 0–17	61.9	27.9	32.7	23.6	12.4	3.4
Pregnant women	8.1	13.4	21.1	21.2	33.2	11.2
The rest of the affiliated population	2.5	19.2	22.3	27.5	22.6	8.4
Total percentage	100.0	26.1	30.9	23.4	15.0	4.7

Note: The population attended to is made up of beneficiaries affiliated to SIS that have been attended to at a MINSA post, center, or hospital.
Source: INEI (2003).

Almost half is destined for the populations of the remaining DISA, and only 11.6 percent of the activity is carried out at a higher level of complexity in Lima and Callao.

Compared with the rest of MINSA, SIS has a higher concentration of poor groups. An analysis of weighted coverage[44] (affiliated members attended to) of SIS reveals that 26.1 percent of users belong to the poorest consumption quintile, while only 4.7 percent is found in the richest quintile (Table 4.12). Nevertheless, when comparing spending quintiles, a lower degree of targeting in Plan C (pregnant women) is observable than that seen in the rest of the plans. In effect, only 14.6 percent of the resources of Plan C are destined for use on the first quintile. Although only 15.1 percent of the same plan is destined for the richest quintile, the principal leakage is produced in quintile 4, which absorbs 38.7 percent of the resources directed toward pregnant women.

SIS devotes 43.8 percent of its resources to the two poorest quintiles, while the richest quintile absorbs only 9.4 percent of total funds. The differences between the lowest number of users and the greater benefits for quintile 5 can be explained by two factors: (a) higher rate of use, and (b) the use of higher-cost health care in the highest income quintiles. Despite this, the distribution among quintiles continues to be progressive.

Nevertheless, compared with other insurance providers, SIS still has the largest number of affiliated members from the low income quintiles. Of the total number of people that indicate affiliation to SIS, 64 percent belong to quintiles 1 and 2. ESSALUD concentrates 76 percent of affiliated members in the highest income quintiles (4 and 5) and the private insurers and EPS concentrate 90.6 percent in quintile 5. The majority of the population from quintiles 1 and 2 are not affiliated with insurance other than SIS (36.8 percent and 31.8 percent of the population in quintiles 1 and 2, respectively) (see Figure 4.8).

Problems and Challenges. Despite its importance, SIS faces a chronic lack of liquidity because the fund transfers from MEF fail to cover the production cost. During 2002–04, the relation between the total of billed services (gross production value) sent to MEF and

44. Weighted by average rates of use per affiliated member and by the average cost of attention under each plan.

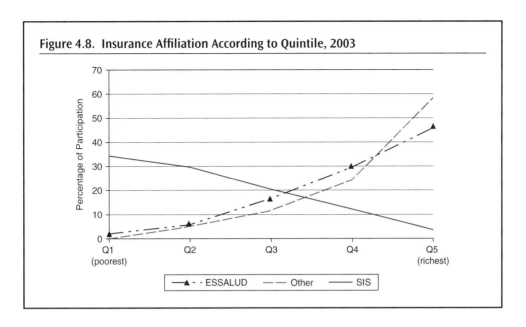

Figure 4.8. Insurance Affiliation According to Quintile, 2003

the financial transfers made by SIS to provider reimbursement was 0.91 percent. This means that, on average, 9 percent of the services rendered by providers and financed by SIS have not been covered due to cash-flow problems.

At the same time, the rate of use diminished, in part due to the growth in affiliations and to the reduction in the number of services rendered. This last factor can be explained by increased targeting and by the decline in the facilities' interest in providing services financed by SIS. A review of the numbers shows that the most significant reductions were produced in Lima and Callao, which would indicate that SIS is willing to protect the poor while tightening its belt financially (see Table 4.13). As mentioned, SIS reimburses hospitals in Lima according to a differentiated format that considers full payment of expenses as variable costs from an accounting point of view. This may be one of the causes of its imbalances.

Table 4.13. Comparison of Affiliations, Number of Consultations, and Number of Consultations per Person in SIS Between 2003 and 2004

Geographic Area	Number of New Affiliations in 2004	Percentage Increase in Affiliations, 2003–04	Reduction in Consultations between 2003 and 2004	Percentage Decrease in Consultations between 2003 and 2004	Rate of Use*	Percentage Variations in Rate of Use between 2003 and 2004
Prioritized DISA	524,844	25.7	−820,374	−21.1	−0.7	−37.2
Lima and Callao	245,117	1.2	−2,038,313	−41.5	−1.7	−50.1
Other DISA	847,565	20.7	−2,676,371	−27.3	−0.9	−39.8
Country total	1,617,526	21.4	−5,535,058	−29.8	−1.0	−42.1

*Rate of use = Consultations divided by affiliation.
Source: SIS, statistics to December 2003 and 2004. *Boletín Semana a Semana*.

The root of the problem seems to be that SIS's objectives and plans are overly extensive and ambitious, as well as unclear and politically vulnerable. SIS's current operating system consists of paying services that are registered by the facilities; these payments, however, have no relation to either the goals set or the plans as prioritized. Services are offered on a universal basis, which conflicts with MEF's budget restrictions. If the policy of providing financial protection to the poor and extremely poor and to other groups denominated as "emergency or targeted groups determined by law" is not backed by MEF, the continuity of this instrument is at risk. The current discontent expressed by health care facilities and the DISA may endanger the progress made by SIS.

One way of solving this impasse, while providing sustainability to public insurance and a more progressive nature to its plans, is to set referential fulfillment goals for each region that take into consideration the poverty levels of the region. For this purpose, it is necessary to maintain information on costs and adequately determine reimbursement tariffs according to official national and regional goals for the number of beneficiaries per plan and services to be covered. This should be accomplished without political interference. In addition, a Guaranteed Plan must be included in the budget used to finance this plan.

Given the inequities in the access to and use of tertiary health care facilities, SIS should consider a specific amount to finance a Catastrophic Illness Fund directed at providing access to specialized institutes in Lima for the poorest families in the interior of the country.

The establishment of a Guaranteed Plan will strengthen the regulatory role of MINSA and permit efforts to make national and regional priorities compatible. The services included in the Plan would be: maternal-perinatal care, check-ups for children, immunizations, and communicable disease control as part of a health care program for the poor.

For various reasons, SIS has made important contributions to sectoral development over the last few years: (a) it has tied financing to activities, encouraging an improved use of resources; (b) it has diminished the economic barriers to access by the poorest members of the population; and (c) it has the operating capacity and has generated valuable and transparent information for the sectoral management of insurance.

Institutional Strengthening. Despite the surprising achievements reached thus far, some policies require consolidation in order to plan a new and improved horizon for public insurance. We recommend:

- *Converting the SIS into an insurer-purchaser institution.* Currently, SIS acts as a payout institution for the attention given at MINSA facilities. This means that a purchasing plan must be drawn up to indicate to the MINSA facilities just where production should be increased and where no change is needed. In this way, SIS will be giving a heads up to the facilities regarding financing priorities. In particular, the prospective purchase approach will require SIS to generate pressure to increase productivity in lower-priority facilities and concentrate its resources on motivating an expansion in service and production offerings in priority areas. To develop this approach, it is necessary to set regional goals within a budget framework.
- *Improving coordination with MINSA and the DISA.* The development of the purchasing function and the execution of the purchasing plan require a coordinated effort by MINSA and the DISA (and their respective networks). The objective is to harmonize increases in purchasing, investment, and other programmed actions

with SIS's financial efforts (which cover only a portion of the variable costs of visits), and in particular with the PAAG for primary care actions. The lack of articulation with MINSA has been reflected in reduced leverage for SIS and PAAG efforts and the Management Agreements—directed toward improving access to services—so that the three principal ministerial policy instruments function in an uncoordinated fashion that fails to generate much-needed synergies.

■ *Strengthening control over the adequate use of insurance, in particular by the providers.* By introducing the concept of free care, the SIS is breaking away from the logic of high co-payments. Strict control over the granting of insurance benefits made by providers to beneficiaries is necessary to avoid fees that exclude the poorest members of the population while delivering services financed by SIS to non-poor individuals who do not qualify for SIS insurance.

■ *Improving SIS's socioeconomic classification systems in order to direct its resources, preferably to the poorest sectors.* It is necessary to formulate a new plan in the SIS that is directed toward providing access—primarily in the regions—to the country's higher-complexity facilities. This plan will be sustained by resources from the budgets of national institutes and hospitals and new financial sources, including regional funds. This will allow SIS to take part of the funds allocated to the population in Lima and direct them toward poorer regions that have less access. In this way, efficiency will be achieved in addition to stimulating improved network performance and patient referral systems among regions, creating a more equitable system.

■ *Promoting a culture oriented toward customer satisfaction and the advocacy and defense of patient rights.* Improving the Peruvian health system will contribute to democratization in society. Thus, it is necessary to create mechanisms through which personal preferences can be expressed in the framework for health priorities established by MINSA and subnational governments.

■ *Establishing provision standards.* The fulfillment of the Plan's specific goals in the poorest departments must be monitored, and management contracts must tie fulfillment to financial incentives. MINSA, SIS, and PAAG experiences can serve as a platform for new developments. Ideally, SIS payments and the MINSA management agreements should be merged into one operating system. The incentives can be designed to reinforce behaviors that extend coverage in the poorest and most isolated sectors and improve both the quality and opportunities for health care.

Regulation of the Health Sector

Formally, the Ministry of Health is the entity that governs and regulates the health system, but in practice, it intervenes little in social security and the private sector. ESSALUD operates as an independent and autonomous entity with its own laws that neither reports to MINSA nor is subject to its supervision. In addition, the Law of Autonomy of 2004 (Law 28006) grants greater independence to ESSALUD that extends to its dealings with MEF, as evidenced by the fact that it is not even obliged to register its budget execution with the Integrated System of Financial Administration (SIAF). With regard to the private sector, MINSA possesses extensive faculties to fiscalize the activities of Private Healthcare Providers (EPS), but these entities cover only 0.2 percent of the national population. Medicines, which are the primary component of private health spending, are produced and distributed within a free-market context, and current legislation contemplates few regulatory mechanisms to ensure adequate quality and competition.

MINSA also performs financing and operating functions that distract it from its regulatory role. The central apparatus of MINSA carries out policy and financing functions through its organizational structure and OPDs. MINSA continues to support DISA's operations outside of Lima, but the budgets of these entities depend on the regions. Nevertheless, MINSA maintains the administration and financing of the DISAs in Lima and Callao (which absorb 38.8 percent of the Ministry's total resources), and that of the hospitals and specialized health institutes.

Decentralization. Given the lack of clarity, the regional DISAs also perform regulatory, financial, and provider functions: they direct the health facilities that depend on them and have the autonomy to organize health care activities in their respective jurisdictions. MINSA's participation in this process is decreasing. Efforts to clarify the responsibilities that fall within each government ambit are progressing slowly as part of the decentralization process, and the stage has been set to strengthen MINSA's regulatory functions and clearly delineate the formulation and decisionmaking process for accountability.

On July 28, 2005, through Supreme Decree 052-2005-PC, the government determined the health-related functions that would be transferred to the regions and local government following an accreditation process. Some of the most significant functions include: the formulation of regional policies according to national guidelines; the formulation and execution of regional health development plans; the "transfer of resources for reimbursement for services"; to "control, monitor and evaluate the fulfillment of insurance processes, attention plans, application of fees, coverage goals and health care service standards;" to "organize and implement healthcare services …."; and "to be responsible for the dissemination of useful information to the population on administration and services." *Nombramiento* of personnel will also fall under the jurisdiction of the regional and local governments. This scheme proposes a model that contemplates a separation of functions that strengthens the regulatory role of MINSA to give coherence to the system and transfer provision responsibilities to the subnational governments. Box 4.3 looks at the possibilities available for separating functions.

Separation of Functions. The first step toward separating functions requires that MINSA detach itself from the DISAs in Lima and Callao and from the national institutes and hospitals. This means that MINSA will give up its provision functions. The principal challenge here lies in defining to which institutions the national hospitals should be attached, which may become autonomous entities or be rendered dependent on the DISAs or on a third entity specifically created to manage them.

The second step is to strengthen SIS's role as a sectoral financing institution by channeling fiscal resources through this insurance as a collection and distribution body for financing, an aspect discussed in the previous section.

The third step is probably more complex. It involves internal reorganization of MINSA to make it a regulator of the entire Peruvian health system and not just the public sector. This requires: (a) defining health policies and strategies for the entire national population, meaning the population covered by the current ministerial structure, the population of ESSALUD, and the population covered by the private sector; (b) fiscalizing the fulfillment

---

Box 4.3: The Separation of Health Functions Increases Accountability

One of the most recognized approaches to operating health systems in the 1990s advocated a separation of functions. Initially developed in the United Kingdom, this focus was extended to different countries such as Colombia, the Netherlands, New Zealand, and Spain. This vision proposes that health care organization systems can be improved if clarity exists with regard to the main functions the system is meant to perform.

The focus on separating functions recognizes three main functions for heath systems: provision, financing, and regulation.

Health care systems exist to promote a healthy lifestyle and to prevent, cure, and rehabilitate. This essential function of all health systems is known as the provision function due to the fact that society organizes its productive forces in hospital facilities, health care centers, laboratories, clinics, and so forth, in order to produce or provide health care oriented toward maintaining or improving the population's health. The organizations that carry out these functions are called providers. The organization of the heath system's productive resources (such as doctors, nurses, beds, and equipment) requires coordination.

It is necessary to provide a degree of direction to the provision function through what is known as the regulatory function. Due to public health reasons and the chronic scarcity of resources that accompany health care activity, society needs to prioritize its problems, concentrating its forces on developing effectiveness. A regulatory role exists and is geared toward setting the standards for fiscalizing, supervising, and evaluating the regulatory function. The components involved in the regulatory function are known as "regulators."

In addition, health care systems require significant consumption of society's resources. Obtaining these resources and their subsequent allocation among institutions within the system is known as the "financing function." Entities that engage in financing are known as "financing bodies or insurers."

Within this analytical framework, it is possible to identify relations among the system's elements. The most important relation between financing bodies and providers is known as the "resource allocation or purchasing function," depending on the degree of separation of functions that exists among the elements.

---

of these policies through independent bodies (this may lead to a redefinition of the role of the Superintendence of EPS or the creation of a Health Superintendence); (c) supervising the development of heath strategies that enable the citizens to have a transparent view of the performance of actors; and (d) evaluating the achievement of sanitary objectives, the adaptation of policies, strategies, and global performance of sectoral institutions.

Strengthening the Regulatory Role. One of the major limitations that MINSA must overcome is not having the necessary and timely information to exercise its regulatory function and issue norms that strengthen other functions. Functions that require bolstering include ensuring that the public funds managed by insurers are sufficient to finance health care for the poor in order to reduce all types of gaps while effectively overseeing public health standards.

Regulation is one of the most important functions of the contract or compact, meaning the relation between policymakers and suppliers. Standards and information are needed to make better decisions, and to monitor and supervise public and private suppliers.

MINSA is making considerable effort to improve its information systems and has achieved significant progress, as is evident in the case of SIS and in the area of sanitary oversight. Nevertheless, it is important to point out two problems: (a) the absence of pertinent information for decisionmaking, and (b) the existing information systems are incompatible and lack timeliness and precision, and in some cases are unreliable. The system is not governed by a vision of management according to results, and tends to overwhelm the suppliers with an excess of requests for information that in the end is not even used.

Several regulatory responsibilities are examined below to provide a clearer idea of the link between regulation and regulatory activities at MINSA with information systems:

- *Oversight of public health and issuance of the pertinent norms to ensure that the target population receives adequate services from the public and private suppliers.* MINSA does not have an adequate registry of the population assigned to the facilities for which it is responsible. In addition, the subregistry of vital statistics, including mortality, makes it difficult to correlate mortality levels with supplier performance.

- *Oversight of public health and outbreaks.* The General Office of Epidemiology maintains a registry of and oversees 17 diseases and provides immediate notification of outbreaks. Nevertheless, it must become computerized and expand its monitoring of preventive actions to avoid the occurrence of outbreaks as opposed to merely informing the population of damages that have already occurred.

- *To correct failures in public or private market supply to ensure the provision of merit goods and the placement of human resources in unattractive areas.* MINSA could decide to correct these failures giving financial incentives to the regions and DISAs. One way to do this is to transfer fiscal resources based on performance measured by indicators of productivity or coverage of services that are of little interest to the supplier (for example, preventive actions in poor areas that do not generate income). In addition, it could regulate the placement of human resources in order to ensure the availability of trained personnel in depressed areas. Achieving this requires confronting two obstacles: the instrument, and the process to register both production and human resources.

  Despite the fact that the Health Information System (HIS) is an excellent instrument for providing information on production that is later consolidated in MINSA, this system has several limitations. HIS registers only visits that take place within the facility, and does not easily interface with other systems. In addition, the search mechanism is not user-friendly, so specialists from the statistical unit must be consulted. Another problem that has not been overcome involves the correct differentiation between and registration of "visits" and the registration of "patients atendidos" as managed by HIS. In the face of this confusion, the registration of "visits" is generally used. HIS, however, is not a universally used instrument. Other parallel systems have emerged, including program production registries, the production sheets used by some of the DISAs, and the systems for production registration used by SIS.

  The Master List of Personnel is a database that allows for the individual identification of health workers according to codes, profession, contract status, or labor relation with MINSA, and the location of the health care facility and DISA to which they have been posted. This is a very important database that, due to the management and coordination problems experienced by the parties that feed it, fails to effectively consolidate the information needed to develop an overall view of human resources. For example, personnel codes are repeated for two or more professionals and an individual may appear on the Master List more than once due to misspellings and incomplete name registration, among other difficulties. Also, no distinction is made between type and duration of contracts. The interface with HIS is not automatic, and when attempts are made to analyze worker productivity and performance, many observations are lost due to poor registries in the databases.

The PAAG has an information system for contratado personnel and has attempted to collect more data, but this effort has not been universal. In summary, it is difficult to follow up on human resource productivity, which limits any performance-based merit system. Each DISA collects this information and processes it for operating purposes, but no system is in place to provide either sanctions or incentives.

■ *Regulating tariffs and monitoring costs for purchasing of services.* MINSA, as part of its efforts to correct market failures and monitor increases in costs, or out of an interest in purchasing services for the poor through insurance plans, needs to know costs and their relation to standard costs and tariffs with which it can buy or finance services for insurance plans.

One of MINSA's current challenges is to facilitate the consolidation and registration of financial flows, the budget executed in the health facilities, and the automatic reporting of these financial instruments to the DISA and subsequently to MINSA. The CLAS are responsible for consolidating financial information from different sources for accountability purposes, but traditional facilities fail to consolidate information on the funds they are allocated and spend. One comment on this: while the DISA, as SIS intermediaries, send funds directly to the CLAS in cash, funds sent to the other facilities are in the form of materials or inputs. Something similar occurs with the management of fees that are collected directly by the facility. The health care facilities' managers have no control or decisionmaking instruments. At a micro level, this problem impedes efforts to identify each facility's costs, which in turn affects the ability to make appropriate decisions throughout the system and reduces the ability of both DISA and MINSA to manage the sector.

■ *Allocation of public funds.* MINSA should ensure that funds are allocated in an equitable, efficient, and effective manner. This task, however, is currently blocked by a lack of adequate budget information stemming from an absence of coherency among the concepts of prioritization within the realm of public health (collective health and individual health) or attention levels (primary, secondary, and tertiary) that MINSA uses and those seen in SIAF. Furthermore, the decentralization process brings with it the challenge of incorporating local governments into the SIAF GL. This opportunity will allow us to better understand health spending in the local ambit. If the unit cost per service is unknown, health and DISA facilities are unable to aspire to one day having a budget that is realistic instead of merely historical.

In summary, MINSA is a regulatory entity that lacks enough information to make better decisions and execute appropriate policies. As such, the challenge lies in obtaining better information. In addition, the decentralization process complicates matters and makes the necessity of clarifying responsibilities for registering and managing information at a regional and local level even more pressing, particularly with reference to supply availability in different jurisdictions. The transfer of health functions once accreditation has occurred (Supreme Decree 052-2005-PCM) paves the way for the regions to take charge of their information systems, which will undoubtedly require MINSA's leadership to effectively articulate all regional activities.

Finally, it is important to point out that MINSA must be convinced that the use of an effective information system will provide instruments for performance-based management to correct market failures, and so forth. In addition, it makes little sense to generate information if it is not shared with the population, whether for user-patient purposes or as a means of involving citizens in vigilance and political voice. Transparency and information availability will contribute to improved accountability processes.

Review of the Peruvian Literature on the Health System

Peruvian authors have produced a copious and noteworthy literature on the health system that includes both a diagnostic and a set of policy recommendations. Table 4.14 provides information from only a small selection of these texts. Information produced by national and international organizations and think tanks specializing in the social sciences has not been included. This is because the principal purpose of this chapter is to present a sample of Peruvian intellectual thought on health care in order to determine how others perceive the problems, and to test whether the recommendations in this chapter are in keeping with other findings in this area.

Analysis of the literature reviewed indicates that: (a) the findings of the diagnostic of the health care system are widely shared by the authors, who invariably indicate that (i) progressive improvement has been made in the health of the population over the last decades, (ii) slow progress has been achieved in mother-child coverage (particularly in the area of professional attention for deliveries), (iii) inequitable access to health remains a problem, (iv) fees constitute the principal barrier for access to health care, and (v) fragmentation and scarce coordination continue to cause difficulties both in the sector and in MINSA itself; and (b) Peruvian experts generally concur in their policy recommendations to extend coverage of professional attention for deliveries, make improvements in the quality and problem-solving capacity of services, generate improvements in the referral network, and drive measures that tend to diminish inequity (primarily by targeting resources geographically and individually), emphasizing actions in the rural areas, where the worst health indicators are registered.

Recommendations

The evaluation of social service provision, and in this particular case, of the public health sector of MINSA, reveals that no channels and processes exist for accountability purposes, and, if some do exist, they are weak on the supplier side (health care professionals and facilities) to the regulating and financing sector, and from the authorities of the sector to the users and patients. This is due, in part, to the lack of a clear definition of the actors' responsibilities, the weak position of MINSA, and the absence of standards and goals for which the actors must be responsible. Next, the recommendations will be enumerated and grouped into three general strategies linked with health care functions, with the intention of improving the situation described. The recommendations will be based on the accountability triangle (see Figure 4.9).

Table 4.14. Main Findings on Health Care in Peruvian Literature

Topic	Author	Diagnostic and Recommendations
Health and population	Bardález (2001:165)	■ There has been improvement in the Peruvian population's health in recent decades. ■ Slow growth in coverage for mother-care attention (neonatal mortality is elevated in cities). ■ Recommend an increase in attention for deliveries and neonatal, and for hospitalization in general. ■ The diversity in health scenarios demands decentralized management.
	Guzmán (2002:185–238)	■ The main cause of maternal death is inadequate access to health care and the limited problem-solving capacity of the sector. Clandestine abortions account for nearly a third of maternal deaths. ■ Limited access to reproductive health care, principally by adolescents. ■ A combined strategy is needed: improvements in education, access to services (professional attention for deliveries, access to quality emergency obstetrical care, access to family planning services), and improvement in the economic and social status of women. ■ Drive the problem-solving capacity of services and public insurance, and access to obstetrical care. Prenatal control currently provides limited capacity to predict complications. ■ Need to prevent undesired pregnancies and extend coverage to family planning.
Health policies	Francke (1998)	■ Services with high externality and services for mothers and children should be assigned geographically based on risks. ■ Primary care services in rural areas must combine targeting with universality. ■ Apply exemption to a set of services for the poor. ■ Control the abuse in using tariffs to generate income.
	Francke (2001:21–24)	■ Making health care a right for all Peruvian citizens requires: a democratization of the State, prioritization of universal access to quality services, and reorganization of services and health systems. ■ Reorganizing the health system requires: engaging in coordinate planning of all health services, organizing MINSA and ESSALUD facilities to delimit the services provided, and granting autonomy to and decentralization of primary care networks and hospitals (the CLAS must widen its coverage, particularly at the primary-care level).
	Johnson (2001:95–132)	■ The main problems of the health sector are: absence of a systemic vision, lack of coordination among MINSA subsectors, instability in public and technical posts, poor qualifications of personnel, an absence of a multidisciplinary focus, the vertical and traditional character of MINSA, and the functions are mixed (regulation, provision, and financing). ■ Separate functions and specialization in MINSA. ■ Replace MINSA's pyramid structure with a model for flat organization.

(continued)

Table 4.14. Main Findings on Health Care in Peruvian Literature (*Continued*)

Topic	Author	Diagnostic and Recommendations
Health care financing	Alvarado (2002:41–85)	■ Inequity of access and sanitary results and the current distribution of resources. ■ Apply geographic targeting to sectoral funds, apply individual targeting to attention in centers and hospitals, build databases for targeting, and introduce charges and exemptions for users within the Integral Health Insurance.
	Petrera (2002:86–139)	■ Modify the financing structure of health care to contemplate fiscal resources and compulsory contributions. ■ Develop a public insurance fund to organize SIS financing. ■ Develop the purchasing function of the health care insurance fund. ■ Restructure the health sector to render it more effective, efficient, competitive, and transparent. ■ Develop improved synergy among the sector's resources through public interaction and the incorporation of private sector providers.
	Madueño, De Habish, and Jumpa (2004)	■ Economic barriers exist to insurance market access for the 20 percent of uninsured, independent, low-income workers. ■ MINSA's tariff policy provides no incentives for *potestativo* insurance (paid by the individual) to act as "implicit insurance," so the expansion of the insurance market is limited. ■ Apply a segmentation strategy to the market encompassing the remaining 80% of independent workers and establish institutional arrangements that allow for an expansion of the insurance market. By benefiting diverse market agents, particularly middle-class users, it becomes more politically viable to diminish the resistance of this segment with regard to efforts to redirect public subsidies to the poorest populations.
	Guzmán (2003)	■ Create a Unified Social Security System based on solidarity for health care governed by MINSA. ■ Financing could be provided by funds coordinated by a board made up of representatives from the different institutions that compose the fund. ■ Services could be provided through public and private providers. ■ Regulation could be the responsibility of the National Health Superintendence. ■ Define a Guaranteed Basic Health Plan for the entire population that covers the most urgent problems and priority sanitary issues. ■ Affiliation would be obligatory and multiple payment mechanisms would be used.
	Sobrevilla, Loo, Telyukov, and Garavito (2002)	■ Strengthen those MINSA initiatives designed to structure a simple system of individual classification of services. ■ Strengthen the Integral Health Insurance program, providing a variety of ways through which services can be financed. ■ Strengthen shared administration and the CLAS by improving the structure of activities that will be purchased.

Table 4.14. Main Findings on Health Care in Peruvian Literature (*Continued*)

Topic	Author	Diagnostic and Recommendations
	Valdivia (2002:11–16)	■ Inequity in access to health care services and serious errors in the targeting of public subsidies.
		■ One possible effect of the tariff policy could be the detouring of the demand of public and private suppliers and decreased recovery in the face of high elasticity of demand in higher socioeconomic groups.
		■ This same policy could have a positive effect on quality and drive increases in demand, creating a space for cost recovery.
		■ Improve information systems to incorporate other effects on the demand for services.
Hospital policy	Palomino (2001:95–132)	■ No common hospital policy exists and each hospital is managed independently.
		■ Organize the MINSA hospital system into three levels: a first level consisting of primary care and provincial and departmental hospitals, a second level made up of hospitals corresponding to the macroregions, and a third level consisting of national hospitals and institutes.
		■ Organize the country into departmental networks with assigned populations.
		■ Strengthen hospital regulation.
		■ Create an entity that provides financing for hospitals and that hands over the administration of national and regional hospitals to nonprofit organizations.
		■ Finance hospitals through per capita allocation to the first level and an allocation for cases attended to at the second and third hospital levels.
		■ Develop management agreements between the different levels and actors of the system.
CLAS model	Altobelli (2004)	■ The CLAS have better coverage with SIS financing than non-CLAS facilities.
		■ The rural CLAS show better performance in mother-child plans.
		■ The CLAS produce 1.6 and 1.2 times more than the non-CLAS in urban and rural areas, respectively.
		■ The CLAS collect two times more per inhabitant than non-CLAS.
		■ Help the CLAS take better advantage of SIS financing.
	Casavalente (2005)	■ Comparison of CLAS and traditional facilities with better or poorer performance. The CLAS with better performance attend to less-impoverished patients than the CLAS with lower performance and the traditional facilities with better performance.
		■ The CLAS with better performance provide more services, with plans for pregnant women and children under 5, compared with the rest of the groups.
		■ There is no difference in patient satisfaction.
		■ There are no differences in waiting times between traditional facilities and the CLAS with better performance. The opposite is true for lower-performance CLAS.
		■ CLAS schemes are both equitable and efficient.

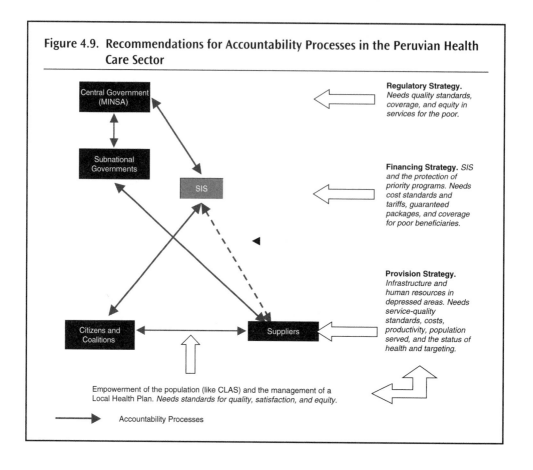

Figure 4.9. Recommendations for Accountability Processes in the Peruvian Health Care Sector

Strategy for Regulation and Decentralization

In theory, MINSA is the body responsible for regulating the Peruvian health care system. This Ministry, however, intervenes little in ESSALUD and the private sector. In addition, the fact that MINSA performs financial and operating functions distracts it from its regulatory role, in part because it is highly focused on providing services in Lima and Callao, including hospitals and specialized institutes. The process of clarifying responsibilities according to government ambit, which is fundamental to achieving an increase in accountability, is progressing slowly as part of the decentralization process. This provides a perfect scenario in which to take advantage of an opportunity to strengthen MINSA's regulatory function, SIS's financing function, and the provision function of subnational governments.

In addition to this multiplicity of roles—and the subsequent weakness performing each of these roles—MINSA lacks the necessary and sufficient information to exercise its regulatory role. Said absence impedes MINSA from establishing standards with which to monitor and supervise the adequate functioning of the sector, and renders it unable to request accountability from suppliers and workers. Accordingly, the population is uninformed and incapable of demanding accountability for services provided under MINSA's jurisdiction.

One of the major challenges for MINSA is to have, as soon as possible, timely information to fully exercise its regulatory function. The different attempts to develop information systems have allowed for a certain degree of progress in, for example, the sanitary oversight system and the SIS registry systems. This progress, however, has been isolated. An integral approach must be adopted to deal with this problem and lend transparency to the relations and transactions among the agents of the system: regulators, financing entities, and public and private suppliers. This corresponds to the long route of the accountability triangle. It is also urgent to define the standards needed: type and level of services that will be offered, coverage of the target population, costs, and productivity in provision, among others.

The challenge over the next five years is to have information on:

- *Vital statistics of the population and the identification of the characteristics of demand.* MINSA makes estimates of the beneficiary population without precise knowledge of the users of the different services it administers (preventive, curative, and rehabilitation). This requires making progress toward a means of identifying the population that facilitates adequate follow-up, based on access and impact criteria, and on the status of health and health care interventions. In addition to the identification efforts, it would be wise to develop socioeconomic classification mechanisms applicable to the beneficiary population that will enable a clear understanding of whom to subsidize, what to subsidize, and how much to subsidize.

- *Service production in public facilities.* The statistics on outpatient attention are extremely weak and those related to hospital discharges are good only in certain hospitals; in addition, this information is not consolidated by MINSA. An effort is needed to coordinate the information bases that SIS generates with those handled by MINSA.

- *Supply of services.* Since the infrastructure census of 1996, only partial efforts have been made to identify the physical characteristics of the health care supply in MINSA facilities, and no attempts have been made with regard to the sector's suppliers. With the separation of functions slated to accompany the decentralization process, the regions will become responsible for maintaining updated information on supply availability in their jurisdictions. This information is indispensable to monitoring the performance of health care services.

- *Financing and budgeting.* The statistics relative to the budget can be studied through the SIAF, but MINSA's budget structure does not allow for the use of this information to analyze the quality of its spending or that of the regions that report directly to SIAF. With the current system, it is impossible to examine the use of funds according to health care priorities (for example primary, secondary, and tertiary health care) or according to equity in fund distribution among jurisdictions. It is also impossible to establish the cost-effectiveness of service units (cost and production of specific hospitals, geographic networks, or individual services).

- *Productivity of human resources.* The lack of information on productivity impedes efforts to build a culture of accountability of human resources to management, facilities to the networks, and the networks to the DISA. Currently, MINSA and the DISAs conduct no follow-up on human resource productivity, and, even if they were to attempt to follow up, they would be unable to do so quickly due to problems in HIS and the Master List of Personnel. This database of human resources suffers from duplication in codification that limits its interface, even manually, with other databases. Under this information system, it is impossible to apply an incentive and merit plan based on better performance.

■ *Cost-tracking systems.* No information system on expenditure, salaries, and locations of health personnel exists that allows for a determination of the connections between the availability of human resources and production and an analysis of costs and subsequently of tariffs. Without costs and tariffs, SIS cannot set reimbursement amounts according to real costs, nor is it feasible to set standards under which suppliers should operate.

Working with simple indicators facilitates dialog, social contract, and transparency regarding the organization's goals. If MINSA has the needed information, it can report to the population on the services it can finance or buy from SIS (as a guaranteed package) and what can be expected from health care facilities with regard to equity, quality, and costs. This measure would grant the population a significant tool of empowerment (the short route on the accountability triangle).

Once the information systems are functioning, it will be easier to set goals and monitor the indicators established by the MDGs. The sector's culture of accountability could begin with the monitoring of sanitary priorities related to the services needed by the poor, such as an increase in deliveries at health care facilities to reduce maternal mortality. The yearly goals for the country can be set, with regional variables. The national priorities could be complemented and financed by the regional governments, which is a way of empowering the regional governments.

Financing Strategy

This financing strategy will be complemented by the regulatory and decentralization strategy in the sense that it will help to clarify the responsibilities of different agents linked to financing and the purchase of services. Four areas that deserve attention have been identified:

1. *Maintaining a protected and independent budget for public health programs with population goals (immunizations).* This independence will protect purchases of vaccines and other key inputs from spending pressures emanating from other budget areas.
2. *Strengthening SIS institutionally as an insuring entity.* SIS could be in charge of the purchase of health care services throughout the country, allowing MINSA to concentrate on its regulatory function. An initial attempt has been made to separate SIS from the financing function. This attempt notwithstanding, SIS has yet to be fully constituted as an insurer, and it mostly functions merely as a payout body. SIS could continue to be financed by MINSA and by the users that pay affiliation premiums, thus creating channels for accountability to its two financing bodies, while improving SIS's progressive character.
3. *Financing a Guaranteed Priority Plan with SIS.* To do this, it is essential to ensure that: (a) legislation guarantees the existence of a plan, the costs of which are known, that establishes official national and regional goals for the number of beneficiaries and health care services that will be covered; (b) a budget exists that allows for the financing of a Guaranteed Plan for the number of identified beneficiaries and the

corresponding coverage; and (c) SIS considers an amount to finance a Catastrophic Illness Fund directed toward providing access to specialized institutes in Lima by poor families in the interior of the country.

Establishing a plan will generate a powerful regulatory instrument for MINSA that will aid in efforts to make national and regional priorities compatible. The services this plan could include are: maternal-perinatal care, check-ups for children, immunizations, and the control of communicable diseases.

4. *Implementing a national tariff policy.* It is necessary to regulate charges to users of hospitals and heath care posts and centers. These entities must have systems that provide socioeconomic identification of patients to increase equity and efficiency of access to hospitals and primary health care. This effort will generate transparency in how funds are used.

Provision Strategy

Human Resources. The recent *nombramiento* of personnel with contracts in rural areas and the elimination of access to the specialized residencies provided by SERUMs will produce a considerable loss of personnel in rural and poor areas. This demonstrates the urgency of developing new mechanisms and formulas that attract health care personnel to poor and isolated areas. Any effort is this direction must contemplate short-term economic incentives, such as the restructuring of some of the mechanisms for medical residency (for example, the granting of higher points and privileges for SERUMs physicians that work in areas far from medical residencies).

Infrastructure. What is needed is: (a) to strengthen primary public health care in areas where it is currently scarce, mainly in rural and poorer areas, and (b) to strengthen the supply of emergency obstetric care and emergency care in hospitals located in the poorest regions. The mortality of women during pregnancy and delivery and of women who have recently given birth continues to be a major public health concern in Peru. The majority of the causes of maternal death indicate a deficit in the access to and quality of care during the prenatal and postpartum stages. Almost all of these problems can be prevented if the care during delivery is provided at a health care institution with adequately trained personnel and appropriate equipment.

Empowerment of Users. The CLAS model, which is a management model that is administered and supervised by the community through its Association and Council of Directors, has proven that, among other things, it possesses effective channels for accountability that translate into higher user satisfaction, greater access for the population assigned to the facility, more intramural and outreach activities, longer opening hours, and more productive personnel as measured by the number of visits per day. Strengthening this model and considering using its channels for accountability are recommended. The success of this model lies in the feasibility of working around a local health care plan as a standard that considers the product goals expected of a health care facility.

Annex—Services Covered by SIS

Following is a list of the services covered in all the plans. Different combinations of health services and exams apply depending on the plan. Please see www.sis.minsa.gob.pe for more detail.

- Immediate care for newborns without health problems
- Hospitalization for newborns with pathologies
- Hospitalization with surgical procedures on newborns
- Check-ups for newborns with low birth weight
- Immunological exam for newborn whose mother is HIV-positive
- Immunological exam for newborn whose mother is RPR-positive
- Integral health care (*Control de Crecimiento de Niño Sano, Programa Ampliado de Inmunizacones*)
- Dental hygiene exam
- Iron supplement
- Anti-parasitic treatment
- Treatment for HIV-AIDS in children
- External consultation
- Restoration and simple dental treatment
- Restoration and combined dental treatment
- Dental extraction
- Outreach work (home visit)
- Triage
- Emergency care
- Emergency care with observation
- Outpatient medical-surgical intervention
- Hospitalization in a healthcare facility
- Hospitalization with minor surgical intervention
- Hospitalization with major surgical intervention
- Hospitalization in the intensive care unit
- Blood transfusion (one or more units)
- Peri-urban emergency transfer
- Rural or costal emergency transfer
- Sierra-jungle emergency transfer
- National transfer (child and accompanying adult)
- Burial.

CHAPTER 5

The Social Safety Net

Cornelia Mihaela Tesliuc

This chapter assesses Peru's social safety net (SSN) and describes how to build a safety net to complement economic growth and public interventions, such as health and education, to contribute more effectively to the reduction of current and future poverty.

Safety nets are formal and informal measures that protect people from the worst effects of low income and poverty. Internationally, they include cash transfers, food programs, workfare, price and other types of subsidies, and programs that ensure access of the poor to essential public services, such as school vouchers or scholarships, fee waivers for health care services, and social funds. In Peru, the SSN consists mainly of food assistance and workfare programs. In addition, in Peru, social funds play an important role in ensuring access of poor households and communities to health, education, water, sanitation, roads, and electricity.

Two analytical techniques are used to understand the key strengths, weaknesses, and options of the SSN sector: (a) an assessment of the effectiveness and efficiency of public transfers in redistributing income and reducing poverty; and (b) an assessment of the accountability mechanisms. This chapter investigates the design of the system (overall level of funding, spending/program mix); the design of key programs (missing the relevant priority group, inadequate coverage, or low adequacy); implementation (differences between the provisions of the laws and regulations and how the programs are implemented in the field); and the effectiveness of the accountability mechanisms.

An innovative aspect of the *Rendición de Cuentas para la Reforma Social de Perú* (RECURSO) is its combination of qualitative and quantitative data sources, which are valuable each in its own right, and yield important synergies when used together. The primary source of quantitative information is the Living Standards Measurement Survey (*Encuesta Nacional de Hogares*, ENAHO 2003), including a special community-level module, which was conducted by the *Instituto Nacional de Estadistica e Informatica* (INEI). The chapter also draws on the results of a Qualitative Power, Voice, and Service Delivery Study (QPVSD) in 18 provincial and district municipalities in three departments that cover the three geographical regions of the country (sierra, coast, and jungle). The QPVSD was designed to complement the ENAHO with in-depth information of perceptions of client power, voice, and how service delivery is affected by decentralization.

We start by summarizing the key policy recommendations, followed by a diagnostic of the main issues in the sector and an overview of the main findings and recommendations emerging from previous studies. Finally, we present in more detail the key recommendations and options emerging from our analysis and the rationale for the proposed policy changes.

Main Policy Recommendations

The recommendations in this document are largely for short-term reforms in the SSN, and take into account existing institutions and programs. These reforms are likely to better cover the priority groups within existing financial and institutional resources. In the longer term, it will be desirable to identify programs and interventions expected to have greater impact on the educational, health, and nutritional status of the poor. Most likely, such interventions will require increased funding and greater capacity.

1. *Clarify objectives of the SSN policy, define achievable results, and strengthen accountability.*

   ■ Focus on key priority groups. Focus the policy interventions on the groups with the greatest cumulative disadvantages—children and their families living in poverty. Children are the age group with the highest incidence of poverty, and constitute the largest group of extreme poor. Many poor children experience several forms of deprivation in addition to consumption poverty, such as high rates of malnutrition, low academic performance, and school dropout.

   ■ Focus on a few key interventions to strengthen investment in human and physical capital, moving away from *asistencialismo*. Gradually change the focus of food programs from assistance (coping) to delivery of assistance linked to investment in human capital or in physical assets. Moreover, these should complement other sector programs to ensure that all poor children have basic nutrition, healthcare, and education.

   ■ Revise the policy of using social programs with the objective of subsidizing producers of milk and agricultural products. A more efficient and transparent procurement policy could substantially reduce input and intermediation costs, allowing an increase in the number of beneficiaries reached with the same budget and in the quality of the products.

   ■ Set in place an SSN to help protect households from the negative effects of various shocks. Shocks generally require quick responses, and SSNs have been largely seen as the best form of response to covariate shocks. The existing workfare program in urban areas could act as a countercyclical intervention with further adjustments in its design.

■ Improve accountability. Establish systems of monitoring and evaluation linked to program objectives. Clarify lines of accountability and ensure that monitoring and evaluation information is available to users, providers, and policymakers.

■ Establish strategies tailored to rural and urban areas. In urban areas, focus on programs which use self-selection of beneficiaries; in rural areas, continue using geographic targeting to allocate resources across municipalities and selecting priority age groups.

■ Clarify the roles of the different agencies, levels of government, and beneficiary groups with regard to regulation, financing, implementation, and program monitoring.

2. *In urban areas, improve access of poor children to an improved Vaso de Leche program, linking the program to nutrition, health, and education interventions. Continue using and strengthening the enforcement of simple targeting mechanisms: demographic, program choice, and self-selection. Continue to implement the workfare programs countercyclically.*

■ *Vaso de Leche* in urban areas has a high coverage of the target population and enjoys strong political legitimacy. The government might consider a number of measures to improve the poverty and nutrition impact of this program by linking it with complementary interventions in health and nutrition education. To expand the program within the available budget, it should enforce: (a) exit from the program of families whose children pass the eligibility age (0 to 6 years old), and (b) use of daily distribution of cooked food as a means to assure self-selection. These improvements are likely to generate savings, which could be used to increase coverage.

■ Continue to operate *A Trabajar Urbano* in a countercyclical manner. To further improve the implementation of the workfare program some fine-tuning is required: (a) set the wage rate sufficiently low to ensure that an automatic self-selection will occur; (b) intensify the efforts to select unemployed household heads who are most in need; (c) consider the options for integrating the workfare programs with the municipal investments to ensure quality (in terms of supplementary resources needed to complement the labor production factor) and maintenance of assets created; and (d) consider as possible projects not only the construction of physical assets, but also the provision of social services (caregivers, health promoters) that might increase the participation of women.

3. *In rural areas, find the combination of interventions that effectively enhance the human capital of the poor and improve access to basic services. Use cost-effective techniques to identify the priority groups (geographic and demographic targeting).*

■ Expand coverage of the Supplementary Food Program for Groups at Risk of Malnutrition (PACFO) to cover all children aged 6 months to 2 years in the poorest rural districts identified based on the poverty map. Since it is recognized that feeding programs are not the complete answer to improving nutritional status, to be effective, nutritional programs need to be combined with health programs and micronutrients fortification and supplementation. Education in primary health and nutrition and child-feeding and care practices in pregnancy and infancy are also recommended.

- However, feeding programs are not the complete answer to improving human capital. It is necessary to transform food programs and isolated health and educational programs into an integrated approach that takes advantage of their complementarities and provides certainty to families of achieving a minimum of well-being.
- Continue to finance infrastructure investments to ensure universal access to basic services, building on the National Compensation and Social Development Fund (FONCODES) experience and expanding it to include new municipal investment mechanisms.

4. *Consider increasing the overall financing of SSN programs to close to the average spending in middle-income countries of about 1 percent of gross domestic product (GDP).*
   - A stronger SSN would require increased funding. SSN spending is low compared to both national needs and regional standards. If the government aims to reduce poverty more substantially through redistribution of resources in favor of the poor, and to use the SSN to create synergies with other public interventions, higher spending may be required.
   - No pilot programs should be developed unless they can be financed in a sustainable way at a full level of deployment.

The Accountability Triangle Approach

This chapter embraces the conceptual framework developed in the 2004 *World Development Report* (WDR) that stresses that services will not work sufficiently well for the poor when governments do not feel the pressure to respond to citizen demands or cannot enforce basic performance rules with frontline service providers, and where citizens, especially poor citizens, have no control or choice over service providers. The WDR conceptualizes an approach that focuses on accountability mechanisms and power relations among policymakers, providers, and citizens/users. This approach emphasizes the role of three such relationships: the *political voice* of different citizen groups vis-à-vis policymakers in shaping policy design; the *compact* between policymakers and service providers; and *client power* (either through participation or through choice) of citizens vis-à-vis service providers.

Within such a framework there are two pathways of influence on the availability and quality of services for the poor.

- First, there is a short route of accountability when citizens/clients have a direct influence over service providers, either through participation in production, control over the decisionmaking process (what services are delivered, how, and to whom), or by monitoring their outcomes. The key word for this relationship is client *empowerment*.
- Second, there is a long route of accountability that involves the central and subnational governments as an intermediary agent. For this long route to work well, the government should be accountable to its citizens through the operation of

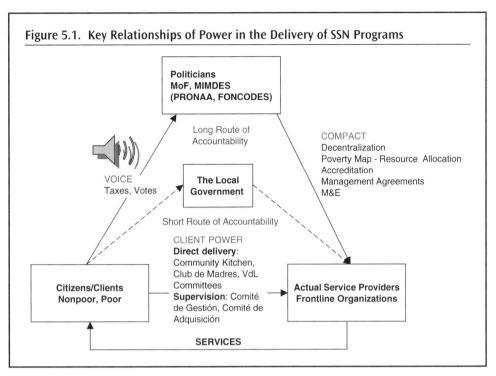

Figure 5.1. Key Relationships of Power in the Delivery of SSN Programs

Source: Based on *World Development Report 2004.*

political institutions that provide voice to and influence of citizens over political decisionmaking. The key word for this relationship is citizens' *voice.* On the other hand, the government should also be able to monitor frontline service providers so that they deliver the services for which they are paid in both adequate quantity and quality, and in a timely manner. The key word for this relationship is the *compact*—a clear and enforceable contract between the policymakers and frontline service providers. Strengthening the three relationships—empowerment, voice, and compact—would create the enabling environment for adequate service delivery, inclusive of the poor (Figure 5.1).

The main objective of accountability is to assure that safety net programs are used for poverty reduction in the short and long term, and to avoid exclusion errors (people that qualify but are not covered by the program) and inclusion errors (beneficiaries incorrectly included in the program), due to elite capture, corruption, rent-seeking, and clientelism.

Peru has taken important steps to establish an accountability framework for social service delivery. Table 5.1 presents the key institutions and accountability mechanisms that govern the provision of SSN services in the country. While the institutional framework for accountability includes a diversity of mechanisms and institutions, most of them apply only to the few programs that are decentralized. Many of these mechanisms are only in their incipient phase, and it is not yet clear how they will evolve.

Table 5.1. Accountability Mechanisms for SSN Programs in Peru

	Institutions/Mechanisms	Observation
Compact	Pro-poor budget allocation—allocation of public spending for food programs and basic social infrastructure to district municipalities using resource allocation index (based on Unsatisfied Basic Needs Index, population density, infrastructure deficit, chronic malnutrition rate for the population aged 6 to 9).	Used for only a few programs
	Accreditation of provincial and district municipalities that have implementing responsibilities following the decentralization of food and infrastructure programs—verification of minimum conditions to fulfill the responsibilities that are transferred (ex ante accountability).	Incipient, very bureaucratic
	Performance agreements (*Convenios de Gestión*) signed every year between the Ministry of Women and Social Development (MIMDES) and each accredited provincial or district municipality—they specify the resources transferred, the purpose for which they can be used, the targets that need to be complied with, and the monitoring requirements that need to be submitted periodically to MIMDES (ex post accountability).	Incipient, untested
	Strengthened Monitoring and Evaluation (M&E). An M&E system for social programs (SIME) is being developed by MIMDES. Main source of information for SIME comes from implementation reports municipalities are asked to submit every semester.	Incipient
Client Empowerment	Participation in service delivery: Community-Based Organizations (CBOs), (*Comedores Populares, Comités de Vaso de Leche, Club de Madres*, Parents Associations) directly involved in the delivery of services (selection of beneficiaries, preparation of meals, service delivery, oversight).	Access of poor beneficiaries is limited
	Participation in management and oversight: Management committee (*Comité de Gestión*)—made up of 3 representatives of CBOs, 1 from the municipality and 2 from PRONAA—role in defining the food basket, management of operations, distribution of food, oversight, preparation of monitoring reports.	Applies only to newly decentralized programs
	Procurement committees (*Comités de Adquisiciones*): Ensure transparency of food procurement; representatives of CBOs or civil society can participate as observers.	Incipient
	FONCODES Núcleo Ejecutor: 3 members are elected by the community and a fourth is appointed by the district mayor. Operates the FONCODES special account, hires project designer, buys inputs, hires skilled workers to execute the project, and oversees execution.	Incipient

(continued)

Table 5.1. Accountability Mechanisms for SSN Programs in Peru (*Continued*)

	Institutions/Mechanisms	Observation
Voice	Local Coordination Councils (*Consejo de Coordinación Local*) (civil society represents 40% of total) in charge of promoting participatory budgeting; facilitates participatory selection of projects to be included in the *Plan de Desarrollo Local Concertado*.	Poor rarely represented
	Mesas de concertación para la Lucha contra la Pobreza: Among other things, can supervise the procurement of food, and execution of infrastructure projects and maintenance.	Only in few municipalities
	Participatory Budgeting: A forum for citizens to be consulted in the selection of local investment projects.	Limited only to infrastructure
	Comité de Vigilancia: Created by Participatory Budgeting—social auditing committees that track expenditure, procurement.	Incipient/untested

Source: Compiled by author.

Despite these efforts, Peru still has a long way to go in developing and monitoring compliance with standards in several key areas: unit costs for interventions, spending level, and performance benchmarks in terms of share of expenditure reaching extreme poor or other vulnerable groups.

Key Issues of the Social Safety Net Sector

The Peruvian SSN is built around three types of programs: (a) food-based programs that distribute food to various target groups and with various objectives; (b) a social fund, FONCODES, that finances basic social infrastructure and income-generating projects in poor rural communities; and (c) workfare programs that offer temporary employment. Combined, SSN spending in 2003 constituted about 0.7 percent of GDP.[45]

Food-based Programs. In 2004, 27 food-based programs were in operation in Peru. The largest programs are the *Vaso de Leche* (Glass of Milk) program for young children, school feeding (school breakfast and school lunch), community kitchen (*Comedores Populares*) for children and adults, and several nutritional programs for infants and pregnant and lactating women. These programs reach 9.5 million beneficiaries, or 35 percent of the population. Spending for food-based programs is around 0.4 percent of GDP. Given the large coverage, the average subsidy per beneficiary is only US$2 per month. About 70 percent of the public spending reaches the poor (the bottom 55 percent of the population) and 30 percent goes to the extreme poor (the poorest consumption quintile; see Table 5.2).

---

45. To place things in context, the 0.7 percent of GDP spending on SSN compares to over 3 percent of GDP spending on pensions, most of it (over 85 percent) covered by public subsidies from the Central Government. In 2004 the Government undertook a Constitutional reform that will reduce the future liabilities of the civil servants pension regime.

Table 5.2. Social Protection Spending, 2003

	Spending		Number of Beneficiaries*		Distribution by Poverty Status**			Average Benefit/Month		Trends 2003/2000
	Mill. $	% of GDP	Thousands	% of Total	Extreme Poor	Poor	Non-Poor	$	US$	
Total Social Protection	**8,049**	**3.82**								
Total Social Insurance, of which:	**6,672**	**3.17**								
Pensions	6,672	3.17	704	2.6				790	239	←
Public subsidy	5,805	2.75								
Total Social Safety Net, of which:	**1,377**	**0.65**								
Food-based programs	**816**	**0.39**	9,520	34.9				7	2	
Glass of Milk (Vaso de Leche)	356	0.17	4,871	17.8	31	38	30	6	2	≈
School Breakfast (Desayunos Escolares)	117	0.06	1,542	5.6	47	33	20	6	2	←
Community Kitchen (Comedores Populares)	98	0.05	871	3.2	22	43	35	9	3	→
PACFO (food supplement for at risk children)	44	0.02	298	1.1				12	4	←
Wawa Wasi (daycare)	36	0.02	40	0.1				75	23	≈
School lunch (Almuerzos escolares)	24	0.01	496	1.8	40	40	19	4	1	≈
Total Workfare, of which:	**237**	**0.11**								
A Trabajar Urbano	157	0.07	77	0.3				300	91	↑↓
A Trabajar Rural	80	0.04	67 in 3 years					300	91	→

Total Social Fund/Community Driven Development	324	0.15				10	3 →
FONCODES—basic social infrastructure investments	204	0.10	n.a	n.a	13		→
PRONAMCHCS—natural resources management	120	0.06	n.a	n.a	87		
Pro Memoria							
Average monthly wage, net						1,628	493
Average net wage, unskilled worker						758	230
Minimum monthly net wage						427	129
GDP, Millions of Soles, 2003	210,746						
Population, '000s, 2005	27,926						

*Number of beneficiaries based on administrative sources.

**Distribution of beneficiaries based on household survey data; FONCODES distribution represents the distribution by district poverty.

Source: Based on data from MEF, Ministry of Labor, and MIMDES.

The Social Fund. The National Compensation and Social Development Fund (FON-CODES) was created in 1991 to finance small local investment projects. Its stated objectives were to generate employment, help alleviate poverty, and improve access to social services. The projects financed by FONCODES are demand driven and involve the community in execution and supervision. The most popular projects are the construction or rehabilitation of schools, health posts, water and sanitation systems, rural roads, secondary electrification schemes, and small-scale irrigation works. The social fund has been widely used in Peru to reach out to the poorest rural communities using poverty-map allocation methods and, in the past, absorbed more resources than those channeled through programs that provide direct transfers to households (meals in the case of food programs, or wages in the case of workfare programs). In 2004, FONCODES programs amounted to 0.15 percent of GDP, less than half of what it spent a few years ago.

Workfare Programs. There are two workfare programs operating in Peru, *A Trabajar Urbano* and *A Trabajar Rural,* which provide temporary employment opportunities for unskilled workers in poor areas, at relatively low wages. The programs provide work for up to six months on temporary public projects undertaken to renovate social infrastructure and perform general community maintenance work. They cover less than 0.5 percent of the population and most of the beneficiaries are from the poorest two consumption quintiles. In 2003, the budget for the two workfare programs amounted to 0.1 percent of GDP.

The Institutional Framework. Social protection programs—pensions, labor market policies, and social safety net programs—are scattered across a number of ministries and agencies, and levels of government. The Ministry of Economy and Finance (MEF) is in charge of the pension system and the largest food program, *Vaso de Leche.* The Ministry of Labor and Employment is in charge of the urban workfare program and other labor market interventions. The Ministry of Women and Social Development (MIMDES) is responsible for all the food-based programs other than *Vaso de Leche,* the social fund for basic infrastructure investments, FONCODES, the rural workfare program, and a number of programs for children and youth at risk, and other vulnerable groups such as internally displaced people and the elderly. Other ministries (housing, energy, and mining) are implementing subsidy schemes (housing, energy subsidy) that conceptually belong to the social protection sector too.

The Toledo administration developed a poverty alleviation strategy—*Guidelines for a Poverty Overcoming Strategy and Economic Opportunities for the Poor*—that outlined a reform of key SSN programs, but its implementation has moved at a slower pace than anticipated. The strategy had two key components: consolidation of food and infrastructure programs under MIMDES, and reorganization of and improvement in targeting and efficiency in the context of decentralized implementation of programs through local municipalities. The existing SSN programs were to be consolidated in three main programs: (a) a Local Development program, to transfer resources to create infrastructure and economic opportunities for the poor; (b) a Solidarity program, to transfer the resources currently used for food programs to improve the vulnerable group's quality of life; and (c) a Family Assistance program, to transfer resources to assist children and youth at risk, people affected by abuse and domestic violence, and families in catastrophic situations. However, these changes have only partially occurred; so far only the food programs and FONCODES have been transferred to MIMDES, and only some of them (community kitchens, food for work, shelters for youth, and FONCODES) have been partially decentralized. MIMDES has a more prominent role in policymaking and in the implementation of SSN policies, and has absorbed several autonomous agencies, including PRONAA and FONCODES. It also reorganized its function along the three pillars of the strategy, but the transferred programs maintained their autonomy and modus operandi, which constrained MIMDES' ability to play a stronger role.

The slow pace, lack of interest, and difficulties observed so far with the decentralization of food programs suggest that it might be desirable to reconsider the pace and extent of decentralization.

The remainder of this section reviews the key issues of the SSN sector in Peru.

Lack of Clear Priorities

The Peruvian SSN is extremely diverse and lacks strategic focus. There are about 30 national programs that address a large range of vulnerabilities (low income, political violence and displacement, domestic violence) or target groups (infants, school-age children, adults, and elderly). Most of these programs, however, have insufficient budgets compared to the problems they are intended to solve, or have only a limited regional focus, and thus are ineffective instruments for solving the problem nationwide.

Many of the programs operate on the false assumption that simple food transfers can solve a host of problems: material poverty, malnutrition, lack of local development, depressed agricultural or food markets, and lack of social capital or empowerment. In addition, nutritional interventions are unilaterally focused on the supply of food or food supplements, and pay insufficient attention to behavioral factors and informational constraints that severely restrict the efficacy of the intervention. Finally, food programs operate in isolation and rarely complement health and education interventions, thus missing synergies reaped by other similar programs in Latin America and the Caribbean (LAC) or other medium-income countries.

The life-cycle analysis presented in Table 5.3 suggests that the group with the highest risk of poverty and other forms of material deprivation are children living in extreme poverty. Children are the age group with the highest incidence of poverty, and constitute the largest group of poor. A majority of poor children are also affected by forms of deprivation other than consumption poverty, such as high rates of infant mortality, malnutrition, school dropout, or low academic achievement. Infant mortality reaches 64 per 1,000 in the poorest quintile, more than twice that in the richest quintile (average of 28 per 1,000 in the region). The rate of chronic malnutrition (stunting) is extremely high among children from extreme poor households (47 percent), and these children accounted for 53 percent of the total cases in the country in 2000. Access to education services, although improved substantially in recent decades, fails the poorest. About one-third of the students from the poorest quintile (in extreme poverty) do not complete primary education by age 14. There is a marked difference between the school enrollment rate for children from the poorest quintile and other children. The poorest children join primary school later, repeat grades more often, and drop out earlier. These behaviors have irreparable developmental costs for both the children and society. Other priority groups are some of the elderly without pensions

Table 5.3. Circumstances Aggravating Poverty and Leading Indicators of Deprivation, by Main Age Group and Quintile

Age Group Years	Circumstances Aggravating Poverty	Indicators of Deprivation	Share of Individuals Affected in Each Age Group, by Quintile (%)					Total ('000s)	
			Poorest	2nd	3rd	4th	Richest	Affected	Population
0–5	Mortality	Infant mortality rate	64	54	33	27	14	26	608
	Mortality	Under-5 mortality rate	93	76	44	35	18	184	3,040
	Malnutrition	Stunting	47	31	17	7	5	775	3,040
	Malnutrition	Underweight	15	7	3	2	1	213	3,040
	Not attending school	Not in preschool (3–5)	61	48	39	29	25	835	1,824
6–11	Low human capital	Not attending school	11	7	5	3	3	273	3,827
	Low human capital	Child labor (10–11)	53	26	19	15	9	342	1,276
12–16	Low human capital	Not attending school	26	18	14	8	8	527	3,125
	Low human capital	Late age for grade	33	27	19	11	7	589	3,125
	Low human capital	Child labor (12–14)	53	26	19	15	9	502	1,875
17–24	Low human capital	Not attending school (17–22)	76	73	70	61	50	2,684	4,031
	Employment	Youth unemployment	15	15	16	15	14	612	4,031
25–54	Low human capital	Illiteracy	22	16	11	7	3	1,131	9,696
	Low income	Unemployment	5	6	8	7	7	648	9,696
	Low income	Without social insurance	99	94	83	71	52	8,010	9,696

55–64	Low human capital	Illiteracy	25	31	23	19	9	366	1,760
	Employment	Unemployment	5	6	8	7	7	118	1,760
	Employment	Without social insurance	97	89	80	67	51	1,348	1,760
over 65	Low human capital	Illiteracy	20	24	28	23	15	395	1,829
	Low income	Elderly working	51	53	42	34	27	723	1,829
	Low income	No old-age pension	95	90	81	74	62	1,425	1,829
	Low income	No pension in HHs	92	82	73	60	41	1,216	1,829
Total population									**27,308**

Note: Infant and under-5 mortality rates are deaths under 12 months or 5 years per 1,000 live births. Stunting rate represents the share of children under 5 whose height-for-age is lower than 2 standard deviations (z score). Underweight is the share of children under 5 whose weight-for-age is below 2 standard deviations (z scores). All indicators for school nonattendance indicate the share of children in a given age group not attending any type of school. Late age for grade is the share of school children with ages higher than the expected age. Late age for grade may be due to grade repetition or late school entry. Unemployment represents the share of individuals aged 14 and older who are not working, are seeking work, and are ready to start working in seven days if they found a job. Prevalence of child labor is taken from World Bank (2004a).

Source: Author's calculations using data from ENAHO 2003 (INEI), and DHS 2000 (INEI).

or other means, the disabled, and internally displaced persons. A large share of SSN spending is focused on children in Peru, which suggests a desire to attend poor children first. This focus seems justified.

SSN Spending is Low Relative to the Poverty Gap of the Poor and by Regional Standards

Peru spends 0.7 percent of GDP on its social safety net. This can be compared with the *poverty gap* of the total poor of 6.3 percent of GDP (the amount the poor would require to afford the consumption basket that would raise them to the poverty line), or it can be compared with the *consumption deficit* of the extreme poor of 1.1 percent of GDP (what would be needed for the extreme poor to live on US$1 a day, so they could afford just a food basket providing minimum caloric intake). It is not expected that the poverty gap of the poor will be covered only through redistribution—a substantial share of them would be able to escape poverty through broad-based economic growth. For a large share of the extremely poor, however, the public safety net is their only hope. The SSN resources allocated in Peru are low even if focused toward this group.

Focusing a larger share of existing resources on the extreme poor (the poorest consumption quintile) may have a sizable impact on reducing the poverty gap for extreme poor households, but it is not sufficient to make a substantial dent in the level of extreme poverty. Even under the perfect targeting assumption—if all public subsidies channeled through SSN programs are captured entirely by households in extreme poverty—the poverty gap would fall by a maximum 40 percent of its current level (Figure 5.2).

In spite of being low, SSN spending has decreased since 2000 (Figure 5.3). The economic crisis that hit the country in 1998 and the recession that followed found the country unprepared to protect the level of SSN spending, precisely at a time when it was most needed. The incidence of poverty increased by one-third between 1997 and 2001, reaching over 50 percent of the population, but SSN spending was not adjusted to these new circumstances, or even after the economy started to recover, though poverty remained stagnant.

SSN spending is also low by regional standards. Peru spends almost half of the average for the LAC region of 1.5 percent of GDP (Figure 5.4). With lower spending, Peru covers a much larger fraction of the population than other countries in the region. This implies that the few public resources are overambitiously split across a large number of beneficiaries, which means that the average value of transfers represents a small fraction relative to the consumption deficit of the poor households.

The actual budget transferred to the population is further reduced by high administrative costs associated with administration of food programs. The administrative costs of food-based programs tend to be high relative to the size of the net benefit for households. On average, the food distribution agency PRONAA spends about 15 to 18 percent on administrative costs at the central level. Additional costs to bring the food to the beneficiaries are borne at the provincial and district levels by the municipalities or the beneficiaries themselves. The administrative costs are substantially higher than for cash transfers, where they range between 5 and 12 percent, including the targeting costs (Castaneda and others [2005] for Latin America; Tesliuc and others [2005] for Europe and Central Asia). An even greater cost is probably imposed on the programs by the use of procurement rules that are

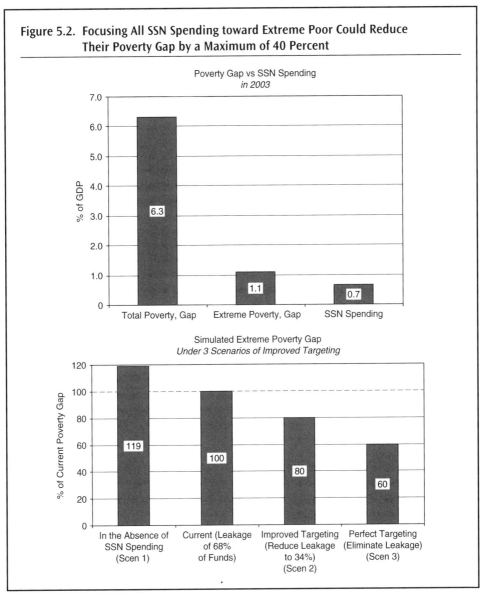

Figure 5.2. **Focusing All SSN Spending toward Extreme Poor Could Reduce Their Poverty Gap by a Maximum of 40 Percent**

Note: In the right panel, comparisons are to the current level of the poverty gap (the one measured in ENAHO 2003, which reflects the current distribution of public subsidy associated with SSN programs) with a simulated poverty gap for households in extreme poverty under three scenarios: in the absence of SSN (scenario 1); improving targeting, that is, reducing leakage by 50 percent (scenario 2); and under perfect targeting, that is, eliminating leakage (scenario 3).
Source: Author's estimates based on ENAHO 2003/04 data.

not sufficiently competitive and transparent. Much more food would be available to the beneficiaries if simple and transparent systems were implemented and if purchases were made in larger markets than is the case today, when purchases are fragmented into hundreds of small transactions and no comparisons are made among the prices paid in different locations.

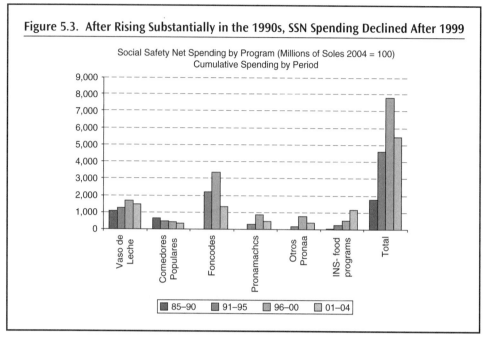

Figure 5.3. After Rising Substantially in the 1990s, SSN Spending Declined After 1999

Note: The spending includes *Vaso de Leche*, FONCODES, PRONOMACHCS, and food programs adminis-tered by PRONAA or the NIH.

Source: Cuanto (1992, 1994, 1997, 2004); Naranjo (1992); PRONAA database 1992–2004; FONCODES (2003); PRONOMACHCS (2004); MINAG (http://www.portalagrario.gob.pe/seg_alimentaria/seg_cap4.shtml).

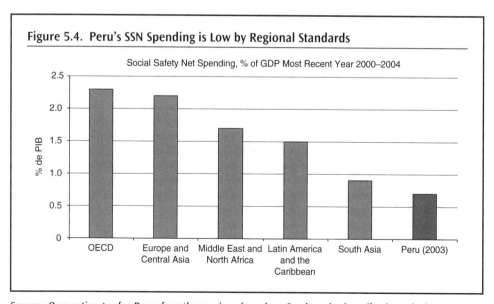

Figure 5.4. Peru's SSN Spending is Low by Regional Standards

Source: Own estimates for Peru; for other regions based on Grosh and others (forthcoming).

SSN Programs Have Relatively High Coverage but Transfer Extremely Small Benefits

Compared to other SSN programs in the LAC region, Peruvian food programs have high coverage, but low adequacy (Figure 5.5). Adequacy means the ratio of the SSN transfer relative to the consumption of the beneficiary. Over 40 percent of the Peruvian population lives in households where at least one member benefits from some type of food program. The coverage of food programs in Peru is higher than the overall social assistance coverage in countries such as Argentina, Brazil, Chile, and Columbia, countries known for having well-developed systems of social assistance. However, with lower public spending and higher coverage than in other countries in the region, the immediate outcome is that the average value of transfers per person is between 5 times and 20 times smaller in Peru than

Figure 5.5. Compared to Other LAC Countries, Peru's SSN Programs Have High Coverage, But are Not Generous

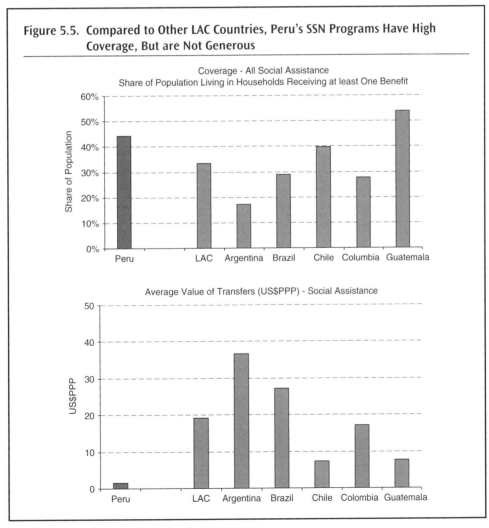

Source: Based on Lindert, Skoufias, and Shapiro (2005, forthcoming).

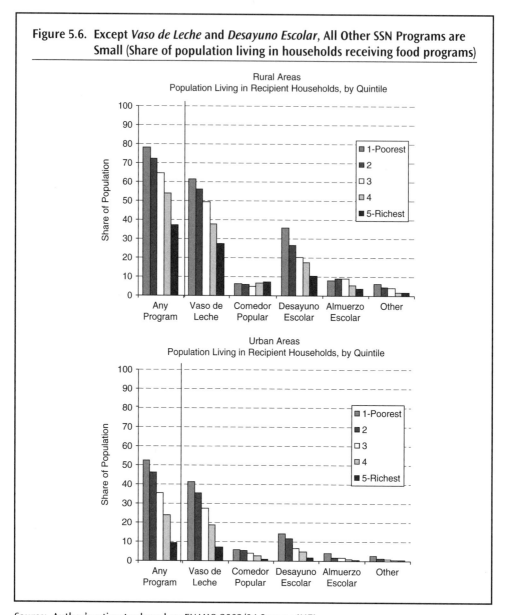

Figure 5.6. Except *Vaso de Leche* and *Desayuno Escolar*, All Other SSN Programs are Small (Share of population living in households receiving food programs)

Source: Author's estimates based on ENAHO 2003/04 Survey, INEI.

in other countries (Figure 5.5; lower panel). The monetary equivalent of the food programs represents less than 2 percent of total household consumption of beneficiary households. The most popular program, *Vaso de Leche*, transfers, on average, less than US$2 per month per beneficiary, or the equivalent of 5 percent of the extreme poverty line of about US$1 per day.

In the aggregate, Peru scores high on coverage of the poor with SSN programs compared to other LAC countries, and this is almost entirely due to two programs: *Vaso de Leche* and *Desayuno Escolar*. All other programs cover substantially less than 5 percent of the population. Consolidating some of these tiny programs may economize on scarce human and financial resources, and capture economies of scale.

Rural residents are better covered than urban residents. This is a positive feature of the Peruvian SSN system, given the higher incidence of poverty and extreme poverty in rural areas (Figure 5.6). Although the coverage of poor children in rural areas is relatively higher than in urban areas, reaching out to the remaining poor children in rural areas could prove very difficult and costly given the complicated geography in certain areas.

The correct way to analyze how effective the food programs are in reaching their beneficiaries is to analyze the coverage relative to the target group of each program. For example, the primary target of *Vaso de Leche* is children under age 7, *Almuerzos* and *Desayunos Escolares* targets school-aged children in poor areas, and *Comedores Populares* targets all poor households.

With the exception of *Vaso de Leche* and *Desayuno Escolar*, which cover 44 percent and 17 percent of their target groups, respectively, all other food-based or workfare programs are not effective in covering their target group (Figure 5.7). To cover its target group of "all poor households," the budget of *Comedores Populares* would have to grow by more than 10 times—clearly an unfeasible scenario. If programs are small compared to their target groups, they fail to accomplish their objectives, and the selection of beneficiaries is prone to political manipulation.

Recently, the government announced its intention to introduce a new program—*Juntos*—to provide 100 NS per month to poor families with children conditional on attending school and using preventive health services. The intended goal would be to cover about 10 percent of the population. If perfectly targeted to the extremely poor, about half of them could benefit. At the moment, the design of the program is not clear, and its financing is only partially secured. Depending on coverage, the cost of the program could be substantial (Box 5.1).

Conditional cash-transfer programs are becoming increasingly popular in several countries, and emphasize the use of demand-side interventions to directly support the poor and encourage investments in their own human capital. There is clear evidence of success from the first generation of programs in Colombia, Mexico, and Nicaragua in increasing enrollment rates, improving preventive health care, and raising household consumption (Rawlings and Rubio 2005). Nevertheless, their success in other countries depends on the implementation capacity to administer a conditional cash transfer and on the coverage and quality of the supply in the health and education sectors.

While SSN Programs in Peru Have Better Targeting Performance Than Some Argue, It can Still be Significantly Improved

Many analyses of the food programs in Peru point to inadequate targeting and large leakages toward unintended beneficiaries (Vasquez 2005; Alcazar 2003). This report, however, points out that while most of the resources do not reach *only* the extreme poor, a large part of benefits go to the extreme and moderate poor. In fact, relative to other food programs in LAC, the food programs operating in Peru have *better* targeting performance. As illustrated in Figure 5.9, Peru's food programs outperform similar programs in Colombia and Guatemala. (See Box 5.2 for an explanation of how Peru achieves good targeting performance.)

However, targeting performance of feeding programs is below that of other cash programs in LAC, the Europe and Central Asia (ECA) region, and Organisation for Economic

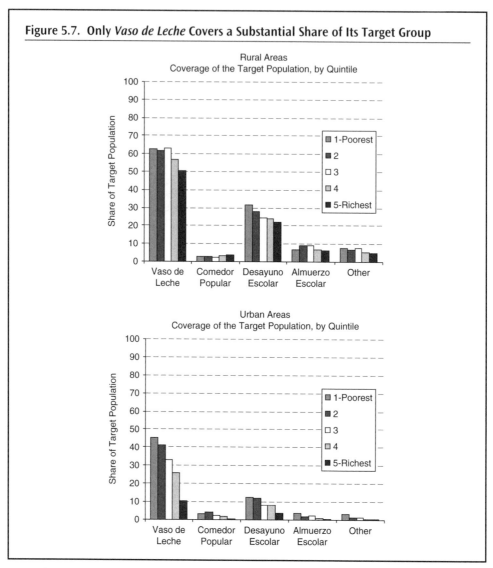

Figure 5.7. Only *Vaso de Leche* Covers a Substantial Share of Its Target Group

Note: The target group for *Vaso de Leche* is children aged 0 to 6 and pregnant and lactating mothers; for *Comedor Popular* it is poor families; for *Desayuno* and *Almuerzo Escolar* it is children aged 7 to 13. The category "other" includes PACFO, PANFAR, and WAWA WASI and targets children under age 3.
Source: Author's estimates based on ENAHO 2003/04 Survey, INEI.

Co-operation and Development (OECD) countries (Figure 5.10). There are two factors that might explain the underperformance of Peru's food programs. First, by design, the relative income threshold used to target SSN benefits is substantially higher in Peru than in OECD, ECA, and some LAC countries. Peru's programs target the poorest 50 percent of the population. In contrast, most programs in OECD and ECA countries target the poorest 10 percent of the population, while the other LAC comparators focus on the poorest 20 percent. Second, only a few (and small) programs in Peru use targeting methods associated with higher targeting performance, such as individuals or household-level targeting (means or proxy means tests).

Box 5.1: *Juntos:* A Conditional Cash Transfer—Cost and Potential Impact on Poverty

Coverage. The government proposal suggests that the program would cover 128,000 poor families with children in 70 rural districts in the initial phase (September–December 2005), and could reach 600,000 households (3 million individuals) when fully deployed, by May 2006. To place things in the context, in 2003, 6 million Peruvians were extremely poor (one-fifth of the total population of 27 million) and 85 percent of the extremely poor households (of about 1 million) have children. This implies that the program could cover about 10 percent of the total population or, if perfectly targeted, 50 percent of the extreme poor. *Juntos* would rank as the third-largest program, after *Vaso de Leche* and *Desayunos Escolares*, based on coverage.

Financing. The program cost is estimated to be US$37 million for the initial stage, of which, 60 percent represent the direct transfers, 30 percent the cost of health supply interventions, and 10 percent administrative costs. The cost of direct transfers could reach US$225 million by 2006, or 0.34 percent of GDP when the program would be fully implemented, making it the largest SSN program in terms of budget.

Potential Poverty Impact. The maximum redistributive impact of *Juntos* could be achieved if the program covered only the rural areas. A well-targeted transfer to rural households with children (about 630,000) could make a substantial dent in the level of extreme poverty, both among the recipients and at the national level. The poverty headcount among beneficiaries could decrease by 25 percent, while the poverty gap could decrease by as much as 40 percent (Figure 5.8). However, this simulated impact on poverty would have to be considered as a maximum level that could be achieved under the strong assumption of perfect targeting and no exclusion errors.

Figure 5.8. Simulated Reduction in Extreme Poverty

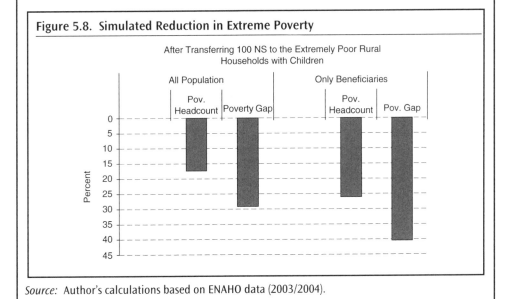

Source: Author's calculations based on ENAHO data (2003/2004).

Overall, Food Programs Have Low Impact on Reducing Poverty

The small amount of public resources allocated to food programs are spread too thinly among a large share of the population, which limits their impact on poverty and inequality (Figure 5.11). In the absence of food programs the poverty headcount would increase from 54.7 percent to 55.2 percent, a change that is not statistically significant. The impact of food programs is larger on extreme poverty; in the absence of the programs the headcount would increase by 4 percent. Food-based programs also have a modest impact on reducing inequality

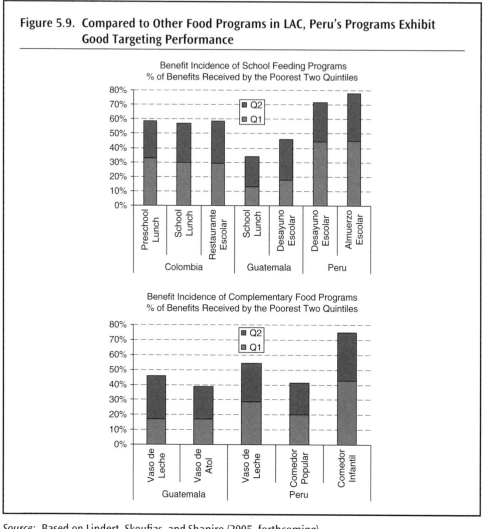

Figure 5.9. Compared to Other Food Programs in LAC, Peru's Programs Exhibit Good Targeting Performance

Source: Based on Lindert, Skoufias, and Shapiro (2005, forthcoming).

Box 5.2: How Peru Achieves Good Targeting Performance

Peru's comparatively good targeting performance of food-based programs is due mostly to high-quality geographic targeting. The country has a long history of developing and using poverty maps to target expenditures to poor areas. The first map was produced as early as 1977, based on an index of unmeet basic needs. Since 1991, FONCODES developed district-level poverty maps based on unmet basic needs (UBN) techniques, and used them to redirect social expenditure toward the poor areas. After 1996, INEI developed improved poverty maps based on census and survey data used by the Ministry of Economy and Finance to allocate pro-poor spending toward the poorest rural areas.

Nowadays, though all public spending on SSN is allocated using a pro-poor allocation index, frequent adjustments are made to continue historical allocation (such as for community kitchens) or to comply with legislation that protects the resources for some regions (such as legislation requiring that one-third of the *Vaso de Leche* budget be directed to Lima and Callao).

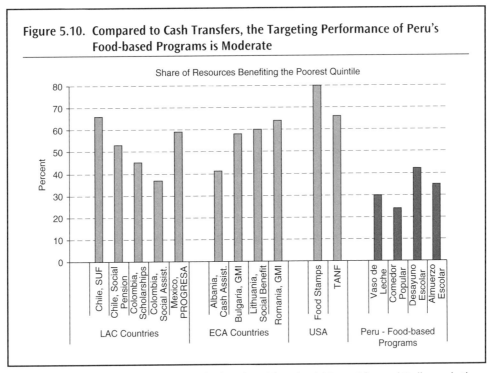

Figure 5.10. Compared to Cash Transfers, the Targeting Performance of Peru's Food-based Programs is Moderate

Source: The author for Peru; Castaneda and others (2005) for other LAC countries; and Tesliuc and others (2005, forthcoming) for the ECA region.

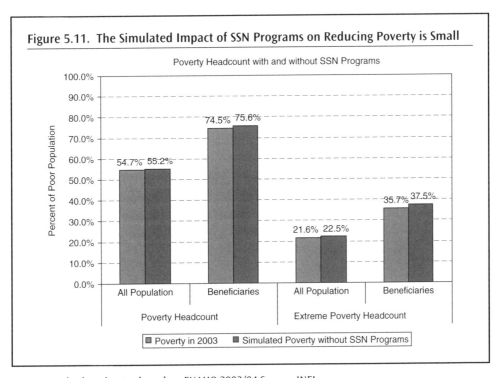

Figure 5.11. The Simulated Impact of SSN Programs on Reducing Poverty is Small

Source: Author's estimates based on ENAHO 2003/04 Survey, INEI.

(they contribute 0.5 percent to the reduction in the Gini index of consumption per capita). The small impact on poverty or inequality reduction is due to the fairly low level of the overall budget, and to the low level of the public subsidy transferred to a beneficiary.

Food-based Programs also Proved Ineffective in Reducing Malnutrition

Despite implementation of several food programs, the malnutrition rate in Peru continues to be high. Child malnutrition, although halved between 1991 and 2000, persists at high rates among the poor: while overall, 26 percent of children suffered from some degree of chronic malnutrition (by the height-for-age standard), 47 percent of the children in the poorest quintile were affected in 2000. The question is, Why does so much malnutrition coexist with so many food programs?

One reason is that only a few of the programs target children under 2 years of age. While malnutrition can be combated effectively for children under age 2 and for pregnant and lactating women, the largest share of benefits goes to older children, and even adults. Moreover, Peru devotes a disproportionate amount of its food and nutrition program budget to simply purchasing and distributing food, as opposed to supporting the longer-term strategies that focus on prevention, promotion, and sustainable behavior-based solutions. The mere transfer of food is too often taken as equivalent to nutritional benefit, even though there is no evidence of their nutritional impact, and less attention is given to debilitating micronutrient deficiencies.

In rural areas PACFO is a program with high potential to prevent the debilitating effects of malnutrition. From the plethora of food-assistance programs, only one program—the Supplementary Food Program for Groups at Risk of Malnutrition (PACFO)—focuses specifically on the age group when malnutrition can be combated effectively. PACFO's impact evaluation revealed excellent targeting performance and relatively good nutrition outcomes (Maximize and Cuánto 2003). The program, however, has a small budget and operates only in eight departments, which implies that important groups among the poor children at risk of malnutrition are not covered. In addition, it appears that after the transfer of the program from the National Institute of Health to PRONAA, the health education component of the program has been weakened.

To improve the nutritional outcome of the program, as suggested by the impact evaluation, it is important to strengthen the health and nutrition education for mothers with regard to food preparation, hygiene conditions, complementary feeding, intrahousehold distribution, and improving knowledge and practices around childcare during infancy.

The existing food programs are hard to reform because they enjoy legitimacy and because very often their role and performance have been misunderstood.

The implementation of food-based programs via community-based organizations (CBOs) brought substantial advantages in the early stages of development: it avoided the creation of a large public administration apparatus and induced a multiplier effect in terms of population covered and resources mobilized, which contributed to social capital and to the empowerment of women. Many of Peru's food-based programs emerged as a survival strategy when massive migration from rural to urban areas produced large impoverished squatter settlements on the outskirts of large cities. The rural migrants and the urban poor formed clubs and service organizations to improve their conditions, and only later benefited from government or donor support. The government focused more on the geographical distribution of resources using poverty maps, a tool that could be implemented by the central authorities in Lima and which could be monitored easily without the need to maintain a large public administration, and relied on the CBOs to reach the poor within a specific area.

With time, however, this model reached its limits, and many poor people remain underserved. Some programs have been captured by those beneficiaries who gained access to the public subsidies in the first place. The government did not enforce exit policies, fearing loss of political support, and even legislated loopholes allowing beneficiaries to continue to remain in the program after they were no longer entitled (such as the *Vaso de Leche* legislation that allows a "secondary" target group—children aged 7 to 13—to benefit from a program that is intended primarily for children aged 0 to 6). Since the program budget is fixed, the low exit rate from the program means that many poor households with younger children are not entering the program, though they may need the benefits offered.

Currently, the CBO-based model is conducive to an inflexible spending allocation. The government has very little space to reorient spending toward new and poorer constituencies; in fact, only the marginal increase in the program budget could be assigned to poorer areas, as happened during 2001–04. The flexibility to allocate funds to the poorest areas greatly depends on whether the program has an established constituency of beneficiaries, as shown in Figure 5.12.

- ■ When programs target only districts with a high risk of deprivation and attend beneficiaries only for a very short period of time (as in the case of PACFO), the allocation is very progressive: the poorest 20 percent of the population receives 60 percent of the resources.
- ■ The geographic allocation is very progressive when programs do not operate through an ingrained constituency, and therefore is not influenced by the historical allocation in the previous years. This is the case of FONCODES, where the project cycle starts all over again every year, and does not depend on the previous allocation.
- ■ In the case of *Vaso de Leche,* the distribution is moderately progressive, while for *Comedores Populares,* it is almost regressive, suggesting that the distribution of funds is close to the one that will occur in the absence of any geographic targeting. Most likely this is because the government finds it difficult to stop serving existing beneficiaries, and only the marginal increase in the budget is allocated based on pro-poor criteria.

Although programs implemented through CBOs are hard to reform, there are measures that could improve their performance without generating much resistance. For example, implementation of *Vaso de Leche* could be strengthened in urban areas to keep within the program's intended objective. In its original design, the program includes a feature that is a key for self-selection of the poor into the program but which works well mainly in urban or densely populated areas. The food is cooked early every morning by a rotating group of mothers. Beneficiaries either participate in the cooking of the food or (if it is not their turn to cook), they must collect the cooked food, usually at around 6:00 a.m. Cooking or collecting the food involves a significant cost in time and effort. Given that the benefit is relatively small, only families that truly need the food are willing to pay the costs of participating in the program.

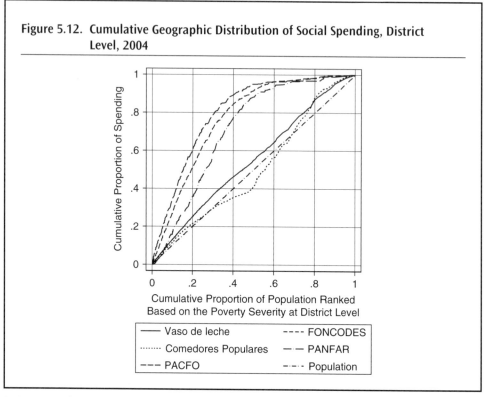

Figure 5.12. Cumulative Geographic Distribution of Social Spending, District Level, 2004

PACFO = Supplementary Food Program for Groups at Risk of Malnutrition.
PANFAR = Food and Nutrition Program for Families at Risk of Malnutrition.
FONCODES = National Compensation and Social Development Fund.
Source: Author's calculations based on MEF data on geographical allocation of resources (2004).

The main issue with *Vaso de Leche* is that over time there has been a weakening in pursuing the original objectives of the program. First, a large share of the beneficiaries (as many as 80 percent in rural areas) receives the benefit in bulk at large intervals, often in the form of evaporated milk, which is more expensive and increases the chance that the product will be shared within the household (as documented by the 2003 public expenditure tracking survey) or used in barter for other goods or services (as revealed by discussions in focus groups). Second, the priority group (children aged 0 to 6) was crowded out over time by beneficiaries in other age groups. In 2003, according to the Comptroller General's Office, only 58 percent of the beneficiaries were from the priority group of children aged 0 to 6, compared to 69 percent in 2001.

FONCODES and the Provision of Infrastructure Investments: A Model Upon Which to Build to Improve Access to Basic Services for Poor Rural Areas

A number of studies (Schady 2005; Apoyo 2000; Paxon and Schady 2002) have shown that, by financing infrastructure investments preferred by local communities, FONCODES expanded access to basic social services, and that investments have reached the poor districts and poor households within those districts. In 2004, the poorer 40 percent of the population lived in districts receiving almost 80 percent of FONCODES resources. Peru's FONCODES cumulative geographic distribution is also more progressive than that of social funds in other countries in the world, such as Bolivia, Nicaragua, Honduras, Zambia, or Armenia, largely because of its predominantly rural focus and the use of poverty maps in selecting the districts (Rawlings, Sherburne, and Van Domelen 2004). The innovative modus operandi of FONCODES (simplified procurement rules, demand-driven community projects, and targeting of investments using "poverty maps" to assign resources to small rural communities) translated into over 40,000 projects for the construction or rehabilitation of schools, health posts, water and sanitation systems, rural roads, and secondary electrification schemes for a total of more than US$2 billion over 14 years of operation.

During the Toledo administration the FONCODES resources have been reduced by half compared to the previous decade, and its institutional capacity has been weakened. Between 1991 and 2001 FONCODES had a working methodology that favored establishing direct links between the Central Government and rural community groups, but had two major drawbacks: (a) its bypass of local governments, and (b) its autonomy in setting sector policies independently of the relevant sector line ministries. Both aspects had negative consequences for institutional development and investment impact and sustainability. Since 2001, the government has taken several measures to address these shortcomings. First, the autonomy of FONCODES in setting up its policy was gradually diminished by removing its executing agency power and integrating it into MIMDES. Second, an attempt was made to transform FONCODES into an implementation agency that is subcontracted by sector line ministries to carry out investment projects according to rules defined by those ministries. Neither of these measures, however, improved the coordination with respect to infrastructure investments at the municipal level.

Starting in 2003, as part of the strategy to decentralize social programs to municipalities, FONCODES was among the first social programs to be transferred to district municipalities, but the decentralization has been conducted so far in an ad hoc manner, without first developing the fundamental elements of the new model of decentralized provision of small-scale infrastructure. Rushed by a tight deadline for starting the transfer process, and in a context of reorganization of MIMDES, so far the decentralization of FONCODES has consisted of only marginal increases in the role that local governments play in the FONCODES project cycle. The new "decentralized" project cycle still falls far short of the expectation of delegating investment responsibilities and resources to district governments. At the root of these problems is the fact that the transfer process has been driven more by the logic of transferring individual subprojects to district governments than by a new, concerted model for decentralized provision of small-scale infrastructure.

Review of Research-based Peruvian Literature

There is a rich domestic literature that analyzes the performance of Peruvian SSN programs. Most policy analyses have focused on such issues as how well the programs are targeted to the poor, what the nutritional impact of food programs is, what impact workfare programs have on household earnings, and the allocation of basic infrastructure investments toward poor communities. Table 5.4 summarizes key policy recommendations from a subset of this rich literature, focusing on the most recent, and Table 5.5 reviews the results of impact evaluation studies.

Table 5.4. Summary of Policy Recommendations in Peruvian Literature

	Vásquez	Franke	Blondett	Bustamante	Chacaltana	Trivelli	Alcazar & Wachtenheim	Valdivia
Clarify objectives of food programs	✓	✓					✓	
Focus on key priority groups and areas:								
■ Children	✓	✓						
■ Extreme poor	✓	✓			✓		✓	
■ Rural areas		✓						✓
■ Outside of Lima								
Increase spending on social assistance		✓						
Establish distinct strategies for rural and urban areas		✓						
Enhance *Vaso de Leche* by adding complementary interventions				✓				
Consolidate nutritional programs and emulate the PACFO model to be used in rural areas	✓							
Redesign, merge, or close programs with substantial leakage	✓						✓	
Restructure all feeding programs into a unified intervention							✓	
Develop new interventions to stimulate the accumulation of human capital/conditional cash transfer	✓						✓	

Recommendation						
Improve targeting:						
Individual targeting	✓					
Categorical (age)		✓				
Geographic targeting		✓		✓		
Self-selection/type of food						
Work test						
Create a Beneficiary Identification System	✓					
Work with CBOs to accept graduation/exit rules	✓	✓			✓	
Offer services to CBOs to help them generate income and become self-sustaining	✓		✓		✓	
Programs should take advantage of existing organizations and social networks			✓		✓	
Design different instruments for chronically poor (transfers) and transitory poor (insurance)				✓		
Enhanced monitoring and evaluation	✓	✓				✓

Table 5.5. Summary of Impact Evaluations of SSN Programs in Peru

Program	Evaluation Period	Coverage	Data	Evaluation Method	Authors/ Year	Main Results
Vaso de Leche	1999–2000	National	ENNIV 2000, 1993 Census, Census of health infrastructure, FONCODES poverty map	Quasi-experimental—propensity score matching	Gajate and Itunirregui 2002	The dependent variable considered is the height-for-age as a measure of chronic malnutrition. ■ The impact of the program was significantly negative for different model specifications. The authors acknowledge the possibility that the results are affected by (a) omitted variables such as the nutritional status of the mother or the birth order of the child and (b) selection bias—only mothers with severely malnourished children participate in the program due to stigma (reverse causality).
Vaso de Leche	December 2001–April 2002	Ancash, Arequipa, Cajamarca Cusco, Loreto y Piura	Program monthly spending registries, ENAHO 1998–2000, ENNIV 1994 and 1997, DHS 1996/ 2000	Quasi-experimental—instrumental variable	Stiefel and Alderman 2003	The study asks, If a community-based, multistage targeting scheme is progressive, is it possible that the program can achieve its nutritional objective? The dependent variable considered is the height-for-age. ■ *Vaso de Leche* (VdL) program is well targeted to poor households and to those with low nutritional status. ■ The impact of VdL beyond its value as income transfer is limited, however. Transfers of milk and milk substitutes from VdL are inframarginal for approximately half of the households that receive them. ■ The study finds no impact of the VdL expenditure on the nutritional outcomes of young children, the group to which the program is targeted.
Vaso de Leche	2002	National	ENAHO Public Expenditure Tracking Survey	Public expenditure tracking survey	Lopez-Calix, Alcazar, Wachtemheim (2002)	■ Very small leakage during the transfer from the Central Government to the municipalities and from municipalities to the local committees. ■ Important leakage in the distribution from the committees to the households; further dilution intrahousehold. ■ Targeted beneficiaries get on average 29 cents of each dollar initially transferred by the central government.

Program	Year	Location	Instrument	Design	Author	Findings
Desayuno Escolar	1993	Huaraz	Specialized survey—treatment and control group: baseline, first- and second-round measurement	Experimental design: 10 schools systematically selected—5 rural schools in the control group (151 students) and 5 in the treatment group (201 students)	Pollit, Jacoby, and Cueto 1996	Targeted beneficiaries get on average 29 cents of each dollar initially transferred by the central government. The study measures the impact of the program on caloric intake, school attendance, and cognitive capacity. Findings: ■ Significant increase in caloric intake for children in the treatment group. ■ Significant increase in school attendance. ■ No significant differences in cognitive capacity as measured by testing in reading comprehension, vocabulary, and mathematics.
Desayuno Escolar	1998	Apurimac y Cusco	Survey done by evaluators	Quasi-experimental design Treatment group in Apurimac (300 4th grade students) and control group in Cusco (290 4th grade students)	Cueto and Chinen 2001	The study measures the impact on height, weight, enrollment, and school dropout, school attendance, cognitive aptitudes, and performance in math and reading comprehension. ■ Body mass index, standardized height-for-age and weight-for-age are not statistically different between the control and treatment groups. ■ Positive impact on hemoglobin level. ■ No significant difference between groups with respect to cognitive aptitudes, except for short-term memorizing aptitudes. ■ School attendance is higher in the treatment group. However, because no baseline information was available, the difference cannot be attributed to the program. ■ Instructional time was reduced because time was allocated for the students to consume the food, and teachers had to dedicate time to preparing the *Desayuno Escolar*.

(*continued*)

Table 5.5. Summary of Impact Evaluations of SSN Programs in Peru (*Continued*)

Program	Evaluation Period	Coverage	Data	Evaluation Method	Authors/ Year	Main Results
PACFO	2002	7 depart-ments		Treatment group in Apurimac Ayacucho and control group in Ancash	Maximize/ Cuanto	▪ Low leakage (9%) and high coverage (73%) of the target group (children aged 6 month to 3 years). ▪ In two departments (Cusco and Puno) a statistically significant reduction in the incidence of chronic malnutrition. ▪ In two other departments (Apurimac and Ayacucho), no significant change in the incidence of chronic malnutrition.
A Trabajar Urbano	2nd round May 2002	Ancash, Cusco, Junin, La Libertad, Lima, Loreto, Piura, Puno, and Ucayali	Beneficiary survey and ENAHO 2002	Quasi-experimental—propensity score matching	Chacaltana (2003)	▪ Most of the beneficiaries are poor (75% of the resources went to the poorest 40% of the population). ▪ The net gain to workers is a small share of the nominal wage paid; in the absence of the program, the beneficiaries could have obtained 80% of the wage paid by the program by engaging in other activities. ▪ The wage was set too high to promote self-selection. ▪ Labor intensive—70 to 80% of the project costs were labor costs.
FONCODES	1996–99	Rural area in 17 departments	Survey done by evaluators	Quasi-experimental	Instituto Apoyo	▪ *Education:* The number of enrolled students increased by 34, the number of classrooms increased by 1, the number of grades by 1.6; the probability of offering secondary education increased by 15%. ▪ *Water and sanitation:* The probability of diarrhea among children decreased by 3%; the latrines had no effect on the incidence of diarrhea; the sewage projects had no significant impact on the incidence of diarrhea. ▪ *Electrification:* The value of housing increased by 2,000 Soles.

Other nonexperimental

Food programs	2000	National	ENAHO 2000	Nonexperimental average and marginal benefit incidence analysis	Valdivia (2005)	▪ Large leakage: 40 to 50% of beneficiaries fell outside the target group either because they were not poor or because they were outside the age range; the leakage is higher for VdL and urban areas. ▪ *Desayuno Escolar* and VdL are very pro-poor at the margin despite having a very mediocre targeting performance on average.
Food programs	2001–03	National	ENAHO	Nonexperimental benefit incidence analysis	Vasquez (2003, 2004, 2005)	▪ High share of target group is not covered (undercoverage ranges from 67% for VdL to 98% for *Comedor Infantil*). ▪ High leakage ranging from 26% in VdL to 47% in *Almuerzo Escolar*.

Source: Based on Yamada and Perez (2005); Alderman and Stifel (2003); Vazquez (2005); Valdivia (2005); Instituto Apoyo (2000); Chacaltana (2004).

This summary represents only a small part of the literature. Most studies that analyze the food programs emphasize the lack of clarity of the objectives of many of the programs, the very low coverage of and the poor targeting toward the extreme poor, the low impact on nutrition, and the lack of understanding of the role of CBOs. Most analyses focused on a particular program or a particular problem (mostly related to targeting). Other issues, in particular sectorwide analysis of program mix and adequacy of financing, have not being studied extensively. In interpreting Table 5.4, the reader should keep in mind that some issues (rows of the table) are not checked not because there is disagreement about or lack of interest in the topic, but because the issue has not yet been analyzed.

Policy Recommendations

Even with improved social services in health, education, and nutrition, some groups may remain vulnerable because they are already living on the edge—such as high-dependency households lacking able-bodied adults or employed workers, or whose heads can find only low-productivity jobs in household services or agriculture. For these people, well-designed SSN programs could complement the two main elements in the fight against poverty— promotion of broad-based growth and more equitably distributed social services. The government can strengthen the SSN by improving the existing programs as a short-term solution. In the longer term it will be very desirable to identify programs and interventions that are likely to have greater impact on poverty reduction but which will necessitate increased funding and greater capacity.

Clarify Objectives of Social Safety Net Policy and Define Achievable Results

For the SSN to contribute to more robust economic development and to reducing the intergenerational transmission of poverty there is a need for a social protection strategy and clear assignment of responsibilities within the central government, and between central government and municipal authorities with regard to regulation, financing, implementation, and program monitoring.

Strengthen the SSN in Urban Areas

In urban areas, ensure full coverage of the poor children with an improved *Vaso de Leche* that could have greater impact through viable reforms. Continue using simple targeting mechanisms: demographic, program choice, and self-selection.

Despite widespread criticism, *Vaso de Leche* could become a good urban program with further strengthening. *Vaso de Leche,* given its budget and relative size—over $100 million or half of the overall budget for food assistance and almost 5 million beneficiaries—has captured a lot of attention and has often been criticized for having high leakages toward the non-poor or non-intended beneficiaries. This report emphasizes that the targeting of the program is better than previously acknowledged. The government may want to review the implementation arrangements for the *Vaso de Leche* program which, given its budget and size, has the greatest weight in defining the overall performance of public spending on food programs. It should become linked to basic nutrition, education, and health programs to ensure that the program contributes to the creation of human capital among the beneficiaries. The implementation could be strengthened by restricting eligibility to children aged 0 to 6, improving procurement, ensuring supplies sufficient to cover seven days a week instead of the actual practice of fewer days to cover more beneficiaries, and distributing ready-to-use daily rations instead of bulk distribution.

Continue to operate *A Trabajar Urbano* in a countercyclical manner, by maintaining a minimal program during periods of economic growth than can be scaled up during recessions or in the aftermath of natural disasters. *A Trabajar* was designed and implemented in response to the 1989–2001 crisis as a temporary solution, and the performance of the program was adequate. With the resumption of growth, the administration has considered discontinuing the program. International experience, however, suggests that it is hard to scale up such programs during crises. The best approach is to maintain minimum program capacity during normal times, to facilitate a quick response during an economic downturn or natural disasters.

To further improve implementation of the workfare program some fine-tuning is required: (a) set the level of wage rate slightly lower than the prevailing market wage for unskilled labor to promote self-selection; (b) intensify efforts to select unemployed households heads who are most in need; the communities could play an important role in individual selection rather then the actual practice of random selection; (c) consider the option of integrating the workfare programs with municipal investments to ensure quality (in terms of supplementary resources needed to complement the labor production factor) and maintenance of assets created; and (d) consider as possible projects not only the construction of physical assets but also the provision of social services (caregivers, health promoters) that might increase the participation of women.

Strengthen the SSN in Rural Areas

Find the combination of interventions that effectively enhance the human capital of the poor. Use inexpensive techniques to identify the priority groups (geographic and demographic targeting).

Expand coverage of the nutritional program, PACFO, to cover all children aged 6 months to 2 years in the poorest rural districts identified based on the poverty map. With further improvements and expansion in coverage, PACFO could help more poor children at risk of malnutrition, especially in areas with fairly good health service coverage and adequate infrastructure to allow warehousing of food commodities at health centers.

Consolidate overlapping programs while preserving budgets, and build on the existing good programs such as *Desayuno Escolar* and PACFO. Some of the food programs have high coverage, others are tiny and overlap with larger programs in terms of beneficiaries and type of interventions. There is scope to consolidate them. The government already has a strategy in place to pilot some demonstration projects to consolidate school feeding programs (school breakfast with school lunch) and to better target nutritional programs (PACFO, PANFAR) to the age groups where these programs can be more effective, but progress has been hampered in the context of decentralization.

However, feeding programs are not the complete answer to improving nutritional status or human capital. It is necessary to transform food programs and isolated health and educational programs into an integrated approach that: (a) assures the simultaneous provision of a basic package of health, education, and nutrition; and (b) takes advantage of their complementarities.

Continue Financing Infrastructure Investments to Ensure Universal Access to Basic Services, Building on FONCODES Experience

The comparative advantage that has allowed FONCODES to be an efficient manager of small-scale infrastructure projects lies in the different systems it has developed to manage the project cycle: systems and instruments for designing, appraising, disbursing, and supervising projects, and for hiring project designers, evaluators, supervisors, trainers, and so forth. While the decentralized project cycle gives district governments a few more responsibilities than before, all this decisionmaking power and know-how still remains in FONCODES zone offices.

The "strategy" underpinning the decentralization of FONCODES is not consistent with an approach aimed at devolving responsibilities and resources for small-scale infrastructure provision to district governments, and therefore at developing their capacities to take on this new role. De facto, the strategy transfers very limited responsibilities to district governments, with FONCODES retaining control over the main management systems that regulate the project cycle.

The real contribution that FONCODES could make lies in building the capacities of district governments to forge strong partnerships with communities and local service providers for effective small-scale infrastructure provision. What is currently missing is a strategy and plan to materialize that potential contribution.

Scaling-up the Scope of the SSN Sector for Greater Impact

Consider increasing the overall financing of the sector close to the average spending in middle-income countries of about 1 percent of GDP. More impact on poverty reduction would require more funds for SSN programs. Even if current resources were perfectly targeted to the extreme poor, the poverty reduction impact would be limited. Additional spending could improve the level of assistance per beneficiary and extend the coverage to groups at high risk of poverty (children and working poor living in extreme poverty).

Strengthening the SSN could come via the addition of new programs. The government contemplates the possibility of introducing a conditional cash transfer program that will provide money to poor families contingent on investing in human capital by sending children to school or bringing them to health centers. This type of program could correct some of the observed negative outcomes with respect to equality of opportunity in education, namely the fact that 26 percent of the children aged 12 to 16 in the poorest quintile are not in school, one-third of children aged 12 to 16 are late for grade, and child labor is pervasive among poor children (53 percent of children aged 10 to 14 in the poorest quintile perform some kind of labor).

The addition of new programs should not move ahead of developing the basic prerequisites for good implementation: household targeting mechanisms, a beneficiary identification system (BIS), verification and recertification mechanisms, an appeals process, and a monitoring and evaluation system. Moreover, for BIS to become operational, Peru might need to put in place a process of providing legal recognition through the National Civil

Registry System to a large number of people without personal identification documents (birth certificates or identity cards).

Strengthen Accountability

The government should continue its effort to improve accountability in service delivery. The main challenge for the government after the first two years of decentralization is to weigh the pros and cons and decide whether a decentralized SSN better serves the poor and vulnerable. The *Vaso de Leche* experience of decentralized implementation and the lessons from the first two years after the transfer of *Comedores Populares* should help the government decide how to continue the process of decentralization of food programs. The government should ensure that decentralization does not move ahead of local government capacity to manage funds sensibly and transparently. Peruvians who are served by local governments that have better administration and resources to cover operating costs, and exhibit functioning participatory mechanisms to ensure healthy checks and balances in the approval of government decisions, are most likely to experience the biggest improvement in the delivery of food programs following their decentralization. However, many extreme poor live in small municipalities where local government capacity is weak, the needs are huge, and helping the poor may compete with other local priorities. It is important to ensure that decentralization does not contribute to increased inequality or reduced opportunities resulting from differences in the institutional capacity among municipalities.

Define the institutional arrangements. The reorganization of MIMDES calls for the creation of regional decentralized offices of the minister (*oficinas desconcentradas*) by bringing together at the regional level the deconcentrated offices of three national programs—PRONAA, FONCODES, and *Instituto Nacional de Bienestar Familiar* (INABIF)—in an effort to create state capacity at the local level. The proposal to territorialize the central administration of MIMDES through the creation of *oficinas desconcentradas* in each of the 24 regions makes sense given the perceived need for monitoring and interaction with local municipalities in charge of devolved social programs. Some of the issues the government may want to address before actually "building" the regional MIMDES offices are: (a) to what extent will the new institutions contribute to more synergism among existing programs; (b) what is the rationale for consolidating the administrative apparatus at the regional level when all programs are to be transferred by 2009 to subnational governments (provincial and district) that have no interaction with the regional government; and (c) what is the rationale for keeping the basic social infrastructure investments—FONCODES—under the jurisdiction of MIMDES, when other sector ministries, municipalities, and specialized infrastructure institutes all execute infrastructure investments in parallel.

Strengthen regular monitoring and impact evaluation and nurture a culture of embedding the results into policymaking. The monitoring and evaluation system will have to go beyond the actual practice of tracking the overall level of spending, number of beneficiaries, metric tons of food, and number of food rations, into following what kinds of people get benefits, how much recipients get, how long people typically receive food, and what changes occur in nutritional status and other development outcomes. Moreover, the system could be conceived to cover not only the programs under the jurisdiction of MIMDES, but also safety net programs that consume a large share of the budget (such as *Vaso de Leche*) or any new program proposal before legitimizing it or scaling it up.

CHAPTER 6

Human Resources in Public Health and Education in Peru

Richard Webb and Sofía Valencia

This chapter reports on a study of the causes of poor performance by human resources in public health and education in Peru. The findings are based mostly on unstructured and nonrandom interviews of education and health professionals, government officials, and analysts, carried out between October 2004 and July 2005 in the cities of Cuzco, Lima, and Trujillo, and in rural areas of two provinces in the Sierra, and on available research reports, project evaluations, and official statistics.

The main conclusion is that deficiencies in the delivery of public education and health are the product of a historical and human adjustment process that is not easily reversible. The process was triggered by fiscal collapse, which forced a substantial reduction in real wages for all civil servants. However, the path followed by that crisis, and especially the degradation of the civil service career, was also a consequence of institutional weakness. In one case, it was the government's failure to monitor performance and enforce work rules. In another, it was the incapacity of users to perceive or react against service deficiencies. These institutional weaknesses opened the door to a perverse mode of adjustment: the cutbacks required by fiscal poverty took the form of a reduction in professional effort and service quality rather than in the number of employees or establishments.

Low productivity, low quality, and anti-poor bias in those services have become rooted in institutions, forms of behavior, and life and career arrangements that include parallel business and educational investments and residential decisions. Providers, bureaucrats, politicians, and union leaders have accommodated to a status quo of low wages, lax discipline, informal and illegal practices, falling entry standards, and inadequate levels of effort. The main policy implication is that reform requires the emergence of a new, exogenous source of pressure sufficiently strong to overcome the accommodating preferences of the current players. The creation of public awareness and organizational capacity on the part of service users could bring about that change.

Reliance on monetary incentives, such as general wage increases, or on bonus incentives for specific goals, is not likely to be effective without: (a) institutional strengthening, especially better enforcement of work discipline based on verifiable standards, and increased participation by a more informed clientele; and (b) the re-creation of the public service career of the teacher and health professional by returning to evaluation, merit-based selection and promotion, and other standard elements of career development.

Conclusions and Policy Implications

We have identified four main conclusions and associated policy implications.

1. Need for an External Intervention

Deficiencies in the delivery of public education and health are the product of a historical and human adjustment process that is not easily reversible. Low productivity, low quality, and anti-poor bias in those services have become deeply rooted in service provider attitudes, informal and illegal practices, and life and career arrangements that include business and educational investments and residential decisions. Providers, bureaucrats, politicians, and union leaders have accommodated to a status quo of low wages, lax discipline, falling entry standards, and inadequate levels of effort.

- Providers have adjusted to the lack of incentives by transferring time, energy, and commitment from civil service jobs into private sector work, creating parallel sources of income, often in different professions or small businesses. Provider adjustment has also meant a downgrading of quality in terms of the innate capacities of entrants and of their professional education. In addition, providers have coped by raising the fees charged by their establishments, reorienting their establishments toward a less-poor clientele, and using that fee income as a salary supplement.
- Bureaucrats and politicians take advantage of managerial laxness, nonenforcement, and confused and contradictory regulations for political patronage, personal favors, and corruption.
- Union leaders in the *Sindicato Unico de Trabajadores en la Educación del Perú* (United Education Workers Labor Union, SUTEP) and other unions gain political power to the extent that their members are an undifferentiated mass of workers rather than a professional meritocracy.

The resulting situation can be described as an equilibrium in the sense that none of the actors with a capacity to influence outcomes is likely to press for or bring about major change. Indeed, unions openly oppose reforms while bureaucrats and politicians find less-visible ways to frustrate change. This accommodation to a bad situation, which we describe as a low-level equilibrium, has been made possible because users have been unable to perceive the poor quality of service received and have lacked the organizational capacity to press for improvement.

Not surprisingly, user perception and voice are weakest in the case of the rural poor, thus reinforcing the supply-side causes of an anti-poor bias.

In this context, significant and sustained improvement of the services provided in both sectors requires the emergence of a new, exogenous source of pressure sufficiently strong to overcome the accommodating preferences of the players. Changing the face of the individuals involved would not be enough, since group interests embedded in the system have a life of their own and are likely to capture the new players. This analysis may explain why many previous efforts at partial reform, designed to be carried out by government officials and providers, have had limited impact and short life spans.

The most promising source for an intervention that could break the impasse is the largely untapped power of users. Certainly, without a radical increase in user awareness and pressure, measures to improve service quality are likely to have limited and unsustainable results. This conclusion is consistent with the main hypothesis contained in the accountability-triangle approach recommended in the World Bank's *World Development Report 2004*, which posits that service improvement requires greater monitoring by and voice of the poor. There is a need for the creation of accountability by mobilizing and strengthening user awareness and voice, and through the development of monitoring tools and user organizations. Recent institutional measures provide potential avenues for tapping and mobilizing user voice and power, especially the new *Concejos Educativos Institucionales* (CONEIs), the *Colegio del Magisterio*, and decentralization. In our opinion, however, the most important catalyst for change would be the emergence of a strong nongovernmental monitoring and evaluation initiative that would draw attention to performance and achievement, and thus inform, stimulate, and focus user demand.

2. Restore the Public Service Career

A second policy implication is that there is a need to rebuild public service careers in education and health services. Professionals in these sectors must regain a full-time, professionally and economically rewarding commitment to public service. As a normative and cultural framework, the career gives form to the contractual understanding between professionals and the State; it should induce good-quality students to enter the profession and to invest continuously in skills, and it should motivate quality effort throughout the career. At present, the career has suffered a demotion in remuneration and status, a loss of professional ethos, and a generalized reduction of effort by tenured professionals.

A reconstruction of the public service career will require much more than changes in norms. This study confirms the need for many specific normative reforms recommended in the past, to improve the standards and procedures for recruitment, evaluation, promotion, and in-service training, and the need for a much more differentiated wage structure that rewards experience, performance, and investment in skills. In addition, the reform of monetary incentives must be accompanied by managerial changes that strongly boost non-monetary motivations. But, our findings suggest that reform requires change on a broad front; isolated measures, such as across-the-board wage increases or teacher-training programs, are not likely to succeed unless they are part of a broad package of measures aimed at restoring a career development path. A related conclusion is that normative reforms will not be effective unless they are accompanied by changes in the actual practices used in human resources management. This is because enforcement is likely to remain weak, especially in view of the gradual and poorly defined path that is being followed by the decentralization of human resource managerial authority.

Specific recommendations related to public service career norms and to monetary incentives that continue to be valid are:

- Hiring standards and procedures that are centralized and demanding, and that are administered with a high degree of technical autonomy. As the predominant employer, and in the context of an excess supply of graduates in both health and education, the government has considerable power to impose recruitment standards; signal universities, institutes, and students regarding a more appropriate syllabus for public service; and to introduce accreditation systems of pre-service training institutions.

- A revised wage structure that restores significant wage differentials for experience, skills, performance, and administrative responsibility must be built jointly with a performance evaluation system. To soften the additional fiscal burden, this could be: (a) done gradually, (b) substitute at least in part for across-the-board wage increases, and (c) be accompanied by other administrative reforms that reduce waste and corruption in the social budgets.

- Improved processes and standards for recruitment and selection are insufficient without improving the processes for granting tenure. Nationwide assessments or nationwide appointment of personnel under contracts should not replace the tenure-granting procedures based on merit and evaluation of capacities. In addition, a moderation of tenure to facilitate transfers among locations and firing on disciplinary grounds and for extreme performance deficiencies, as proposed in the government's Teaching Career Law proposal, is needed.

- In-service training programs, scholarships, and other incentives should be tied to career advancement and performance evaluations.

- Enforcement of these specific recommendations will not be possible without substantial improvement in the information available to monitor performance and to support well-informed managerial decisions. At present, personnel data are incomplete and unreliable, and lack information on provider profiles, numbers and current posts, and contractual conditions. An effort should be made to create a new personnel information system.

The current Teacher Career Law proposal contains provisions that move toward an appropriate and integrated policy effort. There are also organizational and personnel system initiatives in the health and education sectors to improve both specific norms and the quality of information. These initiatives are encountering resistance from teachers, health professionals, and managers and administrators of establishments. In addition, there is a lack of capable personnel at the decentralized level to implement the initiatives.

The more difficult agenda, however, is related not to norms and pay scales but to managerial practices as they bear on the enforcement of norms, on efficiency and waste, and on the generation of nonmonetary motivation. The wide spectrum in performance across establishments suggests that there is a potentially high payoff to better management and more attention to nonmonetary motivations, issues that should be at the center of the policy and research agenda. In particular, we propose further research on the components of nonmonetary motivation identified in this study, such as supportive supervision, professional pride, a sense of responsibility, the pleasure of human interaction, solidarity, teamwork and loyalty, patriotism, and other sources of nonmonetary satisfaction. We also propose further research on the mechanisms to acknowledge success and its effect on motivation. A second area for research relates to the prevalence of informal and corrupt practices and the lack of compliance with central norms.

3. Authority and Management

Our findings suggest a need to review and reformulate the structure of authority with respect to human resources management. The following are tentative considerations that could be the basis for further research.

- Establishment directors have wide latitude for performing very well or very poorly—despite, rather than because, of the norms. School and hospital directors are extremely restricted by tenure rules for their staff, a lack of voice in hiring, minimal budgets for nonpersonnel expenses, activist unions, unfriendly judges who freely admit accusations by disgruntled parents and teachers, and aggressive Parent Associations. Yet, simple observation, interviews, and the systematic study of *Fe y Alegría* schools and Local Committees for Health Administration (*Comités Locales de Administración de Salud*, CLAS) clinics all indicate very different performance under those restrictions. Good directors use leadership skills, bend rules, motivate staff, organize activities, raise community funds, and successfully handle multiple sources of pressure. These differences in performance by directors, though difficult to research due to the variety and subjective nature of factors at work, should be studied more systematically across a greater variety of establishments. The implication is that better choice and management of directors, better in-service training and certification of directors, greater financial incentives, and a freer hand for directors could lead to substantial productivity and quality gains, even without major changes in the norms.

- Midlevel managers supplement their limited formal authority with de facto authority which they obtain from two sources: self-financing and short-term contract hiring. In each case, managers expand their freedom to spend and to manage human resources, and much of the initiative displayed by the best managers derives from the use of those de facto resources. However, self-financing, which is mostly from fees, works against the poor, while contract hiring undermines professional ethos by creating a two-tier employment system and by excluding contract workers from key aspects of the public service career. A thorough reform of the public service career should probably seek a midpoint between the overly rigid tenure of tenured personnel (*nombrados*) and the complete absence of security and benefits of personnel under contracts (*contratados*). At present, managers are losing authority as more and more professionals are granted full tenure. CLAS clinics, in particular, are losing much of the managerial flexibility as their staff becomes increasingly tenured.

- The value added by midlevel management in *Unidades de Gestión Educativa Local* (Local Educational Management Units, UGELs) and *Direcciónes Regional de Educación* needs to be evaluated by educational and health management experts. Their work should do much more in the way of classroom and clinic observation, supportive supervision, and one-to-one advice, as distinct from their current emphasis on mechanical control functions based on checklists of formal requirements and on group training courses and seminars.

■ Unions have an inappropriate degree of authority and are major obstacles to reform. SUTEP in particular uses national and regional strikes to impose its group interests and political agenda at the policymaking level, and a network of local union representatives to police and bully midlevel managers at the establishment level. The government shares a responsibility for this undue authority: it strengthens the hand of SUTEP by imposing a payroll deduction of union dues, and by financing the local-level activities of union activists through paid leaves. In the case of SUTEP, government facilitation is even more questionable given the open association between SUTEP and a political organization, *Patria Roja*. The union agenda works to undermine efforts to evaluate teachers, to increase the security of tenure, and to expand the room for lax work discipline, rather than to achieve public service objectives. Yet, as recent surveys have shown, there is substantial public support for a policy of evaluation and greater discipline in the case of teachers.[46]

4. Right Fit for the Poor

The particular needs of the poor—language, culture, inability to pay to obtain access, local economy and life schedules, geographic location, and access to alternative providers—have played almost no role in the selection, education, or motivation of teachers and health professionals in public service. Nor is there evidence of a preferential concern for the poor or of the acceptance of a policy of affirmative action that consciously accepts the greater cost of providing service to rural, dispersed, and culturally different users. Minor efforts in that direction have existed, such as bonuses for teachers and health workers in rural service, literacy programs, and rural education programs, and the short-term labor provided by rural health service professionals (SERUM). The great majority of providers remain poorly prepared or motivated for service to the poor. Though SERUM probably increases the number of health providers in rural areas, it does so using inexperienced recent graduates, most of whom serve unwillingly.

Social policy requires a major reexamination of the way in which teachers and health professionals are educated, selected, prepared, backed up, and motivated to serve in poor areas. Service delivery to the poor will not change substantially with isolated measures, if they are not accompanied by a substantial and poverty-oriented redesign of the entire public service career in both sectors. For instance, rural education and health provision could become a specialty for those who are willing to commit to remaining in isolated areas for some number of years and benefit from tailor-made undergraduate and graduate education scholarships. Yet a supply-side initiative, even one that consists of a highly integrated

---

46. A national opinion survey carried out in August 2005 finds that 96 percent of respondents agree that teachers should be evaluated, and 71 percent agree that a teacher who fails two evaluations should be fired (APOYO 2005).

package of measures, is unlikely to go far if it is not accompanied by an increase in user awareness and voice. In that regard, we also recommend a strong nongovernmental monitoring and evaluation initiative, with particular emphasis on fuller documentation and dissemination of service deficiencies for the poor.

Background

The Scope of this Study

This chapter discusses the role of human resources in the delivery of public social services in Peru. The focus will be on teachers, doctors, and medical support personnel, and the main question is how to achieve more and better service delivery from those resources, particularly for the poor. This chapter is part of the *Rendición de Cuentas para la Reforma Social de Perú* (Accountability in Social Reform in Peru, RECURSO) Project, a multisectoral study of public social service delivery, and so is designed to complement sector-specific chapters on the education, health, and social protection sectors. The conceptual framework used as a starting point is that proposed in the World Bank's *World Development Report 2004*, stressing the role of accountability and user demand.

Methodology

The study was carried out in two stages between May 2004 and August 2005. The first stage, through October 2004, involved the preparation of a concept paper based on a literature review, data collection, and 56 interviews that included teachers and doctors, but mostly officials and experts, all in Lima. This preliminary research led to three hypotheses that were outlined in the concept paper and became the subject of research carried out in the second stage of the study. The major hypothesis was that declining real wages had set off perverse behavioral responses and interactions among human resources, their unions, the government, and users, producing unsatisfactory service performance, described here as a low-level equilibrium. The second and third hypotheses were that the above process had aggravated the anti-poor bias and the overall inefficiency of service delivery.

These preliminary findings were further studied during the second stage, between November 2004 and August 2005. The research design for this second phase reflected two major difficulties identified during the first phase. One was a severe lack of reliable and consistent current and past official data on basic profile variables, such as numbers of professionals employed under each type of employment contract; and remunerations, including a variety of bonuses or payments from different sources; and age, sex, measures of performance, years of service, and training received.

The second obstacle identified in the initial stage was the existence of major discrepancies between the rules of human resources management and actual practice, along with the presence of hidden and/or illicit practices that would not be revealed by standard survey techniques. The methodology adopted therefore was based mostly on fieldwork and a relatively small sample of in-depth interviews. The interview results were complemented by data from a substantial literature and by large-scale surveys on teachers, and a more limited literature on health professionals.

A total of 266 people were interviewed in 121 individual meetings and 28 focus groups, the majority by the authors of this paper, and others were interviewed by a sociologist hired to study unions and by three research assistants. The interviews included 100 teachers, 21 doctors, 16 other health professionals, 25 school principals, 3 hospital directors, 4 union representatives, and 13 experts. Of the total, 73 were government or former government officials. The selection of interviewees was done through introductions and references from personal contacts to increase the likelihood that informants would be candid. We sought to ensure diversity by choosing a variety of locations and participants.

All fieldwork was done in the urban, urban marginal, and outlying rural areas of Ayacucho, Cusco, Huamachuco, Lima, and Trujillo. Interviews lasted between one and three hours. The approach was semistructured; after explaining our research interests, we allowed participants to raise the most important issues from their own perspective, especially in relation to sensitive topics such as coping behavior and corruption.

Role of Human Resources

Careers matter in public health and education delivery for two reasons. One is that those services require professionals who make a substantial educational investment in specialized knowledge. The financial and motivational commitment is especially large in the case of health professionals, and requires continuous updating, but the educational investment and continuous training that teachers should undertake are also important. In practice, this investment is a lifetime choice based on long-term expectations regarding the conditions of employment, including not only remuneration and prospects for income and professional growth, but also place of work and compatibility with family objectives. Another reason is that the performance of teachers and health professionals in these sectors is highly qualitative, hard to measure, and hard to control under any employment compact. Furthermore, inevitably, it is determined to a large degree by nonmonetary motivations and sources of satisfaction, such as professional self-respect and social commitment—in other words, by the more complete set of motivations that distinguish a career from less-committed forms of employment. This section identifies and describes the main categories of service professionals working in public education and health, types of establishments, and contractual arrangements.

Profile of Human Resources

Service providers in education include teachers, school principals, and volunteers (*promotores de educación*). In 2004, the Ministry of Education (MED) reported that 297,000 teachers and principals were working in the public education system at the preschool, primary, and secondary levels, serving almost 7 million students. The number of volunteers, who mostly work in primary school without compensation or for tips, is not recorded. Also, it is not clear whether teachers hired and paid by local communities or municipal governments are included. Information regarding age, educational background, and other specific features of education service providers is either unavailable in MED records, or unreliable and not updated. At the aggregate level, we found only an indirect indicator of teachers' educational background and their geographic distribution (see Table 6.1). Thus, in 2004, more than 80 percent of teachers in urban and rural areas possessed a pedagogical degree. However,

Table 6.1. Education: Geographic Distribution of Teachers

Sector	With PD	Percent	Without PD	Percent	Total
Rural	82,797	81	18,863	19	101,660
Subtotal urban	162,705	83	33,079	17	195,784
Urban	104,927	84	20,343	16	125,270
Urban residential	10,483	82	2,295	18	12,778
Urbano marginal	25,601	82	5,635	18	31,236
New urban settlements	21,694	82	4,806	18	26,500
Total (Urban + Rural)	245,502	83	51,942	17	297,444

PD = Pedagogical Degree.
Source: Estadísticas Básicas de la Educación, 2004, Ministerio de Educación.

a pedagogical degree is not necessarily an indicator of the quality of a teacher's educational background, since many deficiencies have been found in the institutes and faculties that educate teachers, as will be explained later.

In 2003, there were 247,056 tenured teachers representing 84 percent of the total number of public teachers. The remaining 16 percent had a fixed contract. This percentage is greater than in 2001, when 78 percent of teachers had a permanent contract.[47]

Health service providers are doctors, nurses, obstetricians, technicians, other health professionals, SERUM workers, and volunteers. Their geographic distribution is heavily skewed to Lima and urban areas: 58 percent of doctors work in Lima. Nurses and other professionals are more evenly distributed, with 42 percent in Lima (see Table 6.2).

The SERUM program was created in 1997 in an effort to improve health service delivery to poor and rural areas.[48] Under this program, young health professionals are contracted for a year and assigned based on health facilities needs. In 2004, the SERUM program offered 848 posts of which 40 percent were assigned to doctors. Volunteers are community members who at most receive a tip. Their work combines monitoring and signaling health needs to staff at nearby clinics, and providing basic medical assistance.

The Establishments. Teachers work in a variety of establishments, but mainly in schools and *Gran Unidad Escolar* (Large Schools, GUEs). Other teachers and former school directors work in *Unidad de Gestión Educativa Local* (UGELs), *Dirección Regional de Educación*, and MED as administrative officials. UGELs are decentralized implementation units with some degree of administrative autonomy and provincial jurisdiction, and *Dirección Regional de Educación* are specialized units under the supervision of the regional government.

Health facilities are classified into four levels according to different types of service. Among doctors, there are strong preferences for working in establishments with higher levels

---

47. Information on the number of teachers by type of contract for previous years is not available.
48. Serum replaced a program called *Servicio Civil de Graduandos* (Civil Service for University Students, SECIGRAs). The main difference between these programs is that under SECIGRA doctors did rural service before obtaining their medical degree.

Table 6.2. Geographic Distribution of Public Health Professionals

	Total	Percent
Lima Region		
Administrative	4,818	43
Physicians	5,156	58
Nurses	2,586	37
Other technical staff	16,255	43
Total	28,815	44
Total Other Regions		
Administrative	6,409	57
Physicians	3,688	42
Nurses	4,403	63
Other technical staff	21,923	57
Total	36,423	56
Total of the Country		
Administrative	11,227	
Physicians	8,844	
Nurses	6,989	
Other technical staff	38,178	
Total	65,238	

Source: Human Resources Department, 2003, Ministry of Health.

of specialization, and for being the manager of any establishment, given the associated prestige and reputation, particularly in Lima.

The first level provides primary health care and includes health centers and posts, (*puestos de salud*). Some of them are managed by the community and are known as *Comites Locales de Administración Compartida de Salud* (CLAS). "Rural posts" are commonly located on the outskirts of towns, still far from most of the rural population. The second level includes small hospitals with some degree of specialization, but only at the third level are there complex and technological procedures, including surgery and hospitalization. The fourth level covers those hospitals that are highly specialized and that do high-cost procedures.

Health professionals also work as administrative officials at regional and local offices (DIRESAs and DISAs) and in health network units (*Redes*).[49]

Contractual Arrangements. Education and health service providers can be employed by the government under a variety of legal regimes and with a wide disparity in salaries for similar tasks. Some are hired on a contractual basis in nonpermanent positions. Those in permanent positions enjoy a high degree of job stability.

The Civil Service Law (DL No.276) and its regulations (*Reglamento de la Carrera Administrativa*, DS N° 005-90-PCM) are the legal framework for permanent tenured positions (*nombrados*) and temporal positions under specific contractual agreements with the government (*contratados*). However, the Private Labor Code (DL No. 728) is also used for temporary contracts. Establishments in both sectors have long resorted to temporary contracts. The practice increased during the 1990s, due to a ban on hiring into permanent positions, but the trend since 2000 has been to a reduction in the proportion of *contratados*.

In each sector, the Civil Service Framework has been either circumvented or substituted by a series of specific norms and regulations that have also created many exceptions

---

49. DISAs (in Lima) and DIRESAs (in Regions) are executive administrative units. National Hospitals and Specialized Institutes of Lima are under the supervision of MINSA. First- and second-level establishments and Regional Hospitals are under the supervision of DISAS or DIRESAs.

and gray areas, under which establishments usually recruit, select, and hire guided more by de facto practice than by law. For these and other reasons, the management of human resources within establishments and their supervision by central authorities have been very difficult. In the case of *contratados*, hiring is not subject to any required recruitment and selection civil service procedures, and is for a specific period. Tenured personnel enjoy high job stability and benefits associated with a civil service career—including leaves of absence, severance payments, and pensions—that nontenured personnel do not receive.

Most education service providers are also ruled by specific career regulations such as the Teachers' Law (*Ley del Profesorado, Ley* 24029, 1984; modified by Law 25212 of 1990, and its associated norm DS 19-90-ED (1990). Education service providers are ruled by the Civil Service Law as long as it does not contradict what is defined in their specific career law.

Health professionals work under a greater variety of contracts, including special regimes for SERUM and CLAS workers. In addition, career conditions differ and are defined in specific laws for doctors, nurses, obstetricians, and other professionals.[50] These specific laws are applied to all the career aspects that are not addressed in the Civil Service Law.

Low-level Equilibrium

This section examines the causes of the low-quality performance of education and health professionals. The starting point for the analysis is the decline in government wages that began during the 1970s, caused by a combination of rapid expansion in coverage and the onset of fiscal restrictions. The argument centers on the subsequent responses and interaction of each of the key actors involved: providers, unions, government, and service users. Employee unions played a particularly active part. Unable to prevent wages from falling, they focused successfully on an agenda that, in effect, has allowed professionals to compensate for their low official wages through second jobs by, for instance, reinforcing the degree of job stability associated with tenure, and reducing hours and work discipline.

Successive governments played a relatively passive role, neglecting civil service provisions and other norms designed to ensure career development and quality in work performance, changing payroll rules to delink performance from remunerations, and acceding to union demands for exaggerated tenure rights. For most users, especially the poor, the resulting decline in service quality has not been visible. Instead, public demand focused on visible inputs, notably the construction and staffing of more and more schools and clinics. In this context, education and health professionals were allowed to compensate for falling civil service wages by resorting to second jobs and other coping strategies, which, in effect, severely compromised their public service careers. The process thus developed into a spiral of declining quality and effort, in which responses and interactions have produced a situation that could be described as a low-level equilibrium.

Though the long-run results are perverse, the process is driven by the rational self-interest of each of the main players. Providers have adjusted to low wages by developing parallel careers.

---

50. The career of health professionals is ruled by specific regulations such as Health Professionals Law (*Ley de los Profesionales de la Salud*, DL Nº 23536), the *Ley del Trabajo Médico* (DL Nº 559) and its regulation DS Nº 024-2001-SA; the *Ley del Trabajo del Enfermero* (*Ley* Nº 27669); and the *Ley del Trabajo de la Obstetriz* (Ley Nº 27853) and corresponding norms such as DS 057-1986, which determines levels.

Union leaders provided a facilitation service by pushing for and obtaining contractual terms that reduced work obligations and government capacity to enforce discipline. In exchange, union leaders have been able to build an organization to pursue their radical political agenda. For both government and unions, accountability to the general public is weak while the opportunity for political gain is large. Their interest does not lie in better quality or better coverage of marginal groups with scant political voice, but rather in the political mileage gained from wide-scale patronage (enjoyed by union leaders as much as by the authorities).

Poor pay and lack of incentives, in turn, tended to degrade and demoralize these professions. The loss of self-respect may have been as damaging as the fall in monetary remuneration. Because quality is hard to measure or control in service jobs, and because the users of social services have few choices, to a large extent performance is at the mercy of professional pride and personal commitment.[51] A recent study by the *Organismo Andino de Salud* points out that the loss of self-image and discontent among doctors is an international trend (Yglesias 2003:127).

Other elements reinforced this downward spiral.[52] Repeated efforts to reform were hampered by the ceaseless change of authorities and rules, the excess perfectionism of norms, and the vulnerability of officials who innovate. As noted in recent World Bank reports, Peru's institutional setting is markedly inimical to "doing business," but it should be understood that this applies as much to public sector management as to private business. A second factor was the nature of Peru's labor market, in which three of four members of the labor force are self-employed or are relatives or employees in small family firms, and for the most part work outside the law. It is a labor market that easily accommodates teachers and doctors seeking part-time or flexible working arrangements, as employees or as small businesses, to supplement their government salaries.

The government, in turn, adapted to the administrative limitations created by job tenure and fiscal poverty by also resorting to informality: many teachers and doctors are hired as short-term or contract workers, thus evading its own payroll taxes and benefits. In this way it gained some room for improved management, rapidly expanding primary health delivery during the 1990s, for instance, but created a two-class public labor force. Finally, the general public accommodated to the declining quality of public services by resorting more and more to private suppliers. Elites, in effect, opted out of public schools and health establishments, thus removing themselves as stakeholders.

This historical interpretation of the low-level equilibrium is elaborated and documented below. The process has differed between education and health workers, and the evolution has not been linear. The role of SUTEP is far more visible and consistent over time than that of health worker unions, which are fragmented and were far less active than SUTEP during the 1990s. The process has also had phases. During the most recent, since 2000, the government conceded major benefits to teachers and medical worker unions. Wages have risen substantially, *contratados* have been granted tenure, and the degree of job stability associated with tenure has increased.

---

51. Chiroque (2004) insists that the incentive system for teachers must go beyond wages.

52. The concept of a downward spiral and tradeoff between teachers' salaries and job tenure is an interpretation suggested by Juan Fernando Vega, (2005). The historical analysis draws on Ansion (2001: 279–97).

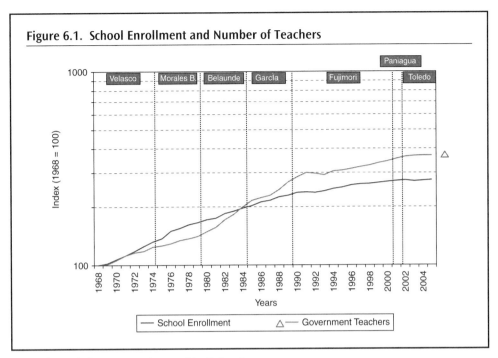

Figure 6.1. School Enrollment and Number of Teachers

Note: The periods correspond to presidential regimes.
Source: Vega (2005).

This section reviews the basic causes that have driven the downward spiral, and then examines and documents the behavior of each of the key players, providers, government, unions, and users. The outcome is summarized in terms of the way in which the career and service delivery to the poor have been negatively affected.

Causes of the Low-level Equilibrium

The low-level equilibrium has been produced by four underlying causes: (a) the trigger was a drop in wages; (b) the adjustment path was shaped by weak government enforcement of contract discipline, (c) weak self-defense by users, and (d) professional demoralization.

Wage Decline. Over the last four decades, successive governments have responded to public pressure for the expansion of basic social services. School enrollment grew substantially, first in primary school, where coverage became nearly universal, and later in secondary and university establishments (see Figure 6.1). The expansion of health coverage was less consistent, with a contraction in the late 1980s and strong recovery in the 1990s, but the long-term outcome has been a substantial increase in coverage in both urban and rural areas.[53]

However, since the late 1970s, this achievement of mass coverage in public social services has been carried out in the face of a long period of economic recession and fiscal

---

53. MINSA establishments provided about one-third of all consultations in 1985, and one-half in 2000.

Table 6.3. Indexes of Fiscal Capacity and Social Service Coverage

	1959	1982	2002	% per Year 59–82	% per Year 82–02
Public Expenditures	100	407	428	6.3	0.3
Population	100	189	277	2.8	1.9
Public Expenditure per Capita	100	215	155	3.4	−1.3
School Enrollment	100	398	575	6.2	1.9
Government Teachers	100	338	628	5.4	3.1
Government Doctors	100	333	387	5.4	0.8

Sources: Central Bank annual reports; MINSA; MED.

contraction (see Table 6.3 and Figure 6.2). In the end, the books were balanced by lower public sector wages, which were forced on employees through inflation. The secular decline in wages followed a cyclical trend around successive fiscal crises, periods of high inflation, and electoral recoveries, though wages have been rising since 2001 with the recovery in output and tax revenues (see Figure 6.2).

As is clear from Figure 6.3, the fall in government capacity to finance social spending was especially deep and lasting from 1983 on, breaking the trend of strong and rising social

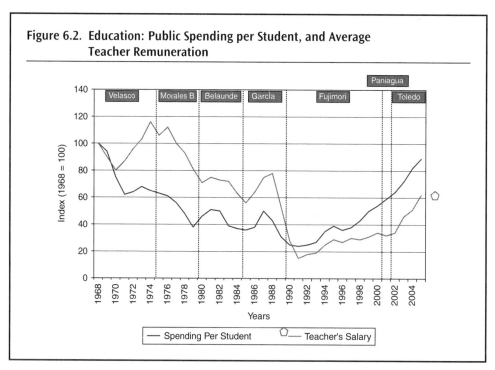

Figure 6.2. Education: Public Spending per Student, and Average Teacher Remuneration

Note: The periods correspond to presidential regimes.
Source: Vega (2005).

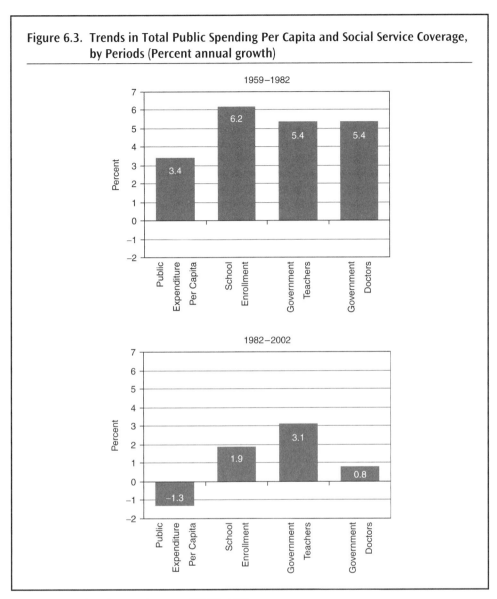

Figure 6.3. Trends in Total Public Spending Per Capita and Social Service Coverage, by Periods (Percent annual growth)

Sources: Central Bank annual reports; MINSA; MED.

spending that had lasted since 1950. This is evident from the per capita public expenditure figures shown in Table 6.3 and Figure 6.3, which serve as an indicator of fiscal capacity to spend on social services. Between 1959 and 1982, total public expenditure per capita rose strongly, at an average annual rate of 3.4 percent, and much of this was used to finance a substantial increase in the coverage of both public education and health services. Public school enrollment rose at 6.2 percent per year, the number of teachers rose at 5.4 percent per year, and the number of doctors rose at 5.4 percent per year, all well above the 2.8 percent annual rate of population growth. During those years, wages fluctuated at levels two to three times higher than current levels. From 1983 to 2002, instead, fiscal capacity declined in absolute terms:

over 20 years public spending per capita dropped at an average annual rate of 1.3 percent. The impact of this adjustment fell largely on teacher and health wages, since governments continued to accommodate demands for growing school enrollment and for broader health coverage. The number of teachers, in fact, grew at 3.1 percent per year between 1982 and 2002, even faster than enrollment (1.9 percent), bringing about a reduction in average class size.

The long-term wage decline for public sector teachers and health professionals is the starting point for this analysis. However, wage trends are poorly documented in both sectors. The most complete series are based on official scales rather than on observed payments. Household survey data are relatively recent and do not provide much detail on the relation of wages to occupational specializations and histories or to employee profiles. Personnel records are incomplete and unreliable in both ministries, with most information available only at midlevel administrative units in different degrees of completion. During the 1990s, efforts began in both the health and education ministries to systematize payrolls using computer databases, but much historical information has been lost. Nonetheless, there is a consensus view that wages have fallen substantially, and it is most clearly documented for teachers. The decline shown by wage series based on official norms was confirmed in our interviews with older professionals in both sectors. Piecemeal evidence from a variety of sources is presented in Figure 6.4. A more detailed series on average teachers' remuneration, shown in Figure 6.4, is consistent with the data in Figure 6.2.

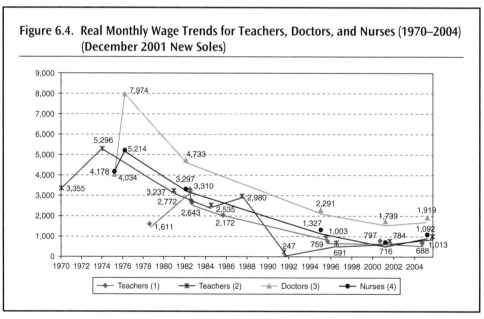

Figure 6.4. Real Monthly Wage Trends for Teachers, Doctors, and Nurses (1970–2004) (December 2001 New Soles)

Source:
1. Teachers: Real wage trend from UGEL Urubamba (Cuzco).
2. Teachers: Real wage trend from INIDEN.
3. Doctors: Real wage trend from Loayza Hospital.
4. Nurses: Real wage trend from Loayza Hospital.

Weak Enforcement. We identify three reasons for weak enforcement of contract discipline by the government: de-legitimization, normative ambiguities, and clientelism and corruption.

De-legitimization: The government's failure to honor its contract obligations, as inflation ate into real wages, has eroded the legitimacy of work discipline. Legitimacy was further undermined by blatant administrative inefficiency, clientelism, and corruption. The government lost moral authority for enforcement, and the demands of providers and their unions for the loosening of work discipline were legitimized. A sense of indignation by employees worked in favor of unions. Even the *Colegio Médico del Perú*, which in previous years had devoted itself principally to matters of professional standards and to the provision of benefits to its members, refocused itself toward issues of compensation. The sense of injustice and of a right to cut corners or find other forms of redress pervades educational and health establishments, as is illustrated in the following statements obtained in interviews:

The director of a large hospital in Lima:

> By 10:30 a.m. most of my doctors have skipped out to their second or third jobs. But, how can I demand [compliance] when I know that on their salary they can't make ends meet.

His own workday began with one to two hours of attention to private patients before the start of his day at the hospital, and included lecturing in the evening, draining time and energy from the extraordinarily demanding requirements that go with being the director of a large hospital. Along the same lines, a school director in a poor district in Lima said:

> One must be tolerant. It is difficult to demand that teachers attend in-service training programs because it would require them to sacrifice their extra jobs. And often I am unable to coordinate with my teachers because when the one o'clock bell rings they rush off. Work discipline is lost.

Another school director said that:

> Coordination and planning problems were particularly acute at the start of the school year in March, when many of my teachers have to attend coordination meetings in their private school jobs.

Normative ambiguities: A second obstacle to enforcement is the confused, often contradictory, ever-changing normative framework for human resources management in both sectors. Officials, faced with contradictions and ambiguities in laws and regulations, were forced to exercise discretion, and often resorted to legally questionable procedures. As a result, actual practice is hard to monitor and is often at variance with normative intent. The overall effect has been to weaken central authority and to encourage creativity by resourceful administrators and politicians seeking ways to attenuate the drastic fall in wages within their own establishments, regions, or subsectors. Disorder is aggravated by a judicial system that undercuts the efforts of directors to impose discipline. Administrative actions are paralyzed and often reversed when employees resort to the courts, accusing directors of "abuse of authority." Díaz and Saavedra (2000) found that public school directors rarely succeed when they try to fire or change a teacher: of 57 directors interviewed, 32 had attempted but only 3 had succeeded. By contrast, in private schools one-third of such attempts succeeded.

Principals and managers are forced to defend their decisions in the courts, which has enormous costs in time, legal fees, and worker relationships. Most directors interviewed for this study, for instance, had faced legal suits. In one UGEL, the newly appointed director discovered a backlog of 2,000 administrative accusations. Another reported finding a similar number, including legal suits and death threats addressed to himself and his closest collaborators.

The cumbersome legal framework and propensity for informal de facto practice is a source of constant managerial confusion, as illustrated in many interviews:

UGEL official in a sierra town:

The appointment of a school principal is based on a public competition held by UGEL. But the selection is made in Cuzco at the Regional Education Directorate. However, the final appointment is made in Lima at MED. Thus, UGEL in practice is not responsible for the selection. However, this is a recent procedure, and the Cuzco Regional Educational Directorate sometimes attempts to make the final decision and to communicate that decision to Lima.

Director of Teacher Pre-service Training Institute in sierra town:

The final decision over appointments was made at UGEL, which is the supervisory authority. However, often principals have to report to both UGEL and the Regional Education Directorate on the same issues, which makes it very difficult to manage even school schedules.

Nurse in charge of a sierra clinic:

My condition as a tenured nurse makes me subject to two and even three lines of authority in regard to human resources management and to the general administration of the establishment. Sometimes, I have to devote extra hours to comply with regulations from DISA, DIRESA, and the Micro-Red. They asked me to fill out forms on the same subject and sometimes contradict each other on particular decisions.

DIRESA Assistant Director:

We have many problems related to human resources management and supervision as a result of the two different types of contracts under which they work. Yet we apply civil service rules to contract workers. We require them to perform like tenured staff, yet they do not receive the social benefits received by tenured workers. We have even more problems with tenured staff; they are very lazy. When I was director of the *Red Norte* I had to transfer tenured doctors out of one establishment so that I could take on contract doctors, and that way the establishment worked better.

President of a CLAS:

DIRESA opposes the CLAS because it wants to control the selection and appointment of human resources. The law says that we are entitled to hire but [DIRESA] denies it. The previous manager was chosen and appointed by DIRESA and we had to accept. We cannot touch tenured staff members in the CLAS; they are the sacred cows of the establishment. We have not participated in recent appointments of doctors for the CLAS and that has affected us financially. We are also affected because DIRESA is allowed to lend out tenured doctors to other establishments, and so we lose personnel. DIRESA wants to manage CLAS staff and the reason boils down to what the director of DIRESA told us: "If we don't give him positions he won't give us authority."

Manager of a rural CLAS:

> There are many legally undefined areas when it comes to managing human resources. DIRESA wants to influence not only the appointments but also our choice of contract workers. In several cases of hiring a contract worker, I have invited DIRESA to participate, even though it was not legally required. When we pay out of our own resources, the law says that we do not need DIRESA authorization, but they require it anyway. In fact, if we want to extend the schedule we have to ask permission from DIRESA.

Clientelism and Corruption: A third cause of weak enforcement is widespread clientelism and corruption: authorities deliberately ignore norms and good work practices for political and personal advantage. For politicians, union leaders, and bureaucrats, 300,000 public education and 65,000 public health jobs represent a rich lode of vote buying, political funding, corruption, and simple opportunities for personal favors—all the more so in a societal context characterized by a scarcity of political and social organization, and an excess supply of secondary-and university-level graduates.[54] It is no accident that through successive governments, public education, the largest and best-organized of these bodies, has suffered from a consistent neglect of real reform. Reforms have been announced repeatedly, and often launched, but little change has been achieved. The most obvious victim of clientelism and corruption has been compliance with recruitment and evaluation norms.

In both education and health, we heard frequent examples of political appointments, especially for administrative posts. One "teacher" was actually a housemaid with political connections. Tenured teachers are often linked to the excessive claims faced by directors of "abuse of authority," and are protected by SUTEP to fight for their rights when they are sanctioned. The control exercised by politicians over appointments in both education and health establishments is illustrated in one region where two political parties, APRA and *Perú Posible*, have a sharing agreement, with each party appointing establishment directors in specified districts. The political competition extends to different factions of APRA, with each faction vying for control of the main regional hospital.

In addition, the regional teachers union, which maintains a highly critical and aggressive public stance vis-à-vis the government, negotiated a private agreement with local education authorities that establishes a monthly payroll deduction of three soles earmarked for the local union, on top of the deduction for the national union, whether or not the employee is affiliated. Union representatives frequently intervene at the establishment and regional level with respect to appointments, reassignments, and disciplinary actions. SUTEP is said to control directors in many schools; however, the union's influence varies a great deal across schools, and to a considerable extent works through the local UGEL. Directors have more scope for imposing discipline when the UGEL is not controlled by SUTEP.

In another region, a history of strong political control by one party (APRA) coincides with the scarcity of CLAS health facilities, which delegate to a local community the management of primary health delivery in that area and thereby remove personnel decisions from the hands of bureaucrats, politicians, and union officials.

---

54. One might add another 100,000 students studying to become teachers in over 300 highly decentralized institutes and universities.

Corruption is also rife. It was mentioned repeatedly in interviews in both health and education sectors, *in all cases* at the initiative of the interviewee, since our policy was not to raise the subject. One doctor, now working for a nongovernmental organization (NGO), recalled that he had been sent to a northern province during the 1990s to establish an evaluation-based hiring process. The system he found, he said, was simply a business:

> Some guy would arrive, and buy the job. His first monthly salary, he would agree with the official, "is for you." Some women offered sex for the job. Having established an evaluation procedure, and turned down a lady in his office, the woman showed up at his house. It was a hard decision, said the doctor, because "she was stunning. And I'm only human." A friend called him up to complain about the new procedures saying, "Hey man, you're ruining the market." The doctor was soon fired by the regional health director.

An interview study by Alcázar and Andrade (1999) of induced demand and corruption in Peruvian hospitals reported that 36 percent of doctors admit to knowing cases of "irregularities" in their institutions, while 21 percent consider that theft is very common. Patronage and corruption are, quite obviously, huge obstacles to any effort to establish a culture of merit-based appointments, promotion, and salaries.

Weak Demand. A schoolroom and a teacher are necessary inputs to produce education, but the output from that resource package can vary enormously, and the same is true of health output. However, the demand for public health and education services has been expressed, and understood by the public, largely as a demand for inputs—for the physical availability of clinics and health professionals and of school buildings and teachers. One reason is that until a few decades ago schools and health facilities did not exist for a majority of the population, so the need for service was naturally conceived above all as a need for the physical instruments of delivery. A further reason is that quality in education or health is difficult to observe, even to the professional eye, and certainly for most users of public services.

Attention to quality has been growing: we recorded complaints from villagers that they had learned to read earlier than their children; recent comparative evaluation data provided by the Programme for International Student Assessment (PISA) are widely known, and allegations of medical malpractice and signs of returning epidemics are steady fare in the media. Greater awareness of quality is understandable in that the physical requirements of service have been satisfied to a large extent, especially in the case of schools, but it is also the result of increased media exposure, surveys, and urbanization. Growing resort to private education in urban areas is perhaps the clearest evidence of concern with quality. Nonetheless, for the most part and until recently, users have not been aware of quality in the education and health services provided by government. This failure to perceive true output facilitated an adjustment to lower wages in the form of a reduction in service provision quality.

Professional bodies have not filled this gap in public perception by acting as watchdogs. The most visible and venerable institution is the *Colegio Médico del Perú*, which, however, admits and certifies doctors without examination or independent standards, in effect endorsing the recent multiplication of low-quality university medical faculties. Many of these faculties lack the resources or will—many are essentially businesses—to train doctors adequately. The *Colegio* recently approved a voluntary, quinquennial recertification requirement for practicing doctors, but has not adopted a strong, quality-oriented professional role.

The parallel organization for nurses, the *Colegio de Enfermeras*, plays a similar role, acting more as a union and benefit society than as a professional guardian. Until the very recent creation of the *Colegio del Magiterios*, teachers lacked any such organization. The profession, rather, has been dominated by a powerful union, SUTEP, which is openly antagonistic to evaluation, merit-based wages, and other measures necessary to raise teaching standards and performance.

A long view reveals considerable change in the nature of the demand for *public education*. From the late 19th to the mid-20th century, education was a political banner, closely associated with visions of productive and democratic modernization and of national integration, and with a diagnosis that identified the backwardness of the nation with the "state of its population," meaning the immense mass of ignorant and impoverished mestizos (Romero 1962). Yet, over this period schooling spread slowly; landlords and local elites actively opposed it, and the majority of the population, still predominantly rural, did not yet see in schooling a realistic investment, or even saw teachers as one more form of abusive elite.

Much later, in 1949, a member of the Cornell University anthropology project, arriving at the mountain community of Vicos, found that a primary school had been in operation during nine years, but he was unable to find a single child of primary-school age who could read or write. In any single year the total school population had never exceeded 15 to 20 pupils out of a possible 350. An account of this project states that mestizo teachers often treated the children as inferior and put them to work as servants and gardeners.

By mid-century, however, the demand for education had begun to explode. According to Contreras (2004):

> The common Indian population rapidly came to realize, to the point of exaggeration, that education was the key to progress. It was during the decade of the sixties that education began to figure as their principal demand. Before the lack of drinking water, health services, poor roads, it was the state of the local school, the bad teachers or the fact that the school lacked higher grades of primary, that was pushed to the top in their demands. The state, which had begun the century chasing campesinos to get them to send their children to school, ended up sixty years later, as in an act of vengeance, chased by them to get more and better education.

For three to four decades, the government raced to satisfy that demand and to meet the logistical and budgetary challenge. The population did not simply wait for government school construction. They often built schools themselves, and even hired teachers. From 1959 to 1982 school enrollment grew at an average annual rate of 6.2 percent, while the number of teachers rose at 5.4 percent. With the government freeze on hiring in the 1990s, communities have been increasingly hiring teachers directly, with community or municipal funding. However, as noted, it is only in recent years that "having education" has been understood in terms of much more than having a schoolroom and a teacher and, eventually, a certificate. The efforts of Parents Associations (APAFAs), for instance, are still almost entirely devoted to the maintenance and improvement of physical infrastructure.

In the case of the demand for health, quality is perhaps even more opaque. Users rely heavily on beliefs, tradition, and reputation, which are created by external signs that correlate poorly with actual quality. At the same time, the demand for curative health is far more urgent than that for education. This urgency, together with the inability to perceive quality, perhaps explains why users across the income spectrum are far readier to turn to private providers, and also why there is little check on the real quality of government provision.

Demoralization. Service workers respond to monetary incentives and managerial enforcement. However, in large part their performance depends on nonmonetary motivation—professional pride, a sense of responsibility, the pleasure of human interaction, solidarity, teamwork and loyalty, patriotism, and other sources of nonmonetary satisfaction. Successful performance, and its acknowledgement by others, is important. A "well-done approach" by directors, middle managers, and government authorities is seldom observed in the existing organizational culture in either sector. It is not surprising therefore that unsatisfactory service performance has been associated not only with falling wages and weak discipline, but also with demoralization, a loss of ethos, and a sense of being let down.

Demoralization has several facets and is both a cause and effect of the low-level equilibrium. One aspect is a loss of status or prestige: three or four decades ago teachers and doctors were *señores*; today they are proletariat. A closely related facet is a loss of pride, of a sense of self-realization. This in turn is related to their sense of being pushed by circumstances into cheating on their professional obligations, by moonlighting, and, in many cases, outright corruption. Finally, there has been a loss of ethos or service commitment. The most obvious cause of demoralization is the fall in real income, but other factors have contributed to this result.

The drop in status has been a trend over several decades and was a running theme in our interviews. It was signaled in a 1974 study of schoolteachers by the *Centro de Estudios y Promoción del Desarrollo* (DESCO): "The truth is that the teaching profession has been losing its relative earnings *capacity and its prestige*" (Ballon, Riofrio, and Roncagliolo 1974; emphasis added).

A school director said that teaching "used to be" a profession. It was not only a matter of money. Status meant that teachers wore suits. A doctor said: "[T]welve years of studying to end up as a taxi driver."

Perhaps the most poignant reference to this fall in the social ladder appears in a 2004 study of the daily life of teachers, where the author observes how impecunious teachers can often be seen: "lining up at the neighborhood charity restaurant (*comedor popular*)" (Anchi 2005).

The loss of image is associated with a loss of pride and self-respect, and a term that we heard repeatedly was "frustration." In 1999, the *Colegio Médico del Perú* expressed its concern and proposed a study of the subjective effects of the economic crisis on motivation: "The profession…is in distress, and feelings of frustration and dissatisfaction are associated with the loss of status" (Hernandez 1999).

Sigfredo Chiroque, an authority on the teaching profession, insists that the incentive system for teachers must look beyond wages, saying that teachers "need to be someone" (Chiroque 2004).

A 1989 United Nations Educational, Scientific and Cultural Organization (UNESCO) study acknowledged the prevalence of moonlighting:

> The teacher is frustrated when he realizes that he will not fulfill his earnings expectations. . . . His status falls and he works basically to survive . . . *pushed* into working in other occupations to obtain additional income.
>
> (Tovar, Gorriti, and Morillo 1989; emphasis added)

In 1988, the *Colegio Médico* also pointed the finger at moonlighting as a cause of dissatisfaction, in a proposal for a study on the Bio-Social Situation of the Peruvian Doctor:

> From the beginnings of the eighties, the medical professional, so as to maintain his status, is required to work in a greater number of health establishments, forcing himself to work longer hours . . . accepting job situations that are not in keeping with his specialization and professionalism, including positions that are exploitative and of an ethically unsatisfying nature, either for himself or for the health system.

(Hernandez 1999)

The director of a large public hospital in Lima saw a loss of morality in the profession and attributed it directly to the economic pressures suffered by doctors. The early 1990s crisis, he said: "taught us to obey the law of the jungle; every man for himself."

The problem of isolation and lack of support was emphasized by the religious director of an *Instituto Superior Pedagógico*, who trains most of the teachers in a province in the sierra. He excused the deficiencies of those teachers, saying that they had been abandoned by the State, getting no supervision, materials, or retraining. This sense of not being backed up is also strong in the case of rural doctors and nurses. Even in urban establishments, chronic shortages of medical and teaching materials and inadequate infrastructure and equipment create a similar perception among professionals of lack of support.

On the other hand, there are teachers and health professionals who are making a difference in service provision. These exceptional professionals are seldom recognized or their success acknowledged outside their schools or their communities. In this way, significant public service experiences are seldom shared or known by other professionals. In addition, there are important project initiatives where teachers, given no more pay, but other working conditions, give extraordinarily of their time and effort. Such projects have provided supportive, ongoing coaching, have encouraged teachers to work together to solve problems, and have shown them that their efforts can result in improved learning by their students (Hunt 2001).

Reaction of Human Resources

Teachers and doctors work less, care less, and seek alternative sources of income. Lower wages meant lower prestige and lower educational and personal standards for entrants into these professions. At the same time, extreme job tenure reduced the efficiency and quality of the labor force by making reassignment almost impossible, whether among locations or among specific placements. Discipline and motivation were undermined by rigid tenure laws and by the disconnection between performance and reward.

We describe three principal responses to low wages: (a) individual workers adopted coping strategies centered on additional sources of income; (b) quality deteriorated as better students turned away from these careers and emigrated from the public sector; and (c) professionals found ways to supplement their salaries by raising fees and through misappropriation and corruption.

Coping through Second Jobs. Professionals responded to the loss of real wage and status in several ways. One was a second job. This alternative is especially accessible to doctors, who can easily obtain and treat private patients, but for teachers, part-time jobs in private schools or as tutors are also relatively accessible. This section will review the evidence on the prevalence, causes, and effects of multiple occupations. Other coping strategies include corruption, which is documented above.

Prevalence of multiple occupations: Our sources for this issue were: (a) three surveys of teachers carried out between 1998 and 2001; (b) the Living Standards Measurement Survey (*Encuesta Nacional de Hogares*, ENAHO) 2003 household survey; (c) an anthropological study by Anchi (2005) specifically on the issue of multiple occupations of teachers; and (d) in-depth interviews by the authors of this study. The nature of these sources did not lend itself to a precise estimate of incidence. However, we deduce that, at the very least, over half of professionals in both sectors have a second occupation that is a source of additional income, and our best guess is that the figure is closer to two of every three professionals.

Our estimate is higher than the figures reported in earlier findings of two surveys of teachers, one by APOYO in 2001, which interviewed teachers outside of Lima, the other by Rivero (2002), which was national in coverage. When asked whether they held a second job, only 15 percent said yes in the APOYO study, and 14 percent said yes in the Rivero survey. A third survey in 1998, limited to Lima, by the Group for the Analysis of Development (GRADE), reported the much higher figure of 41 percent holding a second job. Another source is the 1997 ENAHO, which reported a figure of 31 percent (Table 6.4).

However, we believe that teachers underreport multiple occupations in sample surveys. Rivero (2002) makes the same point: "After consulting several opinions, it seems possible that some teachers inhibited themselves from giving real answers to this section of the questionnaire." The most probable reason is that, in most cases, moonlighting implies some degree of cheating on the responsibilities of a full-time public sector job, and is therefore an embarrassing and potentially risky admission. In addition, some hold two jobs simultaneously in the public sector, which is illegal. Also, much secondary activity, such as helping in a family business or tutoring students for a few hours a week or driving a taxi, would not be considered a second "job." A third reason is simply that most respondents conceal income and sources of income when asked point blank, and for that reason the most reliable way to estimate income is through expenditures.

A different approach was therefore applied for this study. Using data from ENAHO 2003, we compared the reported government salary of teachers and health professionals with the reported total expenditure of their households. The results are shown in Tables 6.5 and 6.6. As would be expected, family dependence on the government salary

Table 6.4. Estimates of Prevalence of Multiple Occupations Held by Teachers

Survey	Percent with Second Job
INIDE (1980)	20
Diaz and Saavedra 2000 (Lima)	41
APOYO 2001 (provinces; excludes Lima)	15
Rivero 2002	14
ENAHO 1997	31
Valencia-Webb	60–65

INIDE = Instituto Nacional de Investigación y Desarrollo de la Educación.
Source: Instituto Nacional de Investigación y Desarrollo de la Educación (1981:103); Diaz and Saavedra (2000:36); ENAHO 1997: Encuesta Nacional de Hogares 1997, published by the Instituto Nacional de Estadística e Informática.

Table 6.5. Government Teachers' Salary as Percent of Total Household Spending According to Degree of Dependence on Official Salary

Teachers	Least-dependent Quartile	Second Quartile	Third Quartile	Most-dependent Quartile
All	22	38	54	98
Lima	18	38	56	85
Provincial Urban	23	38	54	93
Provincial Rural	21	37	54	112

Note: Total of 1,166 teachers.
Source: ENAHO (2003).

varies a great deal, partly because spouses and others contribute to household income, and partly because the professionals themselves have multiple occupations.

In general, the degree of household dependence on the official salary is low if measured by the average ratio between teacher and health worker salaries and their household spending, which are 41 and 53 percent, respectively. As shown in Table 6.7, half or more of household income is covered by other sources. If looked at, not in terms of the average but of the situation of most professionals, the degree of dependence appears even lower. For the least-dependent quartile, the salary covers only 22 percent and 24 percent, respectively, of teacher and health professional household spending (Tables 6.5 and 6.6). In the second quartile measured in terms of dependence, the ratios are 38 percent and 40 percent, respectively. Only one in four of these families has a high level—close to 100 percent—of dependence on the official salary.

The ENAHO data suggest that multiple occupations are more common than reported by earlier surveys. A more definite conclusion requires a disaggregation of the contribution to household income from extra jobs and of the earnings of other working members. However, the small size of the sample, and the unreliability of responses to direct income questions as distinct from spending questions, mean that little additional certainty would be produced from such an analysis, and that the issue of multiple occupations should be

Table 6.6. Government Health Professionals' Salary as Percent of Total Household Spending, According to Degree of Dependence on Official Salary

Health Professionals	Least-dependent Quartile	Second Quartile	Third Quartile	Most-dependent Quartile
All	24	40	57	118
Lima	24	40	63	86
Provinces	24	40	57	119

Note: Total of 111 health professionals.
Source: ENAHO (2003).

Table 6.7. Average Net Monthly Salaries and Household Spending, in New Soles (Reported in ENAHO 2003)

Spending	Salary	Household	Percent
Teachers			
Lima	736	2,364	31
Provincial urban	755	1,867	40
Rural	634	1,081	59
All	737	1,787	41
Health Professionals			
Lima	1,665	4,009	42
Provinces	1,392	2,103	66
All	1,598	3,014	53

Source: INEI.

resolved rather using a larger study of the family finances of service professionals.

However, the more important implication of the ENAHO data does not hinge on the incidence of multiple occupations. Independent of who in the family is providing the extra income, it is clear that work and career decisions of education and health professionals, such as location, schedule choices, investment in training, and acceptance of administrative duties, will be determined not only by the government salary, but also by the occupational requirements of other family members.

Felix Anchi, an anthropology student at the Catholic University, studied the daily life of primary school teachers in the district of San Juan de Lurigancho, an urban marginal area of Lima. Of 32 teachers, 12 were housewives with no other occupation. The other 20 had the following remunerated occupations: tourism, tutoring, union activism, teacher in private school, selling clothes, selling chickens, social worker in a jail, psychologist in an NGO, administration of parents' properties, administrative work in a church school, administration of a small market, wine business, tailor, photographer, taxi driver, seller of gold jewelry, seller of cosmetics, clothing business, shoe sales, and computer services. Of the 32, 25 were women, most of who lived with a man who supplemented the family income.

In addition, some of the teacher "housewives" had occasional jobs carried out at home, such as tutoring. Anchi notes that teachers tend to have professional and social skills that allow them to take up different professions, including politics and community work, and so often it is teaching that becomes their second or complementary activity.[55] A major study of the teaching profession by the German Agency for Technical Cooperation (GTZ) reported that half of all those who train teachers in universities or *Institutos Superiores Pedagógicos* (Teacher Training Institutes, ISPs) have second occupations. Future teachers are thus introduced by the example of their mentors into the multiple occupation world of teaching (Arregui, Hunt, and Díaz 1996).

The issue of multiple occupations was touched on in almost all interviews.

Director of Human Resources in a large Lima public hospital:

> Doctors don't want to hear that they have duties as well as rights. They don't respect their schedule, they punch their timecards and then leave, they skip duty whenever they feel like it, and they don't even work their full six-hour shift. They come for short spells, they prefer to teach at university. Out of 100 nurses, 80 manage to get sick certificates and skip work.

---

55. Chiroque (2004) refers to "the diversity of ways by which teachers earn extra money: many sell cosmetics; and men give private classes or work as street sellers (*ambulantes*)."

Rural anthropologist, university professor, did several studies of rural teachers:

> It is not feasible for rural teachers to have a second teaching job, but they engage in nonteaching work, for instance, owning a small farm, a store, and in one case, a teaching couple sold alcoholic beverages.

Psychologist, university professor, research on urban marginal schools, married to doctor:

> Many teachers have second jobs, some as teachers and some as taxi drivers, etc., but when asked they do not admit that other job because they know that it compromises their official work. Public sector doctors tend to have private patients who they sometimes attend inside the public establishment.

Doctor, directed SERUM (rural health service) program, university professor:

> The public service job suffers because medics work in other jobs to supplement their income, but the official job helps the doctor to get patients and provides many opportunities for corruption.

Director of Pedagogy in Lima UGEL in middle-class neighborhood, 33 years' experience:

> When taken to task for not meeting schedule or targets, teachers reply that they do meet targets in their private sector jobs, which pay better.

Doctor in provincial town in sierra, works in hospital with 14 doctors: "All our doctors have a private practice."

School director, new urban marginal district Lima, 33 years' experience:

> The teachers in my afternoon shift have three jobs—teaching, driving taxis, and a family business. For a teacher with children it would be a luxury to have only one job.

Director *Fe y Alegría* school with mostly female teachers, in very poor Lima district: "Of my 20 morning shift teachers, 7 have a second job; of 28 afternoon teachers, 16 have other jobs."

Preschool teacher in provincial town:

> In my preschool, all six teachers have no other paid occupation, but all of us are women and mostly married. But most teachers in this town have commercial activities and rural teachers generally own a small business.

Director of a large Lima state hospital: "All my doctors have a second or even a third job."

In a sierra rural school:

> Director: "I have no time for another job because I direct and also teach classes."
>
> First Teacher: "In the afternoon I have a carpentry shop in [the town nearby]."
>
> Second Teacher: "In the afternoon I work as an announcer in a radio in town."

Reasons for multiple occupations: The obvious motive that drives professionals into multiple occupations is immediate financial need. However, extra occupations serve professionals in ways that go beyond short-term need. Three such functions can be suggested. One is that doctors use public sector jobs at early stages in their career as a springboard for later private practice. Recent graduates develop a clientele and acquire both experience and reputation gradually, working from the security of a public sector job. This rationale is less important for teachers, but many young teachers do have their sights set on a different career and use the teaching job as a way to finance the additional studies.

A second rationale for an outside occupation is the development of a business where the logic is not so much the immediate income from the professional's direct labor, but rather the use of a diversity of resources available to a household, including other labor, personal relationships, real estate, and the family home. In addition, the creation of an own business is likely to be a long-run target, yielding little in the short run, but offering more room for upward mobility over a longer period. Anchi and other informants mentioned the following businesses run by teachers they knew: academies that taught short courses on specialized subjects, market stalls, handicraft workshops, and small farms. Doctors are most likely to invest funds and time setting up their own clinics.

A third logic that justifies an extra occupation is the potential synergy between public sector work and a private business. The most obvious such opportunities are the own referrals of doctors and the teachers that tutor their own students. But more sophisticated opportunities include the manufacture and sale of school supplies and uniforms, school photography, and medical laboratories and supplies, including X-rays.

Effects of multiple occupations: Professionals with second occupations put less effort into their government job, suffer stress, and are more likely to be absent and to engage in corruption.

Effort is a function of time spent on the job. However, in the case of services such as teaching and health care, effort has several other dimensions that contribute to the quality of the desired output, such as the care taken by teachers in the preparation of classes, degree of concentration, emotional self-control, flexibility to accommodate changes in routine or occasional extra-hour needs, professional rigor, and strong commitment to users and the institution. A public sector teacher or health professional occupied in other activities is obviously handicapped in the performance of his or her formal obligations. A paper by Barbara Hunt, an external specialist who visited over 200 primary schools between 1993 and 2001, states that "teachers routinely had one or more other jobs. They generally had to leave school immediately to go to their other work; no one had time out of school for planning, working with other teachers, or correcting papers" (Hunt 2001).

Another study claims that "most teachers work in two places, one of which is a private school, and because discipline there is greater, the teacher often neglects his public sector job" (Lopez de Castilla 2003).

Any additional occupation will drain time, energy, and moral commitment, yet the full-time employment contract of the government professional presupposes a worker that is capable of giving most of his or her working capacity to that job, including the time and effort required for on-the-job training and upgrading. One result of this hustling is psychological stress.

Anchi (2005), for example, writes that:

> The outside activities of public school teachers have a major impact on their lives, because they involve new worlds, require a great deal of imagination and time, and establish a new

relation with their personal lives . . . the teacher's behavior becomes a pretence to preserve "his image" as a teacher in school and community. [Those jobs] are causing (the teacher) a great malaise in his personal life, including exhaustion or fatigue in his daily life.

Corruption and absenteeism have been facilitated by an extreme degree of security of tenure and a relatively short working day. One effect of multiple occupations is a higher incidence of absenteeism, and it is understandable then that a study of absenteeism in hospitals found a rate of 73 percent among tenured professionals, in contrast to a rate of 37 percent for contracted personnel. A major facilitating factor occurred in education in the 1970s, when the rush to increase coverage led the government to introduce two shifts in schools, and even three shifts in some. The effect was to compress and cut the teachers' working hours, leaving the teachers freer to take on second jobs.

A study on corruption and absenteeism by Alcazar and Andrade (1999) says the following:

> A major problem is absenteeism, defined to include time spent on private patients while working in a public institution: 43 percent of doctors and 32 percent of nurses rated it as common or very common, which the authors blame on the high opportunity cost of full compliance with scheduled hours but also on the inefficacy of the mechanisms for monitoring and sanctioning.

Our interviewees provided further examples of how the prevalence of multiple occupations affects the lives and work of human resources.

Director of a Lima secondary school:

> Teachers with outside work do not yield as much, are more careless of the supplies they receive, are more inclined to get stuck in a routine, seek pretexts to avoid participation in committees and other nonclass activities, and when called to account say: "teaching is my extra income; my real earnings come from my business. I come here to insure my old age." I have had teachers who showed up only twice a week, got discounted, but didn't care. These teachers come tired and stressed out and most fulfill only 50 percent of their teaching program.

Focus group of teachers in Lima's low-income district (four teachers repeated the following): "Those with outside work improvise in class, are tired, and come to do the minimum. They do not prepare."

Director teacher in a sierra small town:

> Some of my teachers were reluctant to admit they held parallel jobs in private schools, where they were allowed to be more innovative, but I told them not to worry because they could bring their innovations here.

Official in Lima urban marginal UGEL:

> Many of our teachers are suffering from mental problems, neurosis, and even schizophrenia, related to their overwork. But most refuse a diagnosis, and the rules for these cases are unclear. They cannot be fired. If they are separated for treatment, they appeal and win in the courts. All we can do is to reassign them.

Director of a Lima hospital:

> Doctors have several jobs, even [the illegal] holding of more than one in the public sector.
> They spend the day jumping around from place to place, spending little time at any one place.
> But they spend most time where they earn most.

Dual practice can also encourage corruption in the form of self-referrals by health professionals.

Doctor, former senior ministry official: "There is growing practice of detouring patients to private practice. Doctors and technicians collude in this."

The only traumatologist in a small town, owner of a private clinic, candidly explaining why he works in the town health post: "I'm here to catch patients."

Quality Reduction. The stock of human resources has adjusted to lower wages, not only through coping, but also through a change in composition in the direction of lower quality. This has happened in three ways: the quality of entrants into the professions has declined, top professionals have dropped out of public service, and skills have deteriorated for lack of upgrading and on-the-job training.

This conclusion is tentative, since there is no systematic and reliable measurement of the quality of either the work or the in-service training of education and health professionals. Indeed, the paucity of evaluation and quality measurement is probably systemic; SUTEP in particular has fought all efforts to introduce evaluation, and the *Colegio Médico* has only recently and timidly introduced voluntary recertification. The lack of transparency on quality is instrumental to the official and professional acceptance of low quality. Human resource selection, management, and upgrading have been consistently neglected in the structure and operation of both ministries, partly due to almost nonexistent official personnel records. Nonetheless, the view that human resource quality has fallen is shared by many of the people interviewed for this study, including both analysts and service professionals themselves, and is supported by indirect evidence.

The standard explanation for this trend is the fast growth of health and education services over the last four decades.[56] "Massification" is the term used to describe this evolution from small-scale, mostly urban services into mass-production industries, which now cover not only a huge urban marginal population but also much of the rural sector. To meet the personnel requirements of this service explosion, teacher-pre-service-training institutes and university faculties have multiplied with little concern for standards and very lax certification requirements. The number of ISPs jumped from 86 to 312 between 1985 and 1995, mostly with the creation of little-regulated private ISPs, which mushroomed especially between 1993 and 1995, going from 30 to 198.

Similarly, health services were extended in the 1990s to almost universal coverage in terms of districts, going from 80.6 percent of districts covered in 1992 to 98.3 percent in 1999. The number of health establishments jumped 87 percent between 1992 and 1996, and most of the new establishments were posts in urban marginal and rural areas. A health official admitted to us that because no one had wanted to apply for a vacancy as hospital director in a town in Peru's mountains, it had been necessary to lower the hiring standards,

---

56. This view is forcefully argued for the case of education by Vega (2005).

and that this was a common practice. Throughout most of the period of massification, wages were simultaneously falling. It is not surprising that quality control in recruitment was put aside in the urgency to meet staffing needs.

Some indications of quality decline in the teaching profession are provided by the following studies. Alcazar and Balcazar (2001) quote a 1997 APOYO opinion survey on the prestige attached to different careers by young people in Lima. Those from middle-class and low-income families rated teaching lowest of all professions. The authors conclude that the fact that most of the students studying to be teachers are from low-income families indicates that the career was chosen not for vocational reasons but because it is cheaper and easier to gain entry. According to GTZ, it is "widely known" that universities lower the "cutoff" requirements in university entrance exams for students who choose education. According to Arregui, Hunt, and Díaz (1996:81), entry into the teaching career "requires much less talent, aptitude and knowledge than for almost any other graduate study."

Interviews carried out for this study tend to corroborate the results of the preceding studies.

Director of an urban marginal school, Lima, a veteran age 60:

> The education of teachers has deteriorated. Private ISPs are responsible for proliferation of bad teachers since they never fail students; this dates from 1995–96 laws. The teaching title is easy to get. Anyone can be a teacher. It's all a business.

University professor on an education faculty:

> There is a great deal of localism in the profession: education students and their teachers are mostly of the same region. This is a vicious circle: mediocrity is reproduced and innovation blocked. It creates complacency, but it is also an opportunity.

Ministry senior official, former director of major ISP:

> The growth of private ISPs has been excessive. We're trying to implement a recently approved accreditation program, but I am being sued and my house is embargoed because we prohibited further matriculation in some ISPs that were granting teaching certificates without requiring any class attendance.

Dean of *Colegio Médico*:

> Quality has been deteriorating over the last 15 years as a result of the proliferation of medical faculties. Most new universities do not have the money or staff that is needed. We have had to modify our recertification requirements because university degrees cannot be trusted. The best students don't enter government service. When 5,000 doctors were appointed recently, the examination was a simulation.

Hospital director in a province: "Doctors do not seek retraining and there are no institutional requirements for retraining."

A young doctor in an NGO: "Quality has fallen over the last five years. Recruitment is corrupt. There is no evaluation of personality—some doctors are psychotics."

Fees and Corruption.   A third response to the fiscal crisis has been a turn to self-financing. To an increasing extent, users are paying for services provided by the public education and health systems. The methods range from the legal to the illegal, with a great deal that is dubious. They include outright fees set by establishments, but many charges are less forthright, and even corrupt. It can also vary between practices adopted by the establishment as a whole, and those carried out by individual professionals or groups of professionals within the establishment. In one way or another, service professionals are generating more and more self-financing as a way to supplement government salaries. The spontaneous entrepreneurial reaction by service providers was given official encouragement during the 1990s in the context of a fiscal collapse. Economy, administrative efficiency, and the principle of cost recovery came to the fore. Health posts that did not raise significant revenues were shut down.

As a result, government services are now less accessible to the poor, and financial control and honesty have been weakened. More generally, service establishments have repositioned themselves in terms of their users, moving upscale. To some extent this has simply been a consequence of fees, but in part has been a result of decisions regarding product mix and location.

There is little systematic information on self-financing, even on funds generated by legitimate and published fees. This opaqueness is not surprising, first, because self-financing is for the most part used as a way to supplement salaries, and though authorities are fully aware of the practice, they prefer to avoid public scrutiny.

Second, the entire matter of self-financing is not properly regulated, with respect to both prices charged and the allocation of wage supplements among personnel. In practice, establishment officials enjoy a great deal of discretion and power to tax or benefit both users and their own staff. In the allocation of supplements, for instance, there is a notorious bias in favor of the administrative personnel who manage the collection and distribution. As shown in Table 6.13, senior administrators in Lima receive supplements ranging from 3,458 to 8,658 soles monthly in establishments, when doctors in the same establishment receive only 1,118 soles.

Third, even when fully authorized, as in the case of the *Asignación Extraordinaria por Trabajo Asistencial* (Extraordinary Bonus for Health Care Provision, AETA), salary payments based on revenues generated by an establishment result in horizontal inequalities across regions, establishments, and categories of professionals within the same establishment.

Fees and corruption in health: One indicator of a rising trend in self-financing or own revenues in the central government health sector is provided by the figures in Table 6.8, which show that self-financing doubled as a share of total MINSA income between 1980 and 2003. In addition, several informants reported that costs

Table 6.8. Self-financing as Percent of MINSA Total Income

Year	Percent
1980	6.7
1981	6.2
1982	8.2
1983	7.1
1984	7.2
1995	10.2
2003	13

Note: 1980–84 figures are Ingresos Propios (own revenues) which can include revenues not received from patients; for example, revenues from private providers. Figures for 1995 and 2003 are revenues from patients only.

Sources: 1980–84 from ANSSA-PERU (1986:27). 1995 from Cuentas Nacionales de Salud MINSA-OPS based on "Tendencias en la Utilización de Servicios de Salud," Peru 1995–2002, MINSA-OPS. Data from the Sistema Integrado de Administración Financiera, Ministerio de Economía y Finanzas.

formerly borne by hospitals—medicines, medical supplies, and lab tests—have now become "out-of-pocket" expenses borne by patients.

A study of five Lima hospitals documented a significant increase in self-financing between 1991 and 1995. The unweighted average proportion of hospital revenues obtained from fees and other self-financing rose from 14.4 percent in 1991 to 22.4 percent in 1995 (Arroyo 2000).

At the same time, self-financing practices appear to vary over a wide range, as suggested by data from a 2004 study in four regions. At one extreme, self-financing as a share of total MINSA establishment revenues was reported to be only 0.1 percent in the region of Sara Sara in Ayacucho, and 2.6 percent in Jaen in Cajamarca. At the other extreme, the ratio was 29.8 percent in Paita in the Piura region and 22.7 percent in the city of Cajamarca. However, the study acknowledges that fee income is not well recorded, that it lends itself to "leaks," that the uses of fee income include transfers into Ordinary Revenue, which thus allows them to be used for payrolls, and also "distorted uses and forms of corruption" (Petrera 2005). Those practices, and the exaggerated variability of the numbers, suggest that reporting of fee income is incomplete.

The view that self-financing in health has increased is strongly supported by statements obtained from numerous interviewees, as reported below. The directors of three major public hospitals in Lima, for example, stated in interviews that their establishments had moved away from the poorest in the city to a less-poor clientele:

Director of a Lima hospital (originally a religious charity institution dedicated to the needy):

> Forty percent of our budget is self-financed from fees. It was much less before. Only 1 or 2 percent of our patients are extreme poor. We created an itinerant outreach program to reach the poor in urban marginal areas and in some provinces where the municipalities pay our fares. That's when we discovered the real poor who couldn't even afford the fare to our hospital.

With respect to the distribution of fee income, interviewees admitted that these are mostly allocated as salary supplements, even though the practice is explicitly forbidden by budget rules.

Director of Human Resources unit of a Lima hospital:

> The law says that the ordinary budget is the source of wage payments; however, these resources are not enough, and that is why *recursos directamente recaudados* (self-financing) are used to top up the payroll. That is why there have been no funds to renew equipment since 40 years ago.

Director of Lima Health Center:

> We pay wage incentives using fees, because the ordinary budget is not enough. Only 18 percent of our budget is for goods and services and 2 percent for capital investments. There is no control over fee income.

Several informants spoke of corruption by lower-level technical staff and social workers in establishments.

Director of Human Resources in a Lima hospital:

> Social workers have their own business based on granting [poverty] exemptions from regular fee payments. It is they who get the most out of the exemption system since they charge for their evaluations and for granting exemptions. Administrative personnel do business approving reassignments or certificates. Nurses and nursing assistants have a "ticket carrousel" business [for patients in waiting lines].

Volunteer in a large Lima hospital:

> Patients have to pay nurses to get their sheets changed. With blood donations, recipients are charged for the donation and also for the containers, which are later resold. Many nurses engage in the traffic of medicines. Once we brought special creams to treat cases of burning. The creams disappeared.

The close relationship between fees, wage supplements, and corruption was discussed by other interviewees.

Former MINSA senior official and NGO consultant:

> There has been a considerable increase in doctors' salaries, but the source of that improvement is perverse, because it comes from fees from patients. It has been financed with money from the poorest. There are different types of fees—those that are controlled by the Ministry, those that are not authorized, and under-the-table payments. There is more than one payroll: one is formal, the other is where other benefits are paid. It is known that these second payrolls are paid out of own revenues but it is not known how they are allocated. There are secret payrolls. Professionals thus receive a formal salary and a separate payment. This is more common where the State has less control, as in large hospitals.

Focus group of three NGO doctors:

> Wage policy generates aberrant behavior: doctors have an insignificant wage but are in a position to charge fees. Those fees then become part of the hospital's own revenues and can then be allocated at discretion. In that way, they have been formalized; fee income has been perverted. They are transformed into food baskets for the staff, incentives for emergency duty, for productivity, and travel fares.

Senior official in Nurses Union:

> Staff members press their directors to charge fees because they are turned into salaries. Nurses in particular are the scourge of directors, pressing for higher fees.

Another form of self-financing in the health sector, in addition to patient fees and corruption, has been the commercialization of public sector infrastructure, equipment, and facilities. Some hospitals have created private "clinics" within the public hospital, in which the establishment's public service professionals carry out a private practice using government facilities. Loayza hospital in Lima, for instance, created its private clinic in 1994 on the third floor of the main building, where patients pay rates for consultations several times higher than those charged in the public part of the hospital, and where they can get beds in more private rooms. The hospital collects a rent, but the arrangement generates subsidized private earnings.

Another commercial practice is related to the acceptance of medical students for specialization. The earlier tradition by which public hospitals took in quotas of students from different public universities has given way to a preferential acceptance of students from private universities in exchange for fees or other benefits by which the private university pays the public hospital for the service. As in the case of fees charged to patients, this practice discriminates against poorer public university students and hurts the poor indirectly because it discourages and reduces recruitment from public universities, which are precisely those most inclined to train doctors in public health skills as distinct from the clinical practice orientation that characterizes private universities.

Fees and corruption in education: Teachers have resorted in similar ways to self-financing in the face of declining payrolls. In schools, the most transparent source of additional financing has been the fees collected by APAFAs, which date from 1950, but which have risen over time. "Voluntary" contributions to the APAFA became a way to reconcile fees with the constitutional mandate that basic education is free. Though outright fees are limited to the legal ceiling imposed on APAFAs, school directors, teachers, and parents have been imaginative in creating sources of income to supplement government funds. These include the marketing of snacks in school kiosks, and of uniforms, school insignias, classroom supplies, photographs, textbooks, photocopies, and charges for collective events, all pressed on the parents with varying degrees of force. Some schools in poor districts of Lima charge S/. 1.00 or 1.50 monthly for courses in noncurricular subjects, such as English and computing. Schools also rent out their facilities for private or community events, or, as in one well-known case in Lima, for parking space. At times it is an individual teacher or school administrator that creates a small, private business, such as a workshop to make school insignias or uniforms, but often it is decided and carried out by the establishment as a whole. However, there are no equivalent estimates of the evolution of self-financing by schools.

Interviewees provided the following observations on these practices:

Director of Education for a regional government, with 40 years' experience as a teacher:

> We are in the hands of a mafia. Producing teaching certificates is a mass-production industry. Universities accept students without entry examinations. Ninety percent of the teachers are dedicated to profiteering. Grades are sold. School directors charge the most. Illegal business is the culture due to the low wages. Teachers collude with doctors to get sickness certificates. In Pataz, 23 teachers were sick one day. APAFA members also steal. Some are "false parents" who lie to get elected. Corruption has increased. To get certified, private schools pay US$5,000. I knew that if I took this job I would end up being sued by the mafia.

Focus group of teachers:

> In large high schools (*Gran Unidades Escolares*), own revenues from kiosk sales, photocopies, uniforms, fees for paperwork, rentals of auditorium, pool, classrooms, cafeteria etc., are retained by the director's office to pay for events outside of the school, in-service training, and other such costs. Most of the time, teachers are not aware of how these funds are used, except for the director's travel expenses.

Table 6.9. Share of Private Schools in Total Enrollment

% Private	1955	1964	1981	1993	2003
Total	11.4	10.9	15	15.6	18.7
Primary	8.9	8.9	13.5	12.3	14.9
Secondary	36.3	22.8	18.5	22.1	24.9

Sources: 1955 and 1964 from INP/OCDE (1966); 1981 from *Perú en Números 1991*, Instituto Cuánto.

Auditor, UGEL:

> Corruption is linked to the lack of funds. Several directors have been accused of misappropriation of school revenues and goods. They take advantage of the difficulty in controlling those revenues in situ. They divide the parents and the teachers to be able to do what they want. Teachers resort to unwarranted charges. Some have been denounced for charging for giving passing grades to students who had failed. They also resort to the sale of books: students who don't buy are not allowed to enter the class.

Book salesman met in a school in San Juan de Lurigancho: "Teachers have deals with publishers and receive checks with a fixed payment of a commission of 150 or 200 soles for selling textbooks."

Reaction of Users

Users responded to deficiencies in public education and health services in two ways: by turning to private suppliers, and by taking on part of the cost burden of public services.

Turn to Private Suppliers. The use of private primary schools has been rising since the mid-1960s, and of private secondary schools since the 1980s, as shown in Table 6.9.

One probable consequence of the trend to private schools has been a loss of concern for public education by authorities. Elites have, in effect, opted out of the system and are no longer stakeholders except in the remotest sense. Members of Congress, senior ministry officials, mayors, intellectuals, media owners, and reporters, even midlevel education authorities in regional UGELs, send their children to private schools, or at least to public schools run with considerable autonomy by religious denominations. Even humble rural teachers send their children to private schools when they can.

A public-school teacher in a remote rural school in the sierra said:

> I am a teacher and I know the quality of public education where I live. My life objective is that my children be better educated than me. So I send my children to private schools. Besides, I know that the best public teachers work also in private schools and work better in these schools since there they can be fired.

Another rural teacher in the sierra said:

> I send almost all my salary to my daughter who is studying to be a nurse in a private institute in Trujillo. I complement my salary with income from a farm which I work with my wife and with communal work we both do.

Table 6.10. Physicians in Private Practice as Percent Total			
1964	1981	1985	2002
44	41	53	78

Note: Active physicians only. Includes dentists. Private practice defined as those not employed by MINSA, ESSALUD, or other public sector entities.
Sources: Bustios; Thomas Hall; Colegio Médico del Perú; Censo 1981.

In the case of health, the evidence also suggests a turn to private providers. Physicians not employed by the government or social security have risen as a proportion of the total, from 41 percent in 1964 to 78 percent in 2002 (Table 6.10).

Those numbers are reinforced, first, by the fact that private practitioners have higher levels of productivity than those in the public sector (Harding 2005); manpower statistics thus understate the share of output produced by the private sector. Second, most public sector physicians also have a private practice, and further, the time and effort devoted to those second occupations has been growing, as argued above. Third, the supply of physicians has been growing far faster than government hiring for at least the last 15 to 20 years. Between 1981 and 2002 the number of active physicians rose 5.2 percent yearly, whereas those employed by government rose at less than 1.0 percent, yearly. The resulting labor market glut has sharpened competition and reduced fees in the private sector. Falling private sector fees coincided with the opposite trend in the public sector, toward higher charges in public health establishments. Users have thus been drawn to the private sector by price as well as quality considerations.

With the poor, the response to poor public service is less a turn to private health providers than an unwillingness to detach themselves from traditional providers and switch to public health services. ENAHO 2003 data report that the poorest quintile recorded 13.4 million cases of illness of which only 4.9 million, or 37 percent, sought and received treatment. It is likely, however, that most of the other 63 percent of cases did receive some form of traditional treatment or advice that is not being admitted or registered as a "consultation."

Voluntary Payments for Public Services. Users have responded to public service deficiencies by supplementing government budgets out of their own pockets. We were repeatedly told of cases where a community or municipality had built or repaired a school or health post or bought school or medical supplies or hired a teacher. The mayor of a small rural district near Huamachuco had hired two teachers, on a contract basis but, unfortunately, never paid them. Another rural primary school, however, had opened a secondary section in 2003 with two grades and had applied to the UGEL for four secondary teachers. When the UGEL did not respond, the community went ahead, hiring two young teachers at a monthly salary of 100 soles. In an even more isolated district in that province, there were several schools and 70 teachers, of which 9 were paid between 400 and 500 soles by the community. In one rural classroom in the sierra a sack full of potatoes sat on the floor next to the teacher's desk. The teacher admitted that it had been a gift from the community, and that he received gifts of that sort regularly. He and his colleague at the two-teacher school also shared in the school lunch provided by the community.

According to a UGEL official, there is a growing practice of formal agreements under which the UGEL agrees to give official status to teachers hired and paid by the community or municipality. Wages fluctuate between 100 and 350 soles, and the official named eight communities in the province that had signed such agreements. One community committed itself to providing a share of its harvest as a payment to teachers. It is also very common for the teacher or health worker to be provided a room in the community, though part of the school or health post is sometimes used for that purpose.

Government Responses

As wages declined over the last three decades, governments repeatedly faced major strikes and street demonstrations by both education and health sector professionals. These mobilizations tended to occur during moments of political weakness, when economic collapses undermined regime support and extremist political groups threatened revolution. In that context, the large-scale mobilization and paralysis of basic social services by unions acquired a pivotal weight. SUTEP, for instance, gained widespread legitimacy by spearheading opposition to the military government during the crisis of 1977–79, and was rewarded by the succeeding government with major concessions, including a system of payroll deduction for union fees. It is not surprising that successive governments, unable to satisfy the demands for stable and even rising real wages, hastened to accommodate union agendas. The thrust of their demands was to establish ever-more-rigid tenure and to loosen discipline in human resources management.

The Legal Framework. The past 20 years witnessed a deterioration of Peru's civil service in the public sector. Budgetary and sector laws and regulations have progressively been introduced that have undermined both the original spirit of the Public Civil Service Law and the coherence and consistency of the administrative system created by that law.

Different governments have introduced specific laws for the health and education sectors and for their separate professional groups, with provisions dealing with the management of their human resources. In practice, these specific laws have prevailed over the general provisions of the Public Civil Service Law. Thus, the careers of teachers and health professionals are regulated by the Civil Service Law only as far as it does not contradict what is established by the specific sector laws.

The result is a complex legal framework in which managers, authorities, and professionals in both sectors, either by tradition or self-interest, use the "best available interpretation." In this context, political power or influence in the media and with the courts has been a determining factor over the actual practices by which human resources are managed. Over time, a parallel human resources management system has emerged, which, combined with fiscal pressures, has eroded the public service career of both health professionals and teachers.

Hiring in Education. According to the Teachers Career Law, teachers enter into the public system as tenured teachers (*nombrados*) after a selection process implemented by decentralized education units. Each of these units is required to establish an evaluation committee, which should include a representative of the teachers union. The last time these formal procedures were followed, however, was in 1991. Even before, the formalities of the selection process were often overridden, notoriously during the 1980s when the government hired massive numbers of uncertified teachers: the stock of teachers doubled in 10 years and 85 percent of those hired lacked a teaching degree (Table 6.11). According to some sources, a substantial proportion of those recruits lacked even full secondary schooling, but this is difficult to confirm because personnel records have not been kept and because of widespread falsification of school certificates.

Table 6.11. Education: Evolution of the Number of Teachers with and without a Pedagogical Degree (PD)

Year	With PD	Percent	Without PD	Percent	Total
1950	16,630	68	7,803	32	24,433
1960	29,599	68	14,111	32	43,710
1970	71,559	70	30,170	30	101,729
1980	101,306	81	24,334	19	125,640
1990	126,695	49	129,773	51	256,468

Sources: Indicadores Cuantitativos del Sistema Educativo, Ministerio de Educación.

During the 1990s, budgetary restrictions led to a complete suspension of new appointments, but hiring continued in the form of short-term contracts which, in effect, allowed the government to pay less than the official salary scales, partly because the scales were not binding for contract workers, and partly because those workers did not receive pension and other costly benefits. Moreover, short-term contracts allowed decentralized units to develop their own procedures and criteria, a process that, as it were, formalized informality. Over time, temporary contracts tended to be renewed every school year, and have been gradually converted into tenured positions.

Ministry official:

> In Lima, the number of posts created by decentralized units without proper budgetary authorization, which were originally temporary but ended up being permanent, were 40 percent of the total number of tenured positions.

In addition, those under contracts were not subject to legal recruitment or selection procedures, and many did not have degree titles or they were false, suggesting that academic standards for *contratados* were lower. According to an MED official, in 2002, during a procedure to evaluate who were recently appointed and through which means, it was found that many of the teachers who had been hired under contracts were not actually teachers, and about 45 percent had not completed secondary education.

Despite their academic deficiencies, many *contratados* were offered a shortcut to a teaching title, called *profesionalización*, which could be obtained after a year or less of study, mostly in summer courses, after which they would be eligible for a tenured position. In a study of rural teachers, most of them tenured, 33 percent had obtained their teaching degree in this way, through *profesionalización* programs, which had become a lucrative business for many universities.

Under political and union pressure, in 1994 and 2001, government twice changed its mind on temporary contracts and proceeded to their large-scale conversion into normal appointments.[57] On both occasions, the government established a shortened form of the legally prescribed selection and recruitment requirements. In 2001, an *ad hoc* procedure set

---

57. In 1994, the government appointed teachers based only on the holding of a title and permanence on the job as a teacher under contract for at least two years.

out to regularize teachers under contracts and to hire new ones. Appointments to fill existing vacancies and positions held by contract teachers were to be based on a national written examination organized by the Ministry of Education. However, of 90,000 applicants, only 2,000 passed the examination. In the end, the government backtracked by reducing the original minimum approval grade, and on that basis chose 20,000 teachers for appointment.

Many interviews confirmed and illustrated cases of government concessions to SUTEP pressures, which contributed to a further undermining of key selection and hiring provisions of the law. A common pattern involves the use of strikes focused on a particular region, pressing the local Ministry authorities for the *nombramiento* of contract workers hired without previous Ministry approval. These pressures for the formalization of a de facto situation obtained support from regional political organizations and from public opinion in general. In the case of the mass appointments made in 2001, a former Ministry official explained that:

> SUTEP was pressing for the massive appointment of teachers, but it opposed the examination. Its argument was that a degree is sufficient credential for appointment.

As a UGEL authority, formerly a member of SUTEP, explained, SUTEP's anti-examination position was a "political directive."

Hiring in Health. The career legal framework prescribes a selection process within health establishments. The hiring decision is made by a three-member commission. Doctors must first pass a national-level exam and begin their specialization or residence.[58] Doctors are assigned to a specific public health establishment, depending on the preference of each doctor and establishment vacancies, under a three-year contract. After this period, doctors obtain their specialization degree. To obtain an appointment, they must apply for an available position at any establishment. These merit-based recruitment and selection procedures appear to have been followed to a large extent in many big hospitals.

As with education, budgetary restrictions during the 1990s led to contract hiring.[59] However, the hiring of *contratados* is not subject to the merit-based selection procedure described above, and in practice has been highly discretionary and open to political pressures. Three hospital directors, who had been appointed through merit-based competitions, told us that they were much less vulnerable to those pressures than colleagues whose appointment had not been based on competition. Indeed, to strengthen their independence they had organized an "association of examination-based hospital directors."

In 2004, following a major strike, the government agreed to appoint 3,466 doctors who had been working under contracts.[60] As with teachers, the criteria applied were time in service and budgetary authorization, without a merit evaluation process. The government was responding to union pressures, but the ad hoc hiring process actions undermined a central element of a career development structure: the capacity to attract, select, and hire the best and most qualified to do the job.

---

58. Article 15, DL 559.

59. Most health professionals were hired through the implementation of programs such as *Programa de Salud Básica Para Todos* (Program for Basic Health for All, PSBPT), CLAS, and, in the case of excluded and very remote populations, the introduction of itinerant teams (ELITES). By the end of the 1980s, the PSBPT program had hired under nonpersonal services 10,806 health employees including doctors, nonmedical professionals, and technicians.

60. Press release, MINSA, December 28, 2004, and interviews.

Table 6.12. Health: Components of Monthly Salaries of Doctors, 2004

Level	Base Salary	Incentives				Shifts and Emergency Duties	Total Salary
		AETA	Food Support	Food Bonus	Subtotal Incentives		
1	2,148.03	660.00	300.00	158.00	1,118.00	756.80	4,022.83
2	2,302.64	660.00	300.00	158.00	1,118.00	793.20	4,213.84
3	2,409.04	660.00	300.00	158.00	1,118.00	811.40	4,338.44
4	2,508.86	660.00	300.00	158.00	1,118.00	850.00	4,476.86
5	2,623.84	660.00	300.00	158.00	1,118.00	918.00	4,659.84

AETA = Extraordinary Bonus for Health Provision.
Source: Ministry of Health, and legal norms.

Remunerations. Despite career laws that prescribe wage incentives for experience and specialization, cost-of-living increases in both sectors have been made with a proportional bias toward the entry levels. There is now less room to reward years of experience and other indicators of career merit.

As a result, in 2004, differences in salaries among career levels were quite small. In the case of teachers, the difference between payments to the highest level and the lowest level of teachers with a pedagogic degree is only 8 percent, and the salary structure does not discriminate among specializations or responsibilities. The salary differential between a director and a teacher has been about 7 percent. Even by the late 1980s, teacher salaries had become a flat structure, undermining the monetary incentives needed to motivate and reward performance and effort. These ratios were originally over 100 percent two and three decades ago.

The same flattening effect has been produced by the granting of bonuses that carry no pension obligation, thus evading the pension benefits established by the Professors Law and the Civil Service Law. In each case the bonus is small, but over time, they have come to represent 88 percent of total remuneration. In principle, these bonuses could reinforce the incentive structure, but in practice they have had the opposite effect. The bonuses are approved at regional and local levels, creating a high degree of discretionality. In practice, this has meant that there has not been a unified payroll system; every decentralized unit has had a de facto payroll system guided by their own practices regarding entitlements, and which in many cases have been of questionable legality. As a result, there are many salary differences across regions and between teachers and administrative personnel.

The pattern is similar for the salaries of health professionals, who also receive many supplements justified as incentives that tend to flatten the salary structure by levels. Payments for emergency room service have the same effect.[61] The difference between the salary of the highest category and entry-level doctors is approximately 18 percent before salary supplements and 13 percent after those supplements are considered in the remuneration (Table 6.12).

---

61. In the last three years, there have been increases for hospital emergency guard duty (DS 008-2003-SA, Law 28167, DU 032-2002).

Table 6.13. Health: Monthly Salary Supplements, by Region, 2004

Occupational Group		RD[1]	Lima Region					Other Regions		
			AETA[2]	Prd[3]	AN[4]	Alm[5]	Total	AETA	Prd	Total
Management	up to	8,200			300	158	8,658	150		8,350
Health professionals (doctors, nurses and others)	up to		660		300	158	1,118	150		150
Administrative	up to			660	300	158	1,118		150	50

Notes:
1. Managerial Responsibility.
2. Extraordinary Bonus for Health Care Provision.
3. Productivity.
4. Food Support.
5. Food Bonus.
Source: Ministry of Health, and legal norms.

Salary supplements have created horizontal inequities among health professionals, across regions and establishments. Supplements are not part of the ordinary payroll system. The government sets maximum limits for each supplement, but each region and establishment pays them according to its own resources, most of which are raised from fees which they themselves set. Thus, higher fee income translates into higher salaries, and Lima tops the list. In 2003, the government sought to reduce these horizontal differences by redistributing income raised in Lima to pay a flat transfer of 150 soles to each administrative and health professional in other regions (Table 6.13).

Rigid Tenure. Civil Service law provisions that allow government to reassign, rotate, or fire teachers and health professionals have been undermined by budget limitations and by ad hoc norms which, in practice, have created a higher degree of job stability than intended by the Civil Service law.[62] Once appointed to a specific position, it is exceedingly difficult to reassign or rotate either teachers or health professionals. The following statements from interviews illustrate the problem.

Former MED authority:

> One of those rights is to be appointed to a specific school. There are cases where, across the street from a school with an excess of teachers, there is another with a deficit, yet it is almost impossible to reassign. Many UGELs instead simply contract new teachers.

---

62. In the case of teachers, Law 25212-1990 (article 13) provides stability associated to job post, establishment, and place of establishment. In addition, article 190 (DS 19-90 ED) further defines that stability.

Focus group of doctors: "It is easier to move a health facility than its personnel. We have heard recently appointed doctors say, 'I am a tenured doctor; nobody can fire me.'"

In the case of firing, preliminary evidence suggests that current procedures are cumbersome and open to many interpretations, due to the number and variety of related norms and regulations. For instance:

President of a CLAS:

> The recent conversion from contracts to tenured appointments has negatively affected our ability to manage personnel within CLAS. Now, the *red* (regional network) can reassign personnel without our approval. Before, we fired personnel. Now, our ability to discipline personnel has been limited.

Manager of a CLAS: "Those under contract that do not fulfill their goals can be sanctioned, even fired. We cannot do the same for tenured personnel."

When a school principal sees a need to fire, he or she must prepare a case file containing proof of a serious fault, which is then presented to and must be approved by the UGEL. In many cases, the UGEL simply reassigns the teacher, even in cases of serious misconduct like sexual abuse or stealing. Hugo Díaz (APOYO 2005) writes that he met with 50 school directors in Callao:

> Most were victims of administrative suits that arose because they had tried to fire a teacher for bad performance and then had been countermanded. So, directors often do not even try to fire someone, unless they are very sure of UGEL support and of their own position.

Several managers commented on the effect of excess tenure on the performance and effort of tenured teachers and health professionals.

Director of a DISA:

> Tenured health professionals work six hours or less. They refuse to work on contagious diseases like dengue, whereas personnel under contracts are more flexible. The conversion from personnel under contracts to tenured ones has resulted in less effort and less hours worked within establishments.

Another manager of a CLAS:

> We had personnel under contracts that were willing to go out to poor communities. Most of the tenured personnel refused to work more than six hours or visit poor communities. After the conversion, we had to hire personnel under contracts to compensate for the number of hours lost due to the conversion.

Principal of a rural school:

> Tenured teachers are hard to manage or discipline. They have a culture of rights but no obligations. Most do not identify with their school communities or the parents.

Unions not only demanded and obtained rigid tenure; they act as watchdogs at the establishment and UGEL levels to ensure the strictest possible interpretation of the norms, while refusing to accept responsibility for the quality of work.

UGEL authority:

> SUTEP is interested in job stability but does not say anything about the quality of the service provided by those who have that stability. Its position is essentially a political position. SUTEP does not recognize that stability implies responsibility for the type of service that is being provided.

Weakened Management. In both sectors, there has been a major deterioration in the capacity to impose discipline and manage a career system. The procedures for appointments and evaluation established by the Teachers Law of 1984 were implemented only during one year, in 1990.[63,64] The norms became moot in 1991 when promotions and tenured appointments were suspended. The suspension, in turn, led to a progressive deterioration of the annual evaluation system.

The capacity to evaluate was further undermined by the disappearance of and failure to update information on career records. When circumstances gradually permitted a limited number of appointments and promotions, regional administrative offices applied ad hoc procedures, ignoring the Teachers Law and its evaluation norms, making personnel files even more unnecessary. As a result, records on absenteeism, degrees, training, past experience, and years of service, among other variables, are deficient, even though the information is needed to classify, transfer or reassign, evaluate, and pay personnel.[65]

MED official:

> It is essential to evaluate teachers. However, the instruments to do so are nonexistent. In particular, 80 percent of the information on the personnel files and career records of teachers has been lost. As a result, it is impossible to get any information regarding level of education attained, degrees, specializations, years of service, history of positions held (not even the last two), or on-the-job training received for all teachers.

In the case of health professionals, each professional category has separate promotion and evaluation procedures.[66] There is preliminary evidence that, within some large health establishments, when there is a vacancy, these procedures are usually followed in the case of doctors. But, as in the case of education, the suspension of promotions led to a progressive deterioration of the evaluation machinery at the sector level. A lack of systemic information makes it very difficult to assess whether legal evaluation and promotion procedures have been followed and what are their results. In the same way, paperwork routines have continued to record personnel information, especially in large hospitals. But that information is mostly kept up to date within those establishments. It is not easily available and not always reported to MINSA. Furthermore, since regions and establishments develop their own different practices and rules regarding the reassignment of personnel, central authorities are also unable to track regional numbers and location of staff, among other key management variables.

---

63. This procedure was established in DS 019-90-ED and is discussed in Díaz and Saavedra (2000).

64. A procedure for updating information is covered in article 81-83 of DS 019-90-ED.

65. Studies of absenteeism therefore resort to interviews and surveys, instead of records.

66. In the case of doctors, besides Civil Service Career norms, the procedures are established in articles 15, 16, and 17 DL 559; and articles 36-44 DS N° 024-2001-SA.

In addition, the authority of school principals and managers of health establishments to supervise and sanction personnel within establishments has been progressively eroded. Over time, that authority has been reduced even in the case of basic disciplinary actions.

A key problem faced by principals is their lack of authority over personnel. They may be capable of direct supervision, but their recommendations are not always accepted by intermediate authorities at UGELs, who exercise little supervision (Díaz and Saavedra 2000). Several school directors stated that their job was essentially administrative, and that most decisions regarding personnel were made at the local UGEL. Yet, despite their limited authority over personnel, they are under constant pressure from the different players of the school community to act. The lack of real authority was a common complaint. Authority is curtailed not only by the UGEL; the unions also monitor and exercise pressure over principals and health establishment managers.

Despite the weakness of evaluation and supervision, we found cases of strong motivation inspired by establishment managers, who found imaginative ways to stimulate, reward, and exercise authority. In many of these cases, principals even designed their own supervision mechanisms, such as a principal who involved teachers in the supervision and control of their colleagues and created a "written commitment" to achieve excellent performance. In other cases, CLAS managers or regional directors in *Direcciones de Salud* (DIRESAs) designed nonmonetary incentives to reward personnel according to mutually agreed performance standards. In all of these cases, managers and principals recognized that they got a positive response even in those cases where it seemed impossible that the teacher or health professional would change.

In-service Training.   Another important element of the incentive framework of a career structure is the possibility of being trained to gain more specialized knowledge and thus have the required background to be promoted and assume higher degrees of responsibility.

There are two problems regarding training of teachers and health professionals. One is the poor pre-service training they receive from institutes and universities. The government has on different occasions established academic standards to improve education offered by those institutions and has created public institutions to compensate or improve the original academic background of public teachers and health professionals. However, these initiatives have not been sustained.

Second, a related problem is the in-service training of teachers and health professionals. There have been different training projects, such as the National Plan for Teacher Training (*Plan Nacional de Capacitación Docente*, PLANCAD), funded by international organizations, with mixed results. The in-service training carried out by ministries is difficult to assess due to the lack of information. There is information on the number of training events and participants, but almost none regarding the need for the training, its objectives, and what was finally accomplished.

LLE Outcome: Career Erosion

Civil service incentives, rules, and motivations intended to channel the work of teachers and health professionals have been replaced by careers that do not correspond to the original compact between government and its service professionals. At the same time, motivations differ at different stages of the professional's work life.

Table 6.14. Teaching Career Stages and Motivations

Career Stage	Motivation					
	Social Status	Current Income	Security	Springboard	Synergy	Ethos
Training	Very high	No	Yes	Yes	No	Yes
Pre-*nombramiento*	High	Some	Very high	Yes	Some	Yes
Post-*nombramiento*	Little	Very High	No	Yes	Yes	Some
Mature	Little	High	No	Yes	Yes	Some

Springboard = Use of professional studies and/or practice to move into a different occupation or career.
Synergy = When public service and private occupation reinforce each other.
Ethos = Includes professional vocation, honesty, altruism, political or community or union activism, and team spirit.
Source: Authors, based on observations and interviews.

Tables 6.14 and 6.15 summarize the main career paths that, in practice, have come to replace the civil service career as conceived in the law and as it existed, to a much greater extent, three or four decades ago. The core elements of the civil service structure—commitment to public service and merit-based promotion—have been replaced by largely private objectives and by advancement outside the civil service.

Entry. The decision to become a teacher has been driven by the broad notion of ascension in terms of social status or class, for the most part, from a world of manual labor to that of a "profession." The large majority—82 percent—of education students come from lower-middle-class or lower-class backgrounds (Alcazar and Balcazar 2001:38). A teacher's degree meant income, nonmanual work, and social respect. Security of employment was part of the package. For many students, additional graduate studies in a different career

Table 6.15. Physician Career Stages and Motivations

Career Stage	Motivation					
	Social Status	Current Income	Security	Springboard	Synergy	Ethos
Training	Yes	No	Yes	No	No	Yes
Pre-*nombramiento*	Yes	Some	Very High	Some	Some	Yes
Post-*nombramiento*	Little	Very High	No	Yes	Yes	Some
Mature	Little	High	No	Yes	Yes	Some

Springboard = Use of professional studies and/or practice to move into a different occupation or career.
Synergy = When public service and private occupation reinforce each other.
Ethos = Includes professional vocation, honesty, altruism, political or community or union activism, and team spirit.
Source: Authors, based on observations and interviews.

were also seen as a way to open doors to other possible professions. This last, "springboard" motivation, is probably increasingly important, as the expectations related to the profession have been falling. In the APOYO survey, 42 percent of education students had attempted to enter a different career, and one in three had chosen education after beginning but failing in other professions.

Until the early 1990s, students entering medical faculties were mostly from urban-based middle- to upper-class families. However, the multiplication of medical faculties during the 1990s, combined with the falling income and status of the profession, has shifted recruitment to lower social classes. According to the Dean of Medicine, most students entering that field at the University of San Marcos are residents of the northern marginal areas of Lima.

Pre-nombramiento.   Most teachers work several years before they obtain a tenured position. The wait became longer during the 1990s as a result of a freeze on appointments. Entry into the labor force is actually a gradual process; 40 percent of students had some teaching experience before graduating (Rivero 2002). Work under short-term contracts remains a common first experience for teachers. Contract teachers are willing to work at wages well below those of tenured teachers and in the least-favorable locations, often working by the hour as replacement teachers, since their overwhelming motivation is tenure, with the status and security it brings.

Gaining experience and the good opinion of a community or a school director increases the odds of a quick *nombramiento*, and the self-interest behind this strategy blends well with the often sincere motivation of vocational and community commitment. At this stage, however, teachers must often support themselves, and many already have families, so that immediate and longer-run economic motivations begin to carry more weight and initiate teachers into the world of multiple occupations and the potential synergy between a government position and private occupation. The springboard motive also grows in importance, since partly employed and partly discouraged teachers use their time to pursue studies toward a different profession.

For doctors, the pre-*nombramiento* stage is characterized by similar motivations. By contrast with future teachers, vocation and ethos matter more, social status less, and springboard motivation exists in the form of plans to use early public sector experience as a stepping stone to private practice or to emigration. A major factor during this stage is the intense demand by recent graduates for further specialization, normally obtained through a period of work in a public hospital.

Over the last two to three decades, this motivation was used by the government as a way to induce doctors into spells of service in rural or urban marginal areas; that service, at first carried out through the SECIGRA program and later through the SERUM program, weighed substantially in the criteria for allocating hospital positions for specialization. And, though it is not possible to quantify the prevalence and force of altruism, it is evident from interviews and life histories that social concern both reinforces the willingness to accept a period of rural service and, perhaps more important, is itself wakened or stimulated by that service, creating a minority pool of doctors who are willing to follow a career that continues to be strongly motivated toward public service. Recently, however, the weight attached to SERUM service has been cut, removing a major motivation to accept positions in hardship areas.

Post-nombramiento. Nombramiento brings a radical change in motivations for the teacher, who is immediately relieved from the contract worker's need to market himself or herself to school directors, parents, communities, and UGEL staff. Status and security and a higher income are assured. In the almost total absence of incentives or rewards for any expenditure of additional effort, and the absence also of administrative capacity to evaluate and apply discipline, most teachers and doctors reduce their effort to the minimum required, and turn their energies and aspirations to objectives outside the public school or clinic.

Some female teachers devote themselves more fully to their family and home, but as Anchi (2005) and other sources indicate, most teachers seek additional income from second teaching jobs, usually in private schools or from a variety of business activities. For others, the *nombramiento* means more time and energy for the study and experience required to move into a different principal profession or occupation, an objective that, as noted, was often attempted at an earlier stage but frustrated. A teaching appointment then becomes a springboard. In other cases, teachers exploit the potential synergy between their public school and private work, whether both consist of teaching or when some business, such as tailoring uniforms or selling textbooks or transporting pupils, can profit from the teacher's position.

At this stage, one finds individual teachers in almost any school with high professional and moral motivation, whose effort goes beyond legal requirements or the example of less-motivated colleagues. This may be more often the case with rural teachers, who respond to their students' high level of dependence, and who are also often in a position to assist the community in other ways. Another professional category that evokes social commitment is that of the school director, who, if honest, is out-of-pocket in the job because the additional salary is trivial and does not compensate the large additional effort required of him or her. Many individual directors are strongly committed teachers. Another frequent expression of ethos takes the form of community, union, and political activism—teachers who participate in communal organizations or who become mayors or members of local government councils or union activists. Though we lack the statistics, it is plausible that teachers supply an important share of Peru's local-level leadership.

Doctors at the post-*nombramiento* stage have a similar set of motivations, but the opportunities for synergy between public and private occupations are greater than for teachers, most evidently in the form of self-referrals and in the building of their reputations.

Mature. For both teachers and health professionals, motivations show little change as they approach the end of their public service career. The career incentive to perform well in public service becomes even less relevant, while effort expended on developing a post-civil-service activity grows in importance, particularly because in both sectors the professionals retire early.

Anti-poor Bias

Much of the failure to deliver to the poor is due not to insufficient spending or overall coverage, but rather to delivery systems that contain built-in biases against the poor. The following biases will be examined: (a) bad fit between the service and the poor, (b) cost of access to public benefits, and (c) poor incentives.

Fit

Public education and health packages are designed and delivered in ways that are inappropriate for the particular circumstances and needs of the poor, especially the rural poor.

Culture, Language, and Attitudes. Perhaps the most frequently mentioned instance of misfit concerns indigenous culture and language (APOYO 2001, Tables 2 and 3b). Ministry figures report that only 0.2 percent of all teachers are bilingual. According to APOYO's national survey, 26 percent of school directors said that Quechua or Aymara was the predominant language in their community, yet only 7 percent used those languages in teaching. In addition, an understanding of local economic and social life is an important pedagogic resource, a tool to engage students and create interest and relevance. Effective primary health care for the rural population requires considerable communication to achieve community participation and transmit hygiene instruction, for which both cultural familiarity and language ability are indispensable (Guzmán 2001).[67] Quechua dialects complicate the problem further: a teacher in a high district of Cusco complained that the official textbooks he received were written in the *trivocalic quechua* spoken in the region of Ayacucho, but it confused his students, and a *quechua*-speaking teacher at his school had to devote time learning the dialect (Ruiz n.d.).

There is a long history of criticism on this score in Peru, bearing on both the content and the models of delivery regarding language and cultural appropriateness, and an equally long history of efforts to establish more appropriate models. The cultural attitude of teachers aggravates the technical challenge posed by language. An external evaluation of the *Programa de Educación Intercultural Bilingüe* notes that:

> Participation by the children is a determining factor in learning; that is why it is necessary to improve the affective and verbal interaction with them. But participation is restricted when they are not talked to in their own language.

Dean of education faculty:

> Many teachers have difficulties in teaching poor children. They have a cultural prejudice, believing that poor children do not have the capacity to learn. These teachers rationalize in this way their own lack of capacity to reach those children.

Professor of medicine:

> In rural areas, doctors have to carry out preventive medicine. To do so, a doctor has to gain the trust of the community. It is a hard task, and the doctor must learn the culture of that particular community. It also requires special social and cultural skills. Many doctors are not necessarily prepared to face those challenges and they seldom stay long enough to get to know the community and to gain some of those skills that are learned through practice.

One hypothesis, in the case of education, is that teachers are not well prepared to teach in another language. Furthermore, there seems not to be a consensus about in which language

---

67. According to World Bank (2001), Quechua speakers scored lowest of all regional or language groups on the 1996 mathematics achievement test applied to a national sample of 50,000 fourth graders.

they should teach, how they should teach, and in which language children should learn. An external evaluation of the *Programa Educación Rural y Desarrollo Magisterial* (Ministerio de Educación 2001) states:

> Changes are needed to adapt school materials better to local realities, and to the habits and customs of rural children. The relevance of the materials is questioned especially by school principals and teachers of rural schools.

Formation

Fit is also a matter of appropriate education and in-service training of teachers and doctors for primary and rural service which, in principle, are more easily corrected than the unsuitability of language skills and culture. One aspect is the suitability of specific skills, medical or pedagogic, and the corresponding needs of a poor rural community. Another is the correspondence between the career and lifestyle expectations of personnel selected and the realities of rural community service. In both respects, choices that have shaped current human resources are penalizing the rural poor.

The lack of specific skills and training is borne out by the comprehensive 2001 evaluation of the Bank-financed *Programa de Mejoramiento de la Calidad de la Educación Primaria* (Program for the Improvement of Quality in Primary Schooling, MECEP) by Montero and others (2001), and by a parallel evaluation by Hunt (2001).[68] Both evaluations agree that "school improvement has not reached the rural schools," and that "teachers in rural schools... need special training as well as special materials." Furthermore, 73 percent of all primary schools are multigrade, and 90 percent of rural schools are multigrade. But the formal education of teachers does not cover the teaching methodologies needed within multigrade and one-teacher schools. Those methodologies are required to address, in particular, diversity in terms of age, learning, and language in multigrade classrooms (Sánchez Moreno 2001).

According to a group of UGEL authorities in a small town:

> The MED provides a methodological guide for teachers working in *unidocente* and multigrade schools. But it is not enough. Teachers should receive special training before being sent to those schools, since they lack the knowledge to teach in those types of schools.

The problem of fit is also evident with respect to doctors, whose preparation continues to lack adequate preparation for the public health priorities of rural communities, and most of whom do rural service only as a last choice, for the minimum time possible, and are focused on the standard career goal of specialization, which is inconsistent with rural service. The "complete" and "full equipment" professional who has finished nine years of study in medical school is in fact a very incompletely trained professional for primary rural service.

Group of local authorities of a rural town: "Doctors assigned to rural areas need and must learn social skills. Here, we do not need a 'yanqui doctor.'"

---

68. Hunt's conclusions are based on visits to and observation of well over 200 classrooms between 1993 and 2001.

Former MINSA official and professor in faculty of medicine:

> Most medical students try to learn the most complex cases, but they do not recognize that
> 70 percent of the cases that they will face in practice are colds. Furthermore, many faculties
> emphasize an academic education and focus on specialization and hospital work. Neither stu-
> dents nor faculty recognize the particular needs of primary care, especially in poor areas.

DISA authority:

> Doctors are trained now to work in a hospital, not to work in rural service. Being a public
> health specialist is not good business. A specialist is lost in a small health center. To be effec-
> tive in that type of establishment a doctor must be creative.

Nurse who worked in a rural area: "Most doctors do not know how to diagnose, or how to treat malaria, dengue, uta, or leprosy."

Another group of doctors in Trujillo recalled that during their SERUM years, they had had to work in cooperation with midwives, otherwise they could end up without patients. A professor of medicine in Lima agreed that, "The way to reach a rural community is through the shaman."

Doctor reflecting on his rural experience:

> Soon I had to realize that most of my patients called the midwife and not me. So, I talked to
> her and said: I will call you if they call me first, can you do the same? She agreed and from
> then I had the most rewarding experience. I not only learned from her but I also gained social
> skills that have helped me in my career.

Cost of Access

A second bias against the poor arises as a consequence of the costs required to access and use education and health services.

Cash Costs. Students attending rural primary schools paid $22 annually, according to the 1994 ENNIV household survey (Saavedra, Melzi, and Miranda 1997). These costs included normal and "extraordinary" school fees, APAFA contributions, uniforms, and textbooks, but not writing materials, and in some cases, boarding costs. In the case of health, 69 percent of the poorest-quintile patients had to pay user charges, which in the case of rural health posts averaged 2.20 soles (Valdivia 2002). Additional costs were incurred when patients were required to pay for or supply materials for treatment, such as needles or bandages, and medicines.

In addition, the hidden monetary, time lost, or inconvenience costs of tasks not done, and long trips, can be significant. For the extreme poor, even small payments are often too large and thus exclude them from access to public services. Thus, 66 percent of lowest-quintile families reporting an illness in 2001 did not approach a public health facility for cost reasons, according to an evaluation of the *Seguro Integral de Salud*, created in 2002 (PARSALUD 2003). The *Seguro* has cut user fees, but, as the same evaluation points out, has major problems reaching the poor.

At first sight, the cost-of-access problem appears to be attributable to management poli-cies or to structural factors such as geography, and not to features of social sector human resources. However, health establishments at all levels have an incentive to charge user fees or to transfer costs to users in a variety of ways, such as requiring patients to bring their own food, bedsheets, or bandages, or that APAFAs cover certain costs of school upkeep. As explained, these revenues can be, and indeed are, used to supplement the establishment budget, including the direct or indirect remuneration of personnel, whether or not the rules allow it.[69] The government's tolerance, and even encouragement of self-financing, thus creates a direct conflict of interest between providers and the poor.

User charges (direct or indirect) have acquired a strong legitimacy at the establishment level. The sense of legitimacy is made stronger by being shared among establishment personnel and community representatives, in CLAS boards, APAFAs, *Consejos Educativos Institucionales*, and other instances of participation. The practice is rationalized not only as a legitimate payment for establishment services, but because it is applied in a discretional way that allows for a degree of solidarity toward the local poor. This moral obligation, however, is administered by establishment personnel according to their own criteria for a "poverty line," which of course becomes highly relative to local circumstances.[70] The trend to increasing local autonomy is likely to reinforce this practice and could strengthen the antipoverty bias produced by costs of access.

Distance. Geographic distance elevates the cost of public services for both providers and users. The provider manages this problem by cutting back on quality and by not getting close to the user. The user is forced to bear the added travel and time cost of access, and gets a lower-quality product. One aspect of quality is the reliability of service, which suffers in rural areas. An education supervisor commented:

> Some teachers reside in the community but others commute. Commuters arrive late, and skip days. But those who reside in their community during the week skip Mondays and Fridays, when they go home for visits.

Rural teaching thus involves a huge time and travel cost for both providers and users. We heard of some cases of four-to-five-hour daily commutes to schools. Visits to health facilities often mean even longer commutes. Distance is a structural obstacle that requires affirmative action and expenditure on the part of authorities: if more is not spent per user, the user will receive less service than his or her urban counterpart. With rural schools, supervision, support, and delivery all cost more. Governments, however, have not been willing to bear the extra costs of rural education, and instead have cut back on support, supervision, and provision of materials, as noted by one interviewee (Sánchez Moreno 2001).

---

69. In 2002 MINSA authorized payment of salary productivity and night watch bonuses out of the establishment revenues from such charges.

70. One indication of the degree of discretionality that exists in applying a poverty standard is that the term often used by establishment personnel is not "poor," but the stricter "indigent." The room for local discretion when making means-test decisions is further increased by allowing patients to "owe" and pay in installments or when they are able to pay, which, in credit terms, then allows the establishment to forgive all or part of the debt.

Anthropologist and education specialist:

> Teachers in rural areas have been abandoned. They are isolated. Those who live in rural communities live there without their families. Some supervisors, if they ever reach those communities, only carry out administrative supervision. The lack of support for those teachers shows up in their effort and commitment. We notice the differences when they do receive support. For instance, teachers in special NGO projects or *Fe y Alegría* schools show more dedication and more motivation to work in rural areas. There is an important difference in terms of supervision: MED supervisors focus on finding the mistakes and sanction teachers, but *Fe y Alegría* supervisors first ask: How can I help you?

Incentives

Many of those serving the poor do not have the qualifications and are not adequately prepared to face the challenges of providing service in poor areas. Rural service and some marginal urban postings are undoubtedly a hardship for the majority of doctors and teachers.

The level and structure of remuneration does not act as an incentive for rural service. At present, both teachers and doctors receive additional payments for rural service, but the effective incentive value is not easy to estimate. A 2001 survey by APOYO recorded an average wage for rural teachers of S/. 723, of which S/. 48 (6.6 percent) was rural bonus, whereas the urban average wage was S/. 703. However, the prospect of supplementary family income is a major consideration for teachers, whether in the form of second jobs for himself or herself, or of employment for the spouse or other family member, and that prospect is clearly less favorable in rural areas.

Salary incentives for rural service are minimal, and in fact may not even compensate monetary opportunity costs and lack of payroll benefits of rural service. The evidence suggests that nonmonetary incentives for rural service are also minimal. In fact, there may be strong career motivations to avoid or shorten the length of rural service. One is related to the fact that formal education prepares both teachers and doctors for urban service. Thus, any kind of career advancement is seen outside the rural areas.

Rural teacher:

> I worked previously in a community, an hour from here. Although I had the support of the parents who built a room for me and built new classrooms, I always wanted to move close to the city to advance my career. I am now in a community half an hour away from a small city where I can attend training.

UGEL specialist:

> For a tenured teacher, the next step in his career is to become a director. In rural areas most teachers act as directors or are appointed as such. So what more can be achieved there?

In the case of doctors, anti-rural career motivation is closely related to the possibility of losing career advancement opportunities, especially not receiving specialized training. According to a professor of medicine: "A doctor after five years without training is a menace. In fact, in three years a doctor can fall behind."

DISA authority:

> Rural service could negatively affect a doctor's career. After some years of rural service, the doctor is lost when he goes to city. Rural doctors know this. A rural doctor complained to him, "you are holding me back," and looked for the first opportunity to move away.

Specialization and specialized training implies migration to urban areas and a high turnover of doctors in rural areas.

In the case of doctors, a year of service in SERUM has been a condition for access to hospital internships as a route to specialization. However, SERUM does not necessarily attract the best recent graduates or motivate them to continue in rural service. The dean of a health faculty explained:

> Rural service is a very important experience of a recently graduated health professional. However, currently, SERUM does not provide enough monetary compensation and is not integrated with a health professional career.

Less formally, students studying to become teachers see a rural posting as a route to an eventual urban job (MED 2001).

There seems little doubt that the structure of incentives does not compensate for the disadvantages of rural service and that the probable consequence is that rural poor children are being penalized. Rural teachers are likely to be of lower quality, be absent more, and put in less preparation.[71] With doctors, deficient service is probably more an effect of lack of appropriate formal education, short postings, and high turnover rates, given that effective primary and preventive health in rural communities requires local knowledge and trust-building.

Regardless of all the difficulties of rural service, and the lack of monetary and non-monetary incentives to stay, many doctors and teachers choose to stay for other reasons. A nurse who works more than 12 hours a day in a rural community:

> When I came here, I did not plan to stay. Twice I decided to leave for family reasons, but the recognition I get from the community for my work encourages me to stay.

Teacher working in a remote community, where he can only travel once a month to see his family: "It is very difficult to work here, but I have the support and recognition of parents, which helps me to do my job."

---

71. APOYO (2001:12) reports, however, that teachers in urban schools (*polidocentes*) had lower levels of professional education than those in rural schools (*multigrado* and *unidocente*). In *polidocente* schools (mostly urban), only 31 percent of teachers had attended university or an *Instituto Superior Pedagógico* (*ISP*), whereas in *unidocente* schools (mostly rural), 97 percent had university or ISP training. A study on absence rates by Alcazar and others (2004) did find higher rates of absence in rural (15 percent) and remote (20 percent) schools than in Lima schools (7 percent).

CHAPTER 7

Voice in the Accountability
of Social Policy

William Reuben and Leah Belsky

Main Policy Recommendations

This chapter acknowledges the key role that citizen voice plays in the definition and implementation of social policy, and in making decisionmakers accountable for their decisions and actions. It also acknowledges that civic engagement can increase transaction costs and affect the government's capacity to deliver. The interplay between accountability and delivery depends on a set of factors concerning: (a) the way public decisions are made in a given country, in this case Peru; (b) the way services are delivered; and (c) the way accountability mechanisms are designed, implemented, and used. This chapter focuses on the third factor, and its recommendations address the issues affecting the design and implementation of voice mechanisms in Peru.

The following set of main policy recommendations, and the more specific ones included at the end of the chapter, aim to improve the role of voice in:

- Enhancing the accountability of social policy and the effective delivery of social services
- Making policy design and service delivery more equitable and inclusive
- Developing the local governance framework for decentralized social programs.

The following recommendations build on the overall conclusion of this chapter that Peru's new approach to increasing accountability in social programs is on track and has the potential to overcome the limits of systems supported by previous administrations; that is, an intricate and overambitious model that the government was unable to fully implement during the 1980s, and a model predominantly based on beneficiary participation in service delivery with little or no participation in policy dialog and vigilance during the 1990s. The former led to a low delivery capacity; the latter did not become an obstacle to high delivery levels, but led to unaccountable institutions and illegitimate practices. The current approach focuses on regional and local participation in planning and budgeting. A timely correction of some limitations identified by this and other valuable studies will allow this model to reach the key goal of closing the gap between citizens and decisionmakers while maintaining a balance between an accountable social policy and effective delivery. This can be done as follows.

Clarify Roles and Participation Rights

■ *Opt for channels of plural voice, dialog, and diversity instead of sticking to participation quotas and consensus building.* Given that the new participatory framework assigns voice an advisory and not a decisionmaking role, the restrictions on civil society participation in these mechanisms, imposed through quotas and formal registration requirements, should be relaxed so that a more inclusive and plural voice can be attained. A set of guidelines on how to make voice more inclusive while assuring due process and representation should replace rigid quotas and ceilings. The guidelines prepared for the latest round of Participatory Budgeting are a good model on which others can be based. Similarly, consensus building should not stop plural voice, dialog, and dissent from flowing and influencing decisionmaking. Communicating the voice of civil society only after consensus is reached denies the intrinsic diversity of civil society and can lead to endless discussions and inefficient participation. Methodologies to manage plurality and dissent should be built and incorporated into voice mechanisms.

■ *Avoid confusion and overlap of voice mechanisms by assigning clear responsibilities, creating connections between voice mechanisms and other public institutions at the same level and at higher and lower levels (vertical and horizontal articulation), and increasing versatility of existing mechanisms.* The lack of a blueprint for the decentralization process has led to confusion in the definition and establishment of the participatory mechanisms. This lack of definition reduces effectiveness and prevents large segments of civil society from recognizing their right to participate. Moreover, confusion and overlaps may increase as the decentralization process puts additional pressure on creating new channels of voice. Before proceeding with the creation of new mechanisms, the Government of Peru should evaluate the current situation in order to redefine the scope, roles, and responsibilities of existing mechanisms, creating connections between voice mechanisms and other public institutions at the same level and at higher and lower levels, and consider assigning additional functions to current ones once overlaps are eliminated and each is given a defined role and the appropriate methods and technology to fulfill this role.

■ *Level the playing field for inclusive participation.* Existing social inequality in Peru is a structural hurdle to inclusive and plural voice. However, failure to inform the poor in a timely manner about their right and opportunity to participate and build the needed capacities magnifies existing exclusion. Systematic communication campaigns, presented in native languages, which use local media and community radio and capacity-building activities, can increase participation of the poor.

Reduce the Cost of Participation

▪ *Streamline processes and improve incentives and proximity of participation.* The cost of participation may be big for the State, but it is huge for the poor. Recent experience in Peru shows that: (a) organizing consultations by zones can bring participation closer to communities, thus saving time and transportation costs; (b) providing feedback on the results of participation creates incentives; and (c) using local media and grassroots methodologies can make participation less cumbersome and costly.

Ensure a Stronger Role of Voice in Monitoring

▪ *Improve the quality of information provided and educate citizens about service standards.* Information is the most important factor enabling citizen participation in monitoring public policy and service delivery. The timeliness, reliability, and accessibility of existing information systems need to be improved. Completion of the *Sistema Integrado de Administración Financiera*-Local Government (SIAF-GL) implementation, development and implementation of local versions of *Ventana Amigable* (*Ventana Amigable*-GL), publishing of user-friendly reports of monitoring and evaluation (M&E) systems of the social programs, and disseminating quality standards would enable users and civil society to monitor social policy and evaluate the performance of social services. In addition, a user-led evaluation of *Ventana Amigable* would help improve its user-friendly format and accessibility.

▪ *Pilot and adapt international best practices on participatory M&E methodologies.* Voice should have a much stronger role in monitoring policy implementation, institutional performance, and delivery standards, thus covering the entire policy cycle, instead of just focusing on policy design. Peru could learn from international best practices in this area, in which Peruvian civil society and government have not made notable progress.

▪ *Include voice in public monitoring mechanisms.* Existing and new monitoring systems should use feedback from users as part of their inputs. Two ways of doing this are: (a) using instruments, such as surveys and focus groups, to gather the perspective of citizens on the implementation of specific social policies; (b) and/or including voice in results and performance indicators and the collection of data from existing civil society sources. In both cases, it would be important to link participatory M&E results to incentives and decisionmaking. Efforts in progress like the M&E system under design by the Ministry of Economy and Finance (*Ministerio de Economía y Finanzas*, MEF), and those to be implemented by the social sectors, are commendable and deserve support.

Conceptual Framework: The Accountability Triangle Approach

This chapter on civic participation focuses on the role of citizens and service beneficiaries in the accountability framework described in the World Bank's *World Development Report 2004*. It makes a distinction between two ways in which citizens participate and demand accountability. One way citizens participate is by *influencing policy* through voting, direct

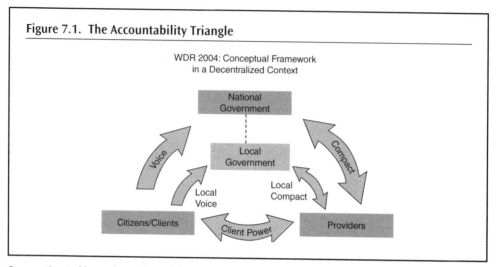

Figure 7.1. The Accountability Triangle

Source: Created by author; adapted from *World Development Report 2004*.

participation in policymaking, and influencing public officials. This type of participation is referred to as *voice*. The second way citizens participate is as clients of public services *implementing policy* and participating directly in service delivery, management, or monitoring. For example, the mothers who participate in Community Canteens cooking, distributing food to others, and receiving food themselves engage in this second form of participation, referred to as *client power* (see Figure 7.1).

Expressing client power is considered a *short route to achieving accountability* because it involves beneficiaries having direct influence and power over services, affecting service delivery without going through the State. Expressing voice is considered a *long route to achieving accountability* because it involves citizens trying to influence service delivery by influencing the State and its social policy. Both types of participation are important and are part of the practice of *social accountability*, defined as the range of efforts by which citizens express their voice, engage in direct management or monitoring of public services, or participate in service delivery (Goetz 2003). As indicated, this chapter focuses primarily on voice.

Tensions between Representative and Participatory Democracy

Often, when public and civil society actors come together through social accountability practices, tensions are created between elected democratic representatives and citizen participants. When citizen participants demand accountability, they contest the decision-making power of elected representatives and challenge the distribution of power between government and civil society. Elected officials and public bureaucracies often resist demands made by civil society, emphasizing that a legitimate electoral appointment grants public officials the power to implement the platform chosen by the electorate.

Tensions are less severe when social accountability mechanisms have an advisory role rather than a decisionmaking role. This study distinguishes between different forms of representation of civil society in policymaking: *direct and collective. Direct representation* takes place in referendums or town hall meetings, where citizens, as individuals, participate in policy consultations or decisionmaking. *Collective representation* denotes processes in which representatives of civil society organizations participate in consultative processes like advisory councils or in ad hoc consultations. *Corporate* bodies are formed when civil society representatives go beyond advising and participate in *decisionmaking*. Each form of participation generates different tensions between elected and nonelected representatives and raises specific concerns about legitimacy.

Tradeoffs between Service Delivery and Accountability

While civic participation can increase accountability and enable effective delivery of quality services to the poor, participation can also reduce the government's capacity to deliver public goods. In some cases, the checks and balances that create accountability systems can work against efficient and timely policy implementation and delivery of public goods, resulting in increased transaction costs and sometimes leading to deadlock situations. Similarly, efficient delivery systems with little or no accountability upset the legitimacy of public institutions, generating frictions that might result in political unrest and social uprising.

Some regimes prioritize either delivery capacity or accountability. Efficient autocracies, for example, will tilt the balance in one direction, while deadlocked democracies tilt in the opposite direction. Figure 7.2 presents a paradigm of political regimes and governance solutions. Ideally, governments will use a more balanced mixture of accountability and decisiveness, and will fall into the upper-right-hand corner of the paradigm (Reuben 2004).

How does a government act both accountably and efficiently? Providing an answer to this question requires consideration of: (a) the public decisionmaking process, (b) the management of service delivery, and (c) the type of control mechanisms by which the government is held accountable. This chapter focuses on the third factor and describes current

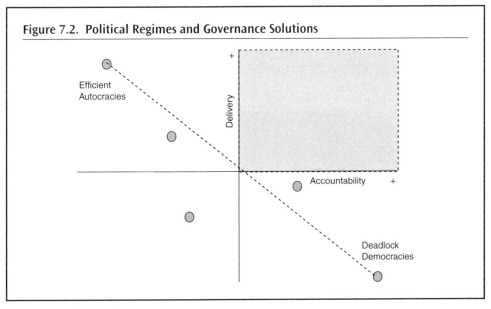

Figure 7.2. Political Regimes and Governance Solutions

Source: Created by author.

Table 7.1. Primary and Secondary Sources

Topic	Primary Sources	Secondary Sources
History of civic participation and governance, and the enabling environment for social accountability		Analyses of constitutional and other legal frameworks, existing literature on governance structures, and analysis of information systems and usage.
National Voice	Interviews with government officials and civil society representatives participating in negotiation spaces at the national level.	Analysis of legal frameworks, existing databases and registries, and literature reviews.
Local Voice	Fieldwork comprised of interviews with key informants and focus groups.	Analysis of legal frameworks, literature reviews, budget reports from local governments in MEF databases, reports from civil society organizations, and Mesa databases.

voice mechanisms in Peru and analyzes how their design and implementation relate to decisionmaking and service delivery, their ability to channel the voice of the poor, and the way they are contributing with local governance and decentralization.

Methodology

The information and data presented in this analysis were gathered by the World Bank team and by *Propuesta Ciudadana*, a nongovernmental organization (NGO) network in Peru. Table 7.1 lists the primary and secondary sources used.

Table 7.2. Fieldwork Sites

Region	Province	District
Cusco	Cusco	San Jerónimo
	Urbamba	Ollantaytambo
	Canas	Tungasuca
Piura	Piura	Catacaos
	Morropón	Buenos Aires
	Ayabaca	Paimas
San Martín	San Martín	Tarapoto
		Juan Guerra
	Lamas	Cuñumbuque
	Tocache	

Field Research on Local Voice. Additional information about the status and function of local voice and empowerment mechanisms was collected through fieldwork, using the following method: Sites were selected in three regions, each of which was located within one of the main geographical regions in Peru—Amazons, Sierra (mountains), and Coast. Within each region, research was performed in three provinces and an associated district within each province, for a total of six sites per region. Of those six sites, three were rural and three were urban (Table 7.2). At each of the sites, semi-structured interviews and focus groups on local voice were performed with the following actors: mayor, director of the local Roundtable for the Fight Against Poverty (Mesa), representatives involved in the Local Coordination Council (CCL) and Participatory Budgeting process, and a civil society representative not engaged in any of the government-sponsored participatory mechanisms. The focus groups were performed with representatives from the local participatory channels, including people excluded or self-excluded from participating in those channels. Indicators were derived from the conceptual frameworks highlighted before.

Issues and Analysis

A Historical Overview of Participation in Governance and Social Programs

Efforts by the Toledo administration to decentralize and democratize the State cannot be fully understood outside of a larger narrative about civic participation in Peru. The governance model being implemented today both builds on and reestablishes elements of the decentralized State created in the late 1980s and largely disassembled by President Fujimori in the 1990s. This section describes the governance models created during the 1980s, and inherited by the transition government, in terms of: (a) the structure established by the 1979 Constitution and its implementation in the late 1980s and early 1990s, and the 1993 Constitution during the Fujimori administration; (b) the forms of representation and decision-making; and (c) the delivery of social assistance and the forms of participation promoted in social programs. These are decisive factors that structure the relationship between the State and citizens.

Democracy in the 1980s: An Unfinished Transition to Regional Decentralization and Incorporating Civil Society in Public Decisionmaking. In 1978, as part of the transition to democracy after 12 years of military rule, the Military Government initiated the creation and approval of a new Constitution. The state structure established by this Constitution was not fully realized until the end of the 1980s and early 1990s. Nevertheless, the democratic model specified is notable for its decentralized structure, multiple and overlapping layers of representation, and incorporation of civil society representatives in public decision-making bodies.[72]

At the national level, the 1979 Constitution established a bicameral Congress. All senators were elected from a single, national electoral district. The House of Representatives (*Camara de Diputados*) was composed of regional representatives. Forty of 180 representatives were elected from the Province of Lima. Departments outside of Lima elected representatives in proportion to population size.[73]

The 1979 Constitution also established regional governments.[74] In the regional governments *civil society was represented within the legislative body,* which was composed of elected representatives, provincial mayors, and delegates of social organizations engaged in socioeconomic and cultural activities. The Regional Congress and president were the

---

72. Regional decentralization and the establishment of regional corporate congresses involving civil society representatives as decisionmakers were actually implemented at the end of the Garcia administration and in the first year of the Fujimori administration in the early 1990s.

73. Constitución del Perú, 1979, at: www.congreso.gob.pe.

74. Chapter XII, articles 252–268.

executive organ of the Regional Governments. However, both were elected by the legislative body, called the Regional Assembly. Thus, a Parliamentary structure was established in which the *Executive Branch of government gained its legitimacy not through direct electoral process but through appointment by the Regional Assembly, and importantly, the civil society representatives therein.*

However, although the model gave power to civil society to participate in decision-making bodies, spaces of participation were limited to those groups and organizations embedded in the economic structure—primarily unions, farmer organizations, and professional associations. In fact, during the 1980s the predominant channels of voice were parallel initiatives led by civil society organizations, influencing through dialog or from the streets. At the local level voice was often channeled through noninstitutionalized mechanisms supported by local mayors. A combination of the late implementation of the regional congresses and their corporate structure and, lately, the excluding nature of the corporate bodies instituted by 1979 constitution, explain this trend.

On the basis of the 1979 Constitution, the National Plan for Regionalization was approved in 1984, in the final stage of the second administration of Fernando Belaunde, and in 1988 the Garcia administration made the decision to implement the plan and called regional elections in 1999[75] (Monge 1998). The regionalization process that took place thereafter was plagued by a number of conflicts. The decision to form the regions on the basis of existing departments and the technical analysis of the National Planning Institute, without consultation with involved populations, created tensions. In addition, the election of civil society representatives from within social organizations generated internal competition among their members. This model of representation of civil society in decisionmaking also undermined the legitimacy of civil society representatives, because representatives did not have obligations to particular electoral constituencies and thus could not be held accountable. Finally, the dependency of the Regional Executive Branch (President and Congress) on the Regional Assemblies paralyzed the capacity of the Executive to decide, act, and govern (Cruz 1996).

By the end of the 1980s, the incapacities of the regional governments were compounded by other factors. Violence continued throughout the countryside as the campaign of the Shining Path divided popular sectors and highlighted the failure of the State to control the use of violence by insurgent groups. The APRA party was further losing its political credibility as a result of the growing economic crisis (Tanaka 2002). By 1990, following a period of hyperinflation and stabilization efforts, social investment had been dramatically reduced (Figure 7.3). As a result of that and of the institutional paralysis mentioned above, the government lost its capacity to deliver social services effectively, failing to meet the expectations of a majority of the population and retain its support.

Fujimori: Centralization and Participation in Social Programs. In 1992, recently elected President Fujimori shut down Congress and regional governments and called for the creation of a new constitution. After defeating the Shining Path and the Tupac Amaru Revolutionary Movement (MRTA) in 1992 and gaining the support of the population, the Fujimori government began to implement a complex political plan by: (a) centralizing the State through dismantling previous bureaucratic structures and layers of political

---

75. Ley 23878 del Plan Nacional de Regionalización; at: www.congreso.gob.pe.

Figure 7.3. Gross Capital Formation in Education and Health in Peru, 1968–1990
(Millions of soles 2004 = 100)

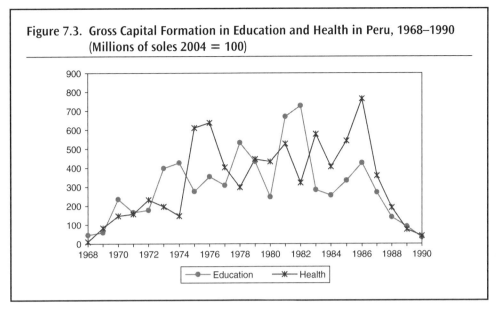

Source: Cuanto (1991).

representation (Pease 2000); and (b) strengthening social programs locally managed by beneficiaries and targeted to the poor, and creating new programs.

At the national level, the 1993 Constitution established a unicameral Congress in which all Members of Congress were elected from a single national electoral district. Direct representation from departments was eliminated. The regional governments were replaced by Transitory Councils (*Consejos Trasitorios de Administracion Regionales*) the responsibilities of which were assigned directly from the Executive power in Lima.[76] By restructuring and centralizing the government and placing all relevant decisionmaking power in the Executive Branch, the Fujimori government eliminated the complex and overlapping representation structures and channels of voice that formerly connected citizens to decisionmakers. By creating one national electoral district, the specific and overlapping ties between elected representatives and their particular constituencies were eliminated. This revision radically changed the structure of accountability and narrowed the routes through which discrete groups of citizens or corporate entities could make demands on the State.

By 1992 the country began to recover from the fiscal collapse of the 1980s, and the Fujimori government assumed its second major task: increasing social spending and strengthening new and existing social assistance programs. The "fight against poverty" and management of social programs was directed by the Ministry of the Presidency. Between 1992 and 1998, the national budget increased by 5.5 times in nominal terms and 1.8 times in real terms, and social expenditure soared from 21 percent to 30 percent of the national budget. Food programs reached more than 10 million people and social infrastructure reached a targeted population of 5,500,000 Peruvians in extreme poverty (see Figures 7.4 and 7.5).

---

76. Constitución Política del Perú de 1993; at: www.congreso.gob.pe.

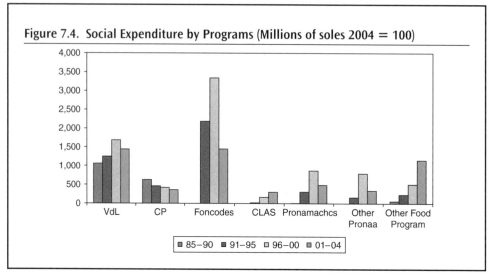

Figure 7.4. Social Expenditure by Programs (Millions of soles 2004 = 100)

VdL = *Vaso de Leche.*
CP = Community Canteens.
Source: Cuanto (1992, 1994, 1997, 2004); Naranjo (1992); PRONAA database 1992–2004; FONCODES (2003); PRONAMACHCS (2004); MINAG (http://www.portalagrario.gob.pe/seg_alimentaria/seg_cap4.shtml.); MINSA http://www.paag.minsa.gob.pe/internet/Transparencia/Transparencia.htm). Dirección Nacional de Presupuesto Publico-MEF database 1993–2004 Instituto Nacional de Salud-INS database 1994–1996 (http://www.sisvan.gob.pe/web/progproy.htm).

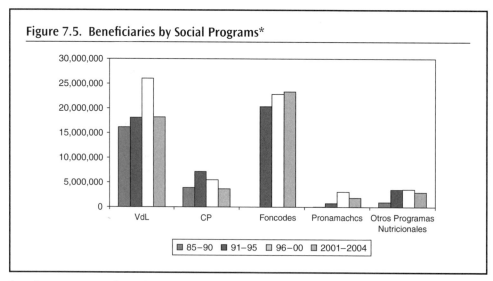

Figure 7.5. Beneficiaries by Social Programs*

*Totals are aggregates for each range of years indicated.
Source: Cuanto (1992, 1994, 1997, 2004); Naranjo (1992); PRONAA database 1992–2004; FONCODES (2003); PRONAMACHCS (2004); MINAG (http://www.portalagrario.gob.pe/seg_alimentaria/seg_cap4.shtml).

While the restructuring of the State eliminated channels for citizen voice—participation in policymaking—the social programs were notable in that they strengthened the second form of participation—client power—allowing users to participate in service delivery. The Community Canteens program, for example, enabled beneficiaries to participate in targeting the poor and preparing and delivering food. The combination of increased social expenditure and promotion of client-power mechanisms linked to social services led to the creation of an organized social basis of support for the government. The governance model thus relied heavily on demonstrated capacity to improve economic performance and deliver social services. However, the limited accountability enabled by the model created conditions for the abuse of power and widespread corruption. This generated civil unrest and public questioning of the administration's legitimacy.

The Fall of Fujimori and Re-creation of a Decentralized Democratic State. Since the fall of Fujimori in 2000, the Transition and Toledo Governments have taken major steps to democratize and decentralize the State. The state structure being implemented today has both similarities to and differences from the model of the 1980s. At the national level, there is stronger regional representation, as the unicameral Congress established in the 1993 constitution remains, but now with regional representation. At the regional level, the model is significantly different. In contrast to the corporate model of representation established by the 1979 Constitution, now, only elected representatives hold decisionmaking power. Civil society representatives hold an advisory role to the President of the Region and legislature. They are centered in the Regional Coordination Council, which is composed of elected mayors and collective representatives of civil society, and which does not have its own operating budget (Table 7.3).[77]

Civil society representatives thus have less power today in formal regional government institutions than they had in the 1980s. However, the Transition and Toledo governments have taken major steps to promote civic participation by institutionalizing the right to citizen participation in governance (Law 26300). In the past three years, in the midst of the new democratic spirit which pervaded the transition governance climate, Peru has seen the creation of a panoply of participatory bodies that bring together civil society and government representatives at national and subnational levels for negotiation and planning. These bodies include: *Mesa de Concertación de Lucha contra la Pobreza* (Mesas),[78] Regional Coordination Councils (CCRs), Local Coordination Councils (CCLs), Participatory Budgeting,[79] and the National Health Council.

While the creation of new participatory spaces is providing new opportunities for citizens to express their voice and channel needs to municipal, regional, and national governments, *direct connections* between the national and local citizens are being weakened. Today, social programs under the Ministry of Women and Social Development (MIMDES) are being decentralized to the municipal level, and local governments are being given more autonomy in managing them. One implication of this is that social programs can no longer be used as a means for the central government to interact directly with local

---

77. Ley 27867 Orgánica de Gobiernos Regionales; at: www.congreso.gob.pe.
78. The history, creation, role, and representation of the *Mesa* program are discussed in the following sections of this report.
79. Law 28056.

Table 7.3. Comparison of State Structure in 1979, Under Fujimori, and in 2005

Level of Government	Constitution of 1979	Fujimori Constitution of 1993	2005
National Government	Bicameral Congress.	Unicameral Congress.	Unicameral Congress.
Form of Representation	House of Representatives: regional representation. Senate: Elected from national electoral district.	All representatives elected from one national, electoral district. No regional representation.	Regional representation.
Regional Government	Executive, Regional Congress, Regional Assembly (elected representatives, provincial mayors, delegates of civil society organizations). Regional Assembly elects Regional President and Congress.	Administrative Body: *Consejos Trasitorios de Administración Regionales.*	Executive, Regional Congress, Regional Coordination Council (Executive, mayors, civil society representatives). Regional Coordination Council advises President and Congress.
Form of Representation	Electoral representation, indirect electoral representation, and collective representation from civil society.	None. Takes orders from Executive in Lima.	Electoral representation (Executive and Congress), and collective representation from civil society.

Source: www.congreso.gob.pe.

populations, thus reducing the potential for clientalistic usage of these programs. As decentralization continues and new governance frameworks are implemented, the precise impact that increased autonomy of regional and municipal governments, potential growth of the bureaucracy, and institutionalization of citizen voice will have on state output is unknown. Perception surveys show that while the post-Fujimori governments have been able to reverse the perceptions of the level of accountability, they are also confronting a decline in the perception of government effectiveness.[80] These data illustrate the complexity of the challenge of creating both effective and accountable public systems.

---

80. The governance indicators presented in Figure 7.6 reflect the statistical compilation of responses on the quality of governance given by a large number of enterprise, citizen, and expert survey respondents from developing and industrialized countries, as reported by a number of survey institutes, think tanks, NGOs, and international organizations. The figure depicts the percentile rank on two of the five governance indicators used by the World Bank Institute. Percentile rank indicates the percentage of countries worldwide that rate below the selected country (subject to margin of error). For a detailed description of the indicators, the sources of information, and the methodology, see: http://www.worldbank.org/wbi/governance/index.html.

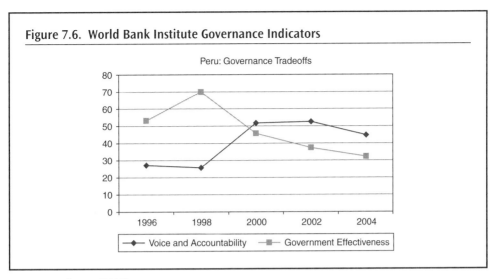

Figure 7.6. World Bank Institute Governance Indicators

Peru: Governance Tradeoffs

Source: Kaufmann (2005).

Analysis. In the three historical periods examined above, governance arrangements employ different modes of civic participation generating distinct tensions between formal and participatory democracy and suggesting tradeoffs between accountability and delivery of public services (see Table 7.4). The governance arrangement of the 1980s failed to solve tensions between formal and participatory democracy, hence, falling short of implementing the decentralization model envisioned by the 1979 Constitution. The regionalization model finally implemented in the early 1990s led to a complex decisionmaking structure. This deadlock political structure tied the hands of the government and prevented it from managing the tremendous security and economic challenges it was confronting and from providing social assistance to vulnerable groups affected by increasing unemployment and economic decline. The governance arrangement of the Fujimori administration achieved high outputs in the social programs but failed to develop transparent and accountable institutions, creating the conditions for state capture, the abuse of power, and the erosion of political legitimacy. The remainder of this chapter will detail the current model and analyze the success and challenges of new participatory spaces in enabling accountability of social services.

The Current Enabling Environment for Civic Participation

The two main contributions that the Toledo administration has made to enabling civic participation are: (a) the institutionalization of citizens' rights to access public information and the establishment of public information systems; and (b) the institutionalization of negotiation and consensus-building spaces—the so-called *espacios de concertación*—where public officials and civil society representatives engage in policy dialog.

Negotiation and Consensus-Building Spaces Linked to the Social Programs. As highlighted above, citizen participation is a fundamental principle reflected in new governance structures

Table 7.4. Historical Overview of Participation in Governance and Service Delivery

	1980s	1990s	2000s
Decentralization and Weight of Regional Representation in National Government	Partially decentralized to local governments. Departmental representation in one house of bicameral Congress.	Centralized. No regional governments, no regional representation in Congress.	Decentralized. Regional governments, departmental representation in unicameral Congress.
Predominant Mode of Participation	Participation in noninstitutionalized mechanisms promoted by local authorities or in parallel processes. Corporate participation of civil society in regional government made effective at the end of the 1980s.	Strong user participation in service delivery. Noninstitutionalized grassroots mechanisms promoted by district authorities or in parallel processes.	Institutionalized voice through specific joint government-civil society spaces promoted by the national government. Establishment of local voice mechanisms and diminished role for client-power mechanisms.
Balance of Power between Elected Authorities and Civil Society	Electoral accountability as the main form of voice. At the end of the 1980s some civil society organizations hold decision power similar to elected representatives in regional congresses.	Executive holds power, beneficiaries of social programs participate in service delivery.	Executive and Legislative Branches hold power, civil society representatives act as advisors in policy dialog.
Social Expenditures and Delivery of Social Programs	Weak	Strong	Moderate

established during the Transition and Toledo administrations and in the legal framework for decentralization. The National Agreement, initiated under the Paniagua administration and signed in July 2002 during the Toledo administration identifies the "institutionalization of dialog and negotiation" as a principle of the State. In addition, new laws (*Ley de Bases de la Descentralizacion-27783, Ley Organica de Gobiernos Regionales-278867, and Ley Organica de Municipalidades-27972*) all recognize citizen participation as an inherent right and principle of regional and local governance.[81]

In connection to the social sectors, five bodies in particular, the Roundtable for the Fight Against Poverty (Mesa), Regional Coordination Councils (CCRs), Local Coordination Councils (CCLs), the National Health Council (CNS), the National Council on Education (CNE), and the process of Participatory Budgeting (PB), realize this principle (Table 7.5).

---

81. Although the National Agreement has been an important space for multistakeholder policy dialog, this report does not analyze it because this space covers a broad agenda that goes beyond the social policy focus of the study.

Table 7.5. New Participatory Spaces for Negotiation and Consensus Building Linked to the Social Programs

Name of Participatory Body/Process	Year: Establishing Law	Functions	Structure/ Composition
Roundtable for the Fight Against Poverty (Mesa)	2001: Presidential Decree 001-2001 PROMUDEH	Build consensus on social policy with focus on gender and equity perspective, increase efficiency in execution of poverty reduction programs, and institutionalize citizen participation in the design, decisionmaking, and accountability of public institutions.	*Structure:* Mesas formed and linked at the national, regional, and municipal levels. *Composition (National):* 8 government representatives, 3 municipal representatives, 12 civil society representatives.
Regional Coordination Council (CCR)	2003: *Ley de Bases de Decentralization* and Law 28013	Provide opinion on annual plan, participatory budget, and regional development plan (including strategic objectives and programs).	*Composition:* 60% provincial mayors, 40% civil society representatives (30% from business and producer organizations).
Local Coordination Council	2003: Organic Law of Municipalities (Law 27972)	Coordinate and develop municipal development plans and participatory budget, identify priorities in infrastructure investments and public services, propose infrastructure and public sector service projects for co-financing, promote local private investment.	Same composition as CCRs.
Participatory Budgeting	2003: *Framework Law for Participatory Budgeting* (Law 28056)	Strengthen relationship between State and society, improve allocation and execution of public spending, commit civil society to actions necessary for effective spending, strengthen monitoring and control of budget management.	6-phase cycle specified in *Reglamento de la Ley* 28056 (DS 171-2003-EF). PB workshops include civil society and government representatives, assisted by a technical committee.

a. Civil society representatives include: 5 from social organizations, 2 from NGOs, 1 union representative, and 2 from cooperative organizations.

Analysis of the legal frameworks for these new participatory mechanisms reveals the following:

Participatory spaces hold an advisory role: None of the new participatory mechanisms hold decisionmaking authority over elected authorities.

Weak or no relationship with horizontal accountability mechanisms: Participatory mechanisms are not connecting with democratic institutions like the National Congress, the Comptroller Office, and the Ombudsperson.

Overlapping objectives: The absence of a blueprint for an integrated design of the new participatory mechanism and their relationship with existing local institutions has led to overlapping objectives and functions: all relate to development planning, but the roles assigned to each mechanism are not clearly determined. In particular, the precise role that the CCRs/CCLs play in Participatory Budgeting is not specified. This increases transaction costs, and participants are asked to assume a sizable burden when the purpose and aims of these efforts are not precisely defined.

Focus of participation is on development planning, and not monitoring: None of the new participatory mechanisms (with the exception of the recently established Vigilance Committees of the Participatory Budget) has a clearly delineated procedure for monitoring public expenditures and implementing development plans and investments.

Civil society participation in local mechanisms is limited: Apart from Participatory Budgeting, all of the new participatory mechanisms place quotas on the number of civil society representatives included. CCRs/CCLs, for example, are composed of 40 percent civil society representatives. Civil society participation is also limited because CCRs/CCLs require civil society organizations to be legally registered to nominate candidates. Given that these mechanisms hold only an advisory role, it is questionable why civil society representation is limited and why quotas are not adjusted to consider specific social history and composition of civil society in a given locale.

Poor vertical and territorial integration: Apart from the Mesa, none of the mechanisms have stable institutional connections that allow views to be aggregated and shared at different levels of government or across different sectors.

Advances in Access to Information. As part of the Toledo administration's efforts to increase transparency and reduce opportunities for corruption, the Congress passed the law of Transparency and Access to Public Information in July 2002.[82] The law requires all public institutions—including all state organs, regional and local governments, public companies, and those providing public services—to provide information on plans, strategic needs, budget allocations, expenditures, and investments. In addition, the Ministry of Finance is required to publish information on public expenditures, including investments and public debt. The Ombudsman Office (*Defensoría del Pueblo*) has been monitoring implementation of the law, and results have shown that while significant advances have been made in making information public, additional steps are needed to implement the law fully. Advances made thus far include[83]:

- ■ *National Level.* By October 2004, 23 ministries had implemented Transparency Portals and 20 had links to respond to citizen questions (*Defensoría* 2005). The MEF has established a Transparency Portal (*Consulta Amigable*) of the SIAF, which

---

82. *Ley de Transparencia y Acceso a la Información.* This includes Laws 27606 and 27927, which were passed to complement the first law.

83. Advances made in information benefited from relevant financial and technical support provided by a wide set of donors and international cooperation agencies. The full report includes an account of main contributions.

is one of the most advanced in the region. It provides information on economic indicators and projections, summaries of the strategic plans of different sectors, central and regional government budgets and expenditures, financial statements of all public agencies, and information on internal and external public debt.

■ *Regional Level.* All regional governments have created Internet transparency portals. An April 2005 evaluation of these portals by *Defensoría* shows that the comprehensiveness of these portals is improving. Twenty-five Regional Governments have included links on their web portals for receiving and responding to requests for information (*Defensoría* 2005). All but one regional government (Tacna) have carried out their biannual reporting to citizens, as required by the law.

■ *Monitoring of Good Governance Efforts.* Since 2003, *Defensoría* has published a series of reports evaluating citizen participation at regional and local levels and presenting recommendations. Between 2003 and April 2005, six reports were published on these topics.[84]

■ *Use of Information.* A 2004 study by Gomero identified 35 civil society organizations with programs dedicated to monitoring that use newly available information, including: NGOs, academic centers, foundations, cooperative organizations, and grassroots organizations. At least 50 percent are located in Lima and the rest are in other parts of the country.

Areas in Need of Improvement

■ *National Level.* Despite important advances made since 2002, improvements are needed to make the SIAF transparency portal—*Consulta Amigable*—more user-friendly; usage of information for monitoring purposes remains difficult for organizations that lack professional expertise. One way of doing this would be to have *Consulta Amigable* regularly assessed by a user panel. The capacity of sectoral ministries to collect and report monitoring information also needs strengthening. Currently, information presented by sectoral ministries and in *Consulta Amigable* is not consistent. An interface is needed to merge this information.

■ *Regional Level.* Information related to the economic management of the regional government, budget execution and expenditures, procurement of goods and services, salaries, and personnel are not yet systematically provided by all regional governments on their web portals (*Propuesta* 2005). Many regional governments do not have systems in place to adequately receive, process, and channel information to citizens. A report carried out by a civil society network, *Vigila Perú*, reports that of 15 regions surveyed, only 3 (Ica, Piura, and San Martin) responded satisfactorily to information requests from citizens. In only 9 of 15 regions were citizens provided an executive summary of government activities before the public assembly. In cases where information was provided, the information was of inadequate quality—often irrelevant, incomplete, not updated, or incomprehensible to a diverse audience (*Propuesta* 2005). An encouraging sign, however, is that almost all regional governments have incorporated recommendations made by *Defensoría*

---

84. www.ombudsman.gob.pe.

after the first year in order to improve audience participation. This includes defining procedures for the process, advising citizens with more notice about upcoming events, and using mass media better in order to reach wider segments of the population (*Defensoría* 2005).

■ *Local Level.* At the local level, SIAF needs to be fully rolled out to capture municipal government expenditures month by month, including spending in social programs in accredited municipalities and directly executed spending in municipalities where programs have not yet been transferred. Also, although the *Law of Transparency* requires all regional and local governments to establish Internet public information portals, the Organic Law of Municipalities exempts local governments that do not have the financial and technical capacity to do it. Indeed, half of all municipalities lack automated systems, and more than three-quarters do not have access to the Internet. A similar proportion is not trained to use email, and half do not know how to use a computer.

■ *Monitoring use of Information and Good Governance Efforts.* Despite the movement to increase government transparency and access, there has not been a systematic effort to identify who is using newly available information and how it is being used. In addition, the *Defensoría* reports are not being applied at the local level.

Overall, while further implementation of the *Law of Transparency and Access to Information* must take place, the capacity of civil society to use this information and monitor government must also be improved. The most recent evaluation of *Defensoría* reveals that despite the existence of the legal framework, many citizens do not insist on receiving information, because they are still unaware of the law and their rights to access public information. MEF or the sectoral ministries should consider assuming the responsibility of training and building the capacity of local governments and civil society to use the newly available information. Finally, information systems would be improved if they also included feedback and evaluations provided by service users and municipal government authorities.

National Voice

This section analyzes the degree to which the voice of civil society is being considered by policymakers in health, education, and social protection at the national level. *An overarching claim on which this analysis rests is that voice heard at the national level in the social sectors should be an aggregate of the views of service users—as citizens—throughout the country, and in particular, reflect the views and needs of the poor.*

Health Sector. The three primary conduits of voice at the national level in the health sector are the National Health Council (CNS), the National Health Forum (FS), and the Doctors College of Peru (*Colegio de Médico del Perú*, CMP). Despite their differing origins and roles in communicating the voice of civil society and influencing health policy, each has a defined purpose and is actively functioning. In addition, each has thematic focuses within the health sector, and a presence at both the national and subnational levels (Table 7.6).

National Health Council: The National Health Council was created as a mechanism for consultation between the Ministry of Health (MINSA) and other health sector actors. It is

Table 7.6. Key Mechanisms for Communication of National Voice in the Health Sector

	National Health Council	National Health Forum	Doctors College National of Peru
What it Is	Consultative body of the Ministry of Health.	Conglomeration of NGOs, academics, and unions with interests in the health sector.	Group to which all practicing doctors in Peru belong.
Formation	August 2002: *Ley del Sistema Nacional Coordinado y Descentralizado de Salud* (SNCDS).	November 2001, initially an informal organization, now an association of NGOs.	1964, *Ley del Colegio Medico.*
Scope	National, Regional, and Local Councils.	One national forum and 19 regional forums.	One national body, a dean in each region.
Objectives	Negotiation and coordination of the SNCDS, develop national health policy, monitor functioning of SNCDS.	Serve as a space for expression of voice of civil society: Channel diagnostics and results from civil society, inform public about status of health in Peru.	Monitor doctors, improve health of collectives and individuals, collaborate with authorities to increase presence of doctors, represent its membership before health authorities.
Financing	Ministry of Health.	Donors, NGOs, consultancy.	Membership fees.
Challenges	Develop Specific Proposals: (a) National Health Plan; (b) Universal Health Insurance.	Establish better mechanisms for identifying needs and voice of the population.	Obtain acceptance of proposals.

dependent on MINSA in three respects: (a) it is financed by the ministry, (b) its thematic groups are directed by MINSA and have MINSA counterparts, and (c) its agenda is defined principally by the Executive Secretary, who is named by the ministry. In addition, the CNS is composed primarily of members of the State (6) or health sector actors employed by the State (2). Among the 9 actors specified by law, there is one civil society representative. For these reasons, the topics on which CNS focuses its work (mental health, health promotion, and medicines) are of interest to MINSA and are also themes around which there is a general consensus (in contrast to more controversial health policy topics like human resources and public-private fragmentation). The CNS is also working on a proposal for universal health insurance, which is part of MINSA's agenda. Of the three actors discussed in this section, CNS provides the weakest representation of voice and is most vulnerable to changes in health sector authorities. However, it is a powerful, key space for the discussion of new health sector policies.

Doctors College of Peru (CMP): CMP participation in health sector decisionmaking is based on its historical influence and legal support. As an institution, it is focused on defending the interests of health professionals, influencing health policy decisionmaking, and improving public health. Although it maintains a privileged relationship with MINSA, it sees itself as acting independently of health authorities. CMP's agenda is determined by the agreements made among the corporate bodies that compose CMP and is articulated in a document entitled *Lineamientos de Políticas de Salud y Seguridad Social 2001–2006*. Among the topics mentioned therein are universalizing social security in health, decentralization, and organization of health services. As a civil organization, CMP expresses its views in "position papers" and acts as a lobby before public authorities. Although it aims to influence MINSA from outside, CMP is an entity with deep roots in the health sector. The majority of the Ministers of Health have been doctors. CMP thus has a powerful influence among policymakers at the national level.

National health forum (FS): FS is the most open and dynamic of the three national voices in the health sector. In its short history it has transitioned from having an academic orientation to aiming to influence health policy at the national and subnational levels and channeling the voice of civil society to public authorities. For this reason it has formed subnational forums to negotiate with Regional Health Councils and subnational health authorities. Its work is nourished by and emerges from the organizations that compose FS. Each year it holds two national conferences, holds regional meetings, writes position papers on specific themes (TB, medicines), drafts legislative proposals (democratization of health management), and declares its policy stance on issues related to human resources and decentralization. At the regional level, specifically in Lambayeque and Ucayali, FS has organized consultations between regional governments and civil society on health priorities. Overall, compared with the other mechanisms, FS has maintained the greatest independence and strives to be a space within which the views of civil society are aggregated and shared. In the future it aims to increase dialog with individual citizens at the grassroots level, and is preparing to take part in the electoral debates.

Conclusions on health sector: Overall, each of these institutions has different strengths and weaknesses when evaluated from the perspective of channeling voice and influencing health policy. The Health Forum and CMP have greater independence vis-à-vis the Ministry of Health compared to CNS, but do not maintain continuous involvement with health sector authorities. In terms of representation, CNS and the Health Forum have the widest representation, and both are poised to influence subnational health policy should they establish more direct relationships with the Regional Health Forums and Committees. In terms of influencing political parties, the Health Forum and CMP are in the strongest position of influence, though CMP's agenda is strongly marked by the specific professional interests of its associates.

Education Sector. Currently, aggregation of voice and influence of policy in the education sector are weak.[85] While an enabling environment for expression of voice is strong, and in recent years new participatory institutions have emerged, their capacity to channel voice is limited by a number of factors. Currently, the main institutions operating within the sector are the Centralized National Association for Parents of the Family, the Education Forum, and the National Education Council.

---

85. Patricia Mc Lauchlan de Arregui (Vocal) and José Martín Vegas Torres (Executive Director) of the CNE were interviewed for the Education Sector review of this report.

National Association of Parents: The Centralized National Association for Parents of the Family (CENAPAFA) was formed in 2001, promoted by the Transition Government as a result of the national consultation on education (*Decreto Supremo* N° 016-2002-ED). It is an association of local parents associations which, until 1998, were led by school directors and worked to support organization of school activities and fundraising, particularly in poor areas. CENAPAFA is one of the two key institutions channeling the voice of civil society in the education sector, and is the only institution that is anchored in the grassroots. However, the association has proven weak in its capacity to influence education policy for two reasons. First, because the organizations that compose CENAPAFA work on the school level and are focused on resource issues as opposed to issues of quality of education and performance, the association lacks a broader perspective and vision on education policy.[86] Second, while in recent years the association has been lobbying to get a seat on the National Education Council, it has been unsuccessful because it is perceived by education authorities as maintaining a close relationship with the teachers union (SUTEP) and political leaders of opposition parties.

Education forum: The Education Forum was formed in 1992 as a space for debate and reflection about national problems in education. It was initially composed of area specialists who supported Gloria Helfer in the Ministry of Education during the first Fujimori administration. Now the Forum is composed of school managers, academics, politicians, and education experts. Since its creation, the Forum has initiated studies in education, helped found the Latin American Forum on Education Policy, and worked on school-based and policy projects. From the perspective of channeling voice, the Education Forum has tremendous potential. Ten members of the Forum sit on the National Education Council, thus giving the Forum the opportunity to influence policy within formal state negotiation spaces as well as from outside. However, the Forum's potential is limited because its members participate as individuals rather than representatives of institutions or of the poor. In addition, the Forum acts only at the national level and is not connected to newly created regional and local participatory spaces. Thus, it is not poised either to aggregate voices from the grassroots or to influence education policy at subnational levels as decentralization proceeds.

National education council: The National Education Council (CNE) was created by the State to consult with independent experts on education policy design and implementation and enable a dialog with education authorities. It was originally cited in the General Education Law in 1982, but was formally constituted by Decree in 2002 (DS N° 07 and 010-2002-ED). CNE is funded by the Ministry of Education and is very much a reflection of its composition, which comes primarily from the Education Forum (10 of 24) and the Ministry of Education. There are important tradeoffs associated with maintaining a close connection to the Ministry of Education. On one hand, the CNE is in a powerful position of influence. However, this link has also resulted in CNE being perceived by others as a structure that does not have autonomy and is thus limited in its ability to provide independent feedback and guidance in the national debate. This is manifested in the limited dialog CNE has kept with key political institutions like the Education Commission of the Congress, political parties, and regional governments.

The ability of CNE to serve as a conduit of voice, connecting with civil society and service users, would be enhanced if it incorporated collective civil society representatives into

---

86. See Figallo (2003) for more details.

its structure. However, the newly formed CNE structure incorporates individual experts rather than representatives. One noted motivation for this is to keep the teachers union and CENAPAFA representatives out of CNE. Finally, while new negotiation and participatory spaces are being created at the subnational level (Regional and Local Participatory Education Councils), CNE has not yet established strong relationships with actors involved in these structures, and is not well poised to influence subnational policy.

Conclusions on education sector: Despite the existence of institutions to channel voice and enable negotiation and incorporation of citizen perspectives in education policy, voice in education is limited. The two civil society institutions—the National Education Forum and CENAPAFA—are disconnected, leaving the National Education Forum without connections to the grassroots and with a structure that does not enable it to incorporate perspectives of civil society institutions. The space for negotiation between the Ministry of Education and civil society, CNE, is disconnected from civil society institutions and the teachers union because it does not incorporate collective representatives, and its degree of independence is questionable. Thus, voice being communicated at the national level is not an aggregation of the voices of service users throughout the country, but represents the perspectives of professionals centered in Lima. Energy is directed toward influencing national policy rather than toward monitoring or influencing at subnational levels.

Social Protection. There are two primary conduits of voice at the national level in the social protection sector: the National Roundtable for the Fight Against Poverty (Mesa) and the Federations of Food Program Beneficiaries.

The National Roundtable for the Fight Against Poverty: The Mesa, established in 2001 by Presidential Decree 001-2001 PROMUDEH, has its antecedents in mechanisms promoted by NGOs and municipalities in the 1980s and 1990s, national dialog spaces like the *Consejo Nacional de Trabajo*,[87] and forums promoted by international organizations like the *Mesa de Diálogo.* It was initiated by CARITAS, an organization of the Catholic Church dedicated to the poor, and presented to President Paniagua by the Episocpal Commision for Social Action as a means of bringing the fight against poverty to the center of the transition agenda (Henríquez 2005). Once presented to Congress, the process of conforming the Mesa began in June 2001, with the stipulation that the Mesa should remain politically neutral.

Unlike the other sectoral participatory mechanisms reviewed, the Mesa has a structure that gives it both horizontal connections to government ministries and vertical connections from the grassroots to the national level. The National Mesa is composed of 8 members of the Central Government, 3 municipal representatives, and 12 members of civil society.[88] These 12 civil society representatives include 5 representatives from social organizations, 2 representatives from NGOs, 1 union representative, and 2 representatives from cooperative organizations. This model is reproduced at regional, provincial, and district levels (Henríquez 2005). The Mesa holds yearly national assemblies where it convenes representatives from Mesas throughout the country. The structure and practice of the Mesa thus enable it to be a powerful mechanism for the aggregation of voice.

---

87. For more detail about antecedents, see Ballón (2005).
88. DS 001-2001-PROMUDEH, DS 014-2001-PROMUDEH.

However, despite this potential role, thus far in the social protection sector, the Mesa has not yet been very active.[89] To date, the main efforts of the Mesa have been focused on supporting decentralization, the design and implementation of the participatory budget, and building the capacity of regional and local agents. Mesa is also following up on the report from the *Comisión de la Verdad*. It has primarily served as a space that collects the reflections, views, and evaluations of the poor and communicates them at the national and regional levels. Currently, the Mesa is acting as an advisor to MIMDES, participating in the Campaign for Infants, and decentralization of social programs, specifically the National Compensation and Social Development Fund (*Fondo Nacional de Compensación y Desarrollo Social*, FONCODES) and the National Food Assistance Program (*Programa Nacional de Apoyo Alimentario*, PRONAA). At subnational levels, Mesas are leading the creation of Joint Development Plans. Once the transfer of social programs has been completed the Mesa aims to assume a stronger role in monitoring, but whether this monitoring will be focused primarily on fiscal accountability at the national and subnational levels or also on collection of feedback from the poor on social services has not been determined.

The role of federations and popular organizations in the aggregation and expression of national voice: Federations of service beneficiaries are another set of organizations that have the potential to serve as a powerful conduit for the voice of the poor, particularly recipients of food programs. In contrast to the sectoral forums, which are composed of NGOs and experts, federations are composed of beneficiary organizations and seek to represent users directly. Discussion of the experiences of Community Canteens and the Glass of Milk (*Vaso de Leche*) Committees reveal insights into the impact and role these federations have played at the national level.

Community Canteens: The Community Canteens—or Clubs of Mothers—are self-managed organizations which, under the leadership of mainly female beneficiaries, collectively organize the purchasing, preparation, and distribution of food to the urban poor. During the 1970s, 1980s, and 1990s, the Community Canteens grew in number and visibility, receiving funding from a mix of public and private sources, until, in 1991, the State created the first Program for the Support of Grassroots Nutrition Programs and after, the National Food Assistance Program (PRONAA) through Law 25307 in 2002.

Since the creation of PRONAA, the main agenda of the Community Canteens at the national level has been to influence the annual allocation of resources to food programs and improve quantity, quality, and size of the basket. In addition, women involved in local community canteens have served as a permanent network of urban women who act as interlocutors with the State on issues regarding health, household violence, and education. The government has further used these networks when launching new campaigns and programs, giving the women additional means through which to influence other social programs.

Yet, while the women involved with Community Canteens have largely maintained a common agenda, an enormous disparity exists in the centralization, organization, leadership, and capacity to influence policy between groups in Lima and those in the rest of the country. Currently, one-third (5,720 of 15,940) of the Community Canteens are concentrated in Lima and Callao (Caballero 2004). Within Lima and Callao there exist three separate spaces for

---

89. Recently, the government asked the National Mesa to play a central advisory role in the design and implementation of the newly established cash transfer program, known as *Juntos*.

national influence: the Club of Mothers, the federation of Community Canteens, and the Federation of Self-managed Community Canteens of Lima and Callao, some of which have explicit or implicit links to political parties. In other regions, comparable networks with shared leadership do not exist. Because Lima is the site of the headquarters of the Ministry of Women and Social Development (MIMDES)—where decisions regarding the social programs are made—Community Canteens of Lima have a physical advantage in terms of being able to organize rallies and communications to the Ministry. These factors have created a situation where the capacity to influence national policy is concentrated in Lima. Finally, the decentralization of the Community Canteen program is creating new venues for influencing the programs. However, because the networks and advocacy capacities of groups outside Lima are weak, decentralization has not yet become a subject of debate across local groups involved in the food programs.

In terms of its national advocacy efforts, the experience of the Glass of Milk Committees does not differ significantly from the experience of the Community Canteens. The major difference between the two programs is that unlike the Community Canteens, the Glass of Milk Committees are completely dependent on municipal decisionmaking. Since their creation the Glass of Milk committees have demonstrated a significant capacity to defend their resources in the National Budget in terms of the quantity and quality of the products distributed by the municipalities. In this way, their agenda has been similar to the Community Canteens. However, at the national level, the major difference between the two organizations is that the major interlocutor in charge of assigning resources to the Glass of Milk program has been the Ministry of Finance and/or the Congress. As in the case of Community Canteens, voice heard at the national level is primarily from *Comités* in Lima. District committees outside of Lima negotiate with their respective municipalities. Thus, both Federations—Glass of Milk Committees and Community Canteens—are playing a limited role as conduits of voice at the national level due to the lack of connection between service users in different locales and the focus these organizations have had on budget protection versus advocacy of broader strategies.

Conclusions on National Voice. There are three main types of national voice mechanisms in the social sectors: (a) those resulting from the formation of national federations of client power mechanisms like food programs and APAFAs in social protection and education, (b) those constituted by individual professionals or NGOs like the *colegios profesionales* and the forums, and (c) those established by the State as mixed institutionalized spaces of dialog and negotiation like the sectoral councils and National Mesa. Each has specific strengths and weaknesses:

- The origin and composition of the federations gives them a special advantage in representing the demand side of service delivery. They are an expression of the social capital accumulated through the participation of users in the client power mechanisms. However, agendas dominated by immediate economic demands and leaderships with scarce access to resources, information, technical expertise, and key decisionmakers have limited their capacity to have a more strategic role in the national debate.
- Professional organizations bring strong expertise to the national debate. They are well funded and have access to both information and decisionmakers. Those conditions have given them the possibility of leading sectoral debates. However, they have not

been able either to connect with subnational civil society or to gather the perspective of poor users of the services of their respective sectors systematically. (There are emerging initiatives to overcome these limitations in *Foro Salud*.)

■ The formation of sectoral councils and National Mesa has followed a top-down approach that has favored an urban and elite-based composition of civil society participants. With the exception of Mesas, which have successfully built a regional and local base, they have not been able to connect systematically with the subnational level or with the poorer users of the social programs. Their credibility is affected by this and by the fact that sector ministries finance operations and appoint their members.

■ One commonality and weakness in each of these mechanisms is that all focus primarily on influencing decisionmaking (influencing policies, planning, proposing programs, and projects) to the neglect of monitoring and evaluating policy and program implementation.

Regional and Local Voice

The new decentralization framework in Peru presents interesting advances for the promotion of civil society voice in regional and local governance, demonstrating an innovative model mixing features of representative and participatory democracy. Breaking with a recent centralist past, in which citizen participation was confined to client-power mechanisms at the local level, the new decentralization framework provides the potential for the accountability triangle to move down to the regional and local levels, opening formal spaces for interaction and feedback among policymakers, users as citizens, and service providers (see Figure 7.1).

In practice, however, the triangle will not be fully functional until the decentralization process has been completed and services such as health and education have been fully decentralized. Until then, the accountability relationships of the compact between service providers and policymakers will be split among the national, regional, and local levels, with those services that have been fully decentralized being accountable to regional and local policymakers, and those that are still centralized to national policymakers.

This section analyzes the newly created local and regional voice mechanisms to explore their potential to become conduits of voice in the newly decentralized setup. It focuses on the Regional Coordination Councils (CCRs) and Local Coordination Councils (CCLs), the regional and local Mesas, and the Participatory Budget. With the exception of CCRs, the analysis draws on secondary information and information gathered in fieldwork study in the Amazons, Sierra (mountains), and Coast of Peru. The methodology and instruments used in the study are described in the Framework Chapter of the report. The report discusses three main aspects of each mechanism:[90] (a) the process of its constitution, (b) articulation with other local mechanisms, and (c) results.

Regional Coordination Councils

Regional authorities resisted the creation of CCRs: The creation of CCRs was preceded by a tense national political debate about the role of voice in the process of decentralization and the power

---

90. In the case of CCRs, this section discusses only their creation, issues of participation and representation, and their current functions.

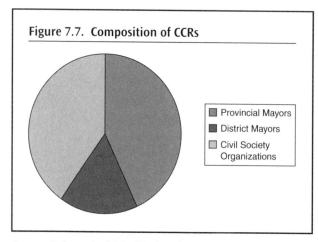

Figure 7.7. Composition of CCRs

- Provincial Mayors
- District Mayors
- Civil Society Organizations

Source: Defensoría del Pueblo (2005).

of elected officials relative to civil society representatives. While Law 27680 was passed in 2002 establishing CCRs, the lack of consensus over CCRs is reflected in the delay of regional governments in implementing CCRs, and in the poor involvement of civil society organizations in elections. The delay of regional governments in forming CCRs motivated passage of Law 28013, requiring that all regional governments establish CCRs by June 30, 2003. Nevertheless, six regional governments (Ancash, Cusco, Junín, Moquegua, Pasco, and Puno) did not establish CCRs within the legal time frame (Ballón 2003).

During the process of electing representatives, 40 percent of the provinces did not register organizations, and in the two most extreme cases, Cusco and Puno, more than 75 percent of the provinces did not register civil society organizations. The failure to register organizations could be the result of a number of factors: lack of incentives or political will on the part of regional authorities, poor notification and education of civil society about the CCR and the opportunity to participate, and structural limitations in the CCR legal framework stating that eligible organizations must have legal status and 3+ years in existence.

Participants in CCRs tend to represent middle-class, urban interests: One of the problems affecting CCRs has been the poor representation of civil society. Generally, civil society representatives tend to represent provincial capital and middle-class urban interests, and there is exclusion of those from poorer groups and more remote districts in the department. Only 27 percent of authorities on the CCRs are district mayors. The civil society organizations that are most heavily represented in CCRs are business and producer associations, at 30.6 percent. If NGOs, professional organizations, and universities are added, organizations representing the middle class comprise 59 percent of civil society representatives on CCRs (Figure 7.7). By contrast, 7.7 percent of representatives are from indigenous and community organizations. On average, 24 percent of representatives in CCRs are women.

There are a number of structural, logistical, and social factors that might explain these figures. The overrepresentation of middle-class interests is partly a product of the legal framework, which imposes a 30 percent quota for business and producer associations, independently of their actual relative strength in a given region. In addition, by requiring proof of legal status and a minimum of three years' institutional activity, the registration requirements give preference to formally established organizations located in provincial capitals. Although the law allows regional governments to modify the registration requirements to make them more flexible, few mayors have taken advantage of this. Ultimately, 40 percent of provinces did not register civil society organizations. Finally, the skewed representation of civil society is also a product of social exclusion and asymmetric capacities within civil society.

The functionality of the CCRs has been diminished by poor specification of their role: In contrast to the Regional Assemblies established by the 1979 Constitution, CCRs hold an advisory role and their responsibilities are limited to participation in the Joint Regional Development Plan and the Participatory Budget. The exact manner in which CCRs are supposed to participate in these tasks is undefined. In some specific cases, like Piura and Cusco, the CCR has formed its own accountability mechanisms, establishing a regional assembly to which the elected members report. Others have increased the responsibility of the CCR by engaging as active members of the regional technical committees of the Participatory Budget (PRODES 2005).

Local Coordination Councils

Participatory budgeting was a strong incentive for the creation of CCLs, which were otherwise resisted by local authorities: Like CCRs, CCLs were initially perceived by many municipal governments as a threat to their authority. However, unlike for CCRs, no deadline was established for their creation and there was no systematic monitoring by the National Council on Decentralization (CND) or the Ombudsman Office. Hence, while the law establishing CCLs was passed in 2003, many municipal governments delayed implementation, and it is estimated that many were not created until 2004, under pressure from Participatory Budgeting requirements. There are no reliable figures on the current number of established CCLs, but CND estimates that to date, 30 percent of municipalities have CCLs, while the national Mesa estimates that they have been created in 59 percent of the districts and 82 percent of the provinces (Arroyo and Irigoyen 2004).

The resistance of local governments to CCLs has resulted in attempts to control the appointment of civil society representatives in CCLs, minimize their functions, and control their operation. It has also been reported that the election process for many CCLs was curtailed by local authorities through the announcing of elections with insufficient notice, not providing adequate information, and informing only those organizations with relationships to authorities. Another way some municipal governments have tried to control CCLs is by keeping their activity to the bare minimum or taking advantage of the law that requires the mayor to convene CCL meetings. Fieldwork reports reveal that CCL activity ranges from no formal meetings to formal meetings as required by law as well as constituent meetings (Table 7.7).

Table 7.7. Activity of CCLs

Frequency and Type of Meeting	Sites	Number
Have not met since creation	Tarapoto, Tungasuca San Jerónimo, Urubamba	4
1 official meeting	Ollantaytambo	1
2 official meetings (as required by law)	Paimas, Buenos Aires, Lamas Morropón, Ayabaca	5
+2 official meetings (more than what is required by law)	Piura, Juan Guerra, Cuñumbuque, Tocache	4
Official meetings and meetings between representatives and constituencies	Catacaos, Cusco	2
	Total	**16**

Source: Voice Field Work Study (2005).

Producer organizations and unions are the primary participants in CCLs, though significant regional variation exists: On average, fieldwork reports reveal that Producer Organizations and unions have strong representation in CCLs—35 percent of representatives are from either group. However, closer analysis of data reveals significant variation among regions. In San Martín, 31 percent of CCL participants are from unions, which show less involvement in Cusco—5 percent. By contrast, in Cusco, 40 percent are from peasant organizations, whereas 5 percent of CCL representatives in San Martín are from peasant organizations. The significant difference in participation trends in these regions may reflect the varied history of social movements in each region. In Cusco, peasant organizations have an important place in the social history of the region, while in San Martín, urban and rural unions have historically played a significant role in influencing policymaking.

On average, only 9 percent of representatives participating in CCLs are from social programs. Women and individuals from rural areas have the weakest representation in CCLs (Figures 7.9 and 7.10). This may be a reflection of social exclusion, discrimination, and poor communication of rights and opportunities to participate, among other factors.

Incentives to participate in CCLs are largely political and range from wanting to monitor authorities to desiring to establish a political presence in government for future campaigns (Table 7.8).

The legal framework for the CCLs gives this mechanism a limited and overlapping role in local governance: The legal framework limits the role of CCLs to participating in local planning and Participatory Budgeting (*Ley Organica de Municipalidades*). This definition of roles has not helped promote the adoption of other accountability functions, particularly monitoring of local public expenditure and performance evaluation of services provided by the municipality. However, in four sites studied during fieldwork (Ayabaca, Buenos Aires, Cusco, and Paimas) CCLs are playing a monitoring role.

In many sites, CCLs have competed with Mesas, because they have overlapping roles: The establishment of CCLs as new mechanisms of intersectoral collaboration has sometimes

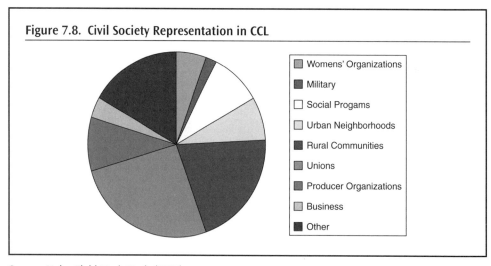

Figure 7.8. Civil Society Representation in CCL

- Womens' Organizations
- Military
- Social Progams
- Urban Neighborhoods
- Rural Communities
- Unions
- Producer Organizations
- Business
- Other

Source: Voice Field Work Study (2005).

created confusion with regard to their role compared to that of previously existing participatory mechanisms, such as Mesas. Many of the informants interviewed found the role of the two mechanisms confusing and overlapping. However, some informants indicated that because of their restricted scope, CCLs do not present competition with Mesas, and that many organizations have opted for continued participation in Mesas because they can serve as a space for broader multisectoral dialog. In some cases, however, mayors have established the CCLs

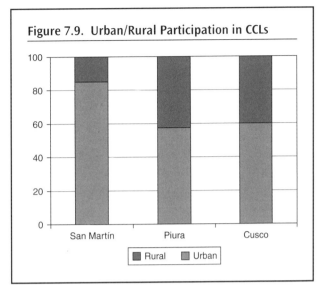

Figure 7.9. Urban/Rural Participation in CCLs

Source: Voice Field Work Study (2005).

as the main mechanism of dialog in the municipality, effectively replacing previously existing spaces.

Roundtables for the Fight Against Poverty

Of all of the participatory mechanisms, Mesas have achieved the widest coverage, but their activity is declining: By December 2003, 1,283 Mesas were established, 26 at a regional level (100 percent of departments),[91] 167 at the provincial level (87 percent of provinces), and 1,090 at the district level (57 percent of districts; Table 7.9). The widespread presence of

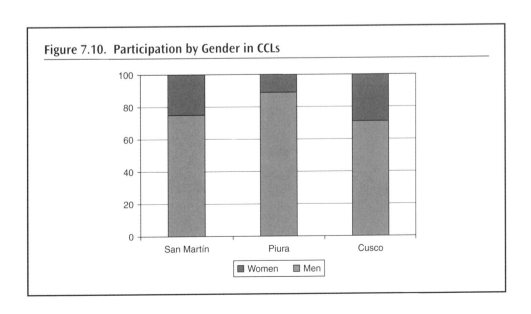

Figure 7.10. Participation by Gender in CCLs

Table 7.8. Incentives to Participate in CCLs

	Political Incentives
Juan Guerra	Obtain specific goals in the municipality
Catacaos	Monitor authorities
Morropón	Jointly govern the municipal council
Piura	Establish a political presence for electoral campaigns

Source: Voice Field Work Study (2005).

Mesas across the national territory reflects the fact that this is the oldest participatory mechanism, created during the Transition-Toledo period. The extended presence of Mesas is also a reflection of the pivotal role played by actors like the central government and the Catholic Church in their promotion. As a participatory mechanism created during the transition period, the Mesa also benefited from the enthusiasm and energy displayed by both the transition government and civil society following a period of strong centralization and restricted participation. In addition, Mesas were established at a time when local governments were not yet redeveloped. This meant that Mesas did not receive as much resistance as that received by the CCLs and CCRs. In fact, Mesas played a central role in the design and establishment of the new participatory mechanisms, namely CCRs, CCLs, and Participatory Budgeting, initiating dialog between local authorities and civil society and building the capacity of both local governments and civil society organizations to engage in planning and budgeting.

The database of the National Mesa and the fieldwork reports reveal a variety of relationships between Mesas and local authorities. These range from relationships in which the Mesa is led by the mayor (640 Mesas coordinated by the mayor; Table 7.10) to others in which the Mesa represents an alliance between the coordinator and opposition parties. In other cases, Mesas have played a role in conflict, mediating between parties, like in Morropon and Lamas; other times they have become a space of dialog or opposition. In Ayabaca, for example, the Mesa evolved from being a space for dialog between conflicting parties divided over mining activity to a body captured by those against mining activity and deserted by the opposition.

As decentralization continues, Mesas will have to redefine their role in local governance: While Mesas had broad coverage at the regional and provincial level, 100 percent and 87 percent, respectively, in 2003 and 2005, fieldwork revealed that 5 out of 11 Mesas studied have limited activity now or are no longer operational. One of the primary reasons mentioned by informants is that Mesas do not have a clear scope, and thus the incentive to participate is weak. The new local participation mechanisms, like Participatory Budgeting and the CCLs, are competing with Mesas, since they all share similar objectives, including discussing local development plans and participating in the allocation of budgetary resources. However, local Mesas from Ayabaca, Morropon, and Piura seem to have maintained a more active role and continue to enjoy a high level of credibility. One of the reasons seems to be the prominent role of the church in the Mesa, which is seen as a neutral actor amidst regional and local conflicts.

---

91. The Constitutional Province of Callao is considered here as a department or region.

Table 7.9. Constitution of Mesas, by Year, at Each Administrative Level

Levels	2001	2002	2003	Total Administrative Areas	%
Regional	26	26	26	26	100
Provincial	161	167	167	197	87
District	432	1,043	1,090	1,828	57
Total	619	1,236	1,283		

Source: Base de Datos de la MCLCP (Henríquez 2005).

Despite the National Mesa's claim that the Mesas have a wide and flexible agenda that can be adapted to changing realities and local contexts and needs, analysis of field data suggests that many participants do not see the scope of Mesas as going beyond engaging in local development planning and supporting Participatory Budgeting (see Table 7.11). Potential functions, like serving as spaces of dialog and conflict resolution or as a monitoring mechanism, were seldom recorded. Thus, even though monitoring progress in the fight against poverty and social policy is a high priority for the National Mesa, field data suggest that this has not been adopted as a priority and operationalized by local Mesas.

Mesas' flexible participation requirements contribute to reflecting social regional heterogeneity in their composition: Across regions, there is significant heterogeneity in the composition of the Mesa. In a sample of 309 Mesas the number of participating organizations per region ranges from 540 in Huanuco to 15 in Callao. In some regions like Huanuco or Piura, the central government has

Table 7.10. Composition of Coordinators of the Mesa, December 2003

Sector	Coordinators	% of Total
Central Government	186	14.50
Education	63	4.91
Health	32	2.49
Agriculture	8	0.62
Interior	44	3.43
MIMDES	0	0
FONCODES	2	0.16
Other	37	2.88
Regional Government	12	0.94
Local Government	640	49.88
Civil Society	246	19.17
Social organizations	140	10.91
NGOs	19	1.48
Chuches	69	5.38
Cooperative organizations	1	0.08
Businesses	10	0.78
Professional associations	2	0.16
Media	2	0.16
Universities	3	0.23
Type of Org. Not Indicated	199	15.51
Total	1,283	100

Source: MCLCP database.

Table 7.11. Functions of the Mesa, at Selected Fieldwork Sites

Function	Area
Develop proposals and formulate development plans	Paimas, Ayabaca, Tungasuca, Tarapoto, Lamas, Cuñumbuque
Technical assistance/PB training/organizations of PB	Tarapoto, Tungasuca, Juan Guerra, Cuñumbuque, Ayabaca
Discuss topics of local relevance and mediate local conflict	Ayabaca, Morropón
Monitor agreements among municipal institutions	Ayabaca, Morropón, Buenos Aires

Source: Voice Field Work Study (2005).

a strong presence in the Mesa (38 percent and 40 percent of all member organizations, respectively). By contrast, in other regions like Junin or Huancavelica, organizations representing the central government account for only 21 percent and 14 percent, respectively.

Similarly, the presence of social organizations varies by region. In the same sample of 309 Mesas, Figure 7.11 illustrates the variations of civil society representation across Apurímach, Ayagucho, Piura, and San Martín regions and between them and the national average.

When compared with other participatory mechanisms, there is a significant difference between the composition of the Mesa and the other mechanisms. Overall, there is a high percentage of central government and social organization representatives relative to local government representatives in Mesas. This profile is a reflection of the weak local government structures in place when Mesas were established and of the less restrictive rules regarding participation of civil society organizations. The composition of Mesas thus makes them a more suitable space for negotiation between local civil society and central government agents, and more a plural space of engagement and dialog. In contrast to CCLs and CCRs, Mesas have

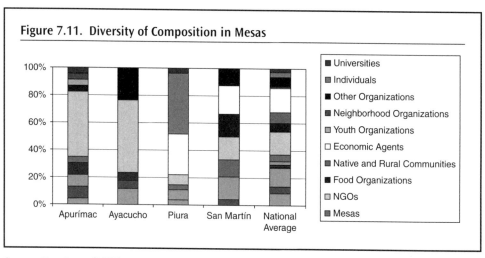

Figure 7.11. Diversity of Composition in Mesas

Source: Henríquez (2005).

served as a positive space for the discussion of local concerted plans involving a wide variety of stakeholders beyond local actors, including national and local authorities, donors, the business sector, and NGOs. Peasant and farmer organizations have a strong presence in Mesas (25.31 percent). This shows that compared with CCR/CCLs, Mesas also have a more balanced rural-to-urban composition.

Women's organizations also have a greater presence in the Mesa, representing 23.57 percent of civil society organizations (Henríquez 2005). The number of unions and business organizations participating in Mesas is considerably lower (4.6 percent). This number contrasts with the figures reported by the fieldwork and regional studies on CCLs and CCRs, which show a predominance of unions (CCLs) and business organizations (CCRs) participating (see previous section). It is also notable that political parties do not have a strong presence in Mesas (Table 7.12).

The National Household Survey reveals two trends in Mesa participation: (a) a very small proportion of household representatives is directly participating in Mesas (less than 1 percent), (b) the majority of represented households were from the middle class in 2002, (c) participation of the first and third quintiles considerably increased, and (d) participation of the other quintiles declined in 2003 (Figure 7.12). The primary incentives for

Table 7.12. Members of Civil Society Organizations Participating in Regional and Local Mesas

Social Organizations	Members	%
Farmers and producers	203	25.31
Defense and development	33	4.11
Sports and culture	22	2.74
Unions	39	4.86
Youth	31	3.87
Women	189	23.57
Fishermen	3	0.37
Neighborhood organizations	64	7.98
Other	218	27.18
Total	802	100

Source: MCLP database.

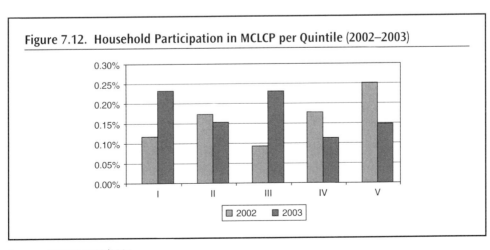

Figure 7.12. Household Participation in MCLCP per Quintile (2002–2003)

Source: ENAHO 2003/2004.

Table 7.13. Duration of Participatory Budget Cycle

1 day	Buenos Aires, Paimas, Cuñumbuque
1 month	San Jerónimo, Cusco, Tungasuca, Piura, Juan Guerra
2 months	Ollantaytambo, Tarapoto
3 months	Canas, Urubamba
5 months	Lamas, Tocache

Source: Voice Field Work Study (2005).

participating in the Mesa are economic. However, social and political objectives, such as achieving gender equity and obtaining a political presence in the district, were also mentioned in the field study.

Mesas have a strong vertical and horizontal articulation: Because Mesas are part of a national structure, there is more articulation between Mesas at the national, regional, provincial, and district levels than between CCLs at different levels and CCRs. With varying intensity depending on the individual cases, there is a flow of information among Mesas at different levels, definition of common agendas, and provision of technical support. There seems to be little articulation between Mesas and CCRs and CCLs. There is, however, a stronger relationship between numerous local Mesas and Participatory Budgeting. Many of the local joint development plans formulated by local Mesas became an important starting point and influential reference for Participatory Budgeting.

Participatory Budgeting

Hesitance of local authorities impacted the inclusiveness and duration of Participatory Budgeting cycles: In 2002, the Participatory Budgeting (PB) process was initiated with pilots in nine regions. However, following the approval of the *Ley Marco de Presupuesto Participativo* (No. 28056), in 2003 and 2004, the process was expanded to all regional governments and municipalities in the country. Like in CCRs and CCLs, many municipal governments were initially hesitant about implementing PB, perceiving it as a threat to their authority and their discretionary prioritization of investments and allocation of resources. This original reaction manifested itself in many regions and municipalities through either weak or no involvement of the president or mayor in PB workshops, weak calls to civil society to participate, or short PB cycles (Lopez-Ricci and Bravo 2004) (Table 7.13).

For instance, in the Regions of Ica, San Martín, and Lima the regional governments did not participate in the participatory workshops, and in Amazonas, Callao, and Moquegua the regional governments represented no more that 4 percent of the total representatives.[92]

However, proportional participation of regional and local authorities vis-à-vis civil society was very uneven across regions (Figure 7.13), revealing differing dispositions of regional and local authorities to engage, differing histories of participation and civic engagement, and varying capacities and power structures. The variation is also a reflection of the flexibility, and in some ways, ambiguity, of the 2004 version of the MEF Guidelines, which do not explicitly describe the process, giving leeway to regional and local authorities to interpret and sometimes distort due process (Lopez-Ricci and Wiener Bravo 2004).

---

92. *Ministerio de Economía y Finanzas* (2005). The registry did not include information on Arequipa, Cusco, La Libertad, and Pasco Regions.

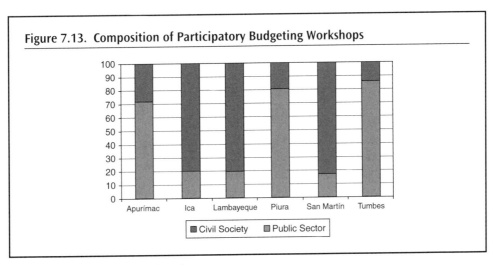

Figure 7.13. Composition of Participatory Budgeting Workshops

Source: Voice Field Work Study (2005).

Civil society participation at the regional and local level shows relevant differences: Analysis of data provided by the MEF's website on civil society participation in 2005 PB for regional governments suggests the following.[93] Economic agents, like business organizations, have the highest level of participation in the PB process (15.4 percent), closely followed by NGO (14.5 percent) and neighborhood representatives (14 percent). Representatives from food programs showed a low rate of participation (5.4 percent). Political parties (0.5 percent), churches (1.5 percent), and universities (2.3 percent) rank among the least represented.

However, a detailed analysis of the data demonstrates that significant regional variation exists. In regions like Apuramac, Ayacucho, and Madre de Dios, economic agents did not participate in PB. In Apuramac and Ayacucho, NGOs show the highest percentage (45.8 percent and 45 percent, respectively), whereas neighborhood organizations are the body with the highest representation in *Madre de Dios* (42.9 percent). This variation in participating agents suggests that factors like the social history of each region, the alliances of the regional leadership with different sectors of civil society, and the differentiated strength of diverse social actors play an important role in the distribution of representation among participating agents of PB.

Analysis of fieldwork information shows that in contrast to the regional level, of the 105 civil society representatives registered in the local PBs, food organizations and economic agents had the highest levels of participation (17 percent each), followed by community organizations (10.5 percent).

Comparisons between the regional level and municipal level in Piura and San Martín suggest the following observation: Food organizations like *Vaso de Leche* and *Comedores*

---

93. When the information was collected (February 2005), there were no registries of Arequipa, Cusco, La Libertad, and Pasco.

Populares have high representation in local PBs (55 percent of total civil society representatives in Piura and 22 percent in San Martín). At the regional level, however, these organizations have no representation in Piura and only 16 percent in San Martín. There is an inverse relationship for economic agents, which have a low representation at the local level (Piura 5.6 percent of total civil society representatives and San Martín 13 percent) and high representation in regional PBs (29.6 percent in Piura and 20.8 percent in San Martín). This suggests that local PBs attract and enable participation from client power organizations, while regional PBs attract greater participation from economic agents, like producer, commercial, and transport organizations.

There are two possible explanations for this trend: (a) the potential scale of investments generates incentives favoring regional versus local PB participation, and (b) proximity of local PBs makes them easy for social organizations to access. Field study data also suggest that as opposed to CCLs, the PB process seems to capitalize and build on existing processes of participation in the locality, including those created during the 1980s and 1990s. Indeed, many PB participating agents originate from client power mechanisms created in those periods.

In the 2004 guidelines issued by the MEF, individuals were permitted to represent themselves directly in PB workshops. In 2004, 3.1 percent of the 1,113 people participated at the regional level, and 3.8 percent (selected sites) were individual citizens. Whereas other local voice mechanisms allow collective representation, PB is the only mechanism that allows individual participation. This might democratize the process further by reducing the potential for monopolization of the process by organized civil society representatives, which may not always be representative of all citizen groups. However, if politically manipulated, individual participation can also pose risks, as in some cases where mayors have ensured that only individuals supportive of their own administrations are participating.

Key incentives for participation in participatory budgeting are economic and political: Ensuring access to budget allocations for investing in local public works and obtaining employment works are two strong economic incentives driving participation in local PB. However, desire to acquire knowledge, and political incentives like improving leadership and knowledge of public expenditure, and participating in local governance, also figured among the primary incentives driving participation.

External and internal factors affect the quality of voice in Participatory Budgeting: While PB is the participatory mechanism in the new decentralization framework that seems to have gained the most credibility, there are still limitations that affect its quality of representation and participation. There are two types of factors affecting participation of the poor in local PBs:

- *External factors.* (a) Incomplete dissemination and lack of timely information about the process; (b) distance and high cost of transportation; (c) non-user-friendly information about the content of the debate (complicated formats, and discussions required knowledge that was not available to all participants); and (d) insufficient time allocated to complete the PB cycle (one-shot or one-week processes mentioned above).
- *Internal factors.* (a) Lack of organizational capacity, and (b) insufficient knowledge to participate (reading and writing is an implicit minimum requirement).

Composition: First, although the participation of women and rural sectors is still poor in PB, it appears to be slightly better than in the other participatory mechanisms. In the municipalities visited by the fieldwork team, the ratio of men to women was 9 to 1 in 3 out of 6 cases, but 6 to 4 for men in one case and 4 to 6, in favor of women, in Tocache. A strategy that appears to facilitate better representation of rural sectors in the PB process is decentralization of consultations (*zonificación*), as seen in some districts in Piura.

Representation: There are cases in which delegates of community and other civil society organizations held consultations about priorities with their constituencies before formulating the list of priority projects and participating in the district or provincial workshops. For example, in Ollantaytambo, community presidents gave copies of MEF priorities to communities and discussed priorities over a month. In Canas and Tungasuca, a system was developed whereby directors must demonstrate that they have held assemblies with communities before participating.

Information: Communication of budget caps to the regions and municipalities before initiation of participatory workshops is a key factor distinguishing participatory planning from a PB process. It is also key for managing expectations and for sound prioritization of budget allocations. In 2003 and 2004, budget caps were communicated after the workshops had been held. In 2005 an increasing number of local governments reported having received the budget caps earlier.

Guidelines: There are also relevant improvements in the subsequent versions of MEF guidelines. The 2004–05 guidelines devote a whole chapter to explaining the importance of articulating the process between the regional and local levels. They also underline the important relationship between the local development plans and the PB, and define the necessary steps of the participatory budget cycle, including: (a) dissemination of necessary information; (b) identification of participating agents; (c) training of participating agents; (d) organization of participatory workshops (at least one to make the diagnosis and identification of the priorities, and another one to prioritize allocation proposals); and (e) dissemination of the PB reports (reporting back to the population).

The articulation of Participatory Budgeting with other mechanisms is loosely defined: Overall, the relationship between the PB process and the other participatory mechanisms has not been well defined. In the past there was an important relationship between Mesas and the PB. Many Mesas have assumed training responsibilities and have supported the preparation of local development plans. The analysis of regional data indicates that 4.2 percent of participating agents in PB were representing Mesas.

The MEF guidelines loosely define the CCR and CCL functions and responsibilities in the PB. There is not a clear distinction between their role and that of other participating agents. Finally, there seems to have been little articulation between regional and local PB processes. The 2006 guidelines have tried to adjust the timelines to facilitate the coordination and feedback among the three levels. However, the legal frameworks may need to be further specified to detail the role and responsibilities of PB at each level.

The small size of investment budgets limits the impact and results of Participatory Budgeting: A key factor affecting the impact and effectiveness of PB is that only a small share of the public investment budget of the country is invested through PB. Table 7.14 shows two possible estimates of the size of the Local Participatory Budget using SIAF-GL's database and *Dirección Nacional del Presupuesto Público*'s (DNPP) 2005 online

Table 7.14. PB as a Percent of the Provincial and Local Budget

	Scenario 1	Scenario 2
Total	5,390,583,787	5,390,583,787
Investments	1,820,546,444	1,820,546,444
In Execution	677,000,000	677,000,000
New Projects	1,143,546,444	1,143,546,444
With Approved Profile		310,406,573
With Profile	639,706,573	
% of Prov/Loc Budget	12	6
% of National Budget	1.30	0.63

Source: DNPP (2005).

database (*Aplicativo 2005 del Presupesto Participativo*). Both scenarios represent very low percentages of the national and provincial/local public budgets: between 1.3 percent and 0.6 percent of the former and 12 percent and 6 percent of the latter.[94]

In addition, while PB is generally perceived as positive by most actors, concerns have been raised about possible atomizing effects on municipal and local investments, which may limit their developmental impact in the long run. The introduction of PB might be leading to an emphasis on small local projects, at the expense of those with provincial or regional impact, reflecting a lack of territorial vision that cuts across local boundaries. With the data currently available it is not possible to conclude whether atomization is occurring. However, a comparison of FONCODES investments between 2001 and 2004 shows an important reduction of the average investment (falling from S./165.000 to S./105.000), which suggests that the combined effect of decentralization and PB might be leading to a reduction in investment size. Indeed, few projects are interdistrict or interprovincial, because participating agents often have more incentives to channel resources to their own locality. The prioritization criteria of the first MEF guidelines may have also increased possible atomization because they favored small/intradistrict over bigger/cross-district investments. This is improved in the 2006 guidelines, which favor projects of wider territorial and population reach.

Finally, although Participatory Budgeting is potentially an important tool of transparency and accountability, municipalities have not always used the process to adequately report their executed projects and expenditures, thereby limiting it to an ex ante accountability mechanism. The creation of the Vigilance Committees, as required by law, should contribute to reversing this trend if they effectively fulfill their watchdog role in monitoring overall municipal expenditures, beyond participatory allocations.

---

94. Table 7.14 was constructed under the assumption that the 2005 Preliminary Budget information followed the same execution ratio as in 2004. It also draws on the 2004 execution information to estimate the share of projects with just profiles and with approved profiles that are likely to be financed. (An annex further detailing the methodology is contained in the full report). Other less-optimistic scenarios, based on the assumption that only projects with an approved feasibility study would see the light, throw even lower percentages of the national and provincial/local public budgets: 0.1 percent of the former and 1.1 percent of the latter.

Local Voice Conclusions

New participatory mechanisms faced temporary resistance from established local political elites: The perception of the new participatory mechanisms as threatening existing power structures and distributions has been an obstacle to their fluid and rapid creation. The way in which authorities responded to this perceived threat varied widely, depending on the leadership styles of regional presidents and mayors and the relative strength of civil society. A combination of top-down compulsory deadlines and budget incentives contributed to enforcing the constitution of CCRs and CCLs and the implementation of Participatory Budgeting.

Overlapping functions are creating confusion: Because the participatory mechanisms were not designed in an integrated fashion, their functions often overlap and cancel each other out, creating confusion about their respective roles and functions. Until an overall framework is created that clarifies roles, agendas, and budgets, these mechanisms have little hope of functioning as an effective participation and accountability system. In addition, decentralization of other social programs could add new mechanisms, thus creating more confusion and overlapping functions.

The poorest sectors of the population are not participating: As many analysts have pointed out, participation has an opportunity cost that the poor cannot afford to pay, unless the time required is reduced to a reasonable minimum, incentives are articulated, information is made available, and the capacity of the poor to participate is strengthened. Currently, participatory activities take place in provincial and district capitals, far away from rural communities; dissemination of information happens in an untimely fashion and often does not reach poor communities; and capacity-building programs are scarce and are delivered in provincial and district capitals.

Social capital built through the implementation of food programs in the past is playing a limited role in local voice: Evidence shows that, solely at *a district level*, experience accumulated over time by participants in the food programs is helping their leaders to participate in Mesas and Participatory Budgeting. This evidence affirms the potential of converting the social capital accumulated through the food programs into local voice, while highlighting that structural limitations in participatory mechanisms can eliminate the potential advantages of previous experience in participation.

As in national voice, regional and local voice is focused on planning, budgeting, and making project proposals: Monitoring does not feature as a priority. In the case of CCRs and CCLs, monitoring was not included as one of their functions, but in Participatory Budgeting, monitoring of actual allocations and expenditures features as the role of the Vigilance Committees. The constitution of these committees is under way, although there is no methodological guidance on how they should perform their duty, and their scope seems to be limited only to tracking allocations and expenditures decided through Participatory Budgeting, instead of the overall municipal budget. Mesas include monitoring of social programs and poverty reduction in their objectives. However, fieldwork data show that they are not yet assuming this role.

Rigid participation quotas are preventing the channeling of a diversity of voices: As stated in the enabling environment section, all local participation mechanisms but Participatory Budgeting have rigid definitions and quotas regulating civil society participation vis-à-vis government representatives, despite the fact that these mechanisms serve only an advisory role. Quotas are not reflective of the composition of civil society in the various locales.

Each mechanism faces specific challenges: CCRs and CCLs are challenged by the vagueness of their role and the rigidity of their participation requirements and quotas. Mesas, despite their pioneering role implementing a new generation of local participatory governance spaces, are becoming less relevant and active in many districts, hampered by competing roles of other more recently created mechanisms. Participatory Budgeting, while showing a more inclusive structure and attractive incentives, risks facing diminishing credibility and fatigue of participating agents due to the small amount of investments made by the mechanism, discrepancy between budget allocations and actual spending, and the potential atomization of the budget.

Many Diagnostics and Recommendations Already Exist in Peru

There is a rich domestic literature that analyzes new participatory mechanisms in Peru. Some of this literature analyzes participation through the lens of democratization, considering the moral value of civic participation in itself. Other analyses, like this one, focus primarily on the more instrumental value of participation in improving public decisionmaking, promoting accountability, and aiding development. Table 7.15 summarizes key policy recommendations from a rich subset of Peruvian literature published during 2004–05. The literature selected is limited to studies examining the new participatory mechanisms established after the fall of President Fujimori, and represents only a small part of the literature of equal quality. It is meant only to give a flavor of the completeness of the analytical work and policy debate that exists.

Specific Recommendations to Improve Voice in the Social Sectors

In addition to the main policy recommendations presented at the beginning of this chapter, the recommendations in Table 7.16 are suggested to improve the inclusiveness and effectiveness of specific voice mechanisms. They are addressed to the Government of Peru and to civil society, understanding that both sides involved in participatory mechanisms need to make changes to improve the role of voice in the accountability of social policy in Peru.

Table 7.15. Summary of Policy Recommendations in Peruvian Literature

Main Issues	Remy (2005)	Gamero and others (2004)	Henríquez (2005)	Chirinos (2005)	Diaz Julio (2005)	PRODES (2004	Grompone (2005)	Leyton and Ricci (2005)	Bardales (2005)
Scope of Participation									
Participation should complement (and not replace) political reform, horizontal accountability, and democratic intuitions.	✓		✓				✓		✓
Voice mechanisms should work to inform, harmonize, influence, and monitor decisionmaking but not to make decisions.					✓				✓
Streamlining Voice									
Avoid confusion and overlapping voice mechanisms through clear assignment of responsibilities and creation of horizontal and vertical connections.		✓	✓	✓	✓	✓	✓		✓
Opt for channels of plural voice and dialog instead of sticking to consensus building.	✓		✓						
Increase functions and versatility of existing mechanisms instead of creating new ones with new legal frameworks and demands for participation.						✓			

(continued)

Table 7.15. Summary of Policy Recommendations in Peruvian Literature (*Continued*)

Main Issues	Remy (2005)	Gamero and others (2004)	Henríquez (2005)	Chirinos (2005)	Diaz Julio (2005)	PRODES (2004	Grompone (2005)	Leyton and Ricci (2005)	Bardales (2005)
Inclusive Voice									
Make participation an effective right through informing, communicating, and building the capacity of excluded groups.	✓		✓	✓	✓	✓			
Avoid participation quotas and ceilings and incorporate flexible criteria to reflect regional and social diversity.	✓	✓		✓	✓	✓	✓		
Increase accessibility to participation through improving proximity, incentives, participation approaches, and streamlining processes (reducing the cost of participating).			✓				✓		
In addition to creating opportunities for local voice, decentralization should become an opportunity to aggregate national voice.	✓		✓				✓	✓	
Voice to Monitor									
Voice should have a much stronger role in monitoring policy implementation, institutional performance, and delivery standards.	✓	✓	✓	✓	✓	✓	✓		
Inclusion of voice in public monitoring mechanisms.		✓		✓		✓			

Quality of Voice

Improve voice inputs through enhancing the quality of information (production, delivery, access, feedback).

Improve voice outputs through enhancing representation, analytical perspective, aggregation methodologies, communication, and impact.

Civil society organizations to establish consistent feedback loops and accountability to their constituencies.

Table 7.16. Recommendations to Improve Inclusiveness and Effectiveness of Voice

Voice at the National Level

Foro Salud and Foro Educativo

- Develop partnerships and a networking strategy with decentralized government and civil society institutions to meet the challenges of decentralization and relationship vis-à-vis negotiation spaces.
- Organize, on their own or in partnership with academic institutions or think tanks, independent analyses and debates of the national budget from the point of view of social expenditure, and more specifically, health and education, like the one developed by *Universidad Católica* in 2002.
- Improve interpretation of needs and concerns of the poor and engage in monitoring and publication of standards and performance using user satisfaction surveys and report cards.
- Strengthen links with client power organizations, like the *Comités Locales de Administración de Salud* (CLAS) networks and CENAPAFA. The relationship should involve both consultation and provision of capacity-building activities and information.
- *Foro Educativo* should explore the possibility of having an individual and an institutional membership to improve credibility and outreach.
- Build stronger links with respective sectoral Congress commissions to provide regular feedback and technical advice.

Professional Associations

- Set up self-regulatory frameworks and codes of conduct and monitor professional proficiency and delivery with a special focus on professional services provided to the poorest sectors of the population.

National Federations of Users' Associations (Federaciones de Comedores Populares and CENAPAFA)

- Improve connection with local users through decentralized consultations and networking, and broaden the scope of advocacy beyond immediate economic issues, incorporating strategic issues such as access to and quality of services to their priority agendas.
- Improve partnerships with specialized forums and professional associations to gain technical capacity and perspective.

Consejo Nacional de Salud and Consejo Educativo

- In collaboration with the forums, continue to make the national and subnational councils institutionalized places for dialog on the improvement of access to and quality of health and education, making monitoring institutional performance and service delivery a priority.
- Contribute as channels of civil society providing participatory monitoring inputs into sectoral monitoring and evaluation systems.
- Establish and fund a challenge fund for independent policy evaluations made by civil society organizations, and use their findings for policy analysis and redesign.
- Incorporate a more diverse membership to gather and channel the views of a plural set of stakeholders linked to the sector, including that of users participating in networks and federations. Because the councils do not have a deliberative function, a broader range of voices from different actors would contribute to better-informed policy decisionmaking and implementation.
- Establish regular links with respective sectoral Congressional commissions to improve dialog and impact.

(continued)

Table 7.16. Recommendations to Improve Inclusiveness and Effectiveness of Voice (*Continued*)

Voice at the National Level (*continued*)

Mesa Nacional de Concertación para la Lucha Contra la Pobreza

- Strengthen its original focus on poverty reduction, advising and monitoring the implementation of poverty reduction strategies, social assistance programs, and Millennium Development Goal performance, and serving as major voice channel and advisory body for MIMDES.

Voice at the Regional and Local Level

Regional Coordination Councils and Local Coordination Councils

- Clarify their definition as advisory bodies and define rules of engagement with regional and local civil society, and establish regular feedback loops and reporting.
- Expand their membership to become stronger channels of plural voice and better reflect local and regional diversity of civil society.
- Define their role as coordinating bodies of regional and local participatory planning and budgeting processes, and avoid overlaps with other participatory mechanisms.
- Overcome current institutional isolation, building horizontal links with other regional, provincial, and district consultative councils and participatory mechanisms, and vertical ties with respective CCRs and CCLs.

Local Mesas de Concertación para la Lucha Contra la Pobreza

- Local Mesas should engage with the regional and national Mesas in a debate to strengthen their definition and profile as local poverty reduction mechanisms of dialog and advocacy.
- Develop local monitoring methodologies to strengthen their role as local mechanisms tracking poverty reduction programs and achievements, and providing upstream feedback to national poverty reduction strategies.
- Support the capacity of client-power mechanisms associated with the social programs to channel their voice to local and regional decisionmaking.

Participatory Budgeting

- Expand the Participatory Budgeting process beyond budget formulation to include other phases of the investment cycle, strengthening the role of Vigilance Committees and providing them with relevant information and methodological skills to perform their job.
- Evaluate and revise the allocation formula of Participatory Budgeting and encourage strategic debate with technical teams to avoid potential investment fragmentation.
- Include, in addition to determining investment allocations, a discussion of recurrent allocations in order to deepen budget debate and the discussion of expenditure tradeoffs.
- Expand monitoring scope and capacity of Vigilance Committees beyond investment tracking to include all local public expenditures.
- Improve inclusiveness of Participatory Budgeting by bringing budget dialog down to the communities using local media and versatile consultation technologies.
- Institutionalize and enforce reporting final allocation and actual expenditure back to participatory agents as a standard phase of the Participatory Budgeting cycle.

References

AANSSA-PERU. 1986. "Analisis del Sector Salud, Financiamiento y gasto del Ministerio de Salud del Perú." Informe Técnico No. 7. Lima.

Abadzi, Helen. 2004. "Education for All or Just for the Smartest Poor?" *Prospects* 34:271–89.

Alcazár, L., J. López-Calix, and E. Wachtenheim. 2003. "Las pérdidas en el camino. Fugas en el gasto público: transferencias municipales, vaso de leche y educación." Instituto Apoyo.

Alcázar, Lorena. 2003. "Monitoring Social Outcomes and Policies in Peru: The Challenge of Decentralization." Background paper for the forthcoming Poverty Assessment of the World Bank.

———. 2004a. "Agenda Nacional De Reformas Económicas En Perú: El Sector Educación." Lima: Group for the Analysis of Development.

———. 2004b. "El Monitoreo y la Evaluación de las Políticas Sociales en el Perú: El Reto de la Descentralización." Peru Poverty Assessment, Working Paper, Grupo de Análisis para el Desarrollo, Lima.

Alcázar, Lorena, and Raúl Andrade. 1999. "Demanda Inducida y Ausentismo en los Hospitales Peruanos." In Rafael Di Tella y William D. Savedoff, eds., *Diagnóstico Corrupción, El Fraude en los Hospitales Públicos en América Latina*. Washington, D.C.: Banco Interamericano de Desarrollo.

Alcázar, Lorena, and Rosa Ana Balcázar. 2001. *Oferta y Demanda de Formación Docente en el Perú*. Working Paper No. 7. Ministerio de Educación, MECEP, Lima.

Alcázar, Lorena, F. Halsey Rogers, Nazmul Chaudhury, Jeffrey Hammer, Michael Kremer, and Karthik Muralidharan. 2004. "Why are Teachers Absent? Probing Service Delivery in Peruvian Primary Schools." Draft. Grupo de Análisis para el Desarrollo, Lima.

Alderman, H., and David Stiefel. 2003. "The 'Glass of Milk' Subsidy Program and Malnutrition in Peru." Working Paper 3089, The World Bank, Washington, D.C.

Altobelli, L., A. Sovero, and R. Diaz. 2004. "Estudio de costo-eficiencia de las asociaciones CLAS." Futuras Generaciones/Perú.

Altobelli, Laura. 1998. "Comparative Analysis of Primary Health Care Facilities with Participation of Civil Society in Venezuela and Peru." Paper presented at the seminar, "Social Programs, Poverty and Citizenship Participation." Inter-American Development Bank, State and Civil Society Division. Washington, D.C.

———. 2004. *Estudio de costo eficiencia de las asociaciones CLAS*. Lima: Futuras Generaciones, Fundación Milagro, and United States Agency for International Development.

Alvarado, Betty. 2002. "Focalización de los recursos públicos en salud." In Juan Arroyo, ed., *La salud peruana en el siglo XXI. Retos y propuestas de política*. Lima: Consorcio de Investigación Económica y Social and Department for International Development (DFID, United Kingdom).

———. 2003. "Transferencias Intergubernamentales en la Finanzas Municipales del Perú." Centro de Investigación de la Universidad del Pacifico–Consorcio de Investigación Económica y Social.

Anchi, Félix. 2005. "Las Actividades Cotidianas del Maestro Fuera de la Escuela, una Estrategia de Sobrevivencia." Ponencia, Masters in Anthropology draft thesis. Pontificia Universidad La Católica. Lima.

Ansion, Juan. 2001. "Los actores de la escuela: hacia un nuevo pacto educativo." In Orlando Plaza, ed., *Perú: Actores y Escenarios al Inicio del Nuevo Milenio.* Pontificia Universidad Católica del Perú. Lima.

APOYO (Instituto Apoyo). 2000. "Sexta Evaluación Ex Post del Foncodes, Evaluación de Impacto y Sostenabilidad." Lima.

———. 2001. *Evaluación de los Efectos y Resultados Intermedios del Programa de Mejoramiento de la Calidad de la Educación Primaria (MECEP).* Final Report. Lima.

———. 2002a. *Hacia una Mejor Gestión de los Centros Educativos en el Perú: El Caso de Fe y Alegría.* Lima.

———. 2002b. "Public Expenditure Tracking Survey: The Education Sector in Peru, Appendix 1: Breakfast Program." Lima.

———. 2005a. Encuesta Nacional, Agosto.

———. 2005b. *Fundación Inca Kola, La Educación Rural en el Perú.* Lima.

Arregui, Patricia, Hugo Díaz, and Barbara Hunt. 1996. *Problemas, Perspectivas y Requerimientos de la Formación Magisterial en el Perú.* Lima: Group for the Analysis of Development.

Arroyo, Juan, and Mariana Irigoyen. 2004. "Desafíos de la Democracia Participativa Local en la Descentralización: Una lectura a partir de doce experiencias." Department for International Development (DFID, United Kingdom)–UNPFA. Lima.

Arroyo Laguna, Juan. 2000. *Salud, Reforma Silenciosa.* Lima: Universidad Cayetano Heredia.

Audibert, M., and J. Mathonnat. 2000. "Cost Recovery in Mauritania: Initial Lessons." *Health Policy and Planning* 15(1):66–75.

Ballón, Eduardo. 2003. "Notas de balance del funcionamiento de los espacios de participación ciudadana a nivel regional y local." Grupo Propuesta Ciudadana, Lima.

———. 2005. "Balance de las experiencias de participación y concertación previas al inicio del proceso de descentralización." Prepared for the World Bank. Grupo Propuesta Ciudadana, Lima.

Ballón, Eduardo, Gustavo Riofrio, and Rafael Roncagliolo. 1974. *El Maestro en la Escuela de Hoy.* Cuadernos Desco.

Bardales, Elisa. 2004. "Por un gobierno de todos." In *La Participación Ciudadana y la Construcción de la Democracia en America Latina.* Lima.

Bardález, Carlos. 2001. "Salud de la población." In Pedro Francke, ed., *Políticas de Salud 2001–2006.* Lima: Consorcio de Investigación Económica y Social, Region-level School Management and Supervisión Unit, Dirección Regional de Educación 201.

Barletti, José, Oscar Chávez, Gerónimo Romero, Lucy Trapnell, and Madeleine Zúñiga. 2004. "Balance y perspectivas de la educación intercultural bilingüe en el Perú." Conclusions presented by the Peruvian delegation at the International Seminar "Balance y Perspectivas de la Educación Intercultural Bilingüe en América Latina" held by the World Bank and el Programa de Formación en Educación Intercultural Bilingüe para

Países Andinos (PROEIB-ANDES), Cochabamba, Bolivia, June 14–17. Accessed at http://www.educared.edu.pe/directivos/index.asp?id_articulo=431 on September 24, 2005.

Beltrán, Arlette and others. 2004. "Informe Final del Diseño de Modelos de Predicción de Cumplimiento de Objetivos del Milenio: el Caso Peruano." Universidad del Pacífico, Lima.

Beltrán, Arlette, Juan Castro, Enrique Vásquez, Gustavo Yamada, and Pablo Lavado. 2004. "Armando un rompecabezas pro-pobre para el Perú del 2015." Universidad del Pacífico, Lima.

Benavides, Martín. 2002. "Para Explicar Las Diferencias En El Rendimiento En Matemática De Cuarto Grado En El Perú Urbano: Análisis De Resultados A Partir De Un Modelo Básico." In: José Rodríguez, y Silvana Vargas, eds., *Análisis de los resultados y metodología de las pruebas CRECER 1998.* Documento De Trabajo No. 13. Programa MECEP. Ministerio de Educación.

Blank, Lorraine, M. Grosh, Guillermo Hakim, and C. Weigand. Forthcoming 2006. "Social Protection Spending Database." The World Bank, Washington, D.C.

Blondet, Cecilia, and Carolina Trivelli. 2004. "Cucharas en alto." IEP.

Bustamante Suárez, Miguel. 2003. "Caracterización del Programa del Vaso de Leche." Dirección General de Asuntos Económicos y Sociales del Ministerio de Economía y Finanzas. Lima, February.

Caballero, Victor. 2004. "El presupuesto 2005 y la transferencia de los programas sociales." Participa Perú.

———. 2004. "Los programas sociales reasistencia alimentaria en el contexto de la fusión y la descentralización." Documento de Trabajo, IEP. Lima.

Carranza, L., and D. Tuesta. 2003. "Consideraciones para una Descentralización Fiscal: Pautas para la experiencia peruana." BCR–Consorcio de Investigación Económica y Social 2003–01.

Casavalente, Óscar. 2005. *El derecho a la salud en establecimientos de salud con administración compartida.* Lima: Defensoría del Pueblo and Department for International Development (DFID, United Kingdom).

Castañeda, Tarsicio, and Kathy Lindert, with Bénédicte de la Briere, Luisa Fernandez, Celia Hubert, Osvaldo Larrañaga, Mónica Orozco, and Roxana Viquez. Forthcoming 2005. "Designing and Implementing Household Targeting Systems: Lessons from Latin America and the United States." The World Bank, Washington, D.C.

Chacaltana, Juan. 2001. "Más allá de la focalización. Riesgos de la lucha contra la pobreza en el Perú." Grupo de Análisis para el Desarrollo y Consorcio de Investigación Económica y Social.

———. 2003. "El Impacto del Programa *A Trabajar Urbano.*"

———. 2005. "La pobreza no es como lo imaginábamos."

Chawla, M., and R. J. Ellis. 2000. "The Impact of Financing and Quality Changes on Health Care Demand in Niger." *Health Policy and Planning* 15(1):66–75.

Chirinos, Luis. 2004. "Participación ciudadana en gobiernos regionales: el caso de los Consejos de Coordinación Regional." In *La Participación Ciudadana y la Construcción de la Democracia en America Latina.* Lima.

Chiroque Chunga, Sigfredo. 2004a. *Conflicto en el Sistema Educativo Peruano 1998–2003. Estudio de Caso.* Lima.

————. 2004b. *Descongelar los Niveles Magisteriales.* Instituto de Pedagogía Popular, Report No. 18. Lima.

————. 2004c. *Para Entender el Debate sobre el Presupuesto Educación 2005.* Instituto de Pedagogía Popular, Report No. 28.

Contreras, Carlos. 2004. *El Aprendizaje del Capitalismo.*

Constitución del Perú. 1979. At: www.congreso.gob.pe.

Constitución Política del Perú. 1993. At: www.congreso.gob.pe.

Cortez, R. 2002. "Salud, equidad y pobreza en el Perú: teoría y nuevas Evidencias." Centro de Investigación de la Universidad del Pacífico, Lima.

Cortez, Rafael. 1998. *Equidad y calidad de servicios de salud: El caso de los CLAS.* Documento de Trabajo no. 33. Lima: Centro de Investigación de la Universidad del Pacífico.

Crouch, Luis. 2005. "Education." Draft report for RECURSO. Washington, D.C.

Cruz, Francisco Santa. 1996. "Notas para un balance de la descentralización en el Perú," *Debate Agrario* (24), CEPES, Lima.

Cruz, Gustavo, Giuliana Espinosa, Angélica Montané, and Carlos Rodríguez. 2002. "Informe Técnico de la Consulta Nacional sobre Puntos de Corte para la Evaluación Nacional 2001." Ministerio de Educación Unidad de Medición de la Calidad Educativa. Lima.

Cueto, Santiago. 2003. "Factores Predictivos del Rendimiento Escolar, Deserción e Ingreso a Educación Secundaria en una Muestra de Estudiantes de Zonas Rurales del Perú." Group for the Analysis of Development, Lima.

Cueto, Santiago, and Marjorie Chinen. 2001. "Impacto educativo de un programa de Desayunos Escolares en escuelas rurales del Perú." Working Papers 34, Grupo de Análisis para el Desarrollo, Lima.

Cueto, Santiago, and Walter Secada. 2001. "Mathematics Learning and Achievement in Quechua, Aymara and Spanish by Boys and Girls in Bilingual and Spanish Schools in Puno, Peru." Group for the Analysis of Development, Lima.

Cueto, Santiago, Cecilia Ramírez, and Juan León. 2003. "Eficacia escolar en escuelas poli-docentes completas de Lima y Ayacucho." Group for the Analysis of Development, Lima.

Cueto, Santiago, Cecilia Ramírez, Juan León, and Oscar Pain. 2003. "Oportunidades de aprendizaje y rendimiento en matemática en una muestra de estudiantes de sexto grado de primaria de Lima." Documento de Trabajo 43. Group for the Analysis of Development, Lima.

Defensoría del Pueblo. 2005. "Reporte de Supervisión de Portales de Gobiernos Regionales." Lima.

Díaz, Hugo, and Jaime Saavedra. 2002. "La carrera del maestro en el Perú. Factores insti-tucionales, incentivos económicos y desempeño. APOYO 2001." In Herrera José Rivero, *Magisterio, Educación y Sociedad en el Perú.* Ministerio de Educación y UNESCO.

Díaz, Julio E. 2004. "Los Consejos de Coordinación Local." In *La Participación Ciudadana y la Construcción de la Democracia en America Latina.* Lima.

Du Bois, Fritz. 2004. "Programas Sociales, Salud y Educación en el Perú: Un Balance de las Políticas Sociales." Instituto Peruano de Economía Social de Mercado.

Edstats. World Bank web page on education statistics at: http://sima.worldbank.org/edstats/.

ENAHO (Encuesta Nacional de Hogares). 1997. Instituto Nacional de Estadística e Informática.

———. 2001. Instituto Nacional de Estadística e Informática (INEI).

———. 2003. Instituto Nacional de Estadística e Informática (INEI).

———. 2004. *Encuesta Nacional de Hogares 2004*. Lima.

Equipo de Análisis de la Unidad de Medición de la Calidad Educativa. 2004. "Factores Asociados Al Rendimiento Estudiantil." Unidad de Medición de la Calidad Educativa. Ministerio de Educación. Lima.

Equipo Pedagógico Nacional de Fe y Alegría. 2003. *Propuesta pedagógica*. Lima: Fe y Alegría.

ESSALUD (Seguro Social de Salud). 2004. At: www.essalud.gob.pe.

———. 2005. "Memoria Institucional 2004 del Seguro Social de Salud-ESSALUD."

Fe y Alegría. 2003. "Fe y Alegría: Movimiento de Educación Popular Integral y Promoción Social." Presentation available at www.feyalegria.org.

Figallo, F. 2003. "Redes Sociales en Educación: el caso de las APAFA." In *De la caridad a la solidaridad*. Universidad del Pacífico.

Fiszbein, Ariel. 2005. *Citizens, Politicians, and Providers*. Washington, D.C.: The World Bank.

FONCODES. 2003. "Indicadores Observados del Plan Estratégico Institucional 2003–2011."

FONCODES Poverty Map. 2004. At: http://www.foncodes.gob.pe/PobrezaPeru/focalizacion.asp. Accessed April 2005.

Foro del Acuerdo Nacional. 2004. Pacto Social De Compromisos Recíprocos Por La Educación 2004–2006. At: http://www.acuerdonacional.gob.pe/Pactos/PactoSocialdeEducaci%F3n.pdf. Accessed on July 2, 2004.

Francke, P., and W. Mendoza. 2001. "Economic Policies and Pro-Poor Growth in Peru." Documento de Trabajo No. 198. Pontificia Universidad Católica del Perú.

Francke, P., and J. Paulini. 2003. "Evaluación de la ejecución del presupuesto del Ministerio de Salud del año 2002." Proyecto AIP-Análisis del Presupuesto Independiente. Consorcio de Investigación Económica y Social, Lima. Processed.

Francke, Pedro. 1998a. "Focalización del gasto público en salud en el Perú: situación y alternativas." Documento de Trabajo No. 155. Pontificia Universidad Católica del Perú.

———. 1998b. "Focalización del gasto público en salud en el Perú: Situación y alternativas." Informe sobre investigación aplicada secundaria no. 1. Partnership for Health Reform, Bethesda.

———. 1999. "Propuesta para una política de empleo." In *Empleo y Desarrollo en el Peru*. Lima: Centro de Asesoría Legal del Perú.

———. 2001a. "Lineamientos de políticas en salud, 2001–2006." In Pedro Francke, ed., *Políticas de Salud 2001–2006*. Lima: Consorcio de Investigación Económica y Social.

———. 2001b. "Políticas sociales: balance y propuestas." Documento de Trabajo No. 194. Pontificia Universidad Católica del Perú, Lima.

———. 2002. "Análisis Independiente del Presupuesto Público 2003 en Programas Sociales: Sector Educación." Proyecto Análisis Independiente del Presupuesto Público 2003. Consorcio de Investigación Económica y Social.

———. 2004a. "Educación pública, salud y descentralización." Universidad Pontificia Católica del Perú. Palestra Web-Site. At: http://palestra.pucp.edu.pe/?id=38 on July 23, 2004.

———. 2004b. "Las políticas sociales y la descentralización."

———. 2004c. "Reforma de programas de alimentación escolar."

———. 2004d. "Reforma de programas nutricionales infantiles."

———. 2005a. "La descentralización de los Programas Sociales: En que Dirección y Cuanto se ha Avanzado."

———. 2005b. "La institucionalidad de los programas alimentarios."

Francke, Pedro, José Castro, and Rafael Ugaz. 2002. "Análisis Independiente del Presupuesto Público 2003 en Programas Sociales." Proyecto Análisis Independiente del Presupuesto Público 2003. Consorcio de Investigación Económica y Social.

Gajate, Giselle, and Marisol Inurritegui. 2002. "El impacto de los programas alimentarios sobre el nivel de nutrición infantil: una aproximación a partir de la metodología del 'Propensity Score Matching'." Grupo de Análisis para el Desarrollo, Lima.

———. 2003. "El impacto de los programas alimentarios sobre el nivel de nutrición infantil: una aproximación a partir de la metodología del "Propensity Score Matching." Grupo de Análisis para el Desarrollo y Consorcio de Investigación Económica y Social.

Galindo, Claudia. 2002. "El Currículo Implementado Como Indicador del Proceso Educativo." In José Rodríguez and Silvana Vargas, eds., *Análisis de los resultados y metodología de las pruebas CRECER 1998*. Documento de Trabajo No. 13. Programa MECEP. Ministerio de Educación.

Gamero, Julio, Zoila Cabrera, Juan Carlos Cortés, and Carolina Giba. 2004. "Vigilancia Social: Teoría y Practica en el Perú." Consorcio de Investigación Económica y Social, Lima.

Goetz, Anne Marie. 2003. "Community of Practice on Social Accountability." Presentation on November 12, The World Bank, Washington, D.C.

Gonzales de Olarte, Efraín. 2000. "Neocentralismo y neolibalismo en el Perú." Lima IEP.

Grompone, Romeo. 2005. "Discutiendo la intervención ciudadana en el presupuesto participativo regional." Grupo Propuesta Ciudadana, Lima.

Guzmán, Alfredo. 2001. "Atención en el primer nivel." *Políticas de Salud 2001–2006*. CIES, Lima.

———. 2002. "Para mejorar la salud reproductiva." In Juan Arroyo, ed., *La salud peruana en el siglo XXI. Retos y propuestas de política*. Lima: Consorcio de Investigación Económica y Social and Department for International Development (DFID, United Kingdom).

———. 2003. *Análisis comparativo de modelos de aseguramiento público y propuesta de un sistema solidario de seguridad social en el Perú*. Lima: Foro Salud y Consorcio de Investigación Económica y Social.

Hall, Thomas L. 1969. *Health Manpower in Peru*. A Case Study in Planning.

Harding, April. 2005. *CLAS and Primary Health Care in Peru*. Concept Note, February 4.

———. 2005. RECURSO background report on Primary Health Care and the CLAS in Peru. May 31.

Harding, April, and Betty Alvarado. 2005. "Peru, Primary Health Care and the CLAS in Peru." Background Paper for RECURSO Study. The World Bank, Washington, D.C.

Henríquez Ayin, Narda. 2005. "Red de redes para la concertación: La experiencia de la Mesa de Concertación para la Lucha contra la Pobreza." Lima.

Hernandez, Max. 1999. *Propuesta para un Estudio Sobre la Problemática de la Profesión Médica*. Para el Colegio Medico del Perú.

Herrera, S., and G. Pang. 2004. "Efficiency of Public Spending in Developing Countries: An Efficiency Frontier Approach. The World Bank, Washington, D.C.

———. 2005. "Estimating the Efficiency Frontier of Public Spending." The World Bank, Washington, D.C.

Hornberger, Nancy. 2000. "Bilingual Education Policy and Practice in the Andes: Ideological Paradox and Intercultural Possibility." *Anthropology and Education Quarterly* 31(2).

Huaman, Josefina. 2005. (Interview). Coodinator of the Mesa de Concertación de Lucha contra la Pobreza de Lima Metropolitana. Lima.

Hunt, Barbara C. 2001. "Peruvian Primary Education: Improvement Still Needed." Paper presented at September 2001 meeting of Latin American Studies Association. Washington, D.C., September 6–8.

Iguíñiz, J. 2000. "Deuda externa y políticas de salud." Documento de Trabajo 189. Centro de Investigaciones Sociológicas, Económicas, Políticas y Antropológicas, Pontificia Universidad Católica del Perú. Lima.

Iguíñiz, J., and R. Barrantes. 2004. "La investigación económica y social en el Perú. Balance 1999–2003 y prioridades para el futuro." Consorcio de Investigación Económica y Social.

INEI (Instituto Nacional de Estadística e Informática). 1996. *Encuesta Demográfica y de Salud Familiar*. Lima.

———. 2000. *¿Ha Mejorado el Bienestar de la Población?* Lima.

———. 2001. *Encuesta Demográfica y de Salud Familiar 2000*. Lima.

———. 2003a. *Encuesta Nacional de Hogares, 2002 IV Trimestre. Diccionario de Datos.* Lima.

———. 2003b. *Encuesta Nacional de Hogares 2003*. Sección Salud (400), preguntas de la 400 a la 420. Lima.

———. 2004a. *Encuesta Nacional de Demografía y Salud, ENDES Continua 2004*. Lima.

———. 2004b. *ENDES Continúa, Resultados Preliminares*. Lima.

———. 2005. *Informe preliminar de Encuesta Nacional de Demografía y Salud, ENDES Continua*. Lima.

Instituto Cuanto. *Peru en Numeros*. Various years.

Instituto Nacional de Investigación y Desarrollo de la Educación. 1981. "El Magisterio Peruano en la Reforma Educativa. Estudio Evaluativo 1972–1980." Ministerio de Educación.

Instituto Peruano de Economía. 2003. "La brecha en infraestructura. Servicios públicos, productividad y crecimiento en el Perú." IPE, Lima.

Jaramillo, M., and Sandro Parodi. 2003. "El Seguro Escolar Gratuito y el Seguro Materno Infantil." Grupo de Análisis para el Desarrollo, Lima.

Jiménez, F. 2002. "El carácter procíclico de la política fiscal: notas sobre la ley de prudencia y transparencia fiscal." Documento de Trabajo 215. Departamento de Economía de la Pontificia Universidad Católica del Perú, Lima.

_____. 2003. "Perú: sostenibilidad, balance estructural y propuesta de una regla fiscal." Documento de Trabajo 225. Departamento de Economía de la Pontificia Universidad Católica del Perú, Lima.

Johnson, Jaime. 2001. "Reestructuración institucional del sector salud." In Pedro Francke, ed., *Políticas de Salud 2001–2006*. Consorcio de Investigación Económica y Social, Lima.

Jung, Ingrid, and Luis Enrique Lopez. 1989. "Sistematización del Proyecto Experimental de Educación Bilingüe Puno (PEEB-P), 1977–1988." Second edition. German Agency for Technical Cooperation, Lima.

Kaufmann, D., A. Kraay, and M. Mastruzzi. 2005. "Governance Matters IV: Governance Indicators for 1996–2004." May 9 Draft. The World Bank, Washington, D.C.

Kuper, Wolfgang. 1988. "Interculturalidad y Reforma Educativa en Tres Países Andinos." *Pueblos Indígenas y Educación* Nos. 45–46. Abya Yala. German Agency for Technical Cooperation. Quito.

Larios, J., B. Alvarado, y E. Conterno. 2004. "Descentralización fiscal. Análisis conceptual y revisión de experiencias en nueve países." Documento Técnico No. 7. Programa Pro Descentralización.

Leyton Muñoz, Carlos, and José López Ricci. 2005. "Plan de Desarrollo Concertado y Presupuesto Participativo 2004–2006: Avances y desafíos a tomar en cuenta?" Grupo Propuesta Ciudadana. Lima.

Lindert, Kathy, Emmanuel Skoufias, and Joseph Shapiro. Forthcoming 2005. "How Effectively do Public Tranfers in Latin America Redistribute Income?" The World Bank, Washington, D.C.

Londoño, Juan Luis, and Julio Frenk. 1997. *Pluralismo estructurado: Hacia un modelo innovador para la reforma a los sistemas de salud de América Latina.* Documento de Trabajo n. 353. Washington, D.C.: Banco Interamericano de Desarrollo.

López de Castilla, Martha. 2003. "*¿Cómo Sobrevive un Docente?*" Instituto de Pedagogía Popular, Informe No. 10.

Lopez, Luis Enrique. 2002. "A ver, a ver ... ¿Quien quiere salir a la pizarra? ¿Jumasti? ¿Jupasti?" Programa MECEP. Documento de Trabajo No. 15. Ministerio de Educación. Lima.

López-Cálix, J. R., L. Alcazar, and Erik Wachtenheim. 2002. "Peru: Public Expenditure Tracking Study." In *Peru: Restoring Fiscal Discipline for Poverty Reduction, Public Expenditure Review.* World Bank and Inter-American Development Bank, Report No. 24286. Washington, D.C.

López-Ricci, José, and Eliza Wiener Bravo. 2004. "Planeamiento y el presupuesto participativo regional 2003–2004: Enfoques de Desarrollo, Prioridades de Inversión y Roles de los 'Agentes Participantes'." Documento Síntesis. Grupo Propuesta Ciudadana, Lima.

Madueño, Miguel, Midori de Habich, y Manuel Jumpa. 2004. "Disposición a pagar por seguros de salud en los segmentos no asalariados de medianos y altos ingresos. ¿Existe una demanda potencial en Lima Metropolitana?" Lima.

Maximize and Instituto Cuánto. 2003. "Evaluación de Impacto del Programa de Complementación Alimentaria para Grupos de Mayor Riesgo." Lima.

MED (Ministerio de Educación). *Cifras de Educación 1998–2003.* Lima.

———. 1989. "Política de Educación Bilingüe Intercultural." Lima.

———. 2000. "Programa Curricular de Educación Primaria de Menores. (Primer y Segundo Grados.) Estructura Curricular Básica de Educación Primaria de Menores." Dirección Nacional de Educación Inicial y Primaria, Lima.

———. 2001a. *Consultoria para la Evaluación de los Procesos Institucionales Existentes en el Sector Rural para la Atención de la Escuela Rural.* Primera Fase.

———. 2001b. *Evolución del Gasto en Remuneraciones, Plazas y Carga Docente.* Lima: PLANMED.

————. 2001c. *Plan de Implementación de un Programa de Incentivos para Docentes de Zonas Rurales y de Condiciones Especiales.* Final Report. Lima: Instituto Apoyo.

————. 2004. "Horas Efectivas de Trabajo Escolar." Report, R. M. No.0189-2004-ED, Lima.

————. 2005. Secretaría de Planificación Estratégica.

MEF (Ministry of Economy and Finance). 2004a. *"Los Sistemas de Pensiones en Perú."* Dirección General de Asuntos Económicos y Sociales.

————. 2004b. *"Plan de Acción de los Sistemas de Pensiones en Perú, 2004–2008."* Dirección General de Asuntos Económicos y Sociales.

————. 2005a. At: www.mef/presupuestoparticipativo. Accessed February 4, 2005.

————. 2005b. Budget Directorate. Requested information.

MEF-SIAF (Sistema Inegrado de Administración Financier). At: http://transparencia-economica.mef.gob.pe/amigable/default.asp. Accessed in 2005.

Mendoza Bellido, Waldo. 2003. "Perú: Pobreza, Política Social y Contexto Macro-económico." Presentation, Dirección General de Asuntos Económicos y Sociales, MEF.

Ministerio de Educación and UNESCO. 2002. *Magisterio, Educación y Sociedad en el Perú, Encuesta de Opinión y Actitudes a Docentes Peruanos.* Lima.

Ministry of Health about PAAG. http://www.paag.minsa.gob.pe/internet/QueHacemos/clas/clas.htm.

MINSA (Ministerio de Salud). 2002. *Bases para el análisis de la situación de salud.* Lima.

————. 2003a. *La mortalidad materna en el Perú.* Oficina General de Epidemiología. Lima.

————. 2003b. *Análisis de la situación de salud del Perú 2003.* Oficina General de Epidemiología. Lima.

————. 2004. *Administración Compartida CLAS, Propuesta Normativa, Programa de Administración de Acuerdos de Gestión.* Lima.

————. 2004. *Análisis de la situación de salud del Perú 2003.* Oficina General de Epidemiología. Lima.

————. 2004. *Hoja de Ruta para la Implementación del Proceso de Descentralización de la Función de Salud.* PARSALUD.

————. *Evaluación de la participación Social en el Modelo CLAS.* Dirección General de Salud.

————. Oficina de Estadísticas e Informática. At: <www.minsa.gob.pe>.

MINSA–OPS (Ministerio de Salud–OPS). 1995–2002. "Tendencias en la Utilización de Servicios de Salud." Peru.

Monge, Carlos. 1998. "Cusco: Regionalización y Desarrollo Regional." In *Debate Agrario* No. 3, CEPES. Lima.

Montero, Carmen, Patricia Oliart, Zoila Cabrera, and F. Uccelli. 2001. *La Escuela Rural: Modalidades y Prioridades de Intervención.* Working Paper No. 2. Ministerio de Educación, Lima.

Montero, Carmen, Patricia Ames, Zoila Cabrera, Andrés Chirinos, Mariella Fernández Dávila, and Eduardo León. 2002. "Propuesta metodológica para el mejoramiento de la enseñanza y el aprendizaje en el aula rural multigrado." Documento de Trabajo No. 18. Programa MECEP. Ministerio de Educación.

OECD/UIS (Organisation for Economic Co-operation and Development/UNESCO Institute for Statistics). 2003. "Literacy Skills for the World of Tomorrow. Further

Results from PISA 2000." Paris: Organisation for Economic Co-operation and Development.

Oliart, Patricia. 2002. "Qué Podemos Aprender de las Escuelas Rurales: Reflexiones Acerca de los Dilemas de la Escuela Rural en la Sierra Peruana." In *Escuelas que Aprenden y se Desarrollan*. Lima: Universidad Peruana Cayetano Heredia.

OPS/OMS. 2002. *Proyecciones de Financiamiento de la Atención de Salud 2002–2006*. Lima.

———. 2003. *Análisis y Tendencias en la Utilización de Servicios de Salud, Perú 1985–2002*. Lima.

———. 2004. *Cuentas Nacionales de Salud Perú 1996–2000*. Lima.

Ormeño, A. 2002. "Balance Estructural y la política fiscal en el Perú: 1990–2002." *Apuntes, Revista de Ciencias Sociales* (50).

Orr Easthouse, Linda. 2004. "Literacy: Freedom Depends on Who Holds the Tools." Wycliffe Canada.

Ortiz de Zevallos, G., G. Pollarolo, H. Eyzaguirre, and R. M. Palacios. 1999. "La economía política de las reformas institucionales en el Perú: los casos de educación, salud y pensiones." Documento de Trabajo R-348, Banco Interamericano de Desarrollo.

Palomino, José. 2001. "Los servicios hospitalarios en el Perú." In Pedro Francke, ed., *Políticas de Salud 2001–2006*. Lima: Consorcio de Investigación Económica y Social.

PARSALUD. 2003. *Consultoria Seguro Integral de Salud*. Documento presentado como producto dentro del marco de Asistencia Técnica y Monitoreo. Lima.

Paxson, Christina, and Norbert R. Schady. 2002. "The Allocation and Impact of Social Funds: Spending on School Infrastructure in Peru." *The World Bank Economic Review* 16(2).

———. 2005. "Child Health and Economic Crisis in Peru." *The World Bank Economic Review*.

Pease, Henry. 2000. "Así se destruyó el Estado de Derecho." Lima.

Pereyra, J. 2003. "Sostenibilidad de la política fiscal: una simulación de la restricción presupuestaria." *Estudios Económicos* (9). Banco Central de Reserva del Perú, Lima.

Perla, C. 2003. "Descentralización y Presupuesto Público 2003." Grupo Propuesta Ciudadana.

Petrera, Margarita. 2002. "Financiamiento en salud." In Juan Arroyo, ed., *La salud peruana en el siglo XXI. Retos y propuestas de política*. Lima: Consorcio de Investigación Económica y Social and Department for International Development (United Kingdom).

———. 2005. "Final Report on Financial Management in the Formulation, Monitoring and Evaluation of the Management Agreements." Associate Consultant, PARSALUD Project.

"Políticas Pro-Pobre en el Sector Público de Salud en el Perú: ¿Cuáles son los Proximos Pasos?" Based on SIAF. RECURSO Project report.

Pollit, Ernesto, Enrique Jacoby, and Santiago Cueto. 1996. "Desayuno Escolar y rendimiento: a propósito del programa de desayunos escolares de Foncodes en el Perú." Background paper. Lima.

Portocarrero, F., and M. Romero. 1994. "Política Social en el Perú 1990–1994: una agenda para la investigación." Documento de Trabajo No. 19. Centro de Investigación de la Universidad del Pacífico, Lima.

Portocarrero Grados, A. 2000. "Redistribución del Gasto Público en salud: 1995–1998." Universidad Nacional Mayor de San Marcos, Lima.

PREAL (Programa de Promoción de la Reforma Educativa en América Latina y El Caribe). 2003. "Informe de Progreso Educativo, Peru (1993–2003)." Lima.

PRODES. 2005. "Proceso de Descentralización 2004: Balance y Recomendaciones para una Agenda Pendiente." Lima.

Propuesta. 2005. "Grupo Propuesta Ciudadana, Vigilancia del proceso de Descentralización (Vigila Perú)." Reporte Nacional No. 7. Lima.

Rawlings, Laura, and Gloria M. Rubio. 2005. "Evaluating the Impact of Conditional Cash Transfer Programs." *The World Bank Research Observer* 20(1).

Rawlings, Laura, L. Sherburne-Benz, and J. Van Domelen. 2004. "Evaluating Social Funds." World Bank, Regional and Sectoral Studies. Washington, D.C.

Red EBI Perú. 1999. "Congreso Nacional de Educación Intercultural Bilingüe 1998." In *Educación Bilingüe Intercultural: Experiencias y Propuestas*. Lima: German Agency for Technical Cooperation.

Remy, Maria Isabel. 2005. "Los múltiples campos de la participación ciudadana en el Perú—Un reconocimiento del terreno y algunas reflexiones." Instituto de Estudios Peruanos. Lima.

RESAL Perú. 1999. "Gasto Social Básico en el Perú." European Commission DGVIII/A/1.

Reuben, William. 2004. "Civic Engagement, Social Accountability, and the Governance Crisis." In *Globalization, Poverty, and Conflict*. London: Kluwer Academic Publishers.

Rivero, Herrera José. 2002. *Magisterio, Educación y Sociedad en el Perú*. Ministerio de Educación y UNESCO.

Rivero, José. 2004a. "Políticas educativas y exclusión: sus límites y complejidad." At: http://palestra.pucp.edu.pe/?id=48. Accessed July 23, 2004.

———. 2004b. "Políticas Regionales Andinas para el Desarrollo de la Escuela Rural." Lima.

———. 2004c. "Propuesta: Nueva Docencia en el Perú." Consultoría preparada para la Dirección Nacional de Formación y Capitación Docente, DINFOCAD. Ministerio de Educación del Perú.

Rodríguez, José. 2004. "Importancia del gasto público de calidad en la educación." Universidad Pontificia Católica del Perú. Palestra Web-Site. At: http://palestra.pucp.edu.pe/?id=25. Accessed July 23, 2004.

Romero, Emilio. 1962. "El Proceso Económico del Perú en el Siglo XX." In Jose Pareja Paz-Soldan, *Visión del Perú en el Siglo XX*. Ediciones Librería Studium, Tomo I.

Ruiz, Lazo Albino. Undated. *La Serpiente de Luz, Tierra y Educación en los Andes*. Instituto Fernand Braudel de Economía Mundial.

Saavedra, J. 2004. "La situación laboral de los maestros respecto a otros profesionales. Implicancias para el diseño de políticas salariales y de incentivos." In *¿Es posible mejorar la educación peruana? Evidencias y Posibilidades*. Group for the Analysis of Development.

Saavedra, J., R. Melzi Ríos, and A. Miranda Blanco. 1997. "Financiamiento de la Educación en el Perú." Documento de Trabajo No. 24. Grupo de Análisis para el Desarrollo.

Saavedra, J., and P. Suárez. 2002. "El financiamiento de la educación pública en el Perú: el rol de las familias." Documento de trabajo 38. Grupo de Análisis para el Desarrollo.

Saavedra Chanduvi, Jaime, Roberto Ríos Melzi, and Arturo Miranda. 1997. *El Financiamiento de la Educación en el Perú*. Working Paper No. 24. Lima: Group for the Analysis of Development.

Sakellariou, Chris. 2004. "The Indigenous/Non-Indigenous Early Test Score Gap in Bolivia, Peru and Mexico." *Applied Economics.* School of Humanities and Social Science. Nanyang Technological University. Singapore.

Sanchez Moreno, Eliana. 2001. "Uso del Tiempo en Escuelas Multidocentes y Multigrados, Informe Proyecto Abriendo Puertas."

SIAF (Sistema de Información de Administración Financiera). 2004. "PIA y Ejecución de la Función Salud 1999 a 2004." MEF, Lima.

Tanaka, M., and C. Trivelli. 1999. "La participación social y política de los pobladores populares urbanos: ¿del movimientismo a una política de ciudadanos? El caso de El Agustino." In Martín Tanaka, ed., *El poder visto desde abajo. Democracia, educación y ciudadanía en espacios locales.* Lima: Instituto de Estudios Peruanos.

———. 2002. "Las trampas de la focalización y la participación. Pobreza y políticas sociales en el Perú durante la década de Fujimori." Instituto de Estudios Peruanos, Lima.

Tanaka, Martín. 2002. "La dinámica de los actores regionales y el proceso de descentralización." IEP, Documento de Trabajo No. 125, Lima.

Tesliuc, E., and Lindert, K. 2002. "Social Protection, Private Transfers and Poverty in Guatemala." Background paper to the Guatemala Poverty Assessment. The World Bank, Washington, D.C.

Tesliuc, Emil Daniel, M. Grosh, D. Coady, and L. Pop. Forthcomming 2005. "Program Implementation Matters for Targeting Performance: Evidence and Lessons from Eastern and Central Europe." The World Bank, Washington, D.C.

Tovar, Teresa, Luis Gorriti, and Emilio Morillo. 1989. *Ser Maestro, Condiciones del trabajo Docente en el Perú.* UNESCO/OREALC, Santiago, Chile.

Trapnell, Lucy, and Eloy Neira. 2004. "Situación de la Educación Intercultural Bilingüe en el Perú." Consultancy for the World Bank. Working document.

Trivelli, Carolina. 2004. "Analizando la encuesta: los comedores de Lima metropolitana en 2003." In *Cucharas en Alto.* Lima: Instituto de Estudios Peruanos.

Uccelli, Francesca. 1999. "Familias Campesinas, Educación y Democracia en el Sur Andino." Instituto de Estudios Peruanos (IEP), Documento de Trabajo, Lima.

Valdivia, Martín. 2002. "Sensibilidad de la demanda por servicios de salud ante un sistema de tarifas en el Perú: ¿precio o calidad?" *Economía y Sociedad* 44 (marzo).

———. 2005. "Peru: Is Identifying the Poor the Main problem in Targeting Nutritional Programs?"

Vásquez, Enrique. 2004a. "Gasto Social en el Perú: un Balance Crítico al 2004." Consorcio de Investigación Económica y Social.

———. 2004b. "Programas Alimentarios en el Perú: ¿Por qué y cómo reformarlos?" Study prepared for the Instituto Peruano de Economía Social de Mercado, Lima.

———. 2004c. "Subsidios para los mas Pobres: serán beneficiados los niños en extrema pobreza?" Los Niños Primero, Observatorio para la Infancia y la Adolescencia.

———. 2005. "Desafíos para el 2005: Una agenda social a discusión." Centro de Investigación de la Universidad del Pacífico, Lima.

Vásquez, Enrique, and Enrique Mendizábal, eds. 2002. "¿Los niños ... primero? El gasto social focalizado en niños y niñas en el Perú: 1990–2000." Universidad del Pacífico—Save the Children, Lima.

Vásquez Huamán, Enrique, ed. 2000. "Impacto de la inversión social en el Perú." Centro de Investigaciones de la Universidad del Pacífico, Lima.

Vega Ganoza, Juan Fernando. 2004. "La autoridad de los padres de familia como base de la política educativa." Articulo de PALESTRA, Portal de Asuntos Publicos de la Pontificia Universidad Católica del Peru. At: http://palestra.pucp.edu.pe/?id=48. Accessed July 23, 2004.

————. 2005. "Para que la educación (pública) eduque." Instituto Peruano de Economía Social de Mercado. Serie Reforma del Estado. Aportes para el debate. Lima.

Vidaurre, R. 2000. "Reflexiones e interrogantes acerca de la reforma tributaria a partir del proceso de la descentralización." Fundación Konrad Adenauer, Lima.

Vigil, Nila. 2004. "Pueblos Indígenas y Escritura."
  At: http://www.aulaintercultural.org/IMG/pdf/indigenas_escritura.pdf. Accessed March 20, 2005.

Vigila Peru. 2004. "Vigilancia del Proceso de Descentralización: Reporte Nacional Numero 7, Enero–Abril." Grupo Propuesta Ciudadana, Lima.

Waters, H. 1998. "Productivity in Ministry of Health Facilities in Peru." The World Bank, Washington, D.C.

World Bank. 2000. "The Challenge of Health Reform: Reaching the Poor, Shared Administration Program and Local Health Administration (CLAS) in Peru." Washington, D.C.

————. 2001a. *Peruvian Education at a Crossroads.* World Bank Country Study, May.

————. 2001b. "Peruvian Education at a Crossroads: Challenges and Opportunities for the 21st Century." World Bank Country Report, No. 22357. Washington, D.C.

————. 2003. Program Document for a Proposed Fourth Programmatic Social Reform Loan to the Republic of Peru.

————. 2004a. "Inequality in Latin America: Breaking with History." Washington, D.C.

————. 2004b. *World Development Report 2004: Making Services Work for Poor People.* Washington, D.C.

————. 2005a. *World Development Indicators 2005.* Washington, D.C.

————. 2005b. www.WorldBank/RECURSO/Compact/Volume_II/Chapter_4.

————. Various years. *Peru DHS Fact Sheet.* Washington, D.C.

Yamada Gustavo, and Patricia Perez. 2005. "Evaluación de Impacto de Proyectos de Desarrollo en el Perú." Universidad del Pacífico, Lima.

Yglesias, Arturo. 2003. "Salud, Gobernabilidad y Retos Estratégicos en la Subregión Andina." Organismo Andino de Salud, Lima.

Zúñiga, Madeleine, Liliana Sánchez, and Daniela Zacharías. 2000. "Demanda y Necesidad De Educación Bilingüe: Lenguas Indígenas y Castellano en el Sur Andino." German Agency for Technical Cooperation, KFW. Ministerio de Educación, Lima.

Eco-Audit

Environmental Benefits Statement

The World Bank is committed to preserving Endangered Forests and natural resources. We print World Bank Working Papers and Country Studies on 100 percent postconsumer recycled paper, processed chlorine free. The World Bank has formally agreed to follow the recommended standards for paper usage set by Green Press Initiative—a nonprofit program supporting publishers in using fiber that is not sourced from Endangered Forests. For more information, visit www.greenpressinitiative.org.

In 2005, the printing of these books on recycled paper saved the following:

Trees*	Solid Waste	Water	Net Greenhouse Gases	Electricity
463	21,693	196,764	42,614	79,130
'40' in height and 6-8" in diameter	Pounds	Gallons	Pounds	KWH